RELIGIOUS LIFE
IN A NEW MILLENNIUM
VOLUME TWO

Selling All

Religious Life in a New Millennium
Volume Two

SELLING ALL
Commitment, Consecrated Celibacy, and Community in Catholic Religious Life

Sandra M. Schneiders, I.H.M.

PAULIST PRESS
New York/Mahwah, N.J.

Procession of the Virgins, detail of gold leaf on glass and colored glass mosaic in Sant'Apollinare Nuovo, Ravenna, Italy, c. 568. ©Archivo Iconografico, S.A./CORBIS

Series design by J. E. Pondo

Cover design by Cynthia Dunne

Library of Congress Cataloging-in-Publication Data

Schneiders, Sandra Marie.
    Selling all : commitment, consecrated celibacy, and community in Catholic religious life / Sandra M. Schneiders.
        p.   cm. — (Religious life in a new millennium ; v. 2)
    Includes bibliographical references (p.) and index.
    ISBN 0-8091-3973-1
    1. Monastic and religious life of women. 2. Celibacy. I. Title. II. Series.
BX4210.5 .S37 2001
255'.9

                                                        2001021372

Published by Paulist Press
997 Macarthur Boulevard
Mahwah, New Jersey 07430

www.paulistpress.com

Printed and bound in the
United States of America

The Reign of God is like a TREASURE
hidden in a field
which a person FOUND...
and out of joy
SOLD ALL she had
to BUY THAT FIELD.
(cf. Mt 13:44)

This volume is dedicated
with love and gratitude

to
Rita and Tom O' Malley,
from whom I have learned so much
about relationship,

and to
their four children,
who are treasures in their life and in mine.

TABLE OF CONTENTS

PREFACE TO *RELIGIOUS LIFE IN A NEW MILLENNIUM* (THREE VOLUMES)

In the fifteen years since the publication of *New Wineskins*[1] the experience of Roman Catholic women Religious, who were the primary intended audience of that book, has broadened and deepened to an extraordinary degree. If, in 1986, it was appropriate and necessary to talk of new wineskins, that is, of new structures and procedures, and even of new theological categories and constructs, to hold and give shape to the new experience of the life that was emerging in the wake of Vatican II, today it is time to speak of the wine itself, the substance of the life, which has matured during the past decade, yielding both excellent vintage and some disappointing results. The new wine that demanded new wineskins two decades ago now needs decanting. It is time to pour, to taste, to analyze, to judge, to choose and reject, to blend and bottle, to store for the future. This task is already underway in a plethora of books and articles that have appeared during the 1980s and 1990s. This three-volume work, *Religious Life in a New Millennium*, is intended as a contribution to that lively discussion.

It is the underlying presupposition of this work that for Religious Life and those who live it in faith there is indeed a future full of hope (cf. Jer 29:11). But if that hope is to be realized Religious must do the difficult work of rethinking their life in the radically new context of a new millennium which many cultural critics are characterizing as postmodern. I say that this is a difficult work because the context is complex, the experience to be examined and integrated is extremely rich and varied, the dialogue partners who can no longer be ignored as irrelevant are numerous and diverse. If Religious Life is to continue to make sense, to be a compelling and energizing life choice for those who live it and an attractive possibility for those contemplating it for themselves, and finally to be able to be presented coherently to those who appreciate it as well as those who do not, it must be examined anew and in depth.

I have been struck in recent years by the qualitative difference between the types of questions Religious were asking two decades ago and those that are at the center of discussions today. It seems to me that the difference is essentially that virtually every question raised today leads directly into the issue of what Religious Life is and means. In other words, whatever the presenting problems or issues—celibacy, permanent commitment, formation, associates, community, vows, ministry, feminism, Church, or prayer—the real question is "What is this life really all about?" Whatever one has to say about the particular issues must originate in and be expressive of what one claims the life is and means. I think the explicit emergence of this question is a very positive development, even though it greatly heightens the stakes in every discussion. It manifests the realization that, finally, Religious Life is a life, not a collection of disparate and separable elements but a coherent whole. The question about the life itself is one about its wholeness, its integrity, its authenticity as a way of being in this world. Consequently, this work is not an easy read. Anyone looking for a possible answer to specific problems will probably be disappointed.

What I am offering is an understanding of the life itself in its contemporary cultural context (volume 1) as the framework for a reconsideration of its constitutive dimensions, namely, lifelong commitment in consecrated celibacy lived in community (volume 2), and an exploration of the way in which the authentic and integrated living of this life can help to transform not only the Religious herself but also the society and culture of which Religious Life is a part (volume 3). This is a dangerous project for a writer because a comprehensive view of any reality invites not only agreement and disagreement with particular points (always a welcome source of both affirmation and improvement) but complete rejection of the project as a whole if the underlying presuppositions are found unacceptable. This is a danger I am willing to run because I am convinced of the value of Religious Life not only to the individuals called to it but also to the Church, which is called to be a light to the nations and therefore to the world itself. Recently someone asked me, "Does Religious Life need the Church?" and I replied that I thought the prior question is "Does the Church (and therefore the world) need Religious Life?" and I am convinced that the answer to the latter question is yes (and for other reasons so is the answer to the first). The realization of the potential of Religious Life, both for the Church and for our endangered cosmos, species, and culture, however, requires a theoretical basis that is clear and compelling. I am not arrogant enough to claim that this work supplies such a basis, much less the only one, but I hope it will generate focused discussion at the level on which I think this discussion must proceed at this point in history.

The primary intended audience of *Religious Life in a New Millennium* is the same as that of *New Wineskins*, that is, North American Roman Catholic women Religious. This is not the exclusive audience, for obviously much of the material in this work, as in its predecessor, is applicable to Religious in other cultures, to Protestant and Anglican Religious and members of ecumenical Religious communities, to male Religious, especially those of nonclerical institutes, to members of Secular Institutes and of secular or third orders connected with Religious orders, to members of Societies of Apostolic Life, and to various kinds of associates of canonical institutes. I have learned from conversations with laypeople, both Catholic and non-Catholic, that much of the material in *New Wineskins* was directly relevant to committed lay life, and I hope that that will be the case with this work as well. Indeed, it should be the case that Religious Life, rooted in and expressive of baptismal consecration and mission, would have more in common with than distinctive from Christian life in general.[2]

The choice of the specific audience is dictated by very practical considerations. First, the forms of life in some way analogous or related to Religious Life are so numerous, and each is sufficiently specific, that "ringing the changes" on everything that is said to account adequately for the variations would make the text excessively cumbersome, even if I were capable of doing it. Those living these other forms of life are much more competent than I to make the appropriate distinctions and qualifications in terms of their own life. Second, this work is a reflection on experience, and even within canonical Religious Life itself, to say nothing of related forms of life, the experiences of female and male Religious, North American Religious and those in Latin America, Asia, Africa, and Europe, and those in clerical and in nonclerical institutes are irreducibly diverse. I cannot speak from experience about and therefore am not competent to analyze the experience of men or of people whose cultures I do not share. Third, the specific experience with which I propose to deal is extensive and varied enough that doing it justice will more than fill the pages of three volumes of reasonable length. Finally, I am taking something of a chance in attempting to include, as fully as possible, in my specifically intended readership, both the so-called apostolic and contemplative forms of women's Religious Life.[3] This will present sufficient challenge in terms of distinctions and qualifications, even though what the two forms of life have in common is much more evident today than it was in preconciliar times.

The choice to write a new work rather than to revise *New Wineskins* was dictated by two realizations. First, the essays in the earlier volume retain their validity as reflections on the experience of the two decades that followed Vatican II and therefore, at least in my judgment, should stand as they are. Second, the experience that now requires reflection is not generated by the same dynamics as was the experience of the 1960s and 1970s. Although this distinction is simplistic, I think it is indicative of something important to say that in the immediate aftermath of the Council, Religious were dealing predominantly with changes *within* Religious Life itself as Religious encountered the "world" from which they had been almost hermetically sealed for centuries, whereas in the last fifteen years the concern has been much more explicitly with the interaction *between* Religious Life and the ambient culture, both secular and ecclesial.

There is a cause and effect relationship between the two phases. As Religious congregations responded to the Council's reaffirmation of the world as the locus of salvation and reconceptualized themselves as existing not out of or separate from the world but in, with, and for the world, they began an extensive dismantling of the structural barriers between themselves and other people and between the privatized culture of preconciliar Religious Life and the surrounding culture. At first, the primary impact of this dismantling was experienced within Religious Life itself. Dress, horaria, dwellings, community life, and ministries changed. This called for revisions of constitutions, and from that followed changes in internal structures, institutional involvements, and relationships within and outside the congregation. Foundational to these observable changes, of course, was a new theology and a rapidly evolving spirituality, but it was the breakdown of the total institution that precipitated what was to follow.

The opening up of the institution interrelated Religious with American secular culture in a new and much more intimate and pervasive way. To invoke only a few pertinent examples, permanent commitment through vows could not be proposed or explained without some reference to the cultural experience of ubiquitous career mobility, familial reconfigurations, indefinitely delayed marriage, and rampant divorce. Poverty had to be seen through the prism of attitudes toward money, lifestyle, and social class in a capitalist culture and in relation to a global economy. Ministry had to take account of the categories of career and promotion, employment and compensation, insurance and retirement. In short, it was not just that ceasing to be a closed system had repercussions for the internal life of the social system we call Religious Life but that the system itself was now in pervasive interaction with its cultural environment in ways that have deeply influenced it. It is primarily this interaction between Religious Life and culture, both ecclesial and secular, that is the focus of this work.

It has seemed to me that this task of analyzing and rethinking Religious Life could best proceed in three phases, the first a consideration of the global or general context (both cultural and ecclesial) influencing Religious Life, the second focusing specifically on the life itself through an exploration of its distinctive and constitutive relationships, and the third focusing on the influence of Religious Life on the context (again both ecclesial and cultural). In the global phase (volume 1) I want to address the larger question of "locating" or situating Religious Life in the multiple contexts that now qualify it in significant ways. It is a question of "finding the treasure" that is Religious Life. This task of "locating Religious Life" is a distinctly postmodern undertaking in the sense that there is no grand scheme or metanarrative within which all the influencing environments can be coherently related to one another and cumulatively create the single "space" or "place" of Religious Life. There was a time when we could describe the relationship between the Church and the world and within the Church the place of each form of life. This enabled us to properly place Religious Life in relation to all its significant publics and/or others: Vatican, hierarchy, local clergy, other forms of Religious Life, other congregations within one's own form, Catholic laity, other "seculars." And none of the relationships overlapped in intrinsically contradictory ways. Religious Life was subject to some, superior to others, in opposition to still others.

Today, Religious Life is situated vis-à-vis a plurality of incommensurable, overlapping, or largely unrelated realities, movements, and structures, and each of these situations may affirm, challenge, or radically call into question the self-understanding and claims of Religious concerning the meaning and significance of their life. How, for example, are Religious related to their obvious analogues in other world religions, such as Buddhist or Hindu monastics or Islamic Sufis? How are Religious related to clergy or to laity within the Catholic Christian community? How are women's Religious congregations related to feminism as a cultural movement? What kind of sociological reality is a Religious congregation? What does the new cosmology and its effect on theological categories have to say to the fundamental Christocentrism of Religious Life?

This list does not exhaust the questions, but it does suggest how different they are from those we were asking in the 1960s and 1970s and how each question pertains to a sphere of reality that may have little or nothing to do with the spheres from which the other questions arise. Responding to one such question sometimes does not seem to help much in responding to another. This fragmentation and pluralism are characteristic of postmodernism, and the pertinence of these questions to Religious Life suggests how involved in the cultural context of postmodernity Religious Life is. It is not possible to put these complexes together into a single, unitary worldview. Rather, they have to be held individually and together in a pluralistic way. This engagement with the diverse universes to which Religious Life is related is the global task of this work and especially of volume 1.

Second, there are the questions that are specific to Religious Life itself but which must be asked and answered differently because of the different contexts in which Religious

Life is situated today. In volume 2, therefore, I will be concerned with the relationships that constitute Religious Life
as a state of life: the multiple relationships established by
the commitment to Religious Life through profession; the
central distinctive relationship to God in Jesus Christ that is
consecrated celibacy; and the relational context in which
Religious Life is lived, namely, celibate community. Struggling with questions about commitment, about the meaning
of consecrated celibacy as the defining and distinguishing
feature of the life, and about the varied ways in which the
reality of community is embodied to form the life context of
this commitment has generated an experience that is ripe
for examination. This experience has been, in my opinion,
predominantly life-giving and liberating, but it has also
been, from some perspectives, frustrating and even traumatic. Wise people can learn from both positive and negative experience. My intention in volume 2 is to examine that
experience in light of history, tradition, Scripture, theology,
and the social sciences, but especially in terms of the spirituality involved in responding to the vocation to "sell all," that
is, to give the all of one's life to the All who is God in this
particular form of life.

Third, major changes within Religious Life have resulted
from the engagement over several decades with new questions in a new context. New horizons have opened; freedom
and responsibility have enriched experience; mistakes have
been made; what once seemed simple is now recognized as
very complex; the relative importance of various aspects of
Religious Life has been/is being reevaluated. The specific
task of volume 3 will be to revisit these areas of concern. I
will be examining the experience of the recent past, especially in the spheres of mission/ministry and personal/cor-
porate spirituality as these shape the life of Religious
themselves and through which Religious influence the ecclesial and cultural context within which they live. Religious
Life is indeed a treasure hidden in the field of this history
and culture, worth the price of one's life, but that price is

offered not just to acquire the treasure for oneself, but also to "ransom the field" itself. Religious Life cannot be lived well today without influencing both the postconciliar Church and the postmodern cultural context in which it is located and lived. As that context has influenced, indeed transformed, Religious Life so Religious Life must influence its context. The hope and the goal of those who, unlike the rich young man in the Gospel, are willing to sell all to follow Christ in Religious Life is nothing short of the transformation of the world by the Gospel.

Needless to say, this work is not the product of one person's reflection. Numerous individuals and groups have offered invaluable assistance with different aspects of each of the volumes, and I will acknowledge them in the appropriate places. However, some people and institutions have played a role in the entire project, and I wish to thank them in this general introduction.

I owe particular thanks to my own Religious congregation, the Sisters, Servants of the Immaculate Heart of Mary, whose support and appreciation of my work have made me both proud and humbly grateful to be a Religious in these challenging times. I want also to thank the Carmelite community of Baltimore for their wonderful hospitality, offered to me on numerous occasions, as I have prayed and reflected on the issues discussed in these volumes.

The actual writing would not have been possible without the combination of financial resources generously provided by the Lilly Endowment and the precious resource of time provided by my home institution, the Jesuit School of Theology at Berkeley. My editors at Paulist Press, Donna Crilly and Lawrence Boadt, have been effective collaborators at every point in the process.

The staff of the Flora Lamson Hewlett Library of the Graduate Theological Union has been generous with time and labor in helping with the research, and I am most grateful to them.

Finally, I wish to thank Bishop John S. Cummins, Ordinary of the Catholic Diocese of Oakland, whose encouragement of theological scholarship in general and of my work in particular has been an incentive and support in the academic and ecclesial vocation I share with my colleagues in the field of theology.

While I have learned much from those who have helped me in many ways as these volumes have emerged into the light of day I have, inevitably, made the final decisions about the content and bear the responsibility for what has resulted. I can only say that whatever limitations they suffer (which are surely many), they would have been much more numerous and serious without such help. I hope my readers will profit from what they find in this work, challenge what is questionable, and go on to enrich the conversation about the treasure of Religious Life, hidden in the field of Church and world, for which some, in their joy at finding it, have unhesitatingly sold all they possessed.

Pentecost 1999
Berkeley, California

ABBREVIATIONS

A.A.   *Apostolicam Actuositatem* (Decree on the Apostolate of Lay People), in Flannery, vol. 1.

CARA   Center for Applied Research in the Apostolate.

CCL (1917)   John A. Abbo and Jerome D. Hannon, *The Sacred Canons: A Concise Presentation of the Current Disciplinary Norms of the Church* (in paraphrase), 2 vols. (St Louis: Herder, 1951).

CCL (1983)   *Code of Canon Law: Latin-English Edition*, translation prepared under the auspices of the Canon Law Society of America (Washington, D.C.: Canon Law Society of America, 1983).

CTSA   Catholic Theological Society of America.

CWS   Classics of Western Spirituality Series (Mahwah, N.J.: Paulist, various dates).

E.E.   *Essential Elements in Church Teaching on Religious Life*, from the Congregation for Religious and Secular Institutes. English translation in *Origins* 13 (1983): 133–42.

E.T.   *Evangelica Testificatio* (Apostolic Exhortation on the Renewal of Religious Life), Paul VI, 1971, in Flannery, vol. 1.

Flannery   Flannery, Austin P., ed. *Vatican Council II: The Conciliar and Postconciliar Documents*, 2 vols. Grand Rapids: Eerdmans, 1975 and 1984.

FORUS   Nygren, David J., and Miriam D. Ukeritis, *The Future of Religious Orders in the United States: Transformation and Commitment*. Foreword by

David C. McClelland. Westport, Conn.: Praeger, 1993.

G.S.   *Gaudium et Spes* (Pastoral Constitution on the Church in the Modern World), in Flannery, vol. 1.

LCWR   Leadership Conference of Women Religious.

L.G.   *Lumen Gentium* (Dogmatic Constitution on the Church), in Flannery, vol. 1.

NCR   *National Catholic Reporter.*

P.C.   *Perfectae Caritatis* (Decree on the Up-to-Date Renewal of Religious Life), in Flannery, vol. 1.

P.G.   *Patrologia cursus completus:* Series Graeca. Paris: J. P. Migne, 1857–66.

P.L.   *Patrologia cursus completus:* Series Latina. Paris: J. P. Migne, 1844–55.

P.O.   *Presbyterorum Ordinis* (The Ministry and Life of Priests), in Flannery, vol. 1.

S.C.   *Sacrosanctum Concilium* (Constitution on the Sacred Liturgy), in Flannery, vol. 1.

S.R.V.   *Sacris Religionis Vinculis* (Introduction to the Rite of Initiation to the Religious Life) of the Sacred Congregation for Divine Worship, 1970, in Flannery, vol. 2.

U.R.   *Unitatis Redintegratio* (Decree on Ecumenism), in Flannery, vol. 1.

WOC   Women's Ordination Conference.

INTRODUCTION

In volume 1 of this work, *Religious Life in a New Millennium*, I attempted to locate Religious Life in relationship to a variety of contexts and problematics that characterize the turn of the century. If that effort was at all successful, if indeed it has helped Religious and others to "find the treasure" that is Religious Life in the cultural and ecclesial field in which it is now hidden, it is imperative to attend to the second movement of the gospel adventure, "selling all" to attain that treasure. Those called to Religious Life, today as in times past, face the daunting challenge of giving themselves totally to Christ, to the exclusion of all other primary life commitments, through the perpetual commitment of consecrated celibacy in community and mission. In the present volume I am assuming the location explored in volume 1 as the context within which to look at the constitutive coordinates interior to Religious Life itself: the process of commitment; consecrated celibacy as its heart; community as the context of this total commitment. The approach to these topics, although taking full account of the ecclesial and cultural context, will be much more explicitly biblical, theological, and spiritual.

I have divided this in-depth examination of the life from within into three parts that allow for the grouping of certain topics and their distinction from others. The grouping itself reveals something about my approach to Religious Life which may not be that of others living, writing on, or discussing the same topics. For example, I treat the topic of profession (that is, the definitive commitment to Christ in Religious Life) separately from the vows (that is, consecrated celibacy, evangelical poverty, and obedience). And I treat consecrated celibacy as the central section of this volume distinct from poverty and obedience, which will be taken up in volume 3. In other words, I do not group poverty, chastity, and obedience together as is traditionally done. I hope the rationale for these and other choices will become clear in the reading. Whether or not the rationale is convincing will be for the reader to decide.

The first part will deal with the topic of entrance into Religious Life from the first moment of experiencing a call or vocation to this life through to final commitment by perpetual profession. Under this heading I will deal not only with the theological concept of divine call but with the human process, psychological and spiritual, of discernment (chapter 1). In this first part I will also examine the process of formation for Religious Life and the progressive incorporation of the candidate into the congregation and the community (chapter 2). Finally, I will deal (in chapter 3) with the challenge of perpetual commitment by profession and the resulting state of life.

In part 2 I will look at consecrated celibacy as the heart of Religious Life. The first task will be to explore that thesis by examining, theologically and biblically, the charism of consecrated celibacy itself (chapter 4). But I also want to discuss the possibility that if consecrated celibacy is understood from the feminist standpoint of women's experience of relationship, and therefore of bodiliness, sexuality, love, and fidelity, it might look very different from the way it has been traditionally presented, that is, almost exclusively by male writers and from the standpoint of male experience of sexuality and of women (chapter 5). Finally, I will explore two dimensions of celibacy as lived spirituality in the context of contemporary first-world culture, namely, the relation of Religious to "family" (chapter 6) and "home" (chapter 7).

In part 3, on community as the context of Religious Life, I explore the theological and prophetic nature of community life both as a gospel imperative shared by all Christians and as a specific realization of that imperative in the community of consecrated celibates (chapter 8). On the basis of the resulting understanding of Religious community itself, especially in relation to the apostolic commitment of ministerial Religious, I raise the sociological and spiritual question of what form(s) of community life, that is, what lifestyle(s) might be appropriate embodiments of the theological reality of Religious community from the standpoint of the individual Religious (chapter 9) and from the corporate standpoint of the congregation (chapter 10).

Obviously each of these topics could be the subject of a book in itself. My hope is not to treat them exhaustively and certainly not to present the only possible approach to them. Rather I hope to open up the topics to a fresh examination and invite ongoing conversation about them. Our experience, both positive and negative, over the nearly four decades since the Council has supplied an enormous amount of data for such reflection and conversation. I am convinced that it is time to put that data into dialogue with the tradition on the one hand and our turn-of-the-century cultural experience on the other in order to develop a renewed understanding of what we are about as contemporary Religious. So I invite the reader to reflect with me, and more importantly to reflect with others, on the treasure that is Religious Life and which both demands and is worth the investment of all that we have and are.

Acknowledgments

It is a privilege and a joy to acknowledge the multitude of people and agencies who have contributed in large and small ways to this work, and especially to the production of this second volume. Most significant has been the continued and renewed gift of financial support from the Lilly Endowment, couched in the enthusiastic interest and confidence in the value of the project of Craig Dykstra, vice president for religion, and the equally valuable gift of time for research and writing from my home institution, the Jesuit School of Theology at Berkeley. President Joseph Daoust, S.J., and Dean George Griener, S.J., as well as my faculty colleagues, all of whom have assumed burdens from which I was released during this research leave, have been immeasurably generous in supporting this work. Most members of the faculty at one point or another have also helped me with data from their respective disciplines that I needed to think through issues or to document arguments. They have also listened to and discussed with me, formally and informally, many topics and theories that have been incorporated into the final product.

The staffs of the Flora Lamson Hewlett Library of the Graduate Theological Union, the Leadership Conference of Women Religious, the Religious Formation Conference, the National Vocation Conference, the Center for Applied Research in the Apostolate, and the archives of Notre Dame University have all been most generous in tracking down information I needed.

Many individuals have read and commented on parts of the work, and various congregations and institutions have invited me to address their constituencies and have discussed with me topics treated in this second volume. I am especially indebted to the western region of the Sisters of Charity of the Blessed Virgin Mary (B.V.M.'s), the Carmelite Community of Baltimore, Maryland, Saint Mary's College in Notre Dame, Indiana, Neumann College in Aston, Pennsylvania, and Aquinas Institute at Saint Louis University. Most important in many ways has been the opportunity to reflect with my own congregation, the Sisters, Servants of the Immaculate Heart of Mary of Monroe, Michigan.

My special thanks to the women in formation in Monroe and at the Baltimore Carmel and to the members of the Fertile Fields project, which is bringing together younger women Religious across the United States, for their sharing with me of the perspectives of newer members of Religious communities.

I will not rename the people I thanked in volume 1, all of whom have contributed to this volume as well as the last, but several others must be added to that list: I.H.M.'s Margaret Alandt, Anne Crimmins, Mary Ann Hinsdale, Virginia Pfau, and I.H.M. Associate Joann Wolski Conn, Dorothy Ettlinger, C.C.V.I., Jeannine Gramick, S.S.N.D., Patricia Wittberg, S.C., and Mary Johnson, S.N.D.deN. I am grateful also to a number of men Religious who have shared with me their particular perspective on our shared life, especially Xaverian Brothers Cornelius Hubbuch and Peter Fitzpatrick, and John Mulligan, S.M., and the Marianist community in Oakland.

Once again I wish to thank Bishop John S. Cummins, of the Diocese of Oakland, for his intelligent and pastoral reflection that is always both a contribution to my work and a tonic for my spirit.

Crucial to my sanity during the work on this project has been the loving hospitality and support of my dear friends Rita and Tom O'Malley and their four wonderful boys, Tommy, Johnny, Danny, and Billy. They know how important to me they are.

Finally, I reiterate my gratitude to those who have helped in the actual production of this volume, especially my editor at Paulist, Donna Crilly, whose enthusiasm for the project has been as valuable as her excellent advice and artistic good taste, and Jan Richardson, my indefatigable assistant, whose research skills are matched only by her electronic wizardry in charming the final product out of the computer. My thanks also to her successor, Annie Russell, who has helped to bring this volume to completion.

To these and many other people whose help in various ways has made this book better than it otherwise would have been I offer my heartfelt gratitude even as I willingly accept responsibility for all the shortcomings that still remain.

August 6, 2000
Feast of the Transfiguration

PART ONE

Commitment

CHAPTER ONE
VOCATION AND DISCERNMENT

I. Vocation to What?

Becoming a Religious is a process that begins with a decision by an individual who feels personally called by God to enter Religious Life within a particular congregation and the corresponding decision of the congregation to accept the candidate for a period of mutual discernment. The interrelation of the realities of vocation and discernment, formation and incorporation, commitment and profession, and the resulting state of life is complex and, in a sense, one could start with any of these terms and be eventually led to discuss all the others. I am proposing to begin with a description of what one enters by entering Religious Life. In part this starting point is suggested by the confusion about and often the tacit obscuring of the full reality of what a candidate is proposing to embrace. And in part this description will function as a point of reference for all that follows. The description will be from the outside in, that is, from the organizational to the relational to the spiritual. Hopefully, this will supply the information that will enable a clearer reflection on the theology and spirituality of the life in subsequent chapters.

During most of the lifespan of North American congregations, that is, the past two centuries, three terms have been used virtually interchangeably and have been at least implicitly synonymous for most Religious and those who interacted with them because, in fact, they were coterminous, that is,

3

they covered exactly the same territory in terms of the people involved. The terms were *congregation, community,* and *Religious Life.* A young woman in the 1950s or 1960s who responded to the question of what she intended to do after graduation from high school or college might have replied, "I am going to enter the convent," or "I am going to become a Sister of Charity," and her interlocutor might well have responded, "Oh, so you're going to become a nun." All three terms, *convent, order,* and *state of life,* were considered equivalent. Furthermore, *entering* (an order or congregation) and *becoming* (a Religious) were also used as synonyms marking a change of state from lay to Religious. The equivalence was both factual and unproblematic. In effect, entering the convent entailed necessarily entering a particular order, and this involved becoming a Religious. The transition from layperson to Religious was so dramatic, sociologically, that there were no gray areas between the two states.

Today the situation is quite different. The dismantling of the total institution of Religious Life and the resulting extensive interactions between Religious and their lay counterparts in and beyond the Church have generated considerable expanses of gray area. Furthermore, the virtual identity between the agenda and processes of the institutional Church and those of Religious institutes that characterized the Tridentine period has given way to frequent if not ongoing tensions between Religious and ecclesiastical authorities. Religious are not simply a ministerial arm of the local ecclesiastical structure. The prospective candidate for Religious Life today, therefore, needs to be very clear about what she is undertaking and its responsibilities. In fact, the vocational process involves relating to three distinct realities of unequal importance that are not strictly coterminous: congregation/institute, community, and Religious Life.

A. Congregation/Institute

Both *congregation* and *institute* are juridical terms referring to a group as a "moral person" in Canon Law. A Religious Institute usually comes into being by the initiative of an individual or group, the founder(s),[1] who decides to establish a particular organization within the broad historical social movement of Religious Life. The founder, usually with the first members, decides on the purpose and way of life of the group, writes a constitution or rule of life that both describes the group and its organization and prescribes its way of life, and then submits these documents to the appropriate Church officials for approval. If the documents receive approbation, the group becomes a diocesan institute (if approved by the bishop) or an institute of pontifical right (if approved by the Vatican).

Between 1917 and 1983, when Canon Law was last revised, the canonical prescriptions governing Religious Institutes were so numerous and detailed that the constitutions of various congregations were virtually identical. Any distinguishing features of the group were relegated to books of customs, directories, or oral tradition that were not part of the official canonical documentation of the institute. Fortunately for all concerned, the 1983 Code reduced the "norms common to all institutes of consecrated life"[2] to a minimum, thereby allowing individual congregations considerable latitude in embodying their own charism and spirituality within their "particular law," that is, their own constitutions and other documents.

Nevertheless, as institutes, that is, as canonical entities, Religious congregations conform to a certain pattern that is more or less standard. The elements all institutes have in common include perpetual (or continually renewed) profession of the vows of celibacy, poverty, and obedience; community life; a governmental structure; the requirement of appropriate formation of new members; and, in ministerial institutes, a commitment to ministry specified in some way. There is also a series of canons[3] governing Religious Institutes as distinct from other forms of consecrated life (such as Secular Institutes and Societies of Apostolic Life), which specify how houses of an institute are established, how institutes are governed, conditions for admission of candidates or departures of professed members, apostolates within the diocesan context, and so on. In other words, Religious Institutes as institutes are "standard." Although congregations may differ in how they understand or provide for the realization of each of these elements, all of the elements are present in any canonical institute and all institutes are governed by the same provisions of Canon Law.

The term *congregation* refers to the same juridical entity as the term *institute* but adds the important nuance of specific identity and dynamic history. When Religious refer to their congregation, they mean their own institute as it is stamped by the charism of particular foundation and the teaching and example of the founder, by the history of the group, its personalities and ministries, its successes and crises, its individual mythology and characteristic symbol system, and so on. One might say that to the Vatican the group is an institute and to itself and the people with whom it actually deals it is a particular congregation. The institute, for example, is an apostolic institute of pontifical or diocesan right; the congregation is the Adrian Dominicans or the Sisters of St. Joseph of Boston.

As institute/congregation the entity is both a canonical reality, that is, a "moral person" in Church law, and a sociological reality. Religious Life is an extremely broad and variegated phenomenon with a nearly two-thousand-year history. Sociologists would call it a social movement, analogous to the feminist movement or the peace movement. Within such broad and internally diversified movements arise what sociologists call "social movement organizations."[4] For example, the Women's Ordination Conference is a social movement organization within the broader social movement of feminism, as Pax Christi is within the peace movement. Analogously, a given congregation is a social movement organization within the Religious Life movement. As such it has its particular agenda or mission, its means of achieving that agenda through its lifestyle and ministry, its own rules and regulations, entrance requirements, style of government, and so on. In other words, there is much about the congregation that does not derive directly from its canonical character but is nevertheless integral to its identity and functioning because it is an organization. That is certainly not all it is, nor is it the most important dimension of what it is, but, as we will see shortly, the fact that it is both a moral person in Canon Law and sociologically an organization has important implications for life as a member.

B. Community

In the Tridentine period of Religious Life (i.e., the four hundred years prior to Vatican II) the terms *congregation* and *community* were used synonymously because they were coterminous. All and only the members of the congregation were considered part of the community. Most Religious made no conceptual distinction between the terms even though there was an affective resonance to *community* that was not as readily attached to *congregation,* and *community* tended to be used for the local group while *congregation* applied only to the organization as a whole. This synonymity of *congregation* and *community* was a natural assumption because the congregation was a total institution, and entrance involved not only actually severing virtually all other relationships but also not forming relationships that were not intrinsically related to one's congregational membership. In fact, of course, individual members and the congregation itself had many relationships with families of origin, coworkers, benefactors, and clients that had deeply affective overtones, but the theory of the total institution usually disguised the participation of these people in the community life of the congregation. They were outsiders.

In fact, community is, in a certain sense, at the opposite end of the organizational spectrum from congregation. And it is prior, both chronologically and theologically, to congregation. Community denotes the affective commitment of the members of the congregation to one another, the bonds of unity in faith, hope, love, ministry, prayer, and daily life that insert the community into the ideal tradition of the early Church, whose members "were of one heart and soul" and held "everything in common" (Acts 4:32). Virtually every congregation began as a community, a group of people who had come together as friends united by a common vocation to the exclusive God-quest expressed in consecrated celibacy, shared life, and the ministerial response to a particular social need. Only after some time of living together did they codify their way of life, seek canonical approbation, and become a congregation. A person considering entering a congregation usually had some affective relationship with the members, for example, as a student or coworker or volunteer, before seeking entrance, and today people joining a congregation usually begin the process by associating with some of its members, getting a feel for the quality of the community. Even after incorporation into the institute, indeed throughout life, the person continues to develop her community identity and relationships.

The quality of community is far more significant theologically than canonical status as a congregation. The reality of Religious Life can be lived without the latter, but not without the former. This became clear, for example, in 1968, when the majority of the members of the Immaculate Heart of Mary congregation of Los Angeles were forced by Cardinal McIntyre to accept dispensation from their vows, that is, to leave their congregation/institute, because he disapproved of their renewal efforts. The sisters immediately regrouped, made private vows, and continued as the I.H.M. Community. Some groups, such as the Sisters for Christian Community, have never sought canonical status as an institute because they do not wish to deal with the ecclesiastical issues that involves. But as a community they are bound together by a shared history and spirit, formal commitment, mutual support, and a concern for one another's life and ministry.

The question for Religious, then, is how congregational membership and community are related. This question comes from two directions: that of nonmembers of the institute who are affectively involved in the community and that of members' relationships to many people who are neither members of the congregation nor participants in the congregation's wider community.

In the postconciliar era congregations have become much more conscious of the wide network of affective relationships enjoyed by their members and, conversely, of the many ways in which nonmembers of the institute are related to the congregation. Family members, clients, friends, benefactors, coministers, professional colleagues, fellow participants in spiritual and social justice movements, people who choose the congregation as a context for prayer and/or resonate with the particular spirituality of the congregation, and many others are often affectively close to the congregation in important ways. In other words, the relational network of community is a far more extensive reality than the juridical entity that is the congregation.

Some nonmembers formalize their relationship to the congregation through a commitment of some kind by becoming an associate, affiliate, or volunteer or in some other way. Some, for example, oblates, even make one or another private vow or promise that relates them to the congregation and its charism in a more stable way. These people are not members of the congregation but are certainly part of its extended community and the question for members is often how their own situation differs and what that difference entails.[5]

C. Religious Life

Much more fundamental and important than either entering a congregation or joining a community is becoming a Religious. Religious Life is not really something one "enters" or "joins" so much as a life one lives. One *becomes* a Religious. Being a Religious is not primarily something one does but something one is. Before there were such things as congregations or orders, before Religious banded together in communities, and long before specific ministries were undertaken by congregations, there were Religious.

Religious Life is a *state of life,* like marriage. Profession establishes a stable set of permanent and distinctive relationships to God, one's congregation/community, and the Church. Although rooted in the baptismal commitment common to all Christians, Religious profession shapes that commitment in a particular way that is distinctive within the Christian community. This state of life is formally initiated, after a lengthy preparation and careful discernment, by formal, solemn, and public commitment which establishes a lifelong condition that affects everything the person will do, every decision she will make, for the rest of her life. Being a Religious is a public situation in the Church, and other members of the Church are entitled to hold the Religious accountable for the commitments made.[6] In other words, becoming a Religious is not primarily a matter of joining an organization (congregation/institute) nor even a choice of companions (community) or of a form of service (ministry). It is a personal, spiritual, and ultimate choice of what one will be.

Part 2 of this volume will be concerned at length with the theology and spirituality of Religious Life. Here our concern is to identify it sufficiently to be able to talk about what discerning a vocation to this life entails. Essentially, Religious Life (again, like marriage) is a way of definitively shaping one's relational capacity in a particular way. It is a choice about Who (not what organization or what group or what work) will be the very center of one's life in an exclusive and absolute way that determines all other loves and all other choices in relation to itself.

The decision about what one will do with one's capacity for love is, for everyone, the ultimate life choice. In marriage it is the choice of one's spouse and the family thereby created. For some people it is a life partner of the same sex. For some it is a project or cause or work. In each case, the central focus of one's capacity for love and self-donation, and thus for self-transcendence, determines the quality and shape of the life.

In the case of Religious the ultimate choice is not of an organization, community, or ministry, all of which can be found and embraced outside Religious Life, but of a Person, of Jesus Christ as the locus of union with God. For some people their experience of the universal Christian vocation to the love of Christ has the unusual character of seeming to call them to an exclusivity in that relationship which makes other primary life commitments (e.g., to spouse or family or life work) not viable for them. The call to consecrated celibacy, that is, to giving themselves to Jesus in an exclusive and permanent union that expresses itself in nonmarriage to anyone else is at the heart of Religious Life.

As we will see in much greater depth and detail in part 2, this is its distinguishing feature, that which is not obligatory for any Christian and to which most are not called.

Because Catholic Religious Life entails, at least in most cases—consecrated virginity in the world and the eremitical life are exceptions—entering a congregation or order and thus forming community with other members of the congregation and its extended community as well as being involved in the congregation's corporate ministry, it is possible for prospective candidates to see one or another or the combination of these dimensions of the life as primary in their decision-making process. This has sometimes led to a failure to bring the vocational discernment process to bear directly on the issue of Religious Life itself and thus to people making profession of perpetual consecrated celibacy as "part of the package" without realizing its true significance. The discernment of whether one is truly called to Religious Life bears most importantly on the question of whether one feels personally called, for religious reasons, to the particular type of relationship with Jesus Christ that is expressed in consecrated celibacy.

II. Vocation and Discernment

Although there were periods in the history of Christianity in which children, both girls and boys, were consigned to monasteries at a very young age (as they were to arranged marriages) and simply grew up expecting to be professed as members of the order, no one drifts into or is consigned to Religious Life today. Becoming a Religious is a very deliberate process freely undertaken by the individual in relation to the congregation she or he proposes to enter. It begins in the experience of what, theologically, has been called a "vocation" or call to the life. That call becomes the subject of a prolonged process of "discernment," which involves reflection, testing, and formation. Only if the discernment process indicates the reality of the call and the capacity and desire of the person to respond to it does it lead to commitment in perpetual profession. Consequently,

in this section we need to explore the correlative terms vocation and discernment.

A. Vocation

The very word *vocation* suggests that the initiative for undertaking Religious Life comes from "outside" oneself, from
Another. It suggests that the person hears some clear divine
communication about her or his destiny. This says both too
much and too little about the beginning of the process. It says
too much because it suggests an experience that very few
people will have, a kind of audible divine summons. It says too
little because it suggests that, in a sense, only one's ears and
mind are involved in the experience of vocation. It also can
lead to faulty decisions in that some might feel that unless they
receive an absolutely unmistakable "sign" from God they are
not truly called to Religious Life or, on the other hand, that if
they do feel they have received such a sign they are no longer
free to say no to the vocation (which, of course, means they are
not really free to say yes either).

When vocation is thought of as a clear call from God indicating what one should do, it carries an implicit threat that
failure to obey will have unpleasant if not dire consequences.
This is a case of bad theology (of vocation) leading to bad spirituality (of responding to divine coercion). If, however, *vocation* is not an explicit divine command, to what does the word
refer? It does suggest that the initiative for considering Religious Life is some kind of "address," something that calls for a
response. But unlike someone suddenly calling my name in a
crowded room, the call is coming both from within and from
without in a way analogous to the felt call to be an artist or an
actor or a scientist. It is a convergence of interior factors such
as attraction, talent, interest, experience, desires, ideals, and
even realistic fears and awareness of personal limitations, with
exterior factors such as people I admire, work that interests
me, opportunity presenting itself, needs that move me, structures that facilitate exploration, invitation from another. This
convergence is usually a rich mixture that is both confusing

and exciting and leads a person to begin to explore what this might mean.

Most experienced Religious know that, if they were to list the factors motivating them when they undertook Religious Life, they would now repudiate some of them. Some were unworthy from the beginning, such as a desire to belong to a spiritual elite. Some were immature, such as hero worship of an inspiring teacher, or unrealistic, such as a conviction that one could single-handedly save the world. Some might have been unhealthy, such as a fear of marriage or of financial responsibility. Some were selfish or egotistical, such as a desire for higher social status or a better education than one's family could provide. But those who have remained Religious know that there were other motivations, perhaps less clear but ultimately more powerful, such as a fascination with the God-quest, love for Christ in himself and in his members, a desire for union with God in prayer, zeal to make the Gospel available to others in an attractive and saving way, love of the Church, desire to be part of a community centered on the spiritual life and committed to an idealistic project.[7] Some of these motivations may have been inchoate at the beginning but as less valid reasons were exposed by experience and progressively repudiated, the genuine, life-sustaining ones surfaced and were embraced. This is not unlike the process that leads to marriage. Infatuation is not a bad thing. It brings people together, generates the excitement, creates the dynamism that leads to the desire for mutual and life-long commitment. Not a few people get married partly to get away from their family of origin, or to gain some independence, or to prove to themselves and others that they can attract and hold another person, or because the other person represents a "catch" that offers increased status or financial security. But unless these inadequate motivations give way to genuine love and friendship the marriage will not last.

In short, no one experiences the vocation to Religious Life in its "pure state." Part of the process of discernment is sorting out, at least in a preliminary way, the tangled skein of motivation. And the formation process is designed to help make motivation more conscious and explicit, to begin the purification of less worthy motives and the enhancement of those that can provide a solid basis for commitment. But most people will spend their lives gradually discovering, healing or affirming, and developing new motivations for continuing in their commitments.

One might ask what this conception of vocation has to do with God, a God who calls and to whom one responds. Believing that God is at work in one's life does not necessarily entail believing that God intervenes miraculously or outside the normal workings of human experience. For a person of *faith,* God is guiding our life and destiny, participating in our exercise of divinely given freedom. The working together of all the factors, interior and exterior, that seem to direct our attention toward a particular commitment is just as much God's work as a thunderclap voice from on high, and probably more credible in the long run. Faith challenges us to affirm not only that God is at work in our life but also that our *freedom* is both gift and responsibility and that trusting our own prayerful discernment process is the appropriate response to that gift.

B. Discernment

Discernment, the process by which one finally decides whether one is called to Religious Life in a particular congregation, is a word that is overused and probably often misused today. Sometimes "discernment" is used to justify doing or not doing what a person has decided to do or avoid well before beginning to discern. Nevertheless, genuine discernment is an absolutely necessary process if a person is to arrive at a life choice of enormous importance, such as commitment in Religious Life.

1. What is discernment? When it bears upon vocation, discernment is a process of coming to an informed decision before God of what I should do here and now. First, it is a *process.* It is not an impulse, an infatuation, or a conclusion one jumps to. This is why the Church and Religious congregations insist that a person thinking about Religious Life spend a very long time, up to nine years in many institutes, exploring, testing, studying, praying, discussing, and experimenting before she or he makes a definitive commitment. It also means that the period of formation and progressive incorporation is necessarily one of probation as well. The candidate is testing her fit into the congregation and its ministry, the community, and Religious Life, and the congregation is testing the candidate's suitability for the life.

Second, it is a process of coming to an *informed decision* about whether or not one is called to this life. Informed takes in a great deal. It must include, to the best of one's knowledge, everything relevant to the decision that can be investigated in a reasonable span of time. For a person considering Religious Life this will include theology of Church, Christ, sacraments, ministry, and Religious Life, as well as psychological assessment, experience in community and ministry, and the study of the congregation's history and charism. Candidates, especially those who are older and more experienced when they apply, sometimes resist the formation agenda or even the very notion of formation. They have, after all, an education and often a profession, considerable experience of managing their own affairs, and a developed personality and spirituality when they arrive, and they are not formless spiritual protoplasm to be molded from the outside into some kind of standard product. But the fact is that one who has not lived Religious Life, no matter what other forms of life she or he may have experienced, cannot know firsthand much of what needs to be taken into account if one is to make a genuinely informed decision. Formation is not about molding automatons but about enabling inner freedom by providing the necessary intellectual, religious, spiritual, and experiential resources.

The formation/probation experience of discernment is meant to lead to an informed decision. It is possible to drift into decisions without actually making them. Inertia, the desire for security, lack of courage, laziness, comfort seeking, avoidance of responsibility, and camaraderie can lead a person to try to decide by not deciding. Every congregation has members who simply never decided to leave and somehow kept on keeping on through reception and profession, hanging around while keeping an eye out for something more attractive, which never came along. Becoming a Religious involves making a serious decision for or against a particular life commitment. At some point that decision needs to be made. This presents a greater challenge today, for many reasons, than it did in the past, and we will deal with this issue later. But the fruit of good vocational discernment is decision.

Third, the decision to which one comes through discernment is made *before God*. It is not a matter of deciding whether one likes the community or enjoys the ministry or sees nothing preferable on the horizon. It is a matter of what God is calling one to do with one's life. For this reason the development and deepening of a life of personal prayer not only before entrance but especially during formation/probation is absolutely crucial. In prayer the person relates, one-to-one, in prolonged intimacy with the One with whom she is planning to spend her life in exclusive self-donation. It is analogous to the time engaged people spend together, getting to know each other in a qualitatively different way than they did when marriage was not an issue. The candidate will be taking part in community life, perhaps in some of the ministries of the congregation, and studying its history and spirit. But no amount of success, excitement, or enjoyment of these dimensions of the life can justify or ground the choice of Religious Life unless the deepening relationship with Christ is suggesting from within that consecrated celibacy, the total, exclusive, and lifelong self-gift to Jesus, is ultimately meaningful for her.

Finally, the decision that one comes to before God is a decision about what *I* should *do here and now*. This is the point at which the process becomes utterly personal and concrete. I am not trying to decide whether, in theory, Religious Life is valid, good, or even the best form of Christian life. I am trying to decide whether I am called by God to this life. And it is not a decision about the vague future. No one knows whether she will live another day or year or half century, no matter how young or vigorous she may be when she makes profession. We cannot know who will remain in the congregation or whether the congregation itself is viable. The Catholic Church will undoubtedly undergo significant changes, maybe for the better but maybe for the worse, in one's lifetime, if that is at all extended. The world itself may explode into total war or implode environmentally. The choice one makes about Religious Life has to make sense now, in the present, in this concrete place, with these real people, in this actual Church and world. The commitment one makes must have the depth and power to enable one to deal with the challenges of the present, be the best decision one can make here and now, in the faith that one will be able to face from within the framework of this commitment whatever the future brings.

2. *What requires discernment?* Although discerning one's vocation to Religious Life is governed more by a psychological/spiritual dynamic than by abstract logic because all dimensions of the vocation are intertwined with all the others and one cannot come to clarity about one before going on to the next, it is important to have a sense of the areas which, by the time one is ready to make a decision, should have been examined. Basically, these include one's relationship to each of the three dimensions of Religious Life described above: the congregation/institute, the community, and Religious Life as a state of life.

a. *The call to the congregation/institute:* In times past most candidates for Religious Life were hardly aware of the fact that entering the order to which they felt called involved entering a canonical institute. The canonical dimensions of Religious Life were the province of superiors who interpreted the constitutions and specified the behavioral implications for the members. Today this issue is perhaps one of the most difficult and critical for Religious and those thinking of becoming Religious. By entering a canonical institute a person establishes a public relationship with the institutional Church that goes beyond that of other laypersons in the Church. While Religious are not clerics and therefore not official agents of the institution and are called by vocation to a prophetic role in the Church, which sometimes involves them in legitimate dissent and consequent conflict with institutional authority, Religious Life itself involves a public role in the Church.[8]

Roman Catholicism is a rich, living tradition, the largest single denomination in the United States, and one of the most influential social phenomena in the world. It has a deep tradition of spirituality, a serious and complex theology, a social justice teaching better developed than probably any other in the world today. However, it also has a long and lively history of intolerance, persecution, misogyny, and injustice. There is no question that many Religious in recent years have left Religious Life because they felt they could not, without compromising their personal integrity, be publicly associated with an institution that they perceived as morally rigid, vindictive and even violent in its dealings with the very people Jesus came to save, hypocritical, and corrupt to the point of preferring its own power and control agenda to that of the Reign of God. And there are Religious who have not left but who agonize over this same issue.

Someone considering entering a canonical institute today cannot afford to ignore this issue or pretend that it is not real. Hoping that if one does not attend to it, it will somehow go away or at least not become problematic in one's own life is naïve, and formation personnel who encourage such an ostrich approach are doing candidates a grave disservice, in fact if not in intention. Catholics today cannot, as they often did in the past, assume that whatever emanates from the Vatican or other ecclesiastical authorities is simple truth and God's will for all the baptized. The contemporary Church is wracked with internal dissension over issues that are of major theological and pastoral import, and anyone who contemplates assuming a heightened public position in this institution requires more than a little courage and ability to sustain disapproval, capacity for hope in seemingly desperate situations, discerning faith that can distinguish between the real Church of Christ and its flawed human institutionalization, heroic love for the People of God which is the Body of Christ, and calm determination to serve that body with joy and commitment regardless of the struggles in which it is involved. In short, a vocation to a canonical institute today is a vocation to the prophetic role in action, and the person who hears that call will undoubtedly have to wrestle with it and within it as did Jeremiah, Hosea, and Jesus, none of whom were immune to the anguish it involved.

The contemporary Church needs its prophetic element, especially perhaps its public and organized prophetic element which is Religious Life. But much more than was the case in the preconciliar Church, the contemporary candidate for canonical Religious Life needs to clearly understand the prophetic dimension of her call and embrace it consciously rather than attempting to deny or disguise it or, like Jonah, to run from it by situating her ministry in a nonecclesial setting.

If prophetic involvement in the Church through entrance into a canonical institute is the external face of Religious Life, becoming a member of a congregation is the internal face of this same reality. Congregational identity, for this reason, has always been a major point of discernment for prospective Religious and their formation directors. One does not enter Religious Life in general but a particular congregation. As congregation it is sociologically an organization and it is distinct from other congregations.

Three implications of the fact that the congregation is an organization are important, especially today, when Religious Life is no longer a total institution nor extended communities strictly coterminous with congregations as institutes. First, one *joins or enters* an organization. One is either in it or not in it or in the process of entering it or in the process of leaving it, and there are socially visible markers by which to know where one is on this continuum. Thus a person is a candidate or novice, a temporarily or perpetually professed member, on a leave of absence or exclaustrated, or dispensed from one's vows and no longer a member. These are legal relationships to the institute, and each involves different rights, duties, and responsibilities within the congregation. Just "being around" a congregation in various ways, being affectively related to various members, or even contributing financially or ministerially to the congregation does not assimilate a person to the institute as a member of the congregation.

Second, as a canonical institute and a particular organization the congregation *defines itself* according to canon law and its own particular law, and all full members are bound by all of the features of that self-definition. This means that there are entrance requirements or conditions that must be met if one is to become a member of the congregation and thus that the candidate must discern whether she feels called to and capable of meeting those conditions. At the present time, for example, Religious Institutes are defined as composed of baptized, confirmed, and practicing celibate Roman Catholics of the same sex who profess celibate chastity, poverty, and obedience and share community and ministry.[9] This means that a Buddhist, a sexually active homosexual, a married person, someone who owns a house in her own name, as well as people in many other situations incompatible with the congregation's self-definition cannot be members of the Religious institute.[10]

Third, because of the enormous variety of congregations, both as to basic types and as to particular spirit or "corporate personality," the *particularity of the congregation* is also a major focus of discernment. A preliminary consideration might well be whether the prospective candidate feels drawn to a large or small group. A congregation with hundreds or even thousands of members has considerably more resources for both community and ministry but might feel, to some people, too unwieldy or anonymous or demanding. A very small congregation may offer greater intimacy with all members and more felt sense of belonging, but for some people such a restricted group would feel claustrophobic and demand too much internally focused energy.

A related issue is whether one feels called to an international congregation or to one that lives and ministers to a large extent within one particular national or ethnic context. The international congregation offers a day-to-day experience of the worldwide character and vocation of the Church, which some find powerfully stimulating, but it also makes every major decision a cultural challenge and working together in ministry across cultural divides not only exciting but difficult. The gravitational pull toward compromise and surrender to lowest-common-denominator solutions in order to preserve a threatened unity are ongoing challenges, as are ethnic and racial tensions. The single-nationality congregation involves a powerful identification with the local Church and provides a cultural basis for unity of perception about needs and shared approaches to ways of meeting them. Shared language and customs can make the full involvement of all members on an equal basis much easier to achieve, and such natural bases of unity can make change and development easier. However, national identity of a congregation can also lead to ethnocentrism and narrowness of vision, even to the assumption of cultural or racial superiority in relation to other local churches.

A major point of discernment is whether one feels called to a stabile monastic congregation or a mobile ministerial one. As I tried to show in *Finding the Treasure,* this is not a choice between prayer and action or between contemplation and apostolate, for these are integral dimensions of both forms of Religious Life.[11] But it is a choice about how one's living of Religious Life will be organized on a day-to-day basis. The monastic Religious belongs to a community that is relatively autonomous, in which daily common prayer and other activities is the norm, in which members remain in the same community over a lifetime, and in which ministry outside the monastic environment is relatively rare or even nonexistent. The ministerial Religious belongs to a variety of local communities over her lifetime, not all of which live together in the same house or are even composed of members of the same congregation. Her primary affiliation is to the congregation itself rather than to any local unit of it, and ministry will call her to occasional or frequent changes of location, to distance from family and friends, to a lifetime of developing new abilities to deal with new situations and needs and changed companions and activities. It will not necessarily provide her with a structured schedule or lifestyle pattern to sustain her spirituality, and she will probably have to assume much more individual responsibility for all of the day-to-day requirements of living.

Each of these forms of Religious Life has its advantages and its challenges. The autonomous monastery provides a stabile environment that fosters growth in prayer and deepening of community, but it can also foster self-absorption, resignation to a kind of well-ordered mediocrity that avoids challenge and change, the superficial tolerance bred by overfamiliarity with one's companions rather than deep relationships, or a low-grade boredom that leads to comfortable routine but minimal growth. The ministerial lifestyle provides opportunity for imaginative creativity in the service of the neighbor, society-transforming agency that can be energizing in itself and that challenges one to continual personal development, and an interesting variety of relationships that promote personal flex-ibility and wide understanding. But it can also foster spiritual shallowness excused by busyness, loss of connection with the very meaning of one's life in contemplative union with God, secularism in lifestyle, alienation from and irresponsibility toward community, excessive individualism, and careerism.

For those who feel called to a ministerial congregation, dis-cernment about ministry is also important. Although most con-gregations today engage in a variety of ministries, they do have historical roots in certain ministries and/or types of ministry, and the charism of the congregation makes some types of min-istry more congenial than others. A person with a strong desire for an intellectual apostolate might not find a congregation tra-ditionally involved in social service the best environment for her gifts, and someone who feels powerfully attracted to cross-cultural ministry with the materially poor would be more likely to find companions in a missionary congregation than in one that historically has been involved in first-world education. Although in the past many people entered the congregation they knew, scarcely noticing what ministry the Religious in that congregation did, and were prepared to do whatever God would ask of them, it is a fact that some Religious spent their entire active lives in work for which they were ill-suited and in which they were both unsuccessful and unhappy. Today it is still important to develop a willingness to serve where one is needed, even at the cost of some sacrifice of self-fulfillment, and a candidate who has a nonnegotiable ministerial project at the time of entrance presents real problems. Nevertheless, all things being equal (which, of course, they seldom are) people will minister more effectively when there is some fit between their gifts and attractions and the work they are eventually missioned to do. Therefore, it seems important to do some active discernment around the issue of ministry both before and after entering a congregation.

Even if one is fairly clear about what type of congregation one is called to, there remains the question of which particular one to enter. For example, both the Religious of the Sacred Heart and the Congregation of Notre Dame de Namur are international and ministerial congregations with long histories in educational ministries, but the differences between them are significant. And even within an international order such as the Carmelites or the Benedictines each autonomous monastery has an ethos that has developed through its own particular history. A person who might find one monastery a perfect fit with her own vocation could not survive in another of the same order. In other words, what has traditionally been called "the spirit of the congregation" is an important focus of discernment, which virtually has to go on after a person has become a candidate because it cannot really be described or known outside actual experience of the group's life. It is an ethos that is cultural, social, spiritual, and practical. It is felt as a powerful determinant of behavior and decisions. It is an indefinable something that makes a person gradually feel "at home" or, on the contrary, feel like a perpetual visitor in someone else's family. But it cannot be isolated or analyzed discursively. In effect, the spirit of the congregation, which is an expression of its charism, is a kind of corporate personality within which a person must find her own way of being if she is to feel truly called to this particular congregation.

It is no longer the case that people who feel called to Religious Life generally assume that the order they know from school, parish, or work is the right one for them. Indeed, many younger Catholics have never had any contact with or experience of Religious in their early years. Careful discernment, including investigation of various congregations, is therefore increasingly necessary. Formation personnel of different congregations have come together in recent decades in the effort to help potential candidates find the right environment regardless of whether that means that a prospective member of one's own congregation goes elsewhere. And some professed Religious have changed congregations as they have come to see that a different order responds better to their own vocation.

Both these developments are healthy. But the necessity for those who feel attracted to Religious Life to discern the congregation within which they will test that attraction probably suggests that congregations need to do considerably more to present their own life for such discernment. Many Religious shy away from anything that sounds like "advertising" or even vocation promotion, remembering with discomfort the aggressive recruitment of their own youth that seemed too much like secular corporation tactics. But this is equivalent to shying away from medical intervention because it seems to call into question God's capacity to heal in response to prayer. Vocations, like health, are God's gift, but that does not obviate legitimate effort on our part to promote them. Especially because so many younger Catholics have had no exposure to Religious in parish or school, there is a real need to present the life to them if incipient vocations are to be recognized and encouraged. If Religious believe that their life is worth living, is indeed a gift of God to themselves, to the Church, and to the world, they should be eager to offer it as a possibility to others. There is a world of difference between inviting and encouraging a person to explore the life and trying to cajole, pressure, or even frighten someone into it as the only sure path to salvation. Many people who have felt attracted to Religious Life at some point in their development say that they simply assumed that the life was too special for them and that no one ever invited them to consider it. If professors challenge their students to consider higher education or research as a life work and doctors invite talented young people to apply for medical school, should not happy Religious invite spiritually idealistic young people to take a look at Religious Life?[12]

b. The call to community: Although the decision to enter a canonical Religious institute and a particular congregation is serious, it bears upon what is perhaps the least important, because the most "external" aspect of a Religious vocation. Discernment about one's call to community bears upon the human relationships that form the affective context within which one will live one's vocation to Religious Life. As already noted, many congregations have extended communities that include people who are not members of the congregation, that is, associates, affiliates, and others with less formal relationships. But the person who is a member of the congregation has a very distinctive relationship to the community that nonmembers do not have.

First, a member of the congregation, unlike other people who may be part of the extended community, makes a choice for the community as the *primary affective horizon* of her life. This choice is analogous to that of persons who get married to make the family that the spouses found the primary affective horizon of their life. Such a choice involves "leaving home" both physically and psychologically. One's family of origin is no longer one's primary affective context. This certainly does not mean that love for parents and siblings diminishes but it does mean that one is no longer primarily a child in a social system that exists to a large extent to foster one's own development. The Religious, like the married person, has become an equal adult in a system that has other objectives which the community pursues together. Practically speaking, once Religious Life ceased to demand the total, and in many ways unnatural, cessation of virtually all contact with one's family of origin, it has become clear that many Religious never made this transition interiorly even though they were prevented from much contact with their families.[13] And it is easy for newer members to fail to make this psychological transition if it is not made a conscious focus in formation. Every lull in ministry finds them "going home," by which they mean returning to their family of origin. They continue to look to their family to meet their financial needs, to provide them with vacations or recreation, and to be the sympathetic ears into which they pour their problems in community or ministry. As is clear from the marital analogue, this unwillingness or inability to leave home can have very deleterious effects on community participation because, in effect, one cannot have two primary affective contexts.

Second, because the Religious makes a total and lifelong commitment within the congregation, her or his *responsibility for the community* and its life is qualitatively different from that of participants in the community who are not members of the congregation. The level of participation of the latter can quite legitimately fluctuate as their own primary relationships demand more or less of their time and energy, as they move geographically closer to or farther from the centers of congregational activity, or even as their desire or need to participate waxes or wanes. But the members of the congregation are ultimately responsible for its community life. They are the guarantors of its ongoing life, of its nurturing of new members and its care of older members, of its availability for participants who affiliate at different times and in different ways. The members of the congregation have a right to depend on one another for the love, support, understanding, forgiveness, challenge, and encouragement that everyone within a primary affective system needs and deserves. And the Religious community as Religious bears a special responsibility within the Church to give public witness to the quality of community life to which all the baptized are called.[14]

Religious members of the community face the *challenge of belonging* in a way that goes well beyond turning in their salary or putting congregational initials after their names. Affectively and psychologically, the priority of the community's

claim on congregational members shapes the various decisions they must make about other relationships. In ways that
were virtually unimaginable in preconciliar days, when the
congregation was a total institution, other relationships today
make claims that raise serious dilemmas for community. Many
middle-aged Religious are involved in care for aging parents;
presence to relatives in need is a responsibility; the exercise of
professional colleagueship makes demands; participation in
movements and projects as well as one's own ministry is a significant affective involvement. One's closest friendships may
well be with people who are not members of one's own congregation or even part of its extended community. Such
responsibilities and relationships do not necessarily conflict
with community belonging, but they certainly can and often
do. Such conflicts are not peculiar to Religious, as any parent
who has been caught between a spouse's crucial business dinner, a child's recital, a parent's medical emergency, and her or
his own professional commitments knows. But the issue is how
the priority of one's primary affective commitment, namely,
that of the Religious to her or his Religious community, is best
honored and expressed in such situations.

Particularly for members of ministerial congregations, the
contemporary situation is more challenging than it was in preconciliar times, when members always lived with other members
and carried on an identical ministry. Often, for ministerial reasons, members will find themselves living singly or intercongregationally at some distance from other members or from the
congregation's primary areas of life and activity. One's actual
day-to-day relationships may be primarily with people who are
not members of one's congregation or even of the extended
community. How to maintain a lively and effective sense of affective belonging is the challenge. And if that challenge is not successfully met, the Religious can easily become psychologically
and spiritually marginalized and finally alienated from her community. Part of the discernment about community today has to
bear on the capacity of a person to handle the realities of frequent change of residence, distance, lack of immediate support,

properly motivated accountability, willingness and creativity to make the effort to connect with, support, and be supported by others in the community. Again, this challenge is not unique to Religious Life, as many families whose members are all in different states or even countries can testify. But Religious are neither singles who can build whatever type of community suits them wherever they find themselves and leave such community when it is expedient, nor are they married people who take at least their immediate family of foundation with them. Community, for the Religious, is permanent and corporate regardless of where or with whom she finds herself.

In summary, discerning whether one is called to community as a Religious is probably much more difficult than discerning a vocation to the congregation. For a member of the congregation this is much more than a felt affection for the community, a sense of sharing in its charism, an enthusiasm for its ministry, and a desire for solidarity with some of its members, which may all characterize a person who is not a member of the congregation but part of its extended community. All of these are important, indeed absolutely necessary. But there are other questions for the person who enters the congregation as a member and undertakes community life definitively. Is one ready to finally "leave home" and relocate oneself affectively in this community? Is one ready and even eager to throw in one's lot, for the rest of one's life, with this concrete historical group of people who are not perfect, individually or collectively, and to stay the course with them in good times and bad? Can one find real affective human fulfillment in celibate community, that is, without the intense one-to-one, exclusive, and genitally expressed relationship to spouse or life partner, without the ultimate form of self-extension through history in children of one's own? Is one ready to shoulder the responsibilities of a multigenerational community in which at times one will more support than be supported and at other times be profoundly dependent, without resources from independent means and thus limited to what the community can provide? Is one willing to actually hold all things in common without privately providing for one's own security and well-being? Can one live happily and productively into and within the authority structures of this group? This is a discernment that can only be begun in the period of initial formation but it is crucial that these questions be faced in an honest way before a person seriously contemplates full incorporation into the congregation as community.

c. The call to Religious Life: Everything so far discussed is, of course, part of the call to Religious Life, which is the overall reality to which a candidate is discerning a vocation. The rest of this book will be examining in depth the various aspects and dimensions of contemporary Religious Life. The point of singling out, at this point, Religious Life itself as a focus of discernment is to highlight the fact that attraction to a particular congregation, its ministry, community life, or even to an intensified living of one's spirituality is not equivalent to a call to Religious Life itself.

Religious Life as such is a state of life. By entering the state of life one does not simply join an organization, choose companions, or associate oneself with a project. One *becomes* a Religious. This is a permanent and public change of condition, like getting married or becoming a parent. In times past, when all and only people who joined a congregation were Religious, it was easily assumed that if a person "fit" well in the congregation/community and was capable of exercising its ministry she must be called to Religious Life. It all came as a "package." The large number of departures from Religious Life as the distinctions among these realities has become clearer in the wake of the conciliar renewal suggests that insufficient attention was devoted to discernment about the vocation to Religious Life itself. Many who have left have continued in ministry, have remained part of the extended community, feel deeply imbued with the charism of the congregation, and have continued to live a serious spiritual life. They left because they came to realize that they are not, indeed never were, called to Religious Life.

The distinguishing feature of Religious Life, what it does not share with any other ecclesial vocation, is the commitment to perpetual consecrated celibacy as a public state of life in the Church. In part 2 we will be looking at this reality in detail, and it will be clear, I hope, that this is not a negative project. Consecrated celibacy is not about (even though it involves) what one does not do (get married), any more than monogamous marriage is about what one does not do (have sex with people other than one's spouse). It is about Who and how one loves and, of course, the consequences of that choice. But to avoid ambiguity, especially that which can be raised by the mandatory singleness of the clergy in the Western Church, it is well to state clearly what consecrated celibacy entails and therefore what requires discernment.

Consecrated celibacy is the total, exclusive, and lifelong self-gift to Christ which a particular person feels called to express in genitally abstinent nonmarriage undertaken as a free response to a personally experienced and discerned vocation. This definition has implications that must be carefully engaged before a person makes profession. First, consecrated celibacy cannot be validly undertaken purely as an entrance requirement for or as an implication of something else, for example, entering a congregation. Second, it must be freely chosen in response to a personal vocation. Consecrated celibacy is a charism, a gift from God to a person for the fostering of her own growth in holiness and her service of others. It cannot be mandated or imposed any more than baptism or matrimony can be. Free choice to respond to a real and personal gift is the only valid path into this state of life. Therefore, the individual has to discern whether she feels that she can be happy, fruitful, maturely loving as a celibate. Is this the condition in which she is likely, indeed most likely, to grow in love of God and neighbor? If the answer to that question is no, she is not called to Religious Life no matter how generous and self-disciplined she might be (i.e., able to bear an unwelcome burden for a "higher good") or how attracted to other aspects of Religious Life she might be.

Consecrated celibacy will be discerned within the context of congregational community and ministry, and one's experience with the latter will be a major source of input about the former. But to simply assume that because one seems to be getting along well in the life as a whole, consecrated celibacy will take care of itself, especially if one is not experiencing agonizing problems with it during formation, is not only naïve and short-sighted; it is a recipe for vocational disaster. It would be analogous to avoiding the question of whether one is really monogamously in love with one's fiancé(e) and open to founding a family with him or her. No matter how exciting courtship is and how satisfying the prospect of a home of one's own might be, the crucial question concerns the relationship with the person to whom one is engaged. There are many kinds of love, but only one kind can ground a marriage. There are many ways to love and serve God in Christ. Religious Life is one way of loving, and whether that is the way to which one is called is a serious question to which one cannot assume the answer without adequate discernment.

3. Discernment as a global process: The serial laying out of the elements in the process of vocational discernment and the areas upon which discernment bears can create the false impression that the experience is compartmentalized and mechanical. In fact, it is an experiential continuum in which every aspect affects every other aspect in a kind of hermeneutical spiral of interpretation bearing upon oneself, one's relationship with God, and the congregation/community within which one is discerning.

It begins when the first nudges of attraction lead the person to discuss the possibility of a vocation with a spiritual director and/or congregational vocation director. If there seems good reason to proceed, a certain amount of "standardized" discernment will take place through psychological, physical, and perhaps at least informal educational assessments. If the person seems to meet the basic requirements in these areas and to have adequate personal maturity and life experience, there will be exploratory visits to the community and participation in events designed to familiarize the prospective candidate with the life and spirit of the congregation. And finally a statement, usually by letter, to the congregational leadership of a desire to enter will be followed by interviews with the personnel responsible for admission. During this process the inquirer will probably learn at least as much about herself as she does about the congregation, and that will be the pattern if she continues in the process.

After acceptance the candidate will be progressively initiated into the experience of formation for Religious Life. Today that process is more gradual, and certainly less dramatic, than it was in the past, when postulants entered the convent on a certain day, donned a uniform, and ceased all or most contact with the outside world while following a set program of formation. Candidates today may continue in their pre-entrance living arrangements and profession or work while gradually drawing their secular affairs to closure. In some cases this will require some sobering decision making about house, car, credit cards, salary, savings, and the like, depending on the congregation's schedule of incorporation. But in every case this period is one of deepening discernment as the candidates begin to see the implications of involving someone else in decisions over which they formerly had complete control, being expected to expend time and energy on congregational affairs that require making choices for community over personal projects or recreation, accepting some restrictions on travel and companionship, and becoming more accountable in the area of finances as they anticipate beginning a life of economic interdependence.

Formation becomes a full-time process when the candidate is received into the novitiate. If a person gets this far the discernment process will have deepened considerably and the intimate interconnection among all the facets of becoming a Religious will have become clearer. During the novitiate the role of the formation director becomes crucial as she helps the prospective member clarify her motivations; achieve greater psychological balance and interior freedom in assessing them and herself; grow in theological understanding, Catholic culture and practice, and knowledge of the congregation's history and spirit; deepen her prayer life; develop or consolidate skills in group living and grow in responsibility for and accountability to the local community; listen carefully to her feelings around issues of friendship, family, and sexuality; test her capacity for commitment; and develop or stabilize a disciplined and healthy lifestyle that may make serious demands on people not brought up in a climate of self-control or sacrifice. None of these strands in the life pattern the novice is beginning to weave can be dealt with in isolation from the others, and they will often either illuminate or obscure one another. Problems in one area will create problems in others as insights in one sphere will enlighten other aspects of the life. This is precisely why the ongoing presence and skilled assistance of an experienced director who is both psychologically healthy and spiritually mature are essential even for novices who are mature adults when they enter.

By the end of the novitiate the person has to have achieved sufficient self-knowledge (in an integrated psychological and spiritual sense), conviction about God's designs for her, and familiarity with the congregation/community to be able to make an informed decision about whether to make the commitment of Religious profession. Although she will make it for a specified amount of time at this point, usually three years, that temporary profession is only valid if she intends to make it permanent. Consequently, temporary profession is not a stopgap, reprieve from decision making, or experiment, but a real Religious profession. The provision for temporary vows is a prudent expedient to avoid the necessity of canonical dispensation if the first years of Religious Life reveal serious problems that did not surface (and perhaps could not have) during the novitiate. But the gravity of the decision to become a Religious by making profession emphasizes the seriousness of the work of the novitiate and the holistic character of the discernment process as well as the range and depth of the issues upon which that discernment bears. The joy of profession day is not the superficial satisfaction of having made it through a period of testing, but the deep spiritual joy of self-donation to the One who has called and enabled a life-structuring choice for unconditional love.

CHAPTER TWO
FORMATION AND INCORPORATION

I. Introduction

From the time a person becomes a candidate until she or he makes perpetual profession almost a decade later, the person is in a process usually called initial formation.[1] For a number of reasons both members of the term present problems because most candidates for Religious Life today are not "beginners" as human beings, professional people, or spiritual seekers and the term "formation" has coercive and standardizing connotations with which candidates and formators alike are uncomfortable. It is probably correct to say that few aspects of contemporary Religious Life have been as radically affected by the cultural and ecclesial upheaval of the past three decades (which we examined in detail in volume 1 and will presume as background for all that follows) as initial formation. I am particularly diffident about discussing this topic because, although I have worked with novices and temporary professed Religious in workshops, classes, and spiritual direction and have been involved with formation personnel in various contexts, I have never carried the day-to-day responsibility of a formation program. Consequently, I will not attempt to say how the work of formation should be done but rather to offer considerations from the fields of cultural anthropology, sociology, theology, and spirituality that might be useful to those who must plan and implement the process in the concrete for a particular congregation.

II. Formation

A. Factors Influencing a Revision of Initial Formation

Formation programs were fairly standard across congregations at the close of Vatican II and had been for centuries, evolving superficially to some degree in terms of the type of candidates who were entering in a given time period but changing very little, substantively, in philosophy, theology, spirituality, or even actual practice. Things changed radically within a few years when congregations began to revise their constitutions following renewal chapters in the 1960s and '70s. In fact, even someone convinced that the Council and its implications for Religious Life were the most important and positive ecclesial events of the modern period would probably agree that formation was in serious disarray within a few years of the close of the Council. There was no dearth of energy and commitment in experimentation, but no one, formators or candidates, was particularly happy with the results of most of it. Confusion about goals and inconsistency of means were widespread, and the turnover rate (which some frankly admitted was a role-mortality rate) of formation directors was cause for genuine alarm.[2]

Part of the thesis of this book is that Religious Life is entering or perhaps has entered a new period of stabilization. There is some increase in the number of candidates entering as well as a considerable decline in the number of professed members leaving. The commitment to and energy for Religious Life of members in their forties and fifties suggests a vigorous engagement by the people who will carry the life into the future.[3] Media presentations of Religious Life are beginning to reflect the fact that real Religious are not "flying nuns" or "Sister Act" cultural anachronisms but significant contributors to contemporary Church and society living a life that offers possibilities for growth and service to idealistic young people.[4] The problems of the postconciliar period are by no means solved, and no one wants stabilization to suggest a new period of stagnation or sclerosis, but Religious Life seems to have weathered the crisis of extinction. The dinosaur has perhaps become a songbird[5] but it is alive, still beautiful, and essentially healthy. If it is to continue to grow into its new identity and function in the Church, new members must not only enter but mature in the life, and that entails some kind of formation.

To understand and confront the challenge in the area of formation it is important to understand the reasons for the collapse of the preconciliar understanding of formation and the disarray that followed. I will single out three clusters of influences: numbers of entrants, theological uncertainty, and the questioning of the very notion of "formation."

1. Decline in numbers: The sudden decline in the number of entrants into ministerial congregations, in many cases from forty to one hundred or more a year to one or two, with some years in which there were none, radically affected the model of formation and thus every element of the process. Whether called a "class" (which was more common in educational congregations) or a "band" or "set," the basic context of formation was a large homogeneous group much like an entering class of first-year college students. Most candidates entered immediately after graduation from high school (college graduates were the exception and "late vocations" almost nonexistent) and often came from a school taught by the order they entered or had done volunteer work with that order in a hospital or social service settings during high school or college. They tended to be of the same race, and often a majority were even of the same national or ethnic background. They came, in most cases, from two-parent, practicing Catholic families steeped in Catholic tradition and culture and proficient in Catholic piety. Formators could make assumptions that applied fairly well to almost everyone in the group: that they had little or no experience of a professional life or financial independence; that they were sexually inexperienced and espoused traditional Catholic sexual ethics; that they were North Americans with little or no experience of other cultures; that they had the basic religious education supplied by eight to twelve years of parochial school education and were actively practicing the sacramental and devotional life of the Church; that they were good, or at least average, students with well-developed study habits; that they had an experiential sense of the congregation's spirit from prolonged association with some of its members; that they understood Religious Life as a privilege of which they were unworthy and thus as a kind of highly coveted "prize" to be achieved.

Given these assumptions, which were quite valid at the time, formators could approach their charges as a kind of "class" to be dealt with corporately most of the time. What was suitable for one was probably suitable for all, so there was little need to individualize the formation program. In fact, eradicating any tendency of the candidate toward "singularity" was part of the program. Although candidates were more or less mature adolescents rather than adults and were inexperienced in many areas of life and work, they came with a number of foundational elements in place. Most had been Catholic all their lives and knew what that meant. They knew at least a catechism version of Church teaching and theology; they had a prayer repertoire both in terms of content and discipline; they were well practiced in liturgical participation. Furthermore, most were very used to accepting the authority of parents and teachers and saw the formation personnel, who were always significantly older than their charges, as a kind of combination of these roles. There was a sense in which entering the convent was much like enrolling in a very strict boarding school with profession as graduation. Formation consisted of the curriculum and the process of transmitting it, and the formation personnel were the faculty. When their charges eventually fit fairly well into the community, the formators' work was done, and living the life, highly regulated as it was, would do the rest.

This entire picture became obsolete, seemingly overnight, when the entrance "class" was suddenly one or two individuals who did not exhibit most of these traits. They were often older, sometimes previously married and widowed or divorced, and therefore sexually experienced. Some were recent converts, but even "born Catholics" may have been away from Catholic practice for many years, bringing with them into Religious Life either a preconciliar Catholic traditionalism or virtually no Catholic culture at all.[6] Some had never learned standard prayers, rarely attended Mass, and perhaps had never been to confession. Most had been living independently of parental authority for some time both socially and financially, were professionals or graduate students or at least part of the workforce, not used to any supervision of their private lives. For many, entrance was their first prolonged contact with the congregation itself, so they had little instinctive sense of what was and was not acceptable or expected.

In short, candidates tended to be both more humanly mature and experienced (and thus less psychologically malleable) and much less religiously formed in Catholic faith and practice (and thus more in need of basic Christian as well as Religious formation). But, paradoxically, they were sometimes considerably more developed in terms of spirituality than their earlier counterparts. They might have come with an extensive acquaintance (often uncritical) with Christian and non-Christian mystical literature (though often little if any with the ascetical literature) and a wide exposure to spiritual practices in the form of Zen sitting, yoga, transcendental meditation, centering prayer, or a strictly personal collection of experimental spiritual disciplines but not know how to make the Sign of the Cross, recite the Apostles' Creed, or participate in the Eucharist.

In any case, the formation program had to be radically individualized, not only because there might be only one or two candidates who might differ widely from each other in age, background, and experience, but also because most of the traditional formation curriculum was inapplicable to the kind of candidate entering. Attempts to involve candidates themselves in the planning of their programs was predictably unsettling because it gave the impression that the formators did not know what they were doing (which the candidates often suspected from the outset anyway). The lack of a peer group that would normally have absorbed and relativized correction or criticism as the shared experience of those going through the same initiation process made even mild disapproval seem like a personal attack on the candidate herself. And candidates had no social context for peer complaint that might have defused some normal fear of or anger at authority figures. Candidates and formators thus often became locked into highly personalized conflicts that had as much to do with personality and diversity of experience as with vocational growth, and the asymmetry of power and authority between people often close in age exacerbated the situation.

A tragically ironic situation that became public only infrequently was nevertheless not rare. Some formation personnel were appointed at critically young ages, in their thirties or early forties. The intent was to put people into formation work who belonged to the same age cohort (although at its upper end) as the candidates, and thus reduce the perception of irrelevance that an older director might engender. But a formation director in her thirties, encountering the much wider experience of an adult candidate close to her own age, especially in the areas of relationships and sexuality, was sometimes forced to examine her own convictions, which might have been formed in an experiential vacuum at a very young age. Understandably, the personal crises and the resignation or even departure from Religious Life of formation personnel was traumatic for many candidates who had several directors over the course of the relatively brief initial formation period.

2. Confusion about theology of Religious Life: At just the time it became necessary to completely reconceive the whole process of vocational formation, a second undermining factor came into play, namely, considerable theological confusion about the identity and function of Religious Life in the Church.[7] In the preconciliar era the ideal of the mature congregation/community member was clear and shared by all in the congregation (at least at the conscious and public level). Formation personnel knew what their charges were supposed to achieve

and become before profession and could articulate it clearly to
the candidates. The directors had inherited both a program
and a process for helping the candidates reach these goals.
Although the formation process was often painful to the point
of trauma, there was at least the reassurance, for both candidates and directors, that they were involved in a time-honored
and well-tested process that had produced wonderful community role models who were healthy and holy women or men.

In the wake of the Council and the turmoil of renewal, professed members were experimenting with widely divergent
models of community, forms of prayer, types of ministry, to say
nothing of dress, lifestyle, and spirituality. Not only was the
process of formation undergoing radical revision from a collective to an individual model, but its goal, what it was supposed
to produce, was no longer clear or certain. Was the novitiate to
produce a psychologically well-adjusted individual who would
be capable of figuring out for herself what it meant to be a Religious? Or a committed community member whose primary
loyalty was to the group whatever she might believe about Religious Life? Or a deeply spiritual person who would pray and
discern her way to maturity as a Religious? Or a theologically
well-grounded minister? Or some combination of these?

To make matters more complicated, the formation personnel often received conflicting directives from the leadership
and the membership of the congregation who were developing different theories of Religious Life on the basis of rapidly
expanding experience. Whatever program or process the formator developed or implemented, someone would be highly
critical of it, and the unspoken stricture against professed
members interfering with the formation program that was
operative in preconciliar congregations no longer held. The
traditional enclosure of initial formation which kept the
entrants from any prolonged personal contact with the professed was scarcely viable when candidates had no peer group.
They could not be isolated from either the "outside world" or
from the rest of the community for years on end. The critics
often felt free, even obligated, to augment (or subvert) the

candidate's formation with their own opinions and example and even to side with the candidate against perceived abuses in the formation program or shortcomings in the director. Many directors could not sustain the tension of pleasing no one most of the time, and the turnover in office was extremely rapid. This exacerbated an already unstable situation by precipitating a reinvention of the formation program every two or three years as one formator left under a cloud and another tried, with no better resources, to improve the situation.

3. Hesitation about validity of "formation": Finally, a third closely related factor that kept formation in turmoil was the profound hesitation of many Religious about the validity of the very notion of formation. This hesitation was theological, psychological, and sociological. As Religious reappropriated the essentially baptismal character of their life and repudiated the earlier claim of its superiority to other ways of living the Christian vocation, they began to wonder why a special formation beyond that of life in the local ecclesial and Religious community was necessary. Were Religious being initiated into some kind of esoteric version of Christianity not shared by others? And if so, could that be justified in light of the Council's call of all the baptized to one and the same holiness and to active participation in the mission of the Church?[8]

Many Religious were most articulate about their psychological hesitations. The very idea of "forming" another person, as if she were some kind of inert or passive matter to be "informed" by an ideal imposed from without, seemed violent. (This impression was especially vivid for some Religious who remembered their own formation as an experience of coercion and/or deformation of their natural gifts and personalities.) Furthermore, many of those few who were entering were already adults, experienced in life and spirituality, and the idea of forming them seemed faintly ludicrous if not disrespectful. One might have to form children or even adolescents but hardly a divorced fifty-year-old grandmother!

As we will see below, the traditional model of formation was, sociologically, initiation through a ritual of passage which transferred the person from the secular state to that of Religious Life in a particular congregation. Much of the process was devoted to assimilating the candidate to the group. She had to relinquish her "worldly" dress, relationships, ambitions, ways of behaving (even to such details as how she ate, walked, talked, looked, bowed, etc.) and take on the ways, relationships, and responsibilities of the congregation so that she could function as an adult member within it. Uniformity was an important feature of this ideal. So called "singularity," standing out in the group in one's individuality, was not encouraged. Even tilting one's headdress in an unconventional way was noticed and corrected!

As Religious involved in the renewal became psychologically and sociologically sophisticated, they became very critical of the extreme external uniformity that had been such a prominent feature of preconciliar Religious Life. They recognized the suppression of personal gifts and creativity that such standardization of virtually every element of life had effected. Many became passionate advocates of diversity in dress, living environment, entertainment, personal relationships, prayer forms and styles, educational experiences, and so on. If the ideal of an externally uniform congregation whose members looked alike, acted in unison, traveled together, and spoke as one was abandoned, what was the purpose of formation that to a large extent consisted in socialization into the congregation? A candidate could grow in prayer, learn to live in community, develop as a minister without spending time in a special environment separated from the rest of the congregation. Such separation was primarily a sociological condition of a kind of initiation that now seemed not only unnecessary but counterproductive.

B. Results of the Crisis in Formation

Not surprisingly, the upheaval in formation programs during the renewal decades had multiple effects with which communities continue to deal. The wide variety of experimentation certainly had unsettling and even confusing effects on many who underwent formation during these years and probably had some relation to the high dropout rate among younger Religious during that period since, in such a turbulent context, it was extremely difficult to assure adequate preparation for profession or to make sound judgments about the readiness of candidates for lifelong commitment. Among those who stayed, the continuous revisioning of the process made for little continuity from year to year, and therefore Religious who were professed during the '70s and '80s often lacked not only a formation class or set but even common experience as a cohort.[9] A resulting experience of loneliness in the community has led some who are deeply committed Religious to be peripheral to congregational life and to center their energy in their ministerial settings.

In the past five years there has been an encouraging movement among "younger" Religious to deal with their unique experience and to appropriate at renewed depth their vocation, their commitment, and their community membership. Religious in their forties and fifties are beginning to experience themselves as a cohort, a group who did not go through formation together or through the same formation successively but who now constitute the lower age group in their communities and have every intention of staying the course and keeping Religious Life and their communities alive and productive. In some cases members of the same community who entered during the postconciliar decades are regrouping among themselves and also making their experience, training, and insight available within their congregations. In other cases Religious of the same age group are bonding across congregational lines to help each other experience the existence and vitality of a younger cohort in Religious Life, which tends to be obscured by the fact that they are a minority in their respective congregations. They are asking vital questions about how to live Religious Life today and about community life and ministry in the immediate future. These initiatives bode very well for the future of Religious Life and of particular congregations.[10]

Although the turmoil of the '70s and '80s left much confusion in its wake, the experimentation also provided a great deal of data about formation, both positive and negative, which is now being used in the attempt to meet the needs of a slowly increasing number of mature women in their late twenties to forties who are investigating Religious Life. The importance for formation personnel of personal maturity and life experience, and thus the undesirability of placing very young Religious in such positions, seems clear. The quality of the living group in which formation takes place and its primary focus on the formation process and the people involved in that process are also seen as central. And there is increasing clarity about what the formation process does and does not intend to do and therefore what it needs to involve in terms of content, a point to which we will return below. While mature candidates can and should contribute appropriately to their formation, it seems clearer today that the program itself should be primarily in the hands of the congregation and the formation personnel it appoints and not left up to the candidates' invention or the opportunities that happen to arise.

C. The Need for Formation

If the process of formation is to be effective, both candidates and formators must be convinced of its necessity and importance. Formation is not a set of hoops to be jumped through in order to meet certain canonical requirements nor an obstacle course designed by mildly sadistic guardians of some sacred turf to separate the tough from the weak. As already remarked, when older applicants, especially those with considerable life and/or professional experience, replaced traditional high school graduates as candidates for Religious Life, some people on both sides of the formation process began to question whether it was possible or even made sense to try to "form" such people. Should they not rather continue in their professions and even living conditions as they picked up the culture of the Religious Institute from participation in ministry or congregational events? Some congregations experimented with such ideas but my impression is that most have reaffirmed the necessity of a

structured formation program for all candidates regardless
of age or experience. In my opinion, this is a valid judgment.

Without doubt, formation programs must be individualized
in terms of the candidate's background. Someone who enters
with a master's in theology should not have to take undergradu-
ate theology courses that might, on the other hand, be absolutely
necessary for a lawyer or psychotherapist with little or no formal
theological background. A physician probably should be allowed
to keep up her certification requirements during formation even
if she does not maintain a regular clinical practice. And no one's
prayer life should be retarded or reversed to fit some standard
program of formation in meditation. All this should go without
saying. And it will obviously demand considerable flexibility and
creativity on the part of formation personnel to design a program, especially if there are several candidates, that can take all
of the critical individual differences into account. Nevertheless,
there are a number of very good reasons to hold to the necessity
of a common formation program.

First, maturity and competence in one area does not necessarily imply competence in another, even when the former is
closely related to Religious Life, such as theology, psychology,
or spirituality. The RCIA for example, which is designed
specifically to initiate adults into Catholic Christianity, is used
for all candidates for baptism and often for those transferring
from other Christian denominations, even if they are religiously mature individuals who are highly trained professionals. Often, beginning doctoral students are in their thirties
and forties and are experienced professionals in fields other
than the one they are entering. A forty-year-old engineer who
decides to get a doctorate in biblical studies will go through
the same program as a twenty-three-year-old M.A. graduate
who may actually take the lead if her master's is in theology.
Graduates of medical school go through intensive internships,
and if an experienced physician changes countries or area of
specialization he or she will go through further formation and
testing for certification. In other words, there is nothing
intrinsically infantilizing or demeaning about participating in

a formation program when one enters a new area of life and/or commitment. In fact, it is the normal process, and it would be strange if something as serious as Religious Life required anything less.

Second, Religious Life is a very serious adult project that involves, eventually, a personal life commitment and public ecclesial responsibility. Not only does the person need to have a fairly deep understanding of the obligations and responsibilities she proposes to assume but some realistic experience of living them to the extent that such experience is possible before profession. She needs to know, in theory and in practice, what resources are available for helping her to live this life and how to access them. A candidate needs to become deeply knowledgeable, in both the intellectual and the affective sense, about the congregation she proposes to enter. She needs ministerial development that is not strictly coterminous with professional competence. While this is not an exhaustive list of "curricular content," it is meant to suggest that no matter how mature, educated, and experienced a person is at entrance, there are many areas in which she requires formation simply because she is undertaking a life that is new to her.

Third, it is important in any congregation that all members have some common background, both theoretical and experiential. Especially today, when most new members will not have a large group of peers in formation, it is important that there be some continuity of experience among those who enter over a period of years. Completely diverse formation programs from year to year, or even within one year, create congregational monads who lack the connective links that support genuine incorporation. Many elements of an individual's formation program may be unique to her, but there is also much that must be learned and practiced by everyone who enters regardless of her previous life experience.

Fourth, the process of entering into any permanent project or lifeform requires some kind of mentoring by someone more experienced in the life and/or work. The music teacher (even of a prodigy), the doctoral director (even of a genius), play crucial roles in initiating the person into not only the formal content of the field but into the life and challenges, the professional processes and important connections of the field. The one-to-one mentoring that goes on in formation as the candidate encounters the challenges of the interior life, congregational incorporation, and community is irreplaceable. In short, the candidate is a beginner in the life no matter what her chronological age or how competent or experienced in other areas she may be. One does not "pick up" Religious Life by osmosis.

D. Finding a Model for Formation: The Artistic Analogy

Preconciliar formation programs proceeded according to a traditional model that had become standard as the fruit of long experience. The sudden decline of numbers and change in type of candidate entering made the model obsolete virtually overnight. But recognizing that something no longer works does not necessarily suggest a substitute. Much experimentation resulted more from the conviction that certain attitudes, processes, practices, and elements needed to be abandoned than from any clear vision of what needed to replace them. Infantilizing authoritarianism, personality negating uniformity, legalism, abstract theology, routine religious practice, alienation of responsibility through collectivism were among the features easily repudiated, at least in theory. But developing an alternative model proved very difficult.

Actually, the model abandoned was probably never analyzed as such. Elements and features were clearly dysfunctional and to be discontinued. But it could be helpful to realize why they suddenly appeared counterproductive after serving well for centuries. I would suggest that preconciliar formation was sociologically a kind of tribal initiation, using some techniques of both the military and the educational versions of this process. The question is, what did this model accomplish that was positive and how can that be incorporated into a better overall model even as the dysfunctional aspects are abandoned?

The sociologist Victor Turner, in his now-famous monograph, described the process in primal societies by which young members were initiated into tribal adulthood.[11] The adolescents who, up to this point, are considered children without responsibilities for the tribe are taken apart to an inviolable location for a specified period during which they are sequestered from family and other members of the tribe. The peer group of initiands are stripped of all distinctions, rendered radically equal in a community of formation. Together they undergo instruction in the history and ways of the tribe and the rights and responsibilities of their gender within it. They are also gradually initiated into the mysteries and rituals of the tribe which, heretofore, had been kept secret from them. They undergo painful ordeals, tests of endurance, obedience, courage, ingenuity, loyalty and so on, with just enough support to assure survival. They are required to rely completely on their guides without resistance, question, or explanations. Sometimes they are marked with physical wounds or scars that bespeak victory in trial, tribal identity, or group status. Often they are renamed and symbolically reclothed at the end of the process, when they are finally led back into the celebrating community as newly minted full members with adult rights and responsibilities.

The initiation process as Turner describes it consists in a deliberate breaking down or deconstructing of previous patterns of expectations, ways of behaving, seeing, judging, and responding, even sense of right and wrong as it has been inculcated in the family. Relationships are restructured with the tribe rather than parents and siblings becoming the primary context of belonging, while tribal cohort or peer group, among whom one will finally assume responsibility for the future of the tribe, becomes the focus of loyalty. Obligations and responsibilities are no longer merely individual but communal. Rights commensurate with responsibilities denote full membership. In short, the person is "undone" as a child of the tribe and "remade" as an adult member of the community. Initiation is a total process that is simultaneously cognitive and affective. In order to accomplish the deconstruction and reconstruction the process involves a disorienting mixture of high expectations, shaming and humiliation, exaltation and praise, encouragement and restriction that decenter and recenter the individual within the group. Anyone who went through preconciliar formation in a Religious congregation will recognize virtually all these features as characteristic of the passage from postulate through novitiate to profession.

Religious congregations were not the only institutions in modern society to utilize aspects of this process. Military academies and boot camps are notorious for a particularly brutal and even violent process of depersonalizing first-year cadets or recruits in order to induce a militarization of mind and spirit. The resulting willingness to kill other human beings on command within a blindly accepted chain of command and to find ultimate camaraderie and honor in doing so is a good example of how totally a human being can be remade through the initiation process in a total institution. One might well maintain that the military process is a deformation of the essentially sound process of socialization into a tribe, but my point is that the basic dynamic of deconstruction for the purpose of reconstruction in function of social goals of incorporation is not the invention of Religious Life but the assumption within Religious institutions of a model that has a long tradition. It is also not too surprising that some of the harshness of the military deformation crept into some formation programs in the past.

Finally, the preconciliar model of formation was also affected by the school model of formal education. In such a model education is understood less as the maieutic "leading out" of the person through ongoing Socratic dialogue or apprenticeship with a skilled elder and more as the structured inculcation of information and behaviors deemed desirable for members of society and church. Initiation always involves the transmission to the younger generation of the wisdom, history, rituals, and skills of the tribe. But in the ritual process of primal societies this education was more integral to the overall process of initiation. The "school" model in which a separate institution is created to hand on the intellectual heritage, to test its absorption, and to credential people on the basis of their performance in the process is a relatively recent Western development.

Most Religious congregations in North America were founded during the era when the school model of education was becoming the normative ideal in society. Indeed, many congregations were founded to provide this type of schooling for the children of immigrants from Europe. And most candidates entered directly from school, which made the school model easily comprehensible to them. It is hardly surprising, then, that the school version of initiation was incorporated into the formation model of most congregations, involving not only the learning, sometimes by rote, of material deemed necessary for the professed Religious (such as Latin prayers, the rule, customs, etc.) but also testing that determined advance in the program (with the ever present danger of being expelled for poor performance), odious comparisons among candidates, and so on. The patriarchal, agonistic, conflictual character of Western education, which Walter Ong has well criticized, so powerfully influenced the model of formation that many Religious considered profession a kind of victory and themselves survivors of an ordeal.[12]

The repudiation of the traditional model of formation was an implicit recognition that Religious formation is not sociological initiation of adolescents, nor is it boot camp, nor is it a form of postgraduate education. The question that remained unanswered is, what is it? What is its purpose and desired outcome? What model of formation can be developed that will avoid the dysfunctionality of the traditional model and still achieve the transformative purpose of the process?

In the last chapter I suggested that a major purpose of formation is vocational discernment, coming to an informed decision before God about what I am called to here and now, that is, to become a Religious or to follow another path to sanctity. This discernment takes place subtly within a process of incorporation into the congregation. As we will see shortly, the incorporation process actually facilitates the discernment, but at this point I want to suggest a model that might serve as a framework for discussing the context of a formation program.

In a sense, Religious formation resembles the formation of a musician (or artist of any type).[13] The process arises as a need in function of a "talent" or gift that the subject feels she has. But the talent needs testing and development, and the effort to develop it will, in fact, constitute the testing. If, with proper help and adequate resources, the talent blossoms and the person experiences herself as becoming more and more who she feels called to be, that is, a musician, it will be evident that this is indeed her path. If the development process, on the contrary, becomes increasingly stressful, conflictual, distasteful, even deforming, it will be evident that this is not her calling. However, it could be that the process will reveal both that she is quite capable of following this path *and* that it is not what she really wants to do with her life.

The potential musician, no matter how musically talented or how well educated in other areas, needs finally to find a master and begin studying full time with him or her. This requires a kind of self-surrender in faith that is well founded on the fact that the master is an accomplished musician and recognized teacher. In other words, it is not blind but it does have to be genuine relinquishment of control. The student has to give herself over to the process of musical formation with a certain willingness to do what the master suggests or demands without continual second-guessing or resistance. She may think practicing scales or bowing techniques is beneath her since she has been playing for years, but the master is seeing something that requires more work. The process will be arduous. Mistakes will bring criticism, sometimes harsher than seems necessary. The objective is always the growth and development of the student, the nurturing of her talent, not the vindication of the teacher or the satisfaction of some kind of sadistic appetite of the latter.

The master will be concerned with intellectual knowledge of the literature and history of the field, with aesthetic refinement, with technique and skill, with attitude toward work and stamina in commitment, with the purity and passion of the student's love of music and of the instrument. She or he will require performance, rejoice in success and commiserate in failure, introduce the student to other artists and encourage professional participation. In a certain sense nothing about the student from the way she dresses for a performance to the hours she keeps, from her health to her emotional stability, from her choice of companions to her practice schedule, or anything else in her life that is related to her music (and finally that is everything) is beyond the purview of the master. This does not mean that the student becomes a slave or a robot much less a mindless sycophant. Ideally, the student will admire and even love the master not only as a musician but as an artist and a human being. However, there may well be significant personality differences between them that both overcome because the master recognizes the student's potential and the student appreciates the master's ability to foster her gift. In any case, the student is involved in a process of formation that is directed not just to teaching her how to play an instrument correctly but to her becoming a musician from the inside out. It is the student's own talent that is being called forth and nurtured, not an extrinsic behavior that is being imposed. But the calling forth requires full cooperation from the student and full dedication by the master. I would suggest that the relationship of artist and apprentice in the process of musical formation could offer an appropriate model of the process of Religious formation.

E. Components of the Formation Program

When Religious formation was understood primarily as socialization into the congregation, the determination of content was relatively straightforward. The candidates needed to become skilled at acting, sincerely and joyfully, like the professed members in prayer, ministry, and community life. They needed to learn their canonical and congregational obligations and how to fulfill them. And it was fairly easy to judge whether the candidate was making progress toward that goal and seemed basically happy in doing so. The dedication and zeal of formators and their love of their subjects, for the most part, were beyond question. But most probably saw their task primarily as fitting the candidates into the system rather than nurturing the unique gift of the person as together they tested the fit between the person's gift, Religious Life, and this congregation and community. Today the question of content is quite different.

It is not my intent, indeed it would be beyond my competence, to try to describe (much less prescribe) in any detailed specificity what a formation program should include, especially because lifeforms (monastic or ministerial), congregational charisms, and ministries differ enormously from group to group. However, in view of the definition of discernment given in chapter 1 some suggestions might be offered about categories of resources for that process. Because they are the basic resources for dealing with the major dimensions of Religious Life, they would be relevant for any congregation or order. The three categories are spirituality, community, and ministry.

1. Development in prayer and spiritual direction: If the candidate is going to discern her vocation *before God,* her prayer life is of paramount importance. This is the most intimately personal aspect of formation and the one that makes selection of a competent spiritual director so important. Many congregations have come to realize that having the formator function in this capacity can involve a real conflict of interests because the formation director also has an evaluative role in relation to the candidate that can inhibit the candidate's openness in the direction process. However, the congregation has a serious interest in assuring that the spiritual director is a spiritually and psychologically mature person with a good knowledge of and respect for Religious Life and the congregation. During formation a candidate's spiritual director should be known to and approved by the formation personnel. (This is one of a number of features necessary or desirable in formation that will not continue into professed life.) She or he, ideally, should also be a committed and practicing Catholic who can nurture the candidate's development of the kind of Catholic Christian spirituality that is at the heart of the vocation to Religious Life. This is especially important in the case of candidates who may enter with an eclectic or idiosyncratic spirituality that has little vital connection to Catholic tradition and practice. Although the spiritual direction relationship is privileged and utmost confidentiality is the directee's right and the director's duty, there is a delicate and complex relationship between the role of the formator in the life of the candidate and that of the spiritual director. It is probably a good idea to explore this in some explicit way with the candidate at the outset, before conflicts have a chance to arise.[14]

Also integral to the development of the candidate's prayer life is participation in the liturgy of the Church and in community prayer. Through the former the person is involved in a sacramental living of the mysteries of Christ, which she is contemplating in Scripture and interiorizing through meditation.[15] And the latter is an experiential initiation into the spirituality of the community as well as an opportunity to learn how to participate in and lead community prayer. Today both liturgy and community prayer are difficult to provide in many ministerial congregations. Even novitiates situated in a motherhouse or other institutional context are not necessarily assured of a chaplain, and parish liturgical resources often range from poor to dismal. The small number of people in formation at a given time can make community prayer difficult to develop. The creative use of communion services, drawing nearby professed into the formation community's prayer or joining other communities for prayer might be partial solutions as well as helping the candidates learn to plan creative prayer even in the small formation community. Travel to Newman centers or vibrant parishes, especially during the major festal seasons of the Church year, may be necessary if nothing is available nearby. And women's and men's communities might cooperate in the planning of good liturgies for their own members in formation. But, however it is done, developing an ecclesial and congregational prayer life is too important to be neglected on the grounds that it is difficult or in the hope that it will eventually take care of itself once the candidates are involved in ministry. Formation is the time and place when convictions about and patterns of personal and corporate prayer must be developed and stabilized. Prayer supplies the primary data as well as the context within which discernment must take place. Without minimizing the importance of other factors in formation, the development of the prayer life of the candidate is probably the most important single dimension of the formation program.

2. *Psychological development and exposure to congregational life:* Discernment is focused on deciding what *I should do here and now* about a perceived call to Religious Life. This suggests that the formation program needs to provide resources for the candidate to come to deeper self-knowledge not only about her spiritual life but also about her psychological, social, and moral capabilities and to deal with areas of her life that might be in some disarray or in need of healing. Even though most congregations require thorough physical and psychological testing, letters of reference, and extensive interviews before entrance, few young adults today are free of some agenda arising from fractured families of origin, immersion in a hedonistic and consumerist society, lack of moral formation, financial irresponsibility, or unresolved sexual experimentation that requires attention during formation.

For some candidates the formation process itself will be sufficient for identifying areas of conflict and initiating an ongoing process of healing. But serious issues such as addictions (to food, drink, drugs, smoking, spending, gambling, or sex), inability to deal with authority, deep-seated irresponsibility, pronounced narcissism, social/group incompetence, obesity, eating disorders or other psychosomatic health problems, or unresolved issues of sexual orientation or sexual abuse may require professional assistance that should be provided sooner rather than later. In other words, the "I" who is discerning a vocation needs to be lucid and relatively healthy if a good decision to proceed into Religious Life is to be freely made. Religious Life is not a refuge from life problems or even a structure for controlling them, nor is community a form of ongoing group therapy. A candidate who makes profession before recognizing and dealing with major psychological dysfunction will spend her life trying to make Religious Life serve her personal needs, and this is as doomed to failure as is contracting marriage for similar purposes.

Because the candidate is proposing to enter a form of Religious Life and a specific congregation that exists "here and now," not an ideal community or one that might exist at some time in the future, the formation program needs to provide as much actual experience of the community as possible. This is probably more important at the outset than some third-world or inner-city experiences (which many candidates will have had in some form before entrance), however important in itself such experience might be. Candidates need to see how different community members live, the kinds of ministries in which they are involved, how the government of the congregation works and how it incorporates member participation, how vowed members handle financial responsibilities, how the community deals with its sick and aged, and so on.

3. Intellectual and experiential formation: Finally, discernment is a process of coming to an *informed decision* about one's course of action. This raises the issue of what candidates need to learn, both intellectually and experientially, during formation. I would suggest that, although they will be handled differently in various congregations and will be of diverse importance from one group to another, three clusters of "material" should be part of the formation program.

First, the person discerning needs adequate knowledge in the areas of *theology, spirituality,* and *religion* in their interrelationship. Scholars in both theology and spirituality today are increasingly realizing how integral to each other the two fields are.[16] Theology that is not rooted in spirituality, that is, in the personal and corporate religious experience of the Church, is abstract and often barren. But spirituality that is not shaped and informed by good theology is often incoherent, lacking in substance, and insufficiently rooted in a believing community that can guard it against privatistic idiosyncrasy and fanaticism.

Unfortunately, several factors combined to alienate many postconciliar Religious from formal theology even as they were eagerly developing a more vibrant spirituality. The theological upheavals of the conciliar period left many people, including Religious, so confused about what the Church believed and what trends were worth following that they abandoned the whole theological process and decided to wait until the experts had come to some consensus. It seemed preferable to provide people (including themselves and their students) with religiously meaningful experiences rather than with catechism-clear dogma. The abstractness and irrelevance of much of the theology they had been taught in their own formative years led many to turn instead to psychology and the social sciences for resources for their own lives and their ministry to others. Furthermore, the explosion of ministries in response to overwhelming needs among the poor and the marginalized seemed to demand short-term professional and practical preparation that seemed much more immediately useful than lengthy masters' and doctoral programs in theology or religious studies. But whatever the reasons, the last three decades have seen a considerable decline in theological competence among Religious who, in the 1950s to the 1970s, had become some of the theologically best-educated women in the Church.[17]

The lack of theological interest and/or expertise of many Religious appointed to formation work during this period colluded with the antiintellectualism of some candidates emerging from the activist culture of the 1960s to relegate theological formation of new members to a minor place in the formation program, where it was often quite sporadic and haphazard if attended to at all. In my opinion, this situation is spiritually dangerous, not only for the people to whom the candidates will eventually minister who look to them for theologically sound guidance in the religious sphere, but especially for the Religious themselves who have few intellectually solid resources to sustain their faith or hope in times of challenge and conflict, to guide their choices in crisis situations, or to sustain and nourish their ongoing growth in prayer as they mature in the spiritual life.

I would suggest that Religious, before perpetual profession, should have the equivalent of a Master of Divinity (the degree required for ordained ministry in virtually all mainstream Christian denominations in the United States today), which would acquaint them with the sources of Catholic theology (Scripture, tradition, and church history), major methodologies and schools of thought both classical and contemporary, the chief topics (such as the triune God of Christian faith, christology, sacraments, ecclesiology, general and special moral theology), and the theology and spirituality of Religious Life, including not only its canonical status and obligations but also its place in the life of the Church, its history, its greatest figures, and highest ideals. Even if they were not going to exercise any formal ministry, Religious need such theological formation as a resource for their own spiritual life. This has been recognized since at least the beginning of the monastic movement in the third century and is verified in the writings of all the major figures, both male and female, in the history of Religious Life.[18] Furthermore, for Religious who will minister to others, formally or informally, theological formation is an obligation in justice. Just as it was once assumed that Religious destined for teaching should complete a degree in education and those destined for nursing should obtain an R.N., all Religious who will function as ministers need at least the level of theological competence regarded as normative for the Church's ordained ministers.

Beyond this theological formation aspiring Religious should also begin their education in the field of spirituality, particularly through the reading of some of the classics, both ancient and modern, of the tradition as well as (auto)biographies of giants in the faith, both historical and contemporary. Not only is this a source of formative knowledge about the spiritual life; it can nurture the idealism of candidates with the sense of the depth of union with God that is possible and sustain them with the challenging example of their forebears in Christian and Religious Life.

Finally, the particular religious tradition within which candidates intend to become public figures, namely, Catholic Christianity, needs to be deeply interiorized, and for that reason I would seriously question whether formation is the right time for a great deal of experimentation with non-Christian practice. Immersion in biblical meditation, christocentric liturgical and personal prayer, and at least an initial exposure to some of the devotional repertoire of the Catholic tradition,[19] if it is augmented by serious attention to the growing edges of the tradition, that is, social justice, feminism, ecumenism, interreligious dialogue, and ecology, will supply more than enough agenda for the formation years and help the candidate develop a coherent frame of reference within which to integrate wider resources in later years.

A second area of study during the time of formation bears upon the *congregation's history, spirit, ministry,* and *life.* Some of this material will be breathed in through the very experience of participating in the congregation's life. But it seems to me that formal study of the constitutions and other foundational documents as well as the history of the congregation from foundation to the present, with particular emphasis on its postconciliar evolution, is not only necessary in order to prepare candidates for eventual commitment but especially in order to initiate in them the development of a community "personality." The esprit de corps that comes from pride in the ideals and accomplishments of the group throughout history balanced by a salutary recognition of its corporate shadow is part of that indefinable spirit of the congregation that a full member must somehow incarnate. The myths, symbols, stories, heroes, even the in-jokes, songs, and traditional festivities of the group need to be imbibed both through experience in the community and guided study of its sources.

Third, prospective Religious need to begin to learn, both theoretically and practically, about the actual *day-to-day living* of Religious Life in the twenty-first century. The most obvious challenge is that of community life itself (about which much more will be said in part 3). Candidates today rarely enter the community from the role of minor in a family of origin. Indeed, many never had a healthy family experience at all. Some have lived in communes or volunteer communities. Many have been living on their own, sometimes with housemates for purposes of convenience or partners with whom they were sexually involved, for some years before entrance. Somehow people from these very diverse types of living experiences have to learn what genuine community among committed and mutually accountable celibate adults, motivated by religiously based altruism rather than self-interest, expediency, or common projects, means and how it is lived.

Learning to *live in community* confronts the candidate with challenges that might have been much less operative when Religious communities were total institutions and all members lived in houses of common life under a local superior. Community is high on the list of expressed desires of young adults entering Religious Life today. The fragility and dysfunctionality of so many families and the prevalence of divorce, with its trivialization of relationships, the isolation of the modern city and suburb, the alienation of mainstream liberal culture combined with the rampant narcissism of a market-driven social system that has no place for the slower-paced all conspire to create deeply lonely individuals longing for a sense of personal identity, relationship, stability, and caring. One place to which an idealistic person seeking such belonging can be naturally attracted is the Religious community, especially in its stabile monastic form. However, many who feel so attracted want also the active professional involvement in serving others that the mobile ministerial form offers. A major challenge for formation programs today, whether monastic or ministerial, is to capitalize on the experiential sense of the importance of community without being manipulated into becoming cocoons for societal refugees or substitutes for the families some candidates never had. Religious Life is intrinsically communitarian, but it does not exist to provide a surrogate family, social rehabilitation, psychological therapy, or even continual aid and comfort for its members. It is a community of emotionally mature, autonomous but interdependent adults oriented inward in the God-quest and outward in service of the neighbor.

Combined with a sometimes almost pathological need for a "nest" is a narcissism that conceives of the community as revolving primarily around the self. This is not the place to discuss how the culture of narcissism has developed in the first world, but formators need to be aware that an expressed desire for community today, however sincere, does not necessarily imply an outward orientation toward others in love. This can sometimes manifest itself in a resentment of any restriction on personal self-expression, activities, schedule, or behavior and a resistance to any form of accountability (which is viewed as intrusion, interference, or infantilization) combined with a petulant insistence on incessant "togetherness."

Finally, the reality of contemporary Religious Life involves many ways of living community, especially in ministerial congregations, besides that of the self-contained, stabile, common life in a local community that is most characteristic of monastic life. Most Religious will live in a variety of situations over the course of their lifetime, including in large groups, in small groups, singly, or intercongregationally. This means that they must have both a deeply interiorized understanding of the real meaning of Religious community, which cannot be equated with common life,[20] and a developed sense of congregational identity that will sustain them when they are distant from other members. Although formation would seem to require, at least ideally, a group (of candidates and professed) living common life in which one is initiated into the reality of community, this situation cannot be presented as normative in such a way that candidates will either expect to live this way for the rest of their lives or regard members of the congregation not living in such groups as somehow alienated or inferior.

The primary locus of learning to live community is the life itself, but actual instruction involving analysis, some exposure to sociological theory and contemporary reflection, and serious discussion of the theological and sociological reality of Religious community life would seem to be a necessary part of the agenda if candidates are to develop a realistic and healthy as well as deeply spiritual approach to community.

Another area of day-to-day living of Religious Life, closely related to community but distinct from it, is *sexuality*. Community is a matter of relationship, and all relationship is sexually freighted. To pretend that Religious community is a Platonic symposium is disingenuous if not dishonest, as is any pretense that Religious do not also have many relationships outside the community that have their own sexual resonances. Many candidates for Religious Life today bring with them considerable experience of genital sex. And regardless of their personal experience they have all grown up in a sex-saturated culture in which what little relationship between sexuality and morality has survived tends to be the rigid and condemnatory censoriousness of right-wing fundamentalists (which is hardly to be preferred to amoral hedonism). While increased knowledge about sex and gender among young people may be a positive development of the twentieth century, it has not been accompanied in most cases by an increased sense of the sacredness of sex or of personal moral responsibility in this area of human experience.

People discerning a call to a life of consecrated celibacy face numerous challenges in this area that are at least more explicit than was the case for their midcentury counterparts. Homosexuality, which was mentioned only infrequently and with such circumlocution in times past that only the most informed (or involved) would know what was being said, is now an open topic. It is crucial for potential Religious to come to self-knowledge about, and self-acceptance of, their own sexual orientation and to learn, explicitly, what is required of them as vowed celibates, namely, complete and perpetual sexual abstinence. This is just as true for homosexual as for heterosexual candidates. However, the challenges faced in a monosexual community will not be the same for gay or lesbian as for straight candidates. The former need to be helped to discern whether they feel called to celibacy in a sufficiently powerful way as to be able to live in community and work with highly attractive people of their own sex without becoming involved in exclusive and/or genital relationships. The latter need to discern whether they will be sufficiently energized and able to find affective fulfillment in a same-sex community. Much more needs to be said about this in part 2, but the point here is that the discreet silence that cloaked the topic of sexuality in and outside the community in the past cannot prevail in the present.

Another major area of formation and discernment is *authority*. Again, candidates today come from a vastly different context than their preconciliar forebears. The understanding of parental authority is hardly the (at least theoretical) absolute application of the fourth commandment that it was even three or four decades ago, and the frequency of the breakdown of marriages and of remarriages has undermined any sense that such authority is natural or divinely based. Schools no longer even claim to act "in loco parentis," and students often have much more sense of their rights against school authority than their obligations to honor it. Young people have grown up in a society in which fully one-fourth of the population is behind bars at any given time, and the daily newspaper is filled with accounts of numerous and flagrant violations of the law.[21] And the widespread abuse of authority by people in positions of trust from police to clergy has seriously undermined the credibility of authoritative institutions and people and given rise to suspicion and cynicism. In short, there is very little in first-world culture that would communicate to young adults a clear understanding of, to say nothing of respect for, authority.

Again, we can be glad for what is positive in the changed attitudes toward authority, especially that the authoritarian and even violent "divine right" exercise of power in the name of God and corresponding blind obedience by the governed are things of the past. But Religious Life is a community lifestyle, and authority structures are integral to it. Furthermore, Religious make a vow of obedience (to be dealt with in much greater detail in volume 3) which, though understood very differently today than it was in preconciliar times, still requires a significant surrender of independence in the handling of one's personal life.

A person with serious unresolved authority issues should not undertake vowed Religious Life. But helping a person realize that underneath her problems with schedules, elements of the formation program, behavioral expectations, accountability requirements, or financial disclosure is a deep conflict about authority is very difficult. A person who has a problem with authority will have a problem with authority's identification of the problem as one of authority! In any case, no matter how it is dealt with, an inability to relate positively and cooperatively to authority should not be brushed off as late adolescent rebellion or a personality conflict with the formator. Someone proposing to live a vow of obedience for the rest of her life needs to be capable of dealing respectfully and realistically, with courageous integrity and genuine humility, with authority in the congregation and in the Church. Again, some actual study and teaching in this area seems necessary.

A final aspect of day-to-day living, about which a great deal more needs to be said in volume 3, is that of *lifestyle*. In preconciliar times the candidate who entered the postulate found herself instantly devoid of money and cigarettes and dressed in regulation attire. She followed a detailed schedule of prescribed prayers and assigned work in response to a bell that began ringing at 5:00 or 6:00 A.M. and stopped only when everyone retired for the night. She ate only at appointed times and only what was set before her, which seldom included sweets and rarely, if ever, alcohol. She studied when and what was assigned and recreated only with the formation community at the times and in the ways prescribed. A disciplined lifestyle, in other words, was a nonissue for the individual candidate. The discipline was built into the life, and anyone who could not or would not accommodate herself to it was soon dismissed.

Although such uniformity and rigidity no doubt had some deleterious effects and few want to revive it even for new members, the structured formation program also built a solid foundation of lifestyle habits such as self-control, the ability to delay gratification, responsibility, accountability, efficiency, and hard work that mature Religious could count on when the structures were largely abandoned during the period of renewal.

Today few if any renewed congregations confront new entrants with a detailed plan for daily life that removes virtually all choice in regard to dress, food, use of time, and so on. Nevertheless, the person is still preparing to live a life that requires a great deal of self-discipline in the areas of spirituality, education, ministry, community life, and outside relationships. A person who gets up and goes to bed, spends money, relates, prays, eats, and drinks when and as the mood moves her is not capable of or ready for Religious Life.

Many candidates enter with considerable life experience in which they have had to get to work on time, meet deadlines, keep track of their expenditures, and otherwise live a fairly responsible life. But meeting externally imposed requirements in particular situations in order to graduate, hold a job, or get promoted is quite different from constructing and faithfully living a disciplined lifestyle as spiritual practice in order to be continually disposed for prayer and ministry. Learning the difference between appropriate recreation and habitual distraction, between celebration and excess, between liberality and luxury is part of the work of asceticism that is integral to the spiritual life of the Religious. It touches every aspect of life and every choice one makes, but it is no longer mediated by an intricate system of permissions, the social pressure of virtual uniformity, or even established customs. Again, the period of initial formation is the context for beginning to establish a disciplined and ascetical lifestyle that is the framework of the quest for God and the service of the neighbor that is Religious Life.

F. Formation as Probation

Another unfortunate effect of the school and military models of initiation on Religious formation has been the distortion of the notion of probation. To probe is to examine carefully, ideally reverently, in order to make valid and productive decisions. Probing can involve pain, but healing and wholeness rather than suffering is the objective. Furthermore, a poor theology of vocation summed up in the dictum that the only justification for leaving after entrance was dismissal combined with the "seller's market" occasioned by such large numbers of entrants that congregations could afford to be arbitrarily selective about candidates to make formation a kind of obstacle course in which only the fittest survived. It was decidedly one-sided: the congregation testing the candidate, who was trying to avoid being "sent home" (which carried unmistakable innuendoes of failure) or trying subconsciously to be sent home (so she could leave with a clear conscience). In any case, the probation aspect of formation was not its healthiest feature. Consequently, many Religious today are loathe to emphasize, or even recognize, this dimension of formation.

In fact, probation is intrinsic to formation within the model of artistic formation we have been using. No artificial hoops or hurdles are necessary; the formation process itself is probative. And it is a mutual process in which both the candidate and the congregation are testing the former's vocation to Religious Life (not her quality or value as a person).

Like the novice musician studying with the master, the candidate attempts to live the formation program and in the process will find her initial attraction to the life confirmed or challenged. Some people, within a relatively short time, will know that this is not for them. They know they are not happy and never will be in this environment. But, given the extensive and intensive evaluations of the contemporary admissions process, that is much less likely than it was when idealistic teenagers flocked to the novitiate after graduation with little sense of what they were undertaking. Some others will find themselves in Religious Life with such grace and ease that leaving will never be a serious option even though they encounter the normal challenges of the life. For many, however, the discernment will be a complex process requiring serious probation.

A friend of mine started ballet lessons as a child, loved it, and was obviously very talented. I asked her many years later why she did not become a professional ballerina, and she told me that when she started high school it became clear to her that she had to make a choice. Continuing in ballet would demand her whole self. Everything would have to be relativized by and subordinated to ballet if she were going to go beyond dance as a beloved extracurricular activity into a life in the field of ballet. She decided that there were many other things she wanted to be free to do and try and be. She would always love dance, and the effects of her apprenticeship would be part of her life forever. But she decided not to *become* a dancer.

I think this is a very good analogy for many people for whom discernment about Religious Life is difficult and prolonged. Their attraction to the life is real, and they are quite capable of living it well. But they question whether they really want to have religion, in the total and exclusive form expressed by perpetual consecrated celibacy lived in community and ministry, at the center of their life with everything else relativized by and subordinated to it. They may find themselves strongly attracted to marriage and children, to a profession or artistic career, to a cause or project, or simply to being free to pursue independently a variety of possibilities over the course of time. Like my friend in relation to ballet, they may decide that religion, spirituality, and ministry will always be an important part of their life and that the congregation will always hold a special place in their affection but that they do not want to organize their life around it; they do not want to *become* Religious. Others will decide that Religious Life is indeed the native country of their soul and that nothing else can finally satisfy them. It is worth whatever sacrifice it entails. This will not obliterate other attractions nor make the sacrifices painless, but these people will finally decide to "sell all" in response to the vocation they experience.

In the process of probation leading to discernment, the candidate should find support, encouragement, challenge, and affirmation in the formators. It is not the latter's task to erect obstacles or invent tests, much less to threaten or intimidate or undermine the confidence of their charges. Profession is not a trophy for the victorious or the reward of conformity. Ideally, the decision to be professed or the decision to leave should be arrived at peacefully by the candidate and either choice should be equally supported by the formation personnel. In such a climate probation, however arduous, will be embraced rather than denied, resisted, or dreaded.

G. Summary and Conclusions on Formation

Considering the areas that need to be attended to during Religious formation, namely, prayer, psychological maturation and familiarity with the congregation, formal education in theology, the history and spirit of the congregation, and the issues of day-to-day living such as community, sexuality, authority, and lifestyle, as well as the process of probation itself, the project can appear daunting if not overwhelming. A few concluding observations might be helpful in alleviating the sense of overload probably engendered by the foregoing discussion.

First, it is obvious that almost all of these goals will be on the agenda of the Religious throughout her or his life, and no one expects them to be achieved during the first three (or even nine) years. Initial formation might be considered a time when these goals get *onto* the agenda by being recognized and properly understood rather than *off* the agenda by being accomplished. To know what needs attention (both intellectually and experientially) and what resources are available for growth is the essential first step in a lifelong program of vocational development.

Second, formation is not an academic program in which one takes one subject after another, successfully passing a final exam after which one can forget the content if it is not immediately relevant. All of the areas of formation develop together and interactively, even as one or another receives particular attention at a given time. The music student does indeed practice scales at a particular moment or replay the same passage repeatedly until she gets the rhythm right, but in the process the whole person is becoming a musician, simultaneously learning the history and literature of her instrument even as she expands her own repertoire, perfecting technique through practice, learning to perform publicly by observing other musicians and appearing more and more on her own. The result of musical formation is not really judged by testing one or another component (although that might be done at one time or another) but by the increasing beauty of her performance, which does not preclude mistakes and probably never meets her own or her teacher's highest standards. Likewise, the Religious candidate, as she goes through formation, gets more graceful and effective in living the life. Neither she nor the formators are looking for "perfection" in the sense of having everything under control and never making a mistake, but for an increasing ability to live as a Religious with loving freedom and joy. This process is as intuitive as it is rational. It is not primarily one of performing but of becoming.

A third consideration will probably cause serious hesitations (and disagreement) in some people but, in my opinion, it is crucial to accomplishing the purposes of formation. The scope and intensity of initial formation means that it cannot be a part-time occupation fitted into an already demanding professional and social life. Some people, as we have already noted, have suggested that candidates should not be required to pull up stakes geographically and professionally and "enter" a novitiate. This position arises from two important considerations that deserve serious reflection.

First, contemporary candidates, unlike the teenagers who entered in the 1950s and 1960s, usually do not have family backup systems. If they decide, after some time in formation, that Religious Life is not for them, they have to reenter the adult world as independent agents. While canon and congregational law protect the financial assets of the candidate until profession, it is still a very serious matter to dispose of home, car, bank account, insurance policies, retirement benefits, and credit cards and to quit one's job and at least suspend one's professional life for a period of at least three years and sometimes more in order to engage full-time in the process of initial formation.

In most congregations this process of divestment is gradual, beginning with precandidacy, in which the person looks at the implications of community life and perhaps experiments with it in some temporary and limited way, through candidacy or postulancy, in which the person may remain financially and professionally independent but begins to be somewhat more dialogical and accountable for her decisions and actions, until she begins the novitiate. Although still not entirely financially incorporated into the congregation's life, the candidate ceases to exercise most forms of private ownership and begins to divest herself of personal property. The canonical year of novitiate requires cessation of gainful employment and residence in the formation house, which entails common life, however the congregation defines that, from the standpoint of finances and daily activity.

There is no question that these renunciations are radical, especially in our society, which is so marked by financial and occupational insecurity and the deep sense that if I do not take care of myself I will not be taken care of. But Religious Life (as we will see in volume 3) is a deliberate and public challenge to that sensibility and witnesses to the opposite values of interdependence and mutual support by the total and irrevocable commitment involved in the profession of poverty and obedience. It is crucial that the person who proposes to make that profession in the future face the challenge of this choice and make a decision to begin to live it. At some point, in other words, the person must *enter Religious Life,* and that means, in a very real sense, leaving the life situation from which she comes. In my opinion, this choice, this concrete manifestation of intent, is intrinsic to and basic to the formation process. The willingness, even eagerness, to do so is an important touchstone in the discernment process. It is challenging and risky, but so is the life one is entering. I doubt that anything is to be gained by trying to disguise the radicality of Religious Life, even at the beginning, and perhaps we greatly underestimate the idealism and generosity of candidates, their desire to "sell all," when we doubt their capacity for such decisiveness and commitment.

The second concern of those who suggest that formation should not interrupt the candidate's professional life by relocation or suspension of work is that ministry is intrinsic to Religious Life and, once professed, the person will have to work out a way of integrating the Religious lifestyle and full-time work. Why create an "artificial" environment during formation that will not prepare the person for the "real world" of professed life?

The response was suggested above. Formation is not meant to mirror professed life. It is a time of intensive preparation for a life that will be very different from the secular life from which the candidate came and will prove to be extremely demanding. Just as a doctoral student or medical intern or student teacher or clinical psychology supervisee follows an intensive program, submits to criticism of her work, and meets standards set by others that she will never face again after completing her training, the person in formation is undergoing a process of intensive, full-time apprenticeship and mentoring that she will never again experience. This does not make it "artificial" in any negative sense, but it does make it unique. The person who wants to hang around the edges of the life, dipping into it when it does not interfere with previous and prior commitments, participating only in formation activities she judges appropriate has not entered Religious Life, and until she does, formation cannot really begin.

III. Incorporation

The goal of formation is discernment of one's vocation to Religious Life and, if the decision is to become a Religious, preparation for and incorporation into Religious Life within the particular congregation/community. Although this takes place definitively at a particular moment through the formal act of Religious profession (to be discussed in the next chapter), it actually begins with entrance and continues throughout the lifetime of the Religious. It is a gradual and ongoing mutual process in which the candidate becomes part of the "body," the living organism that is the congregation, and begins to "embody" the spirit of the congregation and the reality of Religious Life in the Church.

Traditionally formation proceeded as if incorporation were a one-way transaction. The candidate was to be transformed from a secular into a Religious in the particular order, and if she successfully negotiated the formation program she was admitted to profession. Although the process of incorporation is asymmetrical in that it is not the congregation, which has a well-defined identity and a long history predating the arrival of the candidate, that is apprenticing itself to the candidate but vice versa, it is nevertheless a two-way process in which both partners in the new relationship change. Just as the arrival of a child in a family causes a reconfiguration of all its relationships among spouses, parents, and siblings, so the entrance of a new candidate will change the congregation. This is most obvious in stabile monastic communities, where a new place is literally set at the common table and everyone has to move over in chapel to accommodate the new member, but even in large mobile congregations there will be, over time, real modifications, especially if the candidate eventually attains a position of leadership in the group.

Incorporation is another area in which the school and/or military models operative in preconciliar formation no longer serve us well (if indeed they ever did). Incorporation is not graduation, a license to practice without supervision, the end of learning and accountability, or a commissioning for a position of command. It is a process of ever deepening sharing of lives that gradually transforms the person and the group. We need a new model for imagining this process that recognizes its mutuality, relationality, and ongoing character. I would like to suggest as a possible metaphor the one constructed from post-Newtonian science by Margaret Wheatley in relation to organizations,[22] namely, that of the candidate and the congregation as intersecting "fields."

Field is a familiar but mysterious category. As I discussed at some length in volume 1, Religious Life is an alternate lifeform in the Church, a particular way of living the common Christian vocation. While not superior to other lifeforms, it is nonetheless distinct and specific. In earlier times entering Religious Life was referred to as "leaving the world," relocating (geographically, sociologically, and/or institutionally) one's person and life in relation to secular and ecclesial society. Like the Great Barrier Reef, which can be seen in the ocean even from the moon, Religious Life stands out within the ecclesiastical "sea" even while remaining completely immersed in and surrounded by it. The life of the Church flows through its porous boundaries, nourishing and enlivening it, even as it nourishes the surrounding ecclesial sea from its own rich life.

This organic model encourages us to imagine Religious Life not as a quasi-solid object, as some kind of hermetically sealed thing or machine protected from its environment by impermeable boundaries, but as a living entity characterized by change, growth, and interaction with other systems. To go even further, science encourages us to realize that reality is composed not primarily of stable substances, which undergo modification through accidental or substantial change (as Aristotelian/Thomistic metaphysics suggested and Newtonian science corroborated) but as space, which, under certain circumstances, manifests at the macrolevel as seemingly solid objects.

However, space, the scientists tell us, is not "empty." Rather, "[s]pace everywhere is now thought to be filled with fields, invisible, non-material structures that are the basic substance of the universe."[23] Fields are invisible geometries structuring space, invisible media of connection bringing matter and/or energy into form. We cannot see fields anymore than we can see space, but we can observe the effects of fields on that which enters them or comes within their influence. For example, iron filings that come within a magnetic field arrange themselves in certain patterns. Movements of bodies are influenced by the gravitational field in which they are. Wheatley hypothesizes that persons and corporate groups are also primarily space structured by fields, both positive and negative, and when these fields intersect certain predictable behaviors appear.

This metaphor sheds some light on our very common experience that the same people behave very differently in situations which, exteriorly, do not seem to differ noticeably. Something "in the air," or perhaps more accurately "in the space" affects them. We sometimes call this something morale, positive or negative energy, or social climate. People even speak of being "in good (or bad) space." And a person in "bad space" who enters positive corporate space can either be pulled out of her negativity or can so infect the new space that, socially, it curdles. In other words, social space seems to be a reality and to be invisibly structured in powerfully effective ways.

Wheatley suggests that social fields are generated as people converse, share their visions and hopes, work out their problems, develop modes of interacting, participate in common projects, and elaborate symbols and myths to interpret and articulate their shared identity and experience.[24] In other words, groups generate or create fields and, when these fields are coherent, corporate space is created that draws people together so that they begin to act in corporate ways. Eventually, a group ethos can be recognized in members, not only among themselves but even by outsiders. Such social fields can outlast the individuals or groups which generated them so that the corporate spirit or ethos can be formative of and expressed by successive generations even after the original members have left the corporation or died. This is often enough observed as second and third generations take over family businesses.

Religious congregations are corporate entities with distinctive features that, collectively, are often referred to as the charism of the institute or the spirit of the congregation. In volume 1[25] I suggested that the category of charism as it applies to a congregation is best understood as the ongoing "deep narrative"[26] developed throughout the community's history with its attendant myths and symbols, outstanding events and persons, struggles and triumphs, projects and challenges, psychology and spirituality that the group has developed from its origins to the present and that has become the inner heritage of each member down through the years generating among them a shared identity. In other words, the theological category of congregational charism may well be understood through the scientific metaphor of "field" structuring the corporate space of the congregation. This charism may derive in part from the personal influence of some outstanding founder like Benedict or Teresa of Avila, but that is very often not the case. The issue of charismatic identity is not so much one of "Who founded us?" as "What have we become together by the grace of God?"

When members of a congregation come together in significant events they often experience very powerfully "the spirit of the congregation," which might be understood as the manifestation in feeling and behavior of the charism as it is operative in this situation. The spirit of the congregation is the space-structuring field giving rise, in particular circumstances, to an experience of the corporateness of the congregation. Furthermore, although this spirit is most tangibly operative in corporate events, it is no less active in the day-to-day lives of the members who live in congregational "space" even when they are not physically together. And experience suggests that others who are not members of the congregation but are somehow related to the community, for example, associates or volunteers or benefactors, can also participate deeply in this spirit. The congregation continually generates a powerful field that can influence all who come within its ambit, whether as members or in some other capacity.

When a candidate enters the congregation she is neither an inert object nor a spiritual tabula rasa. She herself is primarily personal "space" structured by a complex configuration of fields: spiritual, educational, professional, social, economic, and so on. As discussed in the previous chapter, it is the interaction in her of these fields and the way that complexus is influenced by external factors (all, of course, under the influence of grace) that has generated the experience of "vocation." She feels that where she belongs, the best space for her, is in Religious Life in this congregation. She then enters the congregational space structured by its fields. In other words, the formation process can be understood, using this scientific metaphor, as the coming together of two complexes of fields, the overlapping of two kinds of structured space, the personal space of the candidate and the corporate space of the congregation.

Wheatley's point about corporate space can readily be applied to the formation process. When personal and corporate fields are compatible, the individual begins to manifest behaviors and attitudes that reflect the corporate vision and ideals. Such a person does not, in one sense, have to be told what to do, much less coerced into conformity. She is energized by the corporate dynamics, feels at home in the corporate space and able to be and become what she feels called to. The person may well have to be trained in corporate procedures or learn various skills, and will undoubtedly need mentoring, including both affirmation and criticism, but he or she has a feel for what it is all about, a sense of the spirit of the group. And conversely, some people feel constrained, ill at ease, or foreign and often generate negative energy in the group situation, even when they are well disposed and trying hard to conform. In other words, the interaction of individual candidate and congregational charism either validates the felt vocation or calls it into question. This process occurs organically, not by means of artificial "tests" or ordeals in which the candidate's performance is judged. In fact, sometimes it is clear that someone who is awkward in her behavior or less talented for the congregation's mission or in some other way seemingly a poor choice for Religious Life or the congregation is nevertheless clearly called to it while another candidate who "has everything" by any objective measure just does not grow into the life. In some mysterious way one "fits" and another does not, and eventually they and the community know it.

Incorporation is this ongoing process of becoming part of the congregation, imbibing the charism and living by the spirit, becoming one spirit with its members until one becomes a member. Various ceremonies and stages mark the deepening of the process, but incorporation is an ongoing and organic growth rather than a transubstantiating event. And, of course, as the new member becomes more deeply part of the body, it undergoes change due to her influence. At the beginning the influence of the congregational field on the candidate is much stronger than that of the candidate on the congregation, but ideally the candidate's influence will strengthen over time so that eventually she will have considerable leverage in determining the future and shape of the congregation.[27] This is the process by which the life of the congregation is gradually committed to the next generation. Assuming leadership responsibilities is a later stage of the incorporation process, which begins with vocation and entrance and ends only with death. In fact, even in death the members continue to both influence the community from "the realms of light" and to be accompanied by the prayer of the living members, who look to the tradition they have received to preserve and re-create and hand on the charism and spirit of the congregation.

CHAPTER THREE
COMMITMENT AND PROFESSION

I. Introduction

The discernment, testing, and nurturing of vocation through formation is meant to lead to commitment expressed in Religious profession. Like formation and incorporation, commitment is a process. Entrance itself, as we have seen, involves a very real commitment expressed in the renunciations required at that juncture. This first commitment is to test the vocation within the context of community life. Proceeding to and through the novitiate deepens the commitment. Today candidates are not permitted to make a definitive commitment by perpetual vows until they have lived the vowed life for a specified period of time, usually three to five years. However, it is understood, even canonically, that "temporary" profession is only valid if the person making the profession fully intends to make her profession perpetual at the end of the specified period. Temporary profession, in other words, is not time-limited in intention. The specification of a limited time simply permits a less complicated manner of terminating the commitment if, once one begins to live vowed Religious Life (which, of course, there is no way to begin living until one makes vows), it becomes clear that the original discernment was not well founded or that something has changed significantly during the period of temporary profession making continuation in the life inadvisable. At the end of the period of first vows either the Religious or the congregation can terminate the commitment by the nonrenewal of (as opposed to dispensation from) vows. Consequently, in what follows, when I speak of profession I mean first profession that is moving toward or has reached its intended final formulation.

II. Commitment

The term *commitment,* even in its more serious form of reference to persons (because we can also make commitments to principles, courses of action, etc.) covers a spectrum from the most casual ("I'll call you sometime") to the most life-shaping ("I take you for my spouse"). In this chapter we will be considering the latter, that is, lifelong commitment or a fundamental life option. This type of commitment, as moral theologian Margaret Farley defines it, is an act of entering into a new form of relationship by giving our word into the keeping of another, giving that other a claim upon us.[1] It brings into play our selfhood, our future, our relationships to other persons, notions of obligation and law, choice and renunciation, responsibility and hope. In short, it is a very complex reality with implications for our integrity as persons and the possibility of fulfillment for our life.

Furthermore, at least in first world cultures at the turn of the twenty-first century, commitment is in serious crisis. Not only do nearly half of marriages (the prototypical permanent commitment in our society) end in divorce but fewer and fewer people are even willing to undertake marriage, preferring to simply live with partners as long as the relationship seems mutually beneficial and/or raise children as single parents.[2] Consequently, continuing to invite people to undertake Religious Life through perpetual, vowed commitment in community and ministry is countercultural in the extreme and candidates need and deserve the resources to arrive at clarity and conviction on the subject.

A. The Two Dimensions of the Commitment

Although most people who undertake Religious Life do so within and according to the constitutions of a particular congregation, it is important to distinguish between the commitment to Religious Life and that to the congregation. For those who enter a congregation the commitment to the congregation is integral to their profession even though entering a congregation is not essential to Religious Life as such. The existence of forms of Religious Life that do not involve congregational affiliation (e.g., consecrated virginity lived in the secular setting and professed hermit life) makes this clear. The importance of the distinction lies in the inequality of the two dimensions of the person's commitment.

Although I am using the shorthand "commitment to Religious Life" I mean the commitment to Jesus Christ (to be discussed below), which constitutes the life, not commitment to a lifeform or an institution. The commitment that constitutes Religious Life is absolute, total, and unconditional, whereas the implicated commitment to the congregation is relative, partial, and conditional. The commitment to Religious Life is a commitment to a person, Jesus Christ, in irrevocable love expressed in a particular form, namely, lifelong consecrated celibacy analogous to marriage, which is a commitment to the spouse in irrevocable love expressed in the particular form of lifelong and total monogamy. This commitment is a total self-gift that has an absolute priority in one's life and begins with no qualifications or loopholes or "if" and "only if's."

The commitment to the congregation within which this total self-gift is made, which forms the context for living it out, is necessarily relative, partial, and conditional. The commitment to the congregation is relative to the commitment to Christ and conditioned by its ability to support and foster or at least not impede that prior commitment. If, for example, the congregation developed in such a way that participation in it made the living of Religious Life itself impossible, the person might be forced to leave it, to transfer to another congregation or found a new one, or to take up another form of vowed life. Or, if the congregation were suppressed or disbanded, one might continue to live the commitment of Religious Life. To say that the commitment to one's congregation is partial does not imply that it does not claim one's wholehearted love and loyalty but only that one does not finally give one's life, one's self, to the congregation but to Christ within the congregation.

B. The Commitment to Christ

The life option expressed by profession is the commitment to love Jesus Christ totally, absolutely, and forever and to express and embody that love (which is the calling, of course, of all the baptized) in the complete and exclusive self-gift of consecrated celibacy (which is not the calling of all the baptized). Because *love* is such an abused word in our culture we must be clear and realistic about its meaning. Love involves emotion, desire, feeling, all of which can and do fluctuate. But love *consists,* as Farley says, in affirming the being of the other, wanting the other to be fully and firmly, saying yes to the truest reality of the other.[3] It is easier to see what this means in relation to another human being to whom one might be united in marriage or friendship. Surely Jesus, risen and glorified at God's right hand, has no need of my affirmation to enjoy the fullness of being.

The point, however, is not that my affirmation brings about the being of the other but that my regard, my focus on the other, has the other, not myself, as its raison d'être. Self-gift is called forth by the sheer worth and lovableness of the other. The person whose experience of Jesus is such that it draws her out of herself, beyond herself, in a movement of unitive desire that consumes all that she is and can be to the exclusion of any comparable or even mediating love of another human being feels the need to commit herself to him by the irrevocable gift of her life. This is a very mysterious dynamic and one that can never be fully explained. The history of Christian spirituality, however, bears eloquent testimony to the fact that it is and has been the experience of a small minority (although a sizable number) of Christians from the first century to our own day.

The yes of profession to the reality of Jesus Christ is a response to his personal call, an affirmation of his own infinite lovableness and his love of me, a reflection in my life of his

completely reliable fidelity. And it necessarily involves a commitment not only to Jesus himself but to all that he loves, namely, to
his body which is the Church and even to the whole world which
he came to save. This explains the natural expression of Religious commitment in ministry that has always been integral to
the life but which is, finally, not its raison d'être. It also grounds
the absolute necessity, for one discerning a call to Religious Life,
to develop a prayer life in which Jesus, real, risen, living, and
present, mediated by the Gospels and the liturgy, is personally
encountered, contemplated, and embraced in an ever deepening
identification. The Religious must so interiorize the life and concerns of Jesus that she is able to say with St. Paul, "It is no longer
I who live, but it is Christ who lives in me" (Gal 2:20). Only such
personal union can ground the kind of self-gift, the kind of commitment, that perpetual profession expresses. And such unitive
love not only justifies permanence in the commitment; it
demands it, not as an obligation or a requirement but as the only
adequate expression of the actual relationship.

C. The Dilemma and the Glory of Commitment

Commitment, then, is the expression of love and the
"undying-ness" of love calls for permanence in commitment.
But this does not obviate, or even diminish, the conundrum
that permanent commitment involves, especially in the contemporary historical and cultural setting. The hesitations
most moderns have about making irrevocable commitments, no matter how strong the love one experiences, cannot be consumed in a blaze of idealism nor dismissed as the
lack of generosity of a narcissistic generation. Few people
contemplating permanent commitment today, whether in
marriage or Religious Life, have grown up in an atmosphere
of lived fidelity. If their own parents are not divorced, those
of many of their friends are. Their pastors, the Religious
they know, and many of the idealistically committed people
they have met in their school activities or volunteer involvements have abandoned their commitments for greener

fields, often within months or a few years of making them. Instability in every sphere of life is the rule, not the exception. And anyone who has come to prize freedom of choice, self-determination, and variety of life experience has to question an irrevocable choice about anything or anyone.

In discussing this vitally important topic it is crucial to keep distinguishing between real questions and rhetorical ones, in other words, between actual problems and the pseudo-problems, which are created by the way we talk about the issues. For purposes of economy and clarity I will discuss three clusters of concern about permanent commitments in each of which we will distinguish between real and imagined challenges. The first concerns the relationship of commitment to time, especially to the future; the second the question of options; the third the issue of freedom.

1. Speaking for the future: The first and usually most anxiety-ridden question a person, especially a relatively young person, contemplating lifelong commitment is likely to raise is, "How can I say what I will do for the rest of my life if I do not know what the future holds?"[4] The answer, of course, is "If you can only speak for what you know you can't even say what you will do five minutes from now." Since we do continually make plans, start projects, or undertake obligations that involve the future even though we cannot predict it, we can suspect that this formulation of the relationship between commitment and the future is ill conceived.

Every commitment, from the most inconsequential to the most important, has to be made without knowledge of the future. To start an academic program, make a purchase with a credit card, conceive a child, or invite someone to dinner next week commits one to action in a future which is susceptible to a nearly infinite range of possibilities that cannot be anticipated or controlled. I could be in the hospital when it is time to start classes, lose my job and be unable to pay any bills, give birth to a stillborn child, or get the flu on the day of the dinner.

The question about the future, framed in terms of knowledge and control of what lies ahead, is a rhetorical or pseudo-question that would negate the possibility of any commitment. In fact, commitment is not about knowledge of the future or control of eventualities. It is about knowledge in the present that grounds confidence in the ability to deal with the eventualities. The issue of promising, of speaking for the future, is very real, but the implication that one cannot speak for the future unless one knows and controls it is unfounded.

Philosophers and theologians have reflected in depth on the issue of how humans are situated within and related to time as personal history.[5] The naïve perception that time is objective, some substance or medium through which we are moving, traveling from the past into the present headed toward the future, is the basis of some simplistic and unrealistic thinking about commitment. The only real time is the present, which is always experienced from within my personal existence. My "past" is actually my present perceived as influenced by events and people no longer present (or present in the same way) to me as independent existents but functioning now as part of my existence. And my future is my present anticipation of what I have not yet experienced. In other words, the meaning of the past and the possibilities of the future, insofar as they are part of my personal history, are constructions of my present. Our concern with the future is real, but how the future does and should influence our decisions in the present is quite different from the way suggested by a naïve sense of the future as an objective and free-standing reality that will simply "happen to me."

Only humans wear watches, carry calendars, and keep journals, that is, relate consciously to time. Inanimate beings, plants, and animals have no pasts and do not make plans for the future. They are "hardwired," programmed by their constitution and/or instincts, to do what their nature demands. In other words, they do not choose among developmental alternatives or make decisions. The rock does not decide to fall from the cliff in an earthquake; the rose does not choose to be red; the lion is not committed to eating meat. Therefore, they make no moral judgments on their behavior.

Weeds do not feel guilty about growing in the wrong place or regret the damage they have caused; eagles do not feel proud of their flight. Humans, however, do have a past. We make choices, feel pride or guilt about them, learn from our experience, appropriate our development as personal achievement or as failure. And this gives rise to our very valid concern about the future.

Humans know by experience that we are capable of lofty aspirations and heroic self-donation. But we also know that we can be intimidated by challenge, fluctuate in our best resolves, and sometimes fail miserably. In other words, we can know what we most deeply desire to be and to do and also know that there will be times when we will feel unable to live up to those desires. On the basis of our past experience we can both identify with our present deep desires and aspirations, count on our capacity to realize them, and realistically fear our capacity to fail. This is the real relationship between time as personal history and the problematic of commitment.

We do not make commitments because we know what will actually happen in the future or because we can in any way control it. We make commitments because we know in the present, at least to a sufficient degree, who we are, what we love, which relationships we want to be a permanent part of our life. Commitment is a wager not on what the future holds but on our present identity and relationships and a realistic expectation of their development. We know that honoring these realities will be difficult, no matter what events actually transpire as our life progresses. To make a commitment to be our truest self in our most important relationships and thereby to honor and foster our deepest desires is an attempt to give a future to our love by our decision in the present. Commitment is a way of making my love whole even as it is becoming whole over a lifetime. By making a perpetual or lifelong commitment we take the whole of our life and being into our hands, temporally, as a concrete symbol of the qualitative whole to which we do not have access until our final breath, because it does not exist as an actual whole until then.

The novice discerning whether to make profession is wasting her time and generating useless anxiety trying to imagine whether her present idealism will fade or the congregation change or the institutional Church become too corrupt for continued association. The real question is whether she has come to know and love Jesus Christ in such a way that she feels called to, and wants to, give her whole self to him in the exclusive and total relationship of consecrated celibacy, come what may. The question is, does she truly desire to live all of the eventualities she will face, the joys and the sorrows, the disappointments and the triumphs, in the single-hearted relationship to Christ, which has become the most important, the absolutely essential, centering reality of her life? If the answer to that question is yes, and the yes is grounded in a careful and valid process of discernment and is validated by congregational authority, she is ready and able to make perpetual commitment.

2. Keeping options open: A second cluster of concerns about lifelong commitment is closely related to that of the future but with the added emphasis on concern with personal development. Our earlier modern predecessors faced a very limited array of possibilities as they approached adulthood in comparison with the seemingly unlimited spectrum of opportunities stretching before even the average person in the first world at the beginning of the twenty-first century. Most North Americans have grown up with the assurance that "You can be (have) anything you want if you're willing to work for it" ringing in their ears. Although this is a very doubtful dictum, especially for the underprivileged or marginalized members of society, it nevertheless captures an important reality, namely, that a person is not necessarily definitively programmed for life by gender, family, custom, finances, or other once virtually determining conditions. The son of a farmer might become an engineer or a career criminal and the daughter of a homemaker might become a prostitute or president of the United States. Furthermore, most young people in the western hemisphere have been conditioned to extremely high expectations.

They expect to have and to use opportunities to realize ambitions that would have seemed totally unrealistic in the 1950s.

This expansion of possibilities and heightening of expectations is usually seen as a great improvement in the life situation of most people, but it can also be experienced as an overwhelming embarrassment of riches as young people try to decide what and where to study, who to marry, what to do with their lives. Because making a choice does not necessarily remove other possibilities from the horizon whence they continue to beckon, alluringly inviting the person to revisit and revise decisions, it is increasingly difficult for a person in our society to make a definitive commitment that really excludes other options. Facing the challenge of perpetual commitment, the person is likely to say, "I think I really want to do this but I don't want to close off my options," or "I want to keep all my options open."

Again, these statements are the rhetorical formulation of a pseudo-problem that, nevertheless, raises a real issue. There is no such thing as keeping one's options open in any absolute sense of the word. From the moment the alarm rings and one decides whether or not to get out of bed, life consists in continuous choosing, and many choices automatically close off other options. To choose to go to work cuts off a day at the beach. To return or not return a phone call can change one's plans for the day or the year. Even the proverbial "couch potato" whose decisions involve nothing more significant than flipping television channels with the remote control is making choices by not making choices. No one believes the couch potato is training to become president. The ideal of keeping one's options open is in no sense even potentially absolute or infinite. Even in the very narrow range where it might apply, for example, waiting to hear if one is accepted by the other colleges to which one has applied before registering at the first one to which one was admitted, it is a time-bound suspension of choice that cannot be maintained indefinitely. As soon as one sends in the registration form one has cut off the other options.

Adolescence is the time of life when we are allowed to keep a certain number of options open while we assess our own capabilities and interests and the range of possibilities that are realistically available to us. We are encouraged both to experiment widely *and* to avoid premature irreversible choices such as teenage pregnancy or contracting HIV. But if we are to get on with our life adolescence has to come to an end, and it does so by a series of more or less serious choices: of college or work, of occupational preparation and position, of living situation, and finally of significant personal relationships. The person who simply continues to hang around the parental home working at occasional odd jobs for spending money and dabbling in superficial relationships and daily amusements is no one's ideal of the truly free person living a mature and worthwhile life. The colloquial expression, "Get a life," is eminently applicable to such aimless individuals.

If keeping one's options open is not even possible, much less desirable, it remains true that there is a value coming to expression in the desire to do so. We recognize the growth potential, the opportunity for personal development, embodied in a variety of life experiences. Travel, education, relationships with a wide variety of people, occupational opportunities, and many other experiences broaden our horizons, increase our capacity to appreciate diversity, enrich our imaginations, deepen our intellectual understanding of reality, refine our aesthetic sensibilities. Some people become virtual "experience junkies," unable to resist the chance to see or hear or visit or try anything and everything that pops up on their experiential screen. Going as a volunteer to a third-world country, betting on a horse race, having sex with an exotic partner, bungee jumping, or art lessons are all in the category of "experience" that one must have, but none becomes the object of a definitive choice. The experience junkie is the professional dilettante who makes adolescence a life's work. But one does not need to be a dilettante to desire enrichment by a wide variety of experience throughout one's life.

The mature person contemplating a life choice, whether marriage or Religious Life or some other permanent commitment, sees clearly and realistically that making such a choice will foreclose many other options. To marry Joe rules out all the other men in the human race as spouses. To have a child is to undertake at least two decades of responsibilities that will take priority over many of the experiences available to the childless person. And becoming a Religious, among many other things, will limit one's access to money and one's discretion in using even what is available, make certain relationships illegitimate, preclude total independence in choice of location, work, or lifestyle. The real question (as opposed to the rhetorical dilemma) is, does it make sense to do so?

One of life's most challenging paradoxes is that unless one makes commitments, closes off options that are potentially developmental, nothing actually productive can be achieved. The artist must choose one size canvas that immediately determines the scale of the painting. She selects a limited palette range, and as she paints she must solve each problem that arises by choosing one color and its shade, intensity, shape, and placement that excludes others until, finally, there are no choices, no options remaining because adding or subtracting another brush stroke will mar the beauty she has created. Success consists finally in eliminating all options through the right choices.

Unless a person, the artist of her own life, makes choices that involve her life in its deepest springs, unless she puts down relational roots through commitment, she continues to drift through life collecting "experiences" that cannot be fitted into any frame of reference within which they have genuine or abiding significance, within which her life becomes a whole. In other words, as long as one remains a seed, a self-enclosed complex of unactuated potential, one's life is fruitless. Only by "falling into the earth and dying" (cf. Jn 12:24), only by taking root in some concrete time and place with some particular people and projects will one grow into a truly fruitful, life-giving person. To "plant dreaming deep"[6] is to forego many side adventures into potentially interesting landscapes. The dilemma of commitment is that the price of integration which is the sine qua non of fulfillment is the foreclosing of some potentially enriching options. Part of growing up is coming to terms with the fact that I am not the lone exception to this universal law.

One focuses both one's vision and one's energies at the high price of what now lies on the periphery. Metaphysically this simply means that the human is not God and no one can choose everything. But coming to terms with this reality so that one can freely make a life commitment is actually the beginning of coming to terms eventually with death, the ultimate foreclosing of earthly options in favor of life eternal. Only the superficial, then, would underestimate the gravity of perpetual commitment. One of the occupational hazards of contemporary life is drifting into ill-considered commitments without acknowledging the full scope and depth of what one is doing and then having to rupture one's own life and that of others to pull out of them.

Making a definitive and irreversible commitment, in other words, is not an act of self-mutilation enthroning lifelong regret for the road not taken in an imprisoned heart. It is an act of courageous self-determination that is the highest expression of freedom in the human being. Rather than allowing others to make the decisions about one's life (which is the temporary situation of the child or the violent situation of the slave) or allowing chance to dictate it as fate, one takes one's life in one's hands and says, "I have only one life to live and this is what I choose to do with it."

It is not sentimentality that brings tears to our eyes as we listen to the words, "I take you for my spouse...until death do us part" or "I vow to God...for the rest of my life." It is the overwhelming sense of being present at the supreme moment of a human life, the moment of total self-possession and self-gift. It is the act for which humans were made and which is meant to be finally ratified by the "It is finished" and "Into your hands I commend my spirit" of our last breath in this world.[7] It is the solemn moment in Jesus' life that the Gospel of John captures so dramatically, "Now before the festival of the Passover, Jesus knew that his hour had come to depart from this world and go to the Father. Having loved his own who were in the world, he loved them to the end" (Jn 13:1). The commitment to love unto the end is the ultimate act of freedom and self-determination. Anyone who faces it without a sense of its glory and its danger, its beauty and its pain is not ready for adulthood.

All this being said, however, it is not out of place to point out to those contemplating the commitment of perpetual profession that even though many options are foreclosed by the choice of Religious Life, many others are opened by that choice. Most Religious alive today could affirm that they could never have anticipated the wealth of experience Religious Life has provided them. Certainly living through the transformation of the life initiated by Vatican II could not have been anticipated by anyone entering before the mid-1960s. Education and professional development, living and/or association with a remarkable variety of people within and outside one's community, increasing and growth-producing responsibilities in work and community, travel, ministerial involvement with significant people and projects, and numerous other life-enriching experiences have filled the lives of most Religious with an often overwhelming variety of demands and rewards. No one enters (or at least no one should enter) Religious Life to acquire professional or personal opportunities or perquisites. But commitment in any worthwhile life is not an option for boredom and barrenness. It is choice of some options rather than others. The person truly called to Religious Life will most likely experience that the opportunities for growth and development inherent in that life are the ones to which she really feels drawn. Discerning a call to perpetual commitment is a matter of "choosing life," not death. But, like the Israelites on the borders of the promised land, choosing life means obeying "the commandments of the Lord, your God...loving [God], and walking in [God's] ways" (Dt 30:16).

3. Commitment and freedom: This brings us to the third cluster of concerns around commitment, closely related to that of options but now with the emphasis not on what is chosen or renounced but on the very capacity to choose, that is, on our

freedom. People facing the challenge of commitment sometimes fear that by committing themselves, especially in a perpetual way, they are binding their freedom, cutting off their
power to choose, and subjecting themselves to an external rule
or obligation that renders them less the subjects of their own
history, less fully persons.

Once again, this fear comes to expression as a rhetorical or
pseudo-problem which, nonetheless, points to a genuine concern. To address the rhetorical problem we must distinguish
between freedom and spontaneity. As its etymology suggests,
spontaneity is the instinctive behavior that springs forth in
response to a stimulus. We spontaneously duck when a projec-
tile comes at our head or scream when confronted suddenly by
a stranger in the dark. There are other quasi-spontaneous
responses that are not totally instinctive but have become second nature. We smile when introduced to someone or reach for
something to eat when we smell certain odors. We can control
those habitual responses if we have good reason to do so and
controlling them, that is, repressing our spontaneity, is an act of
freedom, not coercion. In fact, we regard people who are at the
complete mercy of their instincts and impulses as very unfree.

Freedom, in other words, does not consist in doing everything I *feel like* doing (whether the feeling comes from nature
or habit) but in having the strength of will to do what I really
want to do, even when I do not feel like it, for example, to care
for my sick child in the middle of the night. Freedom is the
capacity to love, to desire the good of what I love, and to act in
favor of that good. Experience, however, soon teaches us that
it is not really possible to maintain without fluctuation, "at
white heat" so to speak, the energy of our loves. So, as we have
already seen, we take measures to assure that we will not fall
away from our love, from what we really desire, when we are
weak, distracted, tempted, or threatened. Commitments,
ranging from minor resolutions to lifelong professions, are
such measures. They give a law to our love that has two important functions as we walk what Farley calls, "the way of
fidelity." First, commitment shapes and educates our living

out of our desires, and second, it protects us from our own weakness when our vision or resolve is obscured.

The notion of law or obligation, however, suggests heteronomy, coercion from without, and thus loss of freedom. This raises a real problem because if this were really the case, that is, that we became less free and therefore less human by commitment, the latter could not be justified. But if we get beyond the rhetoric of spontaneity, we see, as God says to the Israelites, that the laws of committed relationship are not up in the sky or over the sea, that is, outside us as "mysterious and remote" dicta imposed from on high, but "very near to [us], already in [our] mouths and in [our] hearts" (cf. Dt 30:11–14). The laws governing our commitments may be exteriorized as rule or custom, but the exterior formulation mirrors the choices we have made in our own hearts. They reflect back to us from without what we most want to be and do when that interior desire becomes obscured by passion or lassitude or when we do not know what to do in a new or unforeseen situation.

The marvelous comic strip drawn by Bill Watterson in the 1980s and '90s, "Calvin and Hobbes," featured a highly kinetic little boy and his stuffed tiger, Hobbes, who, when Calvin played with it, became a living companion in his hilarious, mostly imaginative, adventures. One recurrent theme of the comic strip was "the game" in which the two friends would start to play, and as soon as one made a mistake or lost a point he would immediately amend the rules to make his error a score, at which the other would retaliate by reversing the reversal until the two were totally confused and collapsed in exhausted delight declaring that "We have the best games in the world." The whole point, of course, was that they had such a wonderful time because they were not playing a game at all. They were surrendered in childish glee to absolute lawless spontaneity that could not possibly move forward (it usually ended with a score of a jillion to a squillion or some such impossibility that rendered any notion of winning or losing inapplicable) but exhausted them in sheer delight at their own incoherence, a wonderful contrast to the orderly and regulated life Calvin had to lead at home and school. The Calvin in all of us "wants" to be totally irresponsible, absolutely spontaneous, and to enjoy unconditional acceptance by an equally unrealistic Hobbes.

But when adults play real games, rules are of the essence. It would make no sense to practice making free throws unless the basket in the real game will be regulation (that is, rule-governed) height and the free throw line regulation distance from it. Rules allow the focusing of the players' energies, enable them to anticipate the behavior of the other players, assure a "level playing field" for all participants, and establish what counts as achievement. The players rely on the rules to help them control their play and measure their progress. In other words, rules or laws of play are in the service of the project of the players, of what they really want to do but would find it difficult to do without some guidelines and even some sanctions for failure to perform appropriately. People play games because they want to, not because they are forced or coerced, and they learn the rules and play by them because that is how they make progress in what they want to do. Freedom is at work throughout, even (or especially) in the obeying of the rules. The most brilliant achievements emerge precisely from the deepest mastery, the most complete interiorization of the rules.

Life commitment, of course, is not a game. But it is analogous to a game in that it is a serious project freely undertaken out of love, which is, nevertheless, challenging and difficult. Making progress in the life chosen, like improving one's game, requires continuous discipline and practice, and it makes sense to establish what constitutes productive effort so that one does not exhaust oneself in Calvin-like exertions whose only purpose is to wear oneself out before bedtime. One purpose, then, of the law one gives to one's love by making a commitment is to focus and sustain one's efforts to love.

But commitment as obligation has another important function. Many people today shy away from marriage, preferring to live together and "renew our commitment to each other every day." It has been suggested that Religious Life could be similarly undertaken by a short-term promise of some kind that would be renewed regularly as long as the person found the life compelling. This seemingly idealistic approach to love is romantically attractive but terribly naïve, as so many people in such relationships have discovered to their great sorrow.

When there is no obligating commitment, every serious conflict raises the real question of whether this is the point at which to abandon the relationship. By contrast, within an irreversible commitment the question raised by serious conflict is not "Should we split?" but "How are we going to handle this?" The commitment to *not* split is already in place and nonnegotiable, for better or for worse, in sickness or in health, for richer or for poorer, in other words, no matter what. And if we are in this for the long haul, no matter what the problems, then we have to figure out how to deal with the challenge in such a way that the relationship, the love, survives and flourishes. In other words, there is an enormous difference, when challenges to a relationship arise, between a nonnegotiable presumption in favor of the relationship that directs our energies toward solving the problems and an always available option to walk away without guilt, before or after making such an effort. And this option to walk away can be (and often is) unilateral. If I want to abandon a nonbinding relationship, that is my right and privilege, regardless of the implications for or desires of the other person(s). The fact that one knows this, that one has no real claim on the partner, undermines the confidence that the worst can be faced without threat of abandonment. In other words, not making a permanent commitment means I can renew my commitment every day, but it also means I have no compelling reason beyond my own satisfaction for doing so.

Throughout this section I have preferred the term *perpetual* to *permanent* as a descriptor of lifelong commitment. This is an aesthetic choice about how to imagine what Religious profession involves. *Permanent* evokes images of a free-standing, unchanging substance or condition. Mount Rushmore is permanent. Having my gall bladder removed is permanent. But *perpetual* usually qualifies movement, development, life activity. I am a perpetual learner no matter how much I know. A person becomes a parent in perpetuity no matter how old the child gets. Perpetuity connotes both stability and change, in other words, what we call development or growth in which an organism, by living, eventually becomes completely other than it was at the outset and yet maintains its identity. At profession a person undertakes an unknown future from within the structure of a lifetime commitment. She has no idea what living that commitment will eventually entail. But she will certainly be a very different person at seventy or eighty than she is now. And yet, by profession, she says that she intends to be the same person because at the end the same relationship will be at the heart of her being as now motivates her act of self-donation.

D. Fidelity in Commitment

In a subsection of a chapter I cannot discuss fully a subject to which books have been devoted[8] but something needs to be said about negotiating the inevitable challenges of life commitment. No matter how one feels on the day of marriage or profession or at the birth of one's child, the soaring elation will inevitably wane as time goes on. One of the most remarkable Religious of our time, Bede Griffiths, wrote to a friend just before his solemn profession in 1937 at Prinknash Abbey:

> I love this place so much that I simply don't know how I would live outside. I love every moment of the day, every stick and stone here, and every soul in the community, more than words can tell.[9]

He wrote to the same friend in 1954, seventeen years later, from Pluscarden Abbey:

> It is quite true that it [i.e., monastic life] came as the fulfillment [...] of all my desires and satisfied my deepest instincts, but the stress and strain has often been appalling. In fact I often look on it as a kind of crucifixion and my prevailing sense is of profound disillusionment—I mean the sense that nothing in this world can ever give real and permanent satisfaction, and that everything—and everyone—betrays.[10]

It is hard to imagine a better articulation of the genuineness of first love and the realism of experience. But the point is that Griffiths persevered. He lived the commitment he had made despite the suffering and died as one of the truly accomplished Religious of our time, a pioneer in interreligious dialogue, an immensely fruitful monastic, a saint by any calculation. What contributes to such fidelity, to such growth?

The first contributing factor, as we have already seen, is perpetual commitment itself. To affirm one's love both to oneself and, by public profession, to the community of congregation and Church is a major safeguard of its permanence. Deciding to make profession means not leaving implicit to myself the meaning and depth of my love. It requires a conscious and explicit choice that I recognize as my own, that I have in fact affirmed. And as we will see in the next section, there is a real difference between the resolution or commitment we make in the secrecy of our own heart and that which we undertake as public responsibility to and before others. Our culture, as perhaps none before ours, is jaded and cynical about commitment. In a way, few really expect a marriage to last. But those who gather for the religious celebration of life commitments are being informed by the very choice of context that this commitment has been prayerfully discerned and that the fidelity of God is invoked and involved in what is being done. The expectation of fidelity is realistically higher and that expectation is a support for the one making the commitment.

The community context in which one proposes to live Religious profession is a second contributing factor to fidelity. Not only the example and wisdom of fellow members who have lived the life fruitfully and happily for decades but also the companionship of others dealing with the same challenges in congregation, society, and Church offer support for the newly professed. Spiritual, psychological, and professional resources are usually more available to Religious in times of struggle, if they have the wisdom to avail themselves of them in good time, than they are to many of their lay counterparts.

A very important factor in fidelity is the process of actually letting go that should take place during formation and is formally finalized at profession but which, unfortunately, some people never really accomplish. Making a choice, for example, for consecrated celibacy, involves a definitive renunciation of marriage. The person who does not really let go of marriage, not only as a reality in the present but even as a theoretical possibility for the future, will be tempted to play with fire in this arena for the rest of her life. The Religious who has truly chosen celibacy is going to relate (and not relate) to people of the other sex (or her own sex if she is homosexual) in particular ways that will make it clear in all circumstances that she is not sexually available nor open to a genitally active relationship. She will not indulge, imaginatively, in forays into the lifestyle she has renounced nor, behaviorally, in flirtation or expressions of affection that lead naturally in a direction she is committed not to go. The same principles govern other aspects of the commitment made at profession. Nibbling away at the renunciation of private ownership by the gradual accumulation of private property, self-marginalization in relation to congregational processes, evasiveness in dealing with community authority, independence that becomes isolation or estrangement are all expressions of not having let go of the options one did not choose. At profession two roads diverge, and one can take only one of them if any progress toward life-integration, toward holiness, is to be made.

All of the foregoing suggests that an important safeguard of commitment is realistic anticipation of hard times. Profession day is not the time to imagine all that can go wrong, but in preparation for commitment there needs to be an undramatic but unvarnished consideration of both the objective and the subjective challenges the novice is likely to face. Different people will be more susceptible to disillusionment with the institutional Church or taking scandal at the failures of fellow Religious. And each person has her own vulnerabilities, such as a tendency to discouragement and despair, scrupulosity or self-criticism, laziness and luxury, making excuses, harsh judgments and hypercriticalness of others, and so on. As these become evident during formation, it is important not only to work at their remediation in practice but to realize that most such limitations are fairly deeply rooted in the personality and each predisposes the person to particular types of temptation to give up in the face of life's challenges. Forewarned is forearmed in this case as in so many. The less surprised a person is by her own or others' weaknesses the less likely her reaction will be a conclusion that her commitment was ill founded or the life impossible.

Finally, and most important, the only real reason for honoring in perpetuity the commitment of profession, regardless of what happens or what else becomes available, is the love relationship between the Religious and Christ. That love, rooted in sustained contemplation of the beauty and lovableness of Christ, is what called her to the life; it is what comes to definitive expression in profession; it is what motivates her ministry to Christ's body; it is what will be lived day to day over a lifetime of joy and suffering. Nothing, then, is more important, indeed ultimately crucial, than the daily nurturing of that relationship, the sustaining of that attention to the infinite worth of the one to whom she has given her life. The person who loses touch with the beloved, who becomes a stranger to the one to whom she is committed, may continue to keep her commitment out of a sense of duty or obligation, but the life has gone out of the relationship and the life itself has no further meaning.

Prayer is to Religious Life what communication, that is, sustained interaction and mutual contemplation, is to any committed relationship. In her meditation on the Scriptures the Religious remembers the history that produced Jesus and was fulfilled in his life and death, and deeply interiorizes his personality, his relationship with God and others, the mysteries of his life, and his teaching. She becomes "one spirit with Christ" (cf. 1 Cor 6:17) in and through liturgical celebration of his life and union with him in Eucharist. She learns to share her life in Christ with others through spiritual direction, shared prayer, and contemplative ministry. In her annual retreats she puts aside everything, even Christ's own work, to be with him in uninterrupted mutual and loving contemplation. Gradually she develops the lifestyle and the disciplines that facilitate and nurture her communication with Jesus and that ongoing communication nourishes the relationship which is at the heart of her life. A relationship that does not grow is doomed, and a life commitment that is not founded on and expressive of a supremely worthwhile relationship is hollow. The priority of prayer in the life of the Religious is the touchstone of commitment and finally the only guarantee of its success.

III. Profession

Religious profession is the act by which a person who has carefully discerned a call to Religious Life and conceived a deep desire to give herself totally to Jesus Christ in lifelong consecrated celibacy lived in community and ministry finally crosses the threshold into the life in a definitive and irrevocable way. It is a supremely important moment, not as an isolated temporal act but as the culmination of a long process of questioning, testing, and choosing and as the initiating moment of the rest of her life fulfilling that choice. Because it is much misunderstood, either as a terrifying act of self-coercion or as an almost casual celebration with family and friends, it needs to be considered in all its gravity and glory.

A. The Act of Profession

1. Profession as transformative action: Before considering the content of profession, that is, the specific vows that are made, it is important to understand the act itself. Although Religious profession in the Catholic Christian tradition has always included implicitly or explicitly the commitment to lifelong celibacy, profession itself has not always involved the making of specific vows. One could become a Religious in the earliest days by committing oneself to Christ in the hands of the bishop or by definitively assuming the Religious habit in the desert setting. Throughout the history of Religious Life and even today different Religious families make different vows. However, the so-called evangelical counsels[11] are presumed to be included in the act of profession.[12] And a number of orders and institutes have a "fourth vow," which stipulates some particular characteristic or practice pertaining to their spirit or ministry.[13] The point is that profession is not constituted by either vows as such or by specific vows. Profession is the act of definitive self-consecration to Christ.[14] It comes to expression in vows because this is the most solemn and binding way human beings have found to verbally express such consecration.[15]

The clearest analogue of the act of profession is the act of marrying, the definitive mutual self-giving of two people, in their entire persons and possessions, regardless of subsequent eventualities, for the rest of their lives. Profession is what philosophers call *performative* language. It is language that not only expresses but actually does something. When, for example, the words are said, "I baptize you..." the person is actually, in reality, incorporated into Christ. When two people exchange the verbal formula, "I take you for my spouse..." they become a married couple, two in one flesh. When the novice says, "I vow to God..." she becomes a Religious. Performative language does what is said, and in this case what is done is *transformative* of the person herself.

2. Profession as entrance into a state of life: Profession is not only performative language that brings about genuine transformation of the person but a solemn, formal, and public commitment that establishes the person in a state of life. In this respect it differs essentially from private vows, promises, associate commitments, volunteer contracts, or any of a number of other kinds of personal engagements. First, Religious profession is *solemn.* This has to do not with where or how the ceremony is carried out (although it is fitting that the ceremony reflect the solemnity of the act) but with the seriousness and gravity of the undertaking. Profession is not simply the graduation ceremony at the end of the novitiate, something that may or may not be significant a few days after the guests have gone home. And it is not an experiment to see whether one likes the life once initial formation gives way to "real life" as a fully incorporated member of the congregation. Profession is the enactment of a serious, irrevocable, personal decision about who one will be and what one's life will mean. It is reached after long and careful discernment carried out in prayer and prolonged testing by both the person herself and the congregation.

It is probably counterproductive to so dramatize the act of profession (as was sometimes done in preconciliar times) that it loses its organic and peaceful continuity with the whole process of probation and formation and takes on such terrifying proportions that a well-prepared novice suddenly quails before the enormity of the actual act and feels that she cannot possibly proceed. Profession should not be traumatic but a gloriously free and joyful experience of maturing love coming to expression. On the other hand, it is also counterproductive to so minimize or even trivialize the solemnity and gravity of the act of profession (as has sometimes been done in the recent past) that the novice has little sense of the self- and world-transforming dimensions of what she is doing. Profession is a solemn act by which a person enters a new state of life that gives new depth and permanence to the relationships it entails to God, self, community, and the wider Church and world.

Second, Religious profession is a *formal* act. This does not mean that the ceremony is stiff or stodgy or that the one making profession is distanced from those participating in the event. It means that it must actually take place, it happens, at a particular time and place. A minute before reciting the formula of profession the person is not a Religious. A moment later she is. She has definitively and irrevocably crossed a threshold that is recognizable to her and those around her. She immediately signs the book of profession acknowledging her place in the congregation for all time.

Society places high value on formal commitment. The swearing in of the president or the chief justice of the Supreme Court, the anointing of the king or queen in a monarchy, the taking of the oath as a witness in court, the sentencing of a convicted criminal, the naturalization of the new citizen, the signing of adoption papers, and of course the making of marriage vows are all formal acts of great significance creating new life situations for those involved, initiating a state of life, or at least a role, that does not exist prior to the formal act even if the reality of it has been being lived for some time. In a perverse way the tendency of Americans to minimize, trivialize, or even avoid the formal acts of commitments of adult life witnesses to the very strong, even visceral sense we have of the seriousness of such acts. The person who says, "We love each other; we don't need anyone to pronounce us spouses; we don't need to sign any papers to prove our love or establish it" can meaningfully be asked, "Why, if your love is so real and your commitment to each other so solid and reliable, do you shy away from making a definitive and formal statement of it?"

The fear of definitive, formal commitment leads directly into the third characteristic of profession, that it is a *public* act. This has nothing to do with the size of the crowd who witness it or where the ceremony is held (although there must be official witnesses) but with the social consequences of the act. Once a person has entered a state of life by solemn and formal commitment she or he is in a new situation in regard to society. The man or woman sworn in as president of the United States is accountable to the American people for the way he or she upholds and defends the Constitution and protects the interests of the nation. We have a right to expect certain types of behavior and levels of performance, and if these are not met the person can be impeached and even removed from office. Married people are rightly held responsible for monogamy and, in our society, a bigamist can be arrested. Marriage has legally enforceable consequences in the realms of finances, property, health care, and child rearing. The person who adopts a child is responsible for supporting and raising that child just as a birth parent is. Similarly, the person who makes Religious profession is not simply giving a shape to her own spirituality or personally associating herself with a group of people in various ways. She is undertaking a specific set of obligations and responsibilities as well as assuming a certain set of rights for all of which she is accountable before the congregation and the Church, and sometimes even the state.[16]

One reason some people want to keep their commitments "informal" is to avoid the accountability that public commitment involves. As long as the commitment is a purely private and informal arrangement (no matter how committed the persons involved may feel or how well known their relationship is) one can walk away without such formal proceedings as divorce, impeachment, or dispensation from vows. In other words, formality and publicity have to do with responsibility definitively accepted in a larger sphere than the individual consciences and private domain of the participants.

Another consequence of public commitment is that it creates a space and constructs a reality in the midst of the Church and the world that realizes, that actually brings about in a particular way, the dream of the Reign of God.[17] Private commitments, informal commitments, temporary commitments do not establish a person in a *state of life* and do not create a lifeform in the Church or world. Public, perpetual, and formal commitment does. In other words, the prophetic character of Religious Life arises in and remains rooted in profession even as it is lived out in community and ministry.

In my opinion these considerations have some implications for the still lively question about whether a congregation should have a vow formula used by all who make profession or whether each novice should compose her own, provided it includes the substance of the three vows as canonically understood. The motivation for the latter position is understandable and even admirable. The novice should have come to a personal understanding and appropriation of the meaning of the vows before she makes them and such understanding cannot be simply "generic." And if she embodies her personal understanding in a unique formula she may identify more deeply with what she is doing. However, I think there are several considerations that suggest the preference for a congregational formula.

First, as I will suggest shortly, the vows are poetic and prophetic language rather than statements of carefully circumscribed legal obligations. For that reason they are something a person grows into, realities whose significance changes and unfolds as a person matures, and whose understanding is affected by changing cultural conditions over time. To make definitive the understanding of a vow that one has at the end of the novitiate is to limit the poetic potential of the coordinates of profession. The person who thinks "simplicity of life" is equivalent to poverty is bracketing out important community, societal, ministerial, and even mystical dimensions of the vow and reducing it to one important but limited facet. The poetic symbol "poverty" is not limited to any of these dimensions but will gradually reveal, over a lifetime, what it means to be a creature related in every fiber of one's being to the All who is the Creator. The same is true of celibacy and obedience.

Second, because profession is a public act, its meaning is in the public forum. It is not my private understanding of the vows that governs my act of self-commitment but the understanding of Religious Life in this congregation as it holds itself accountable in and to the Church. I must certainly learn what that means in my life and gradually personalize it by my own appropriation of it, but I am not creating this state of life out of whole cloth or founding the congregation. I am entering a state of life and a congregation that pre-exist me and within whose self-understanding I have found my identity and vocation. Assimilation to the congregation is signified by making profession according to the pattern established in this community. The president taking the oath of office repeats after the chief justice the established formula that carries the enrichment and the weight of an entire history of interpretation but that also inserts this incumbent of the office into the whole historical reality of the presidency that has been lived by all his or her predecessors. He or she will certainly contribute to the understanding of the presidency during her or his tenure, but the office is undertaken not as a personal interpretation of public service but as a realization of the meaning of this public role as it is understood by the American people.

Third, because profession is not only personal but communal, it is eminently fitting that the act of profession as it is made by each succeeding new member be the same as that of those who preceded her and those who will follow her. Each will live her profession in a uniquely personal way. But they are living the same commitment within the same congregation and in that unity is strength and support, identity and continuity. The congregation is not a collection of spiritual monads each of whom invents a private form of Religious Life and tacks it on to an aggregate. It is a body, an organic entity, into which one is incorporated by formal and public commitment. To pronounce the historic words intoned by our forebears tells us and the community who we now are in this tradition that is ever ancient and ever new.

B. The Content of Profession: The Vows

Profession, the solemn, formal, public self-gift to God in Jesus Christ by which a person definitively undertakes to live as a Religious within a particular congregation, is expressed by the making of vows. Evolution of Religious Life over centuries has led to the quasi-standard form of the profession of consecrated celibacy, poverty, and obedience, which may be explicit (as they are in most congregations) or implicit in an ancient formula (as in the Benedictine or Dominican traditions) or augmented by additional vows (as in the Jesuit or Mercy tradition). But the canonical definition of Religious Life stipulates the triple vows, at least in their content, as constitutive of the life.

1. The vows as legal obligations: For all the reasons discussed in the previous section, the vows are legally binding obligations. They oblige the person to observe the content of the vows as understood and specified by church and congregational law. The vow of consecrated celibacy, in this as in other respects, stands by itself since no interpretation or particular law can alter its fundamental obligation to remain unmarried and to practice chastity in the form of total abstinence from genital sex and whatever leads to or flows from genital sex. Other matters touching on the vow of celibacy are open to interpretation, for example, whether homosexual persons will be accepted and whether the order can have both male and female members and/or branches. But the substance of the vow is not negotiable.

The two vows of community life, poverty and obedience, admit of enormous variety of interpretation among orders. Whether, for example, the vow of poverty renders the person and/or the order radically incapable of ownership or merely suspends the independent use of property, whether it permits limited personal autonomy in the acquisition and use of material goods or requires explicit permission for each and every item used and absolute uniformity among members and/or houses, and so on is all left to particular law. And how obedience operates in any congregation is a function of its particular constitutions and government structure. Both poverty and obedience have minimal definitions in canon law, but there is wide variety of interpretation and practice depending on the history, ministry, and current stage of evolution of the community.

Much more will be said about the content of the vows in part 2 of this volume and in volume 3, but the point here is that the vows do inaugurate legal obligations in a person's life that she did not have before profession. This is a serious implication of profession. However, in my opinion, this aspect of the vows has been so overemphasized that other more fundamental and significant aspects have disappeared from sight. I want to raise up these other aspects without denying or trivializing the legal implications of the vows. But as in a marriage, the significance of the legal dimensions increases in proportion to the breakdown of the relationship. In a healthy marriage little appeal is made to the courts.

The recognition that a legalistic approach to the vows was inadequate was enshrined, in preconciliar times, in the theology of "the vow and the virtue." Novices were taught that the vows each pointed to and encouraged a virtue (called the "virtue of the vow") with the vow being obligatory and the virtue being an ideal. Thus, for example, one was obliged by the vow of poverty to ask permission for new clothing but the virtue of poverty should keep one from asking for anything not really necessary. This distinction was intended to protect the person and the vow by making clear what was (and was not) legally demanded and could be verified and sanctioned in the public forum while encouraging continual spiritual growth toward the ideal in the interior life. But I think that for many people it had the unintended effect of creating, on the one hand, a cramping legalism (and in some cases scrupulosity) about the vows that deprived them of any attractiveness or capacity to inspire idealism and, on the other hand, privatized the spiritual dimensions of the vows.

2. *The vows as poetic and prophetic:* The vows are first and foremost *poetic* language. Words like *poverty* and *obedience* are not literal descriptions, much less prescriptions, of juridical obligations (although since the thirteenth century there have been increasing efforts to specify more and more exactly what is legally implied by them). They are world-creating metaphors that are hyperbolic in the linguistic tradition of the biblical merism.[18] They intend by their literally impossible extravagance (who can be absolutely poor?) to capture the totality of the commitment being expressed. Hyperbole is exaggeration for effect, the use of extreme language to evoke what is beyond expression. Poetry is hyperbolic by nature. Like the persons who say, "I take you for my spouse, for better or for worse, for richer or for poorer, in sickness and in health...till death do us part," intending, by stating the extremes that are meant to include everything in between them, to commit everything they are and have to the new world of their married life, which they are creating by this performative and poetic language, the person who makes Religious vows does not intend to say, "I will do this (or not do that) under these specified conditions under penalty of such and such a sanction," but "I commit my whole self, everything and forever, to the undying love that has claimed me for the transformation of the world."

The vows are also *prophetic* language. I dealt in some detail with the meaning of prophecy in volume 1, chapters 4 and 10, but let me recall here that prophecy is not about foretelling the future but about mediating the three-way encounter among God, people, and culture. It is about identifying what is death-dealing in the culture and calling it into question by publicly lamenting the injustice and violence of the system, evoking the memory of God's promises, and animating hope for an alternative future. Prophecy calls into question the claim of the oppressive powers that the status quo is the only possible way for reality to exist and function and announces that in the Reign of God things can and will be different. Justice, especially for the poor and the marginalized, will be realized. The hungry will have food, the meek will have land, the sorrowing will be comforted, and the unjustly persecuted will be vindicated.

But the role of the prophet is not to "channel" esoteric, privately revealed information from God to the leaders or the people with threats of extermination for noncompliance with the divine will. The prophet, as one of the community, recalls the history of God with the people and lives intensely the questions the people face but in absolute attachment to the divine agenda. Religious Life is essentially a prophetic vocation. We will have occasion to look in detail at the prophetic dimensions of each of the vows in part 2 of this volume and in volume 3, but here I want to speak of profession as a global project that is prophetic by nature.

By profession the Religious enters into an alternate world whose coordinates are pointed to (not defined) by the vows. The three vows bear on the three fundamental coordinates of human experience: sexuality and relationships; material goods and ownership; freedom and power. In regard to each of these coordinates, or spheres of human life and endeavor, the Religious takes an alternative stance that both announces and effects an approach that calls into question the oppressive arrangements of the status quo. The patriarchal inequality of relationships based on a male-dominant understanding of sexuality is challenged by consecrated celibacy; the greed and self-centeredness of an approach to material goods as to be acquired for oneself to the greatest extent possible regardless of the need of the neighbor is challenged by the commitment to evangelical poverty; and the unrestricted use of power to control reality (including people) for one's own advantage is rejected in principle and practice by Religious obedience. By profession Religious choose an egalitarian and nonsexist approach to relationship, sharing as the primary mode of dealing with material goods, and dialogical listening as the way to corporately exercise power for the common good.

Each of these topics requires much fuller discussion, but the point here is that Religious profession is not exclusively about Religious community life or one's own spiritual growth. It is the undertaking of a prophetic engagement with culture by a radically different approach to the dynamics that structure the Church and the world. Culture, however, is not generic but specific to time and place. Consequently, the vows will mean different things, prophetically, in different ages and in different places. For example, the poverty of an early medieval monastery that created the environment for simple but relatively dignified feudal life for the people of the whole surrounding area while preserving and passing on the cultural riches of antiquity in a barbarian culture was very different from the poverty of a modern ministerial congregation buying stock in unjust or environmentally destructive corporations in order to undermine their economic power and call them to social responsibility.[19] But in both cases "poverty" goes well beyond personal detachment or community sharing to bring a prophetic critique and alternative vision to bear upon the culture in which the congregation lives.

Both the poetic and the prophetic character of the vows suggest a reason to prefer the traditional names for the vows, poverty, obedience, and consecrated celibacy[20] to more specific designations that would narrow the meaning of the vow to some particular aspect or practice such as common life, simplicity, accountability, cooperation, and so on. The more poetic terminology has metaphorical power to draw together many meanings and prophetic power to address whole spheres of human reality. If the vows are regarded not primarily as designating legal obligations (in which case the greater the specificity the better) but as evocative of the structure and dynamics of the alternate world, the Reign of God, which they seek to embody and promote, their very "impossibility" is symbolically significant.

3. The purposes of the vows: In different historical contexts the spirituality of the vows has been understood differently and the emphasis has been placed on different aspects or purposes of the vows in Religious Life. This historical development, it seems to me, has enriched the meaning of the vows, and today we can affirm a variety of interactive purposes that the vows serve in the spirituality of Religious, namely, unitive, communitarian or covenantal, and ministerial ends.

If one looks back to the earliest form of Religious Life, that of the consecrated virgins of the first-century Christian communities who expressed their total commitment to God alone by their renunciation of the societal role of wife and mother, we see the primary emphasis on the *unitive* role of the vows, especially consecrated celibacy. We find the same interpretation of virginity as marriage to Christ in both the male and female branches of Religious Life, but especially among the women mystics, in the Middle Ages. Among the desert monastics of the third and fourth centuries poverty, in the form of an extreme self-stripping of all but the barest necessities of life, played a primary role in their spirituality of contemplative union with God. The mysticism of espousal to "Lady Poverty" among the mendicants, especially the followers of Francis, put a different emphasis on the same vow, seeing it as the primary way of imitating Christ in the *vita apostolica.* Benedict's spirituality for monks living in community mitigated the extreme asceticism of the desert monastics and recentered the God-quest in interior humility expressed outwardly in obedience, which became the primary practice in the quest for God. In the post-Reformation apostolic orders obedience took on a special significance as a way of conforming one's will to the will of God, especially in the corporate mission of the society, order, or congregation.

Each of the three vows, in other words, has been understood at one time or another as the primary mediator of the God-quest that is at the heart of Religious Life. Negatively, the practice of purity of heart, renunciation of material goods, or the sacrifice of self-will disposed the Religious for growth in union with Christ. Positively, exclusive and wholehearted love of Christ, total reliance on providence, and active union of will with the will of God embodied, expressed, and fostered that union. Whichever aspect of profession was emphasized in a particular form of Religious Life or a particular order or congregation, the unitive function of the vows is their most intimate and personal dimension. People enter Religious Life to seek God, and it is not at all surprising that profession is seen as the life-grounding commitment to that quest.

Each of the vows also has a *covenantal* or *communitarian* function that has been understood differently at various times and in diverse cultural settings. The unique form of community life which Religious establish, that of shared celibacy, marks the life off from the more normal form of Christian life, that of the family. It was this choice not to found a family and procreate, that is, not to fulfill one's species role in service of the city and the empire, which first drew the negative attention of civil authority to Religious Life among the Christians. Poverty, in the form of total sharing of material goods, was described as the ideal for the entire Christian community in the Acts of the Apostles (cf. Acts 4:32–35) but it was never taken up, as far as we know, as the norm of lay life among Christians. However, it was assumed by Religious virtually from the beginning as their appropriate way of dealing with material goods. By holding all things in common they not only struggled against the concern with material goods that warred against the search for God alone as the one thing necessary, but they abrogated the conditions of selfishness, greed, competition, envy, domination, and violence that warred against the life of love they aspired to live together in fulfillment of

Jesus' new commandment. And obedience, both to the leader of the community who was seen as holding a place in the community analogous to that of Christ among his disciples and to each other in mutual humility and service, was a primary force for unity in the community. The rebellion, self-will, desire to dominate, and recourse to violent coercion that arise naturally among humans as they seek their own will and good were curbed and sacrificed in the effort to create a context of mutual love in which the will of God alone determined how each and all would live.

Finally, the vows have also always had a *ministerial* function, although this often received less attention in earlier times and has tended to dominate disproportionately in post-Reformation congregations. Celibacy, until very recently, was seen as freeing the Religious for a kind of selfless and unfettered service of the neighbor that was not possible for the person "burdened" with family responsibilities.[21] Poverty, which Jesus specifically linked with freedom to preach the Gospel (cf. Mt 10:8–10), was raised to a particularly high level in the ministerial project of the mendicants in the Middle Ages but has played various roles in the ability of Religious congregations to accomplish remarkable ministerial feats with the slimmest of resources. Obedience became the primary vow among ministerial Religious, specifically because of its role in the deployment of Religious in ministry under centralized authority. This interpretation occurred as early as the foundation of the Dominicans in the twelfth century and reached its apex among the Jesuits in the sixteenth century. Most modern ministerial congregations have followed the lead of the post-Reformation clerical orders in seeing obedience as the central vow and virtue of Religious Life, particularly as it operated in the carrying out of the order's ministry.

IV. Conclusion

Profession is the articulation of a commitment that a person comes to gradually through the process of formation. The commitment is first and foremost to Christ, but it includes commitment to and within the congregation. The commitment envisioned by profession is total and irrevocable and consequently is a very serious move that intends to take in a person's entire life. It is not surprising then that it raises all the questions about the possibility and the desirability of commitment that have always plagued human beings but which are especially acute in the context of postmodernity. Commitment is both the highest achievement of and the greatest challenge to freedom that we face. Making a life commitment, especially in our fragmented and relativistic context, requires enormous courage but also allows for the expression of a love that knows no bounds. Those truly called to Religious Life know the eagerness for profession that arises from that love as well as the trepidation it inspires.

Profession needs to be seen primarily as a unitary and unifying act, a solemn, formal, and public act, by which a person takes her whole life into her hands and freely disposes of it in self-gift to Christ and his body within the congregation. Only in this wholistic context does it make sense to think about the vows as distinct promises bearing on particular spheres of life. But even considering the vows in their individuality, and without negating the legal obligations one assumes by profession of consecrated celibacy, poverty, and obedience, we need to maintain our sense of the poetic and prophetic character of the language we use. Religious Life is not primarily about taking on obligations one did not have as a layperson. It is about a relationship that gives a definitive shape to one's life within an alternate lifeform in the Church and which, like the life of Jesus, has the salvation of the world, the coming of the Reign of God, as its purpose.

PART TWO

Consecrated Celibacy

CHAPTER FOUR

CELIBACY AS CHARISM

I. Introduction: Definition and Terminology

For reasons discussed in detail in volume 1, chapter 7, the understanding of consecrated celibacy as a constitutive dimension of Religious Life has been severely obfuscated, and the confusion extends to Religious themselves as well as to those observing the life from the outside. Consequently, the first task of this second part on consecrated celibacy as the heart of Religious Life is to clarify the meaning of the reality in itself and in distinction from realities with which it might be confused.

A. Definition

The definition of consecrated celibacy that will be operative in the rest of this volume is the following: Consecrated celibacy is the freely chosen response to a personally discerned vocation to charismatically grounded, religiously motivated, sexually abstinent, lifelong commitment to Christ that is externally symbolized by remaining unmarried. My contention is that all of these features must be present simultaneously if we are to speak of the consecrated celibacy characteristic of Religious Life.

First, consecrated celibacy is a charism, a free gift, a vocation or call from God to some people. Although singleness or sexual abstinence can be imposed or mandated, celibacy as a charism cannot. Furthermore, it cannot be acquired by one's own efforts or conferred by authority. It is a gift of God, like the vocation to marriage. The person who feels called to consecrated celibacy needs to carefully discern the reality of that call and her or his capacity and desire to respond to it and, if the discernment warrants such a response, must freely choose to embrace the life.

Second, only a genuinely religious motivation for consecrated celibacy is valid in the Christian tradition. There are many reasons for remaining celibate or unmarried in the contemporary cultural context: the desire for personal independence, obligations to parents or siblings, career demands, antipatriarchalism, and many others. Consecrated celibacy as the heart of Religious Life cannot be validly undertaken for any of these reasons even if some of them play some role in a person's attraction to the state of life or supply peripheral advantages in living it out. Just as getting married may strengthen one's financial situation, solve numerous social problems, or provide a partner in various undertakings, none of these is a valid reason for getting married, at least in societies that have renounced arranged marriages. Motivation in vocational choice is paramount in the discernment of the call to Religious Life just as it is in the call to matrimony.

The commitment to complete abstinence from genital sexual activity, whether heterosexual or homosexual, is integral to the commitment of consecrated celibacy. Although historically sexual abstinence has always been assumed in the theology of this state of life, today it is contested by some people within and outside Religious Life. To a large extent this contestation arises from the confusions that have leaked into the understanding of Religious celibacy from its conflation in the minds of many people with the mandatory singleness of the diocesan clergy. Some clergy who feel no personal call to celibacy but accept it as an onerous requirement for ordination assert that if a cleric does not marry or produce offspring (who would have claims on his or the Church's financial resources or would place affective demands on him that would interfere with his ministry), his sexual behavior is a relatively minor matter, sinful perhaps but no more serious than lapses in other areas of morality and perhaps more understandable because of the imposed burden of obligatory celibacy. Homosexual liaisons can seem particularly nonproblematic since neither marriage nor children are involved. The problems inherent in such positions in regard to sexual immorality, infidelity to public commitments in the Church, abuse of women partners, irresponsibility toward unplanned offspring, and the undermining of mental health through duplicity and compartmentalizing are real and serious but not the subject of this chapter.

The point here is that none of this discussion is relevant to Religious Life of women or men. Religious do not undertake celibacy as an imposed condition for entrance into Religious Life; they enter Religious Life because they feel called to give themselves freely to Christ in a way that excludes other primary life commitments, including marriage. This vocation to total and exclusive self-donation is freely responded to and is symbolized by consecrated celibacy. The symbol is vitiated by a sexually active relationship in the same way that the exclusivity of the marital union is subverted by extramarital affairs.

Finally, the lifelong character of consecrated celibacy is implicit in the perpetual commitment to Religious Life itself, which was discussed in the previous chapter. Again, this is not an imposition on Religious, a condition for entrance, but the expression of the very dynamic of the exclusive relationship with Christ established by profession.

B. The Terminology of the Vow

In the period since the Council there has been considerable debate about the appropriate terminology for this vow as for the others. In some cases the desire for an alternative term arises from a sense that *celibacy* seems to be a privative or negative term, an expression of what one is committed not to do or be. A vow of universal and/or inclusive love, or a vow for relationship would seem to be more inspiring.[1] In other cases, the objection to celibacy is theological. Francis Moloney, for example, regards celibacy as a physical state, that of being unmarried, which is neutral in significance. His argument is that chastity, by contrast, is a virtue that is the common call of all Christians (as are obedience and poverty) and that what differs is simply the context in which these universal gospel imperatives are lived.[2] While I am sympathetic to both these concerns, I think they present problems that the term *consecrated celibacy* avoids. I will return to them at the end of this section.

Historically the reality intended by the vow has been called, at different periods, virginity, chastity, celibacy, and consecrated celibacy. All of these terms can certainly be used, but the problems arising from the first three have led to the fourth, which is being used more often today.

Virginity was the term of preference in the earliest centuries of the Church. All of the great treatises on Religious Life from the patristic period are entitled, in one way or another, "On Virginity." From the beginning virginity was understood to consist not exclusively nor even primarily in physical intactness, that is, in the state of never having had sexual intercourse, although physical integrity was a powerfully expressive symbol of the spiritual reality of integrity and self-gift. It was recognized that a person could violate a vow of virginity in her heart or in her behavior without actually having sexual relationships. And conversely, a person who was violated against her will or someone who had been married and widowed might be virginal in the spiritual sense with a "virginity reclaimed." Even in regard to the Mother of Jesus, Augustine maintained that her virginity as her motherhood was primarily a matter of faith and secondarily a physical fact.

In this respect, Religious virginity was understood much the way the Jungian psychologist Esther Harding presents virginity, that is, as an archetypal reality realized as a quality of the person who is "one in herself," whole and undivided, not controlled by heteronomous forces.[3] Virginity speaks of integrity, wholeness, the self preserved or reserved to be disposed of according to one's own free choice rather than according to the will of another. In this sense we speak of spouses offering to each other the gift of their virginity, meaning the gift of themselves that they have reserved for each other.

In the early centuries of the Church's existence the choice by some Christians, especially women, not to marry because they had given themselves to Christ was seen by the Empire as a radical refusal to assume their assigned societal role, to fulfill the duty imposed on them by the state and by their families of continuing the species. The Christian virgins reserved the right to their own persons, which was a startling exercise of autonomy, especially on the part of women in a patriarchal society that assumed male ownership of women's reproductive capacity, and it was therefore viewed as a threat to the very existence of the Empire.[4] This action of refusing to marry because she was the "spouse of Christ" was analogous to, but even more radical than that of the man who refused military service after baptism because he was now a "soldier of Christ," whose call to nonviolence countervened any obligation to fight for the state.[5]

Throughout most of the history of Religious Life the state of life undertaken by solemn vows was understood as virginity. The spousal theme was elaborately developed in the ceremonies of profession, especially of women, and in the classical commentaries on the Song of Songs, in Religious rules, and in spiritual treatises, usually written by men. Furthermore, although the imagery of virginity was feminine, it was assumed to apply equally to men. However, as clerical celibacy became a mandate in the Western Church and apostolic congregations came into being whose members were not cloistered but devoted to ministry, the mystical understanding of Religious commitment as marriage to Christ gave way to a more instrumental understanding of nonmarriage as freedom for service. Furthermore, it was increasingly the case that it was not, as it was in the past, self-evident (barring clear evidence to the contrary) that those who entered Religious Life had no history of sexual involvement even if they had not been married.

In our own times, despite the reinstatement by the Council of the rite of consecration of virgins,[6] the term is probably more problematic than helpful for most Religious. Not only can physical intactness not be assumed even in the case of the relatively young unmarried candidate, but virginity in contemporary first-world culture has the negative connotation of "inexperienced" or "undeveloped" rather than the positive connotation of self-possession and relational autonomy. Although in the abstract *virginity* probably carries better than any other term the true meaning of the commitment to Christ of Religious Life (which we will discuss below) it simply does not seem to "work" in the present linguistic context.

For both these reasons there was a growing preference for the term *chastity* to denote the obligation assumed by Religious. It was understood, of course, that the chastity in question was that of the unmarried, namely, total abstinence. Sometimes it was called "perfect chastity" but this implied that marital chastity was somehow "imperfect" or inferior and implicitly equated the virtue of chastity, to which all Christians are equally called, with sexual abstinence. If for no other reason, the term *chastity* presents problems.

The term *chastity*, however, had at least two advantages: It denoted how the Religious would live from the time of profession without having to address how she or he had lived prior to entering; it clearly expressed the obligation undertaken by the vow, namely, to abstain from all genital activity. It also, as Moloney suggests, indicates the common ideal of all Christians, Religious, and others, in the area of sexuality.

Several problems with the term *chastity*, however, argue against its use even though it has a long history. First, as Moloney recognizes, chastity is the name of a specific virtue, not even the highest of the virtues, charity. Virginity, however, has always been understood as a much more global reality and, precisely, as the expression of the particular kind of love or charity characteristic of Religious Life.

Second, because chastity is a virtue to which all Christians are equally called, it is doubtful that it can be the object of a vow as such, particularly of a public vow. One does not vow to do what is already commanded but to do something that is a matter of free choice.[7] And such a vow would not distinguish Religious Life from any other form of life in the Church, whereas it is clearly the distinguishing feature of the life and has been since the first instances of that life in the first century. Just as the vows of matrimony institute a public state of life which is distinct from that of the unmarried specifically through the spouses' granting to each other full and exclusive access to their person expressed through sexual union, so the vows of Religious institute a public state of life distinct from others specifically by reserving to Christ the relational capacity of the person expressed through nonmarriage to anyone else.

Third, the celibacy of Religious is not, as Moloney would have it, simply a physical state. When Jesus, probably speaking of himself as a model for those who choose nonmarriage, says (in the felicitous translation of the New American Bible) "Not all can accept [this] word, but only those to whom that is granted. Some are incapable of marriage because they were born so; some, because they were made so by others; some, because they have renounced marriage for the sake of the kingdom of heaven. Whoever can accept this ought to accept it" (Mt 19:11–12), he distinguishes freely chosen nonmarriage from a purely physical condition resulting from birth or violence as well as from celibacy chosen for nonreligious motives. Religious celibacy is a state of life. And the use by Jesus of the graphic term *eunuch* suggests that he is speaking not of a temporary or reversible situation but of a freely chosen, perpetual commitment motivated by the reign of God.

Celibacy, however, is also a problematic term in the linguistic context of the first world. It does, in fact, in our culture designate a physical and social situation of being single and has no necessary implications about motivation or about sexual behavior. People who have not yet married (whether living together or singly), the divorced, the separated, the widowed, and an increasing number of adults (especially women) who choose not to marry in order to preserve their independence or to pursue a humanitarian or professional goal, are all celibate, as are many homosexual people who choose not to enter a permanent partnership. No one today assumes the virginity or single chastity of the unmarried. It is very well known that many of these celibate people are sexually active. Consequently, the problem with designating either the state of life of Religious or the type of chastity integral to that state by the term *celibacy* is that it does not communicate anything of significance. It is this "neutral" use of celibacy that seems to be the object of Moloney's objection, and at this point I would agree with him that it is the least satisfactory term.

Consecrated celibacy, however, although it may be a bit unwieldy, comes closest, in my opinion, to expressing what we are talking about. The advantage of the substantive *celibacy* is that it designates the life condition of the actual Religious without necessitating investigation of or comment about her or his previous life. In this way, it seems preferable to virginity, which raises such questions, and to chastity, which refers to a virtue but not to a state of life. The addition of the modifier *consecrated* immediately removes the reality from the realm of circumstantial or chosen singleness that is religiously neutral. It also suggests free choice and permanence. And, of course, it forcefully implies that the chosen state of life involves the practice of the chastity of the unmarried.

For all these reasons, namely, the capacity of *consecrated celibacy* to express what is being done and to communicate it to the Church and world, I prefer this term for the life-constituting public vow by which the Religious gives herself totally, unreservedly, and perpetually to Jesus Christ to the exclusion of all other primary life commitments. Any of these terms can certainly be used with the understanding that they mean what I have just stated. Different Religious families have their own preferences. However, it can be helpful to candidates, no matter what terminology their congregation chooses, to think about all of the terms that have, historically, been used so as to grasp the scope, depth, and complexity of what they are undertaking as well as to become explicitly aware of the countercultural valence of the vow and the necessity they will surely experience to give a reason for their choice as well as to explain it to sincere but puzzled moderns.

II. The Distinctiveness of Consecrated Celibacy among the Vows

Because the triple-vow formula has been in use for centuries and is virtually universal among post-Tridentine ministerial congregations as well as being canonically mandated, in substance if not in form, for all Religious there is a strong tendency to regard the three vows as parallel in scope and equal in significance. I will argue in what follows that this is not the case. Consecrated celibacy is at the very heart of Religious Life and is constitutive of and distinctive within it for a number of reasons. It may not have been particularly important to stress this point in the cultural context of preconciliar times, but for a variety of reasons it is very important today.

The reasons I am claiming that consecrated celibacy (hereafter simply *celibacy* unless that term is otherwise specified by context) is unique among the vows are biblical, theological, and cultural. First, from the *biblical* standpoint celibacy is the only one of the three vows that is, in its content, unique to Religious Life and in that sense a specific charism given to the individual and through her to the Church. Poverty is the Religious form of the common call of all Christians to detachment from and moderation in the use of material goods. Obedience is the Religious form of the common call to discern the will of God in one's life through the structures of mediation particular to one's vocation. But, although all Christians are called to the chastity appropriate to their respective states of life, consecrated celibacy is a state of life to which not all are called. Neither Religious poverty nor obedience constitute a state of life; they are aspects of a state of life constituted by the free choice of nonmarriage for the sake of the kingdom.

In *New Wineskins,* chapter 7, I discussed in some detail the Matthean passage (19:3–12)[8] that has always been considered the gospel basis of consecrated celibacy. I will not repeat that discussion here, but it is important to recognize that the passage about those who "have renounced marriage for the sake of the kingdom" puts the emphasis on two points: that the call to celibacy is not universal, that is, it is not integral to the baptismal vocation of all Christians; that those who do choose it are freely responding to a personal vocation. It is a vocation to a particular state of life that governs everything else in their life the way marriage governs the whole life of the person who marries. In other words, the person is not simply choosing to practice a particular form of chastity, namely, that of the unmarried, but to construct her or his life, in its totality, in a particular way for the sake of the Reign of God.

Throughout Christian history, beginning apparently even in the apostolic period, some people have tried to present celibacy as the only or at least the best way to live the Christian vocation, thus making celibacy mandatory or at least the ideal and thus exalting Religious Life and denigrating marriage.[9] Paul, who apparently chose celibacy for himself (cf. 1 Cor 7:7), acknowledged that it was his particular gift from God and not that of all Christians. He insisted emphatically that while there was a command from the Lord about the indissolubility of marriage (cf. 1 Cor 7:11) "in regard to virgins I have no commandment from the Lord, but I give my opinion as one who by the Lord's mercy is trustworthy....that it is a good thing for a person to remain as he is [i.e., unmarried]....If you marry, however, you do not sin" (1 Cor 7:25–28). This New Testament position has remained constant throughout the Church's history even when rigorist or elitist positions (formally heretical or not) have been proposed. In short, Scripture supports the two features that mark consecrated celibacy, unlike poverty and obedience, as the constitutive and distinguishing feature of Religious Life, namely, that it is a charism not given to all and that it must be freely chosen.

Theologically, the centrality of consecrated celibacy in the life of the Religious derives from the area of anthropology. The Christian understanding of human dignity is that it is rooted in the creation of human beings in the image and likeness of God and that such similarity to God rests primarily in the spiritual nature of the human being as one endowed with intellect and will. Whether or not one wants to discuss theological anthropology in terms of ontologically based faculty psychology, the point is that the specific dignity of the human being among all God's creatures lies in the human capacity for self-transcendence, for reaching beyond oneself toward the other and, finally, toward the ultimate Other who is God, not in order to possess but in order to give oneself in love.[10] The human being is creation become conscious and therefore relational. Thus, the New Testament "definition" of God, that "God is love" (1 Jn 4:16), establishes the pattern and the goal of human development.[11]

Who or what and how we love, therefore, determines the quality and character of our life as human beings and as Christians. Even without Christian revelation we know this. All of the world's great literature testifies to the fact that human greatness—whether that of cultural agents carrying out influential political or military exploits, artists bringing beauty into the world, heroines and heroes who have given their lives for their children or the downtrodden, in the pursuit of peace and justice, or in resistance to evil—is finally rooted in and informed by love. Every significant life is the expression of a great love and, conversely, no matter how striking its effects on history the absence of love marks any life as a failure or worse, as we see well in the case of Hitler or Stalin. Even unwise or mistaken love is preferable to the absence of love. As Dante said so well, human love is finally rooted in "the love that moves the sun and the other stars."[12] Jesus says that, in the end, all will be judged by their love for him expressed in their love for the least of his sisters and brothers, even if they never knew him in himself (cf. Mt 25:31–46).

Consecrated celibacy is not first and foremost about what one does with one's sexuality; it is about what one chooses to love, or more exactly, who and how one chooses to love. For all Christians the ultimate love, the horizon of life toward which self-transcendence continually reaches, is God. The primary life commitment one makes to spouse and/or children, to the arts or the intellectual life, to the welfare of the neighbor, to the care of the poor or the marginalized, to the cause of justice or truth, is the mediation of that ultimate quest for God that is the deepest motivation of Christian life.

The Religious chooses to engage in the God-quest in an immediate way, exclusive of all mediating primary life commitments. The renunciation of the paradigmatic primary commitment, to spouse and family, is the symbolic expression of that exclusive commitment to the unmediated God-quest. Here symbol must be taken in its strong sense as a perceptible reality that renders present what it expresses. Remaining unmarried creates a visible and tangible lifeform, not only expressing the bypassing of mediating primary commitments but actually removing such mediation from the life of the celibate. The immediacy to God and social marginality that ground the prophetic character of Religious Life (discussed in volume 1, chapters 4 and 10) are the direct result of this choice.

Herein lies the radicality and the absoluteness of the choice that gives Religious Life its specificity among vocations in the Church. Jesus' use of the metaphor of the "eunuch" to describe this state emphasizes well the radicality of the choice. Consecrated celibacy, like sacramental marriage, is not a partial or reversible choice (which does not deny that some such commitments are made in error, break down, or for other reasons must be terminated nor does it involve a judgment on those involved in such situations) but a final disposition of one's relational capacity, one's capacity for self-transcendence in love, that determines the shape and quality of one's life.

Consecrated celibacy carries the obligation of sexually abstinent chastity, but this is the consequence, the implication, of the exclusive love of Jesus Christ that is expressed in the choice to remain unmarried for the sake of the Reign of God. It is analogous to the role of sexual fidelity in monogamous marriage. Marriage is not about not having sex with anyone but one's spouse, but the latter is a symbol of the former, a perceptible living of the exclusive love relationship with one's spouse, which is what marriage is about. Similarly, Religious Life is not about not having sex, but genital abstinence expressive of the lived choice not to engage in any other relationship as the primary commitment of one's life is the symbol of the immediate and total self-gift in love to Christ, which is what Religious Life is about.

Another aspect of the uniqueness of consecrated celibacy among the vows is the obvious fact that it is the only one of the vows that can and must be absolute. No one can practice absolute poverty because this would result in death. Furthermore, it is highly doubtful that destitution, even if it does not reach the point of death, is what Religious poverty is meant to effect. And absolute obedience, as Nazism demonstrated, is neither a human nor a Religious ideal. But Religious celibacy does make an absolute demand. The Religious vows not to marry and not to engage in any of the behaviors that lead to or flow from marriage. It has been facetiously remarked that just as one cannot be a little bit pregnant one cannot be partly celibate, but the humorous comparison is, in fact, apt. Although some have proposed a kind of "third way" in which a person vowed to celibacy engages in a sexually active relationship that involves faithfulness to the partner (of the same or the opposite sex) but not marriage, I am of the opinion, as are most theologians of Religious Life of whose work I am aware, that this is no more a legitimate form of celibacy than "open marriage" is a possible form of matrimony.[13]

A final characteristic of consecrated celibacy that distinguishes it among the vows is what I have called its "nonnatural" character. I do not accept the charge leveled by some, especially those convinced that celibacy should not be mandatory for clerics, that celibacy is unnatural, much less antinatural. But it is nonnatural, both statistically and performatively. Relatively few people, it seems, choose celibacy as a lifestyle, and most of these do not choose it for religious reasons or with any intention of permanence in the state. And certainly many who do choose celibacy are not sexually abstinent. Those choosing consecrated celibacy implying lifelong commitment and total sexual abstinence are very few indeed. Thus, consecrated celibacy is statistically not the norm.

This statistical nonnormativity is the manifestation, it would seem, of the fact that the lifeform of consecrated celibacy is performatively nonnatural. It does not run counter to nature, like excessive fasting that results in death. One does not die of celibacy; indeed celibates are no less vigorous physically and mentally than the married. But celibacy is somewhat like high diving in that it springs from a particular charism (or spiritual "talent" that is not due to nor achieved by the person so gifted) and requires an enormous expenditure of personal resources in ascetical and spiritual practice to actually reach the ideal to which one is called. But like the talented diver who must practice and train at high intensity to achieve what most mortals regard as truly beyond human capacities, the person who lives consecrated celibacy over a lifetime is not a freak or oddity or abnormality. But no one would maintain that celibacy (or high diving) is a universal gift or is easily attained by anyone who is willing to put forth a little energy.

A very important consequence of this "nonnatural" character of consecrated celibacy is that people responding to this vocation have, historically, most often chosen to live it in community. Because the celibate life is under constant threat, not only from those who would violate it by force (which was always a concern of Church authorities in their cloistering of women celibates) but by the cultural ethos that has rarely if ever fostered sexual restraint, Religious have found strength in the community of those who have made the same choice. This is certainly not the primary reason for Religious community, but it does help explain why Religious have usually (though not always) sought a community context for their life and why Religious Life has traditionally been a single-sex lifeform. Today many Religious do not live in the day-to-day presence of community companions, and even those who do live in group situations spend much of their time with non-Religious in the professional and ministerial workplace. Consequently, explicit formation in celibacy, its meaning, the challenges to it, and the means of living it integrally, is much more urgent than it might have been in the past. Those choosing this life today need to realize that their choice is not the norm and that they cannot assume understanding of it or support for it among their contemporaries. Many people, even those within the Catholic context, because of the confusion around the mandatory singleness of the clergy, assume that Religious also are unwillingly celibate and therefore, because celibacy is an unnecessary and harsh imposition, violation of the mandate is much less culpable than marital infidelity. When the social context does not support one's choices, personal motivation must be proportionately better-based and stronger.

Finally, consecrated celibacy also has the greatest potential witness value of all the aspects of Religious Life, especially in the *cultural context* of postmodern society. Freely chosen, religiously motivated, publicly lived, chaste nonmarriage cannot fail to raise questions in our sex-saturated and pleasure-obsessed culture. Both poverty and obedience, as we will explore later in volume 3, have high witness value in a materialistic and power-driven society. However, they can be easily seen as directly conducive to community and ministry, which are the most visible aspects of Religious Life. Whether or not our contemporaries correctly understand Religious community or ministry, they can at least understand that people desire connection and support (which might motivate one to community) and that at least some people want to do something with their lives that will make this world a better place both in the present and for the next generation (which might motivate one to ministry). If some kind of common possession and submission to a form of group government is necessary for or at least conducive to community and ministry, they make a certain kind of practical sense. But the choice to willingly forego both marriage and sex is a genuine conundrum within a rampantly narcissistic and hedonistic culture.

Furthermore, as we have already discussed in the previous chapter, lifelong commitment raises a serious challenge to the fragmentation and antifoundationalism of postmodernity. For a person to take her whole life in her hands, choose to give it a definitive shape in terms of an ultimate relational value (the love of God), and act on that choice by perpetual profession of consecrated celibacy challenges the relativism that permeates postmodern culture. Profession incorporates a person into a lifeform that is visible and operative in society and in the Church, thereby calling into question some of the most universally held presuppositions about the pursuit of sex as pleasure, the right to self-indulgence, and the desirability of noncommitment. On the other hand, it makes a powerful statement about the autonomy and value of the individual person and the capacity of the human being for personal self-transcendence in love, about the enduring quality of love as motivation for the whole of one's life, and about the fecundity and value of such love in society and Church.

In summary, consecrated celibacy is the constitutive vow of Religious Life. It creates the lifeform of unmediated quest for God to the exclusion of all other primary life commitments. It integrates the person in terms of a supreme love that makes the life not only make sense to one who chooses it but has the capacity to bring one to union with God and the power to ground a lifetime of service of the neighbor who is Christ. It is not the vocation of all Christians but a special charism that no one acquires for oneself. Both the vocation itself and the capacity to live it are gifts of God that are not superior to other vocations in the Church but are specific and distinct and require, if they are to be lived healthily and holily, an intense life of prayer, asceticism, and commitment.

III. Motivations for Consecrated Celibacy: A Contemporary Conundrum

The contention in the preceding section that consecrated celibacy is the heart of Religious commitment raises a number of very real, concrete, and existential problems that have to be faced. Most people in Religious Life today entered at a time when consecrated celibacy received very little explicit attention in the formation/discernment process beyond a very discreet

attempt to make sure candidates knew in general that Religious
Life meant no marriage and therefore no sex. There seemed to
be a presupposition that any explicit talk about sexuality would
raise problems with which no one wanted (or knew how) to
deal.[14] Consequently, while obedience and poverty were
explored in detail and the candidate's capacity for living these
commitments was tested extensively, most Religious had relatively vague notions about celibacy beyond the fact that they
were "giving up" marriage and expected to observe a chastity
that was not different from that of their preentrance days. In
other words, celibacy was "part of the package" of entering Religious Life, and many who made profession in their early twenties did not awaken to their own sexuality and the radicality of
their choice until their mid-thirties or even later. At this point
questions of sexual orientation, problems with masturbation,
tumultuous experiences of falling in love, or issues of sexual
dysfunction or addiction asserted themselves with sometimes
devastating urgency in previously tranquil lives. And this sexual
awakening for many contemporary Religious who entered in
the 1940s and '50s occurred in the midst of the so-called sexual
revolution of the 1960s and '70s, which seriously undermined
the sociology of knowledge and moral consensus that had
offered some bulwark against sexual acting out.

Part of the fallout of this encounter between sexual naïveté
on the one hand and cultural and personal sexual upheaval on
the other was, of course, departure from Religious Life by
many Religious who felt strongly called to marriage or other
sexual relationships or at least to the exploration and experimentation that had not occurred before entrance. In most
cases these departures were probably valid choices that
addressed a serious lacuna in the original process of entrance
and formation.

However, for many Religious the same experiences did not
lead them to leave their communities but to raise very serious
questions about the meaning and role and especially the
necessity of celibacy in Religious Life. And these questions
were exacerbated by the emergence of feminist consciousness,

which I will discuss in the next chapter. In my opinion, this is a healthy development even though it has created enormous tension in the lives of individuals and congregations and raised a challenge to Religious Life itself as a lifeform. I consider it healthy because it is no longer possible for people to enter Religious Life without explicitly facing the issues of life-long consecrated celibacy, including theological understanding, psychological issues, motivation, personal vocation, moral capacity, and commitment.

But clarity on the part of candidates discerning a call to Religious Life today does not assuage the problem of people who have been in Religious Life for years and have serious doubts about their own vocation to consecrated celibacy, the validity of their choice of it, and the obligations such a flawed or mistaken option carries. They often are deeply committed to their community and their ministry and cannot realistically imagine themselves leaving. But at the same time they may experience agonizing affective frustration in trying to live a reality that they experience as privative rather than productive. Recent studies suggest that most women Religious find consecrated celibacy the most meaningful of the vows,[15] suggesting that whatever their understanding of celibacy at the time of entrance they have grown into a positive appropriation of it into their mature spirituality. However, for those for whom it is not spiritually meaningful in itself there remains a serious problem of motivation for fidelity to its obligations as well as the challenge of finding some place for it in an otherwise dedicated and fruitful life.

As I see it there are two sets of questions raised by this situation. One concerns valid motivation for the choice of consecrated celibacy. The other concerns the delicate situation of people who have made a vow of celibacy, do not actually feel called to celibacy, and yet do not want to leave their Religious congregations. I will deal with the second issue first because, although it is immensely important to the people whose issue it is, it is not the primary concern of this treatment of the celibacy to which Religious are called.

A. Celibacy Not Freely Chosen

It is not my intention, nor my place, to discuss the actual discernment process and decisions that face people who made a vow of celibacy without appropriate knowledge of what they were undertaking. It goes without saying that support, compassion, and whatever assistance is necessary or possible should be the fundamental approach of the congregation that has accepted and benefited by the dedication and service of these Religious over many years. But I think a few points should be clarified for the sake of not perpetuating or repeating an unfortunate situation.

First, a commitment made without sufficient knowledge, even if no one was at fault in such a process, was not made with real freedom and can legitimately be revisited and even reversed without raising the issue of spiritual infidelity, weakness of character, or moral failure.[16]

Second, it is sometimes possible to find a worthy motivation for keeping a commitment even if it is not the "ideal" motivation. For example, spouses who are parents and find that the love that they thought was the ground for their union never existed or no longer exists may decide to maintain their marriage until their children are grown and find in that generous choice the motivation to deal constructively with their very real differences so that the family's life is a nurturing environment for the children. The end result may be that they separate peacefully when their child-raising duties are fulfilled or that they find that their love has been reborn and they are able to renew their commitment to each other in very different terms. Religious who realize that they are not called to celibacy may choose to live celibately in order to remain in their community and/or continue in their ministry, which is a worthy motive in itself, but in the process they may also discover some real value in celibacy, enabling them to make a free commitment to it that they did not make originally.

Third, it seems to me that the conundrum posed by the situation we are discussing should not be allowed to frame, much less determine the answers to, the basic questions that Religious face today about consecrated celibacy and the Religious life-form. In other words, I do not think celibacy should be made optional or temporary in order to open Religious Life to people who do not feel called to celibacy, whether they are now in a congregation or considering entrance. There may be reasons to discuss whether celibacy is intrinsic to Religious Life (and the point of the first part of this chapter was to make a case for an affirmative answer to that question), but the situation of those who find themselves vowed to a celibacy they did not freely choose is not such a reason.

The fact that some people entered a life specified by conse-crated celibacy without realizing what celibacy really meant does not justify redefining the life to include a mistaken com-mitment in the norm. Such a position may seem harsh, and I have no doubt that some people will strongly disagree with it. Some homosexually oriented Religious who want to maintain a publicly recognized and accepted genitally active partner-ship which, because it does not involve marriage or children, seems to them to be compatible with celibacy understood as nonmarriage have made a particular case for a "broadening" of the understanding of celibacy. Others have suggested that a Religious congregation could have, as full members (i.e., those enjoying active and passive voice and other rights and respon-sibilities of canonical membership), both celibates and mar-ried people. Others have suggested that a vow of celibacy might be made conditionally with the understanding that the person remains open to marriage or made temporally with the understanding that at the end of the specified time the question of marriage could be reopened even if that entails leaving the congregation if the person actually decides to marry. All of these issues may require discussion but, in my opinion, the discussion should not be precipitated by nor car-ried on in function of the situation of those caught in the con-flict described above.

Fourth, the difficult situation in which some Religious find themselves as they have come to realize that they simply did not have the capacity to make a free choice of celibacy at the time they made profession should motivate formation personnel and congregational leaders to make every effort to keep current candidates from making such a mistake. Furthermore, what might have been adequate preparation for a sound commitment to celibacy in times past is not so today. The sexual revolution in our culture, especially the sexual emancipation of women and the increasing acceptance of homosexuality as a natural orientation, as well as the very widespread occurrence of sexual activity among young people and the virtual saturation of the media with sexual information and stimulation mean that today's candidate is a very different sexual subject than the relatively sheltered teenagers who entered in preconciliar days. Today's candidate may not need the basic biological information that earlier candidates should have been offered but need far more psychological, moral, theological, and social formation if she or he is to make a wise decision and valid commitment to lifelong consecrated celibacy.

B. Motivations for Celibacy Freely Chosen

Even though the situation discussed in the preceding section is extremely difficult for people involved in it, the subject matter of this section is more central to the consideration of consecrated celibacy in the cultural context of the twenty-first century. It seems to be the case, if we listen attentively to Religious in contexts such as spiritual direction in which they speak freely of intimate matters, that among people who freely chose celibacy and have lived it successfully for many years there are diverse motives for the choice. Theological reflection on this experientially verified situation raises a number of issues. Because Religious in the past were encouraged not to share very much about anything that touched the area of sexuality and to discuss celibacy in unrealistically idealistic terms that seldom included directly one's personal experience, the first task is to clarify the actual situation. Why do/did people choose (as opposed to simply accepting) celibacy?

One motivation, the one discussed in the first part of this chapter, is historically the most ancient and the most fully theorized in the classical literature of spirituality. It has been called the *nuptial* or *mystical* spirituality of consecrated virginity. In the decades just before and after the Council both adjectives, for quite different reasons, were highly suspect terms. While *mystical* suggested singularity at best and mental imbalance at worst (neither of which was welcome in Religious congregations), *nuptial* suggested varieties of repressed, partially sublimated eroticism or generally twisted sexuality. In the decades since the Council *mystical* has been rehabilitated as referring to fully developed spirituality but not in relation to celibacy, while *nuptial* has taken on the added opprobrium of being potentially antifeminist. In the next chapter I will take up the mystical/nuptial motivation in the context of feminism. Here I want to discuss it as the unitive motivation for consecrated celibacy and hope the reader can and will suspend any prejudices against the metaphor of "marriage to Christ" in order to consider this argument.

As already suggested, each of the vows has at least three dimensions: the unitive, the communitarian, and the ministerial. In other words, profession itself and each of its three vows conduce to the spiritual journey into God of the person herself (what I have called the God-quest), to her participation in a certain kind of community life, and to her commitment to promoting the Reign of God. The traditions of different Religious families have emphasized one or another of the vows as the primary locus of each of these three functions. Thus, while the first-century virgins or the female Carmelites emphasized virginity as the primary locus of the unitive function, the Poor Clares emphasized absolute poverty and the male Dominicans obedience. Poverty was primary in the ministry of the male Franciscans, while obedience played that role for the Jesuits. Celibacy is a primary factor in the understanding of community among the Dominicans, whereas obedience plays that role among Benedictines.

In ministerial congregations founded after the seventeenth century the blending of the three aspects and the overlapping of the vows in the triple formula of profession make it much more difficult, or even impossible, to sort out how the individual vows functioned in the overall project of Religious Life which, in virtually all congregations, was expressed in terms of the primary end of union with God and the secondary end of service of the neighbor. It is perfectly understandable that formation, while making clear to the prospective member what obligations were undertaken by each of the vows and what ideals the virtue of the vow envisioned, did not make the kinds of distinctions among the vows that might be helpful today.

Anyone who talks in depth with Religious in contemporary congregations will soon become aware that the role of the individual vows in the life of each person is unique and that members of the same congregation often experience their commitments very differently. For example, some see the primary purpose of Religious Life in terms of ministry; others in terms of prayer and union with God; others in terms of community life. While there seems to be a tendency for male Religious to see obedience as the most important of the vows and for women Religious to see celibacy as most important, or for those men and women who are primarily concerned with ministry among the poor to see poverty as central, the relation of the vows to the three dimensions of Religious Life is not in any one-to-one correlation with these preferences.

By way of example, one person may experience consecrated celibacy as the context and expression of her unmediated and exclusive God-quest (i.e., as related to the unitive dimension of profession), whereas another may see the total gift of oneself through the surrender of self-will in obedience as the primary means to and mode of union with God. Or, while poverty may be the expression of and means to union with the All for one, poverty may be a primary means to unity in the community for another, or the indispensable expression of solidarity with the poor in ministry for a third. For some, especially men, celibacy is a primarily ascetical practice conducing to both prayer and unfettered ministry, whereas for others, especially women, it is obedience that is experienced as the primary form of asceticism in the service of both community unity and ministerial effectiveness.

This actual experience of how the vows are understood in various traditions, what motivates Religious to make and practice them, suggests that we should expect considerable variety among Religious in relation to consecrated celibacy. I think that is exactly what we do find. As the number of new candidates gradually increases (as seems to be the case at this writing), it may be beneficial and even necessary to deal more explicitly with this plurality and to dissipate some of the vagueness and ambiguity. In a cultural context in which Religious do not live and work exclusively with one another and the Religious lifestyle is not enforced by external controls, it is critical that Religious themselves be as clear about their motivation as they once were about their obligations. In what follows I will attempt to describe the various motivations for celibacy among Religious and then make some crucial distinctions among those motivations in terms of their implications.

1. Invalid motivations: We have already discussed the situation of people who undertook celibacy as "part of the package" of entering Religious Life, who never really understood what they were doing and therefore did not make a free decision. But I want also, explicitly, to rule out of our discussion motivations that may have been conscious or unconscious but led people to positively choose celibacy for the wrong reasons. Fear of sexuality, marriage, and/or parenthood (including childbirth itself and/or family commitment and responsibility), fear or hatred of the other sex (whether actual aggression or mild aversion), desire for a same-sex environment in which to act out homosexual desires, denial of one's own sexuality and desires (whether rooted in naïveté or active refusal to develop as an adult), unresolved issues with parents, confusion or anxiety about gender identity or sexual orientation, hope of environmentally controlling one's proclivities to pedophilia or other forms of sexual addiction, or any other dysfunctionalities in the area of psychosexual development are not valid motives for the choice of celibacy.

It seems to me that discernment about the role of any such dysfunctionality in the conscious or unconscious motivation of candidates should be very actively engaged before a person seriously considers a perpetual commitment to celibacy, and formation personnel should be as sure as they can be that such motivations are not in play before recommending a candidate to congregational leaders. Each of us continues, probably through much or most of our lifetime, to deal with various challenges in the area of sexuality, some of which will arise only as we enter different social and professional settings. Marriage, celibacy, a committed partnership, or singleness can provide the context in which to struggle toward human and Christian maturity in this area. The point here is not that a person must have achieved complete sexual integration before professing lifelong celibacy, but that the motivation for choosing celibacy must not be rooted in sexual dysfunctionality.

2. Valid motivations:

THE UNITIVE MOTIVE FOR CONSECRATED CELIBACY, as already noted, is the classical one. The first Religious in Christian history were those women and men who refused to marry because they had consecrated their virginity to Christ. The metaphor of "marriage to Christ" was a natural way of expressing this choice, which was most often regarded by both the virgin's family and the state as abhorrent but was accepted and blessed by the Church as a valid choice in response to a personal vocation and a striking witness to the power of the Gospel to transform the believer. Virginity continued to be understood almost exclusively in these terms until the modern period. This is not to say that no one entered the monastery for conscious or unconscious invalid reasons, including those listed in the last section, as well as the unmarriageability of younger or less attractive children, coercion, political expediency, possibility for education, escape from intolerable family situations, financial security, ambition, or any of a number of other motives. But the theological and spiritual understanding of virginity remained that of a particular, exclusive union with Christ that excluded marriage to an earthly spouse.

It is important to recall here that, in this respect, Religious celibacy in Christianity differed significantly from that practiced in other religious traditions. Celibacy as an ascetical practice conducive to self-control and moral development, meditation or contemplation, study, art, or service was not unknown before or after the advent of Christianity. Celibacy in these cases was relative to what it promoted and required only as long as it served those ends. But only Christian virgins interpreted their vocation as the establishment of a particular kind of relationship with a Person, namely, Jesus. It is this specific character of Christian virginity that gave rise to features that we do not find anywhere else in the religious landscape.

Christian virgins understood their commitment to Jesus Christ as intrinsically perpetual, just as marriage to an earthly spouse was perpetual. In fact, because the chosen Spouse was not subject to the physical or moral infirmities that might make a human union intolerable, the perpetuity of the celibate commitment was, if anything, more absolute. The Church was so convinced of this that solemn profession of virginity, until relatively recently, did not permit of dispensation, and any attempt by a solemnly professed Religious to marry was not only illegitimate but invalid. Fidelity, in other words, was not to a vow but to a Person.

The concern of both Religious themselves and the Church to protect Religious from any attempt to violate their virginity or to coerce them into marriage was also a logical result of the understanding of celibacy as a particular relationship with Jesus Christ. This led, understandably but unfortunately, to an increasingly rigid understanding of enclosure. Whereas the first virgins lived in the context of the local Christian community, in their own homes or common dwellings or alone, women Religious were gradually obliged not only to common life in prescribed dwellings but eventually to perpetual enclosure behind walls and grilles, from which they could not exit and which no one else, especially men, could breach. This development was cemented by Boniface VIII who issued his famous bull, *Periculoso,* in 1298, consigning all women Religious to papal enclosure in perpetuity. Although the patriarchal, political, and practical reasons for this bear analysis,[17] the theological justification was rooted in the understanding of celibacy as a relation to Christ that merited and demanded at least as stringent protection as that of marriage to an earthly spouse.

The emergence of mobile ministerial Religious Life, especially for women, led to a form of Religious profession, that is, simple vows, which did not entail papal enclosure.[18] This development also led to the influencing of the theology of women's Religious Life by male, clerical, apostolic orders within which celibacy tended to be seen in less unitive and more instrumental terms. It would be very difficult to trace the emergence of this subtle influence, but it is not at all difficult to recognize it. More will be said about this in the next section. The point here is that the unitive understanding of consecrated celibacy that was original and virtually universal for sixteen centuries has undergone some change, and that change requires examination.

Finally, it is important to note that in its origins Religious Life was a lifeform organized in function of the choice of virginity, that is, to promote the God-quest to which these virgins felt called. But, as is often the case, the institutionalization of the value as lifeform led eventually to the institution having a certain priority over the value. If people originally organized themselves into communities to protect and promote their choice of a God-quest unmediated by other primary life commitments, it eventually became the case that some people desired the lifeform itself and accepted celibacy as part of that lifeform without necessarily feeling any particular call to consecrated celibacy itself. This was much less likely as long as all Religious Life for women was cloistered and the contemplative pursuit was the relatively exclusive content of the life. It became much more likely as apostolic congregations were founded in which important and exciting ministerial projects were integral to their purpose and life. Women, in particular, who wanted to nurse, teach, or evangelize in the name of

Christ and to whom ordained ministry was not open were often attracted to the institution of Religious Life itself without a particular focus on celibacy.

By way of summary and conclusion I would suggest that consecrated celibacy in the Christian tradition was, from the beginning, an essentially relational reality. The Christian Religious understood her- or himself as responding, freely and personally, to an invitation from Christ to belong to him and to participate in his cause in a way that excluded any other primary life commitment whether relational or occupational. The preferred metaphor for this self-consecration to Christ was marriage, within which fidelity implied totality, exclusivity, perpetuity, and fecundity. This union of the Religious with Christ was externally symbolized by nonmarriage or celibacy, which implied the chastity appropriate to the unmarried state, that is, sexual abstinence. Whatever other advantages might arise from the celibate commitment its primary purpose and effect was union with God, a union that was mystical in its ultimate intention of total transformation in Christ. Consequently, consecrated celibacy was not understood as merely a choice about one's sexuality, nor a choice of a particular kind of community life or ministry, but a choice, through the disposition of one's relational capacity, of one's whole person. It was a choice of Who and how to love that embraced the whole reality of one's life.

THE MINISTERIAL AND COMMUNITARIAN MOTIVES FOR CELIBACY: The ministerial and communitarian dimensions of the vow of celibacy are closely intertwined with each other and with the ecclesial and cultural developments of the period between the Council of Trent and Vatican II, that is, the period in which congregations of simple vows emerged and became the predominant form of Religious Life, especially in the first world. Consequently the two dimensions have to be discussed together and in interaction with each other.

Ministry was the primary point of contact between most candidates and the congregations they entered. They met the Religious they eventually joined in school or parish or as volunteers in health care or social service agencies. They admired the Sisters or Brothers and wanted to be like them and to be with them. This did not necessarily mean that they wanted primarily to be teachers or nurses and, surprisingly, this does not seem to be the case for many Religious who entered in preconciliar times. They wanted the life of dedication to God and to neighbor that was lived by the Religious they knew. Once in formation, furthermore, they were deeply imbued with the primarily unitive character and function of Religious Life. They learned immediately that the "primary end" of the life was the sanctification of the Religious and the "secondary end," the salvation of souls through the work of the order, was relative if not instrumental in relation to the primary end. When they entered ministry many experienced the conflict between rhetoric and practice and within each as a full-time ministry was scheduled around a full monastic horarium making total dedication to either not only difficult but somewhat incoherent. But it is doubtful that anyone persevered in Religious Life who was not convinced of its essentially unitive motivation.

However, and this is a very important point, the understanding of the vows in this modern context was subtly but significantly different from the historical understanding. Poverty was linked strongly with community life, being a major source of the uniformity of lifestyle that was seen as crucial to the unity of the community, and obedience was equally powerfully linked to ministry as the way in which individual members were incorporated into the mission of the congregation, and the latter was effectively organized and efficiently accomplished. Celibacy, however, was treated with such discreet circumspection, generality, and even vagueness that it was seldom a focus of direct attention. Religious practiced poverty and obedience, developed in the virtues of these vows, prayed and read and listened to instruction about them. Celibacy was primarily a matter of general modesty in deportment, extreme reserve in expressions of affection toward family, men, children, or one another, and as little discussion as possible. In other words, the unitive character of Religious Life was associated with the life itself as a whole, not particularly with celibacy. In this respect, formation and practice in ministerial congregations were very different from that of traditional monasticism, especially that of women, where the mystical tradition of nuptial spirituality was explicitly connected with virginity[19] and virginity carried the unitive meaning of Religious Life in a particular way.

In the wake of Vatican II the renewal of ministerial congregations by a return to the spirit of their founders led to an emphatic reappropriation of ministry as intrinsic to the life itself and a corresponding abandonment of those elements of the monastic lifestyle that impeded ministry. In presenting Religious Life to potential candidates, but especially in explaining the life to themselves, Religious tended to place primary emphasis on the role of ministry in their spirituality and to deemphasize if not mute the structured practice of prayer that had been primarily associated with the unitive dimension of the life. Interestingly enough, a number of factors conspired to make the life of prayer even more central, though less practice-dominated, in and among Religious during this period, notably the retreat movement, return to active spiritual direction, and the human potential movement, which helped foster the interest in mysticism coming from other cultural influences such as the '60s search for transcendence in Eastern religious traditions. In other words, while ministry and contemplation grew in significance among Religious, consecrated celibacy receded as a focus of Religious spirituality.

As the revolutions against authority and institutions of the '60s gave way to the narcissism, rootlessness, and alienation of the '70s and '80s, a new cultural situation emerged that gave rise to Generation X. As Robert Schreiter observed in his address at the inauguration of the Center for the Study of Religious Life, this new generation never lived the structured and routinized religious life and never suffered from the excesses and abuses of authority that characterized Catholicism in the preconciliar period.[20] These young adults have few if any fixed points of familial, social, or religious reference, no stable sources of identity, often no practical resources for pursuing the spiritual life. However, they are no less idealistic than the youth of earlier generations. If anything, their quest for meaning, need for commitment, and desire for personal development have a certain "starvation" quality. They feel that life itself may be at stake (as indeed it is!) in finding their way to something larger and more important than their own moment-to-moment pleasure. This quest has many facets and for many young people is filled with contradictions and studded with personal conflicts and dysfunctionalities. But one of its striking features is the felt need on the part of a new generation for community.

The desire for community, for the close-knit family many lost or never had in a culture of multiple divorces and abandonment, for the school ties and enduring friendships that have disappeared or been shattered by sheer size, anonymity, mobility, and violence, for acceptance and belonging and common purpose, has led increasing numbers of young people into communes, cults, covenant communities, and volunteer organizations. It has also led some to Religious communities. In all of these settings older people recognize disturbing features: susceptibility to authoritarianism and even abuse as a price of acceptance, fascination with ritualistic practice, desire for special clothing and titles and status structures, a need for endless, intense, and often invasive soul-baring with an attendant demand for continual "togetherness." These characteristics are not necessarily accompanied by a developed sense of accountability, capacity for team work, or willingness to forego personal satisfaction for the sake of others. Many older Religious see these conflictual characteristics as dangerously conservative throwbacks to preconciliar ideals and practices combined with the selfishness of the narcissistic and individualistic culture in which these younger people have been raised.

But as sociologists studying this generation point out, this is not necessarily the case. These younger people are not clinging to the past, which they never knew, but discovering or reinventing some of the mechanisms of belonging and identity that people who had far too much of these mechanisms have internalized to the extent that they are useful and do not need to emphasize or want to resurrect. And the failures in genuine community of younger people are probably no more irreparable than the analogous selfishness with which candidates to Religious Life of all ages have had to deal. The forms of rebellion or irresponsibility may be different and young people may be less inhibited about expressing them, but that could actually be an advantage in formation. We will discuss this phenomenon in greater detail in part 3 in relation to communities, but the point here is that the community dimension of Religious Life has a much higher profile among the younger generation than it does among the majority of Religious.

The question at this point is what relation this heightened sense of community has to consecrated celibacy. In one sense, the answer seems to be, very little or even none at all. In times past, when virginity as total self-gift to Christ was the central reality of Religious Life, community was the primary means to and expression of the universal love of neighbor that love of Christ entailed. Just as the mark of the first followers of Christ was "see how these Christians love one another," the characteristic form of Religious Life, community, was a sign of what the life was all about. In other words, consecrated celibacy expressed itself in the love of neighbor that was realized in the community and through ministry. The desire for community among some people looking at Religious Life today, as among some seeking community in other settings, is not necessarily closely connected with celibate love of Christ. In fact, the connection may not be made at all unless those who enter primarily seeking community are helped to see the connection. But seeing what the connection might be does not necessarily mean that that connection exists for the person.

Certain conclusions from these considerations seem important. First, unlike consecrated celibacy, *ministry and community are not particular to Religious Life.* They are not a particular, life-constituting charism offered to some but required of none. All the baptized are called to both ministry and community, the forms of which can differ but the content of which is the same for all. Ministry is participation in the identity and mission of Jesus as prophet, priest, and king (i.e., servant unto death) and as such belongs necessarily to the vocation of all the baptized. Community is the lived participation in the Body of Christ, in the Vine of which we are all fruit-bearing branches. It is the fulfillment of the second member of the great commandment of love of God and love of neighbor. No one needs to enter Religious Life to be called to, indeed obliged to, both community and ministry.

Second, *celibacy is not necessary for either ministry or community.* There is no ministry open to nonclerical Religious that is not equally (at least in principle) open to the laity, both male and female. And there are many voluntary, gospel-motivated communities available for anyone who wishes to live focused community life: family itself, parish, small faith communities within or outside parishes, charismatic covenant communities, international communities like Focolare or L'Arche, service-oriented communities of all kinds, communities of hospitality and resistance, and so on. Furthermore, there is nothing to prevent people who do not find what they are looking for in communities already in existence from founding new communities. None of these communities requires celibacy, and virtually all include both single and married members.

In both these respects the relationship between the communitarian and ministerial dimensions of Religious Life and celibacy is not the same as the relationship between the unitive/mystical dimension and celibacy. So, how is consecrated celibacy related to ministry and community? The first answer must be negative: They are not related by intrinsic necessity. There have been Religious (hermits, anchorites, consecrated virgins) who have not lived a group form of community life. There have been, especially among women, Religious whose sole ministry was prayer and who did not engage in any kind of external ministry such as teaching, nursing, social work, social activism, political ministry, or the like. And there have been ministers and people living an intentional form of Christian community who were not consecrated celibates.

This being acknowledged, shared celibacy among the members of a community does create a particular kind of community. Typically, celibate communities are single-sex groups, although this is not always and exclusively the case. This is an important consideration today for many women who want to live and minister with women, especially women who are actively feminist in their sensibilities, organization, commitments, and lifestyle. My experience with younger people considering Religious Life suggests that in some cases this is their primary reason for wanting to be Religious. I think this bears very careful discernment for reasons I will give shortly.

Also, celibacy is, for some people, a very important fostering condition of ministry. Such people know themselves well enough to realize that the intensity of family relationships and the responsibilities of family life would impede their personal ministerial effectiveness. It is extremely important to realize, and to insist, that this is not the case for everybody and probably not for most people in ministry. The married clergy in other denominations as well as the now extensive network of married lay ministers in Catholicism make it abundantly clear that marriage is not only not intrinsically inimical to ministry; it is a primary aid to ministry for many, if not most, people. Many of the tens of thousands of Catholic ordained ministers who have left the clergy in the past few decades have done so not because they no longer felt called to ministry but because they also felt called to marriage. Many have continued to minister and been healthier and happier and more effective in their ministries since and because of marrying.

Finally, when the affective concentration of consecrated celibacy, voluntary (especially single-sex among women) community, and shared ministry combine in a comprehensive lifeform, it is a remarkably powerful social and spiritual phenomenon that can be both very attractive to idealistic persons seeking meaning in their personal lives and can offer a highly effective context in which to make a difference in this world through service to others.

C. Conclusions and a Proposition

It seems to me that the situation today regarding motivation for the choice of celibacy within Religious Life is qualitatively different from that of the first sixteen centuries of Religious Life and even from that of preconciliar twentieth-century forms of the life. It may have been the case, until the 1960s, that some people entered Religious Life seeing it as a "package deal" that included celibacy among other requirements. It was, however, usually the case that, even if the unitive motive was not explicit when the person entered Religious Life, it was quickly identified as the only valid motive for staying. In other words, while it may not have been explicitly attached to conse-crated celibacy, the latter was seen as intrinsic to a life centered on the God-quest in this particular form. Community was the context and ministry the expression of this unitive project.

Today, especially in light of a new generation's need and desire for community, the idealism and commitment of younger people seeking an outlet for their desire to contribute to the building of a just and peaceful world, and feminism's encouragement of women's solidarity in both life and work, it is entirely possible that a person might consider Religious Life primarily or even exclusively because of the possibility it offers for loving community and meaningful service in solidarity with other committed women. It is possible that such a person may not be particularly attached to the Catholic Church or even to the Christian faith. And the fact that most congrega-tions do not oblige their members to a daily horarium of prayer and spiritual exercises that would quickly become oner-ous for a person not especially attracted to religion in general or Christianity in particular, nor do they inquire directly into their members' faith or practice after profession, it would be possible for a person to be a happy and contributing member of the community and a committed and energetic humanitar-ian without having espoused Religious Life as a lifeform within the Catholic Christian faith context at all. Although I am using the subjunctive, I am not constructing a hypothetical case but describing a real scenario that many who deal with younger Religious and candidates, and some of those Religious and candidates themselves, will recognize.

In what follows I will articulate a position on this issue in full awareness that it will be vigorously contested from some quarters. But I think that if Religious are going to have open and productive discussions (which I think are necessary and urgent) about motivation and commitment in Religious Life, it would be helpful to have some starting point that people could either agree with and develop further or reject and suggest alternatives to. Avoiding the issues by diffusing them in clouds of generalized rhetoric or by generating confusion as a smoke screen is counterproductive.

My starting point is that Religious Life is, not exclusively but constitutively, both religious and a life. The *religion* in question is not generalized spirituality or a personal synthesis of elements from various religious traditions. It is Christianity in its Catholic incarnation. The fact that it is a life, or a *lifeform,* was discussed in detail in volume 1, chapter 2, but the point here is that Religious Life is not comparable to the Peace Corps, the National Organization of Women, or a feminist support group. Although service, advocacy, and feminist commitment are characteristic of most Religious congregations today temporary, part-time, or free-will commitment of time and resources is not the form of commitment envisioned by or appropriate to Religious Life, which makes a claim on the whole life of its members, that is, on the totality of their person, their time (both in terms of everyday life and of the whole of a lifetime), and their resources (talent, financial assets, work, and activities).

The implications of this are the following: first, that no motivation for entrance into Religious Life is valid that is not rooted and grounded in faith in and commitment to Jesus Christ within the Catholic Christian tradition, a faith and commitment that need to be explicit, unreserved, and primary; second, that permanent and total commitment within and to Religious Life in the congregation is necessary. I hasten to add that Catholic faith, as the history of Religious Life and especially the lives of its most outstanding members readily attest, does not preclude prophetic criticism and responsible dissent, active resistance to institutional corruption, strenuous commitment to more adequate understanding and expression of the faith received from the apostles, committed dialogue with and engagement of other world religions, and wholehearted cooperation with people of other (and no) religious and spiritual traditions. And it certainly does not preclude spiritual suffering over the state of the Church as institution and even persecution by institutional officials. But there is an enormous difference between a Joan of Arc, Catherine of Siena, Theresa Kane, Thomas Merton, Bede Griffiths, Joan Chittister, or Charles Curran, who struggle(d) with all these issues from within their Catholic Christian commitment and tradition, and people who have abandoned or rejected that tradition, never interiorly espoused it, or who meld some of its elements into various religious or spiritual syntheses that derive from and are responsible to no community of faith or practice.[21]

Against these background assumptions I want to raise the question of how consecrated celibacy can be understood as integral to contemporary Religious Life. If this life is not only to survive but to flourish in a new historical and cultural setting it seems to me that it must, at one and the same time, be fully faithful to its own highest ideals and take realistic account of the new realities it discovers in its midst, one of which is the fact that the unitive/mystical understanding of consecrated celibacy is not the only reason people make this commitment today.

The unitive/mystical understanding of consecrated celibacy, as we have seen, is both the most ancient and the most powerful motivation and has traditionally been expressed through the metaphor of marriage to Christ. This metaphor captured well (and still does for many people) the totality, exclusivity, and fecundity of the commitment as well as its deepest source in the love as strong as death that fuels the life-encompassing God-quest of the Religious. Within this understanding perpetuity is self-evidently integral to the commitment itself as the time dimension of its totality. In my opinion, whether the nuptial metaphor is used or not, this understanding of consecrated celibacy remains the most self-evidently valid, life-sustaining, and publicly defensible motivation for such a choice and is the only one for which we can argue legitimately to its intrinsically perpetual character.

However, consecrated celibacy has (as do the other vows) both communitarian and ministerial dimensions, and it certainly seems to be the case that for some people who enter Religious Life, generously motivated by the love of Christ, the primary expression of that love and the primary locus of their God-quest is community life and/or ministry. The quality of the life and commitment of such Religious, it seems to me and I think to most who live and work with them, constitutes an undeniable testimony to the validity of this motivation. A person can choose Religious Life out of love of Christ primarily experienced through his body which is the Church and all human and nonhuman creation and can desire to live that dedication by wholehearted service within a community of like-minded and equally committed people. That desire can be sufficient, given other provisos I will mention in a moment, to motivate making a lifetime commitment to celibacy if that is the type of lifeform the chosen community espouses.

It seems to me, however, that a very important feature of this motivation is that the perpetuity of the commitment to celibacy, though real and required, is not a self-evident or intrinsic feature of the commitment. It is a choice, freely made, within a global choice of Religious Life which is a celibate lifeform. It certainly seems (and this is the proviso) that the person must feel some attraction for the celibate lifeform as a good and valid choice for her or him because of the type of community it grounds and/or because of their own ministerial self-understanding in which celibacy is more conducive to their ministerial commitment than other forms of life would be. In any case, she must at least not feel an aversion to it if she is not to undertake an onerous and even oppressive obligation that will militate against her own happiness and development and probably her capacity for community and her ministerial effectiveness. History seems to suggest that there are many people for whom celibacy is an attractive option in relation to their life choices. We find such a choice among artists and intellectuals and social activists and people committed to particular service roles such as child care or nursing. In other words, a person may freely and happily choose celibacy for herself without having experienced it as integral to the unitive/mystical relationship with Christ. It would seem that wanting to give oneself to Christ through ministry and life in a celibate community is a perfectly valid reason for deciding to remain celibate.

A person for whom the celibate lifestyle would be truly burdensome has many other options for community and ministry and should not be encouraged (or perhaps even permitted) to make a celibate commitment. Not only can the charism of celibacy not be invented or imposed, but also celibacy is not an entrance requirement for community life or ministry (as it is for ordained ministry). It is an intrinsic and integral feature of one kind of such life, namely Religious Life, which as a lifeform is actually generated by the vocation to consecrated celibacy and which is committed to maintaining the celibate lifeform precisely to promote and nourish the charism of celibacy in the Church (among other things). Religious communities, in my opinion, should not feel pressured to abandon or even mitigate their celibate character because someone who feels no vocation at all to celibacy (for unitive/mystical or communitarian/ministerial reasons) wishes to enter. Unlike ordained ministry, to which there are no comparable alternatives, Religious Life is not the only option for a person who wants to make community and/or ministry the center of her life in a more intentional way than ordinary parish life offers.

Another important consideration, however, is that the perpetuity of the commitment to celibacy is only intrinsic (and in that sense absolute) within the framework of the unitive/mystical

motivation. A person professing celibacy as part of a commitment arising primarily from communitarian and ministerial
motivation freely makes a permanent commitment to that
aspect of the vocation to Religious Life as a whole within a particular congregation. But it seems to me that it has to be recognized that if the life itself ceased to be meaningful or even
became an impediment to further human or spiritual growth
and development, it might be actually necessary for the person
to leave the congregation, and therefore Religious Life, which
would entail the abrogation of the celibate commitment.

Although it would be an impediment to valid profession for
a person to make a life commitment with "fingers crossed" in
the sense of "unless something better comes along" or "as
long as it seems like a good investment," there is the possibility
that a person living the life wholeheartedly and faithfully
might find herself truly unable to continue within it. Such a situation might be one of the following: that the community life
has become genuinely destructive and there seems no way of
ameliorating it at least within a reasonable time; that the congregation has made a nonnegotiable choice regarding ministry or community life which is impossible for the person to
accept and implement in good faith; that the person is faced
by Church or congregational authority with a choice between
violating her conscience or leaving her community; that her
or his spiritual experience has made participation in the
Catholic tradition virtually impossible; that without having
courted temptation or engaged in any infidelity she or he has
discerned a vocation to marriage that simply was not there, or
of which she was not aware, when she made profession; that a
growing awareness of his or her sexual orientation and/or
identity has posed problems in the area of chastity that cannot
be resolved within the celibate context.

I think we see, in some of the choices Religious have made
since the Council, the distinction between the intrinsically perpetual call to consecrated celibacy rooted in the unitive/mystical
God-quest and the sincerely permanent but not absolutely non-
renegotiable commitment to celibacy of someone embracing

Religious Life for primarily communitarian and/or ministerial reasons. Some Religious have left their congregations because they realized that they were never called to the life or that their motivations were not valid at the time they made profession and had not changed since. But others who entered for valid reasons and lived the life faithfully have left for some of the reasons suggested in the previous paragraph or others like them, and their leaving of their congregation was, in effect, also a leaving of Religious Life itself since the congregation was really their primary focus in the first place.

However, others have left their congregation for some of the same reasons but have immediately transferred to another congregation or so-called "noncanonical" (Religious) community or eventually reentered Religious Life in another group. For these people their primary focus was always Religious Life, the unmediated and exclusive quest for God expressed in consecrated celibacy, and the congregation was the locus and context of that commitment. But the commitment to Religious Life did not cease with the necessary separation from a particular congregation. There have been striking examples in recent history of Religious persevering in their commitment to Religious Life, especially to consecrated celibacy, even when their congregation was suppressed or dispersed by persecution, and thus community life and/or ministry became impossible. In such cases the unitive/mystical understanding of consecrated celibacy stands out in bold relief.

In summary, I believe that consecrated celibacy is intrinsic to Religious Life which was developed by, and as the life context of, people who had received that charism in and for the Church. However, as Religious Life became institutionalized as a lifeform it began to attract people whose primary charism was not consecrated celibacy but who felt willing and able to embrace and sustain celibacy in order to participate in the lifeform. Thus, community life and ministry (always part of Religious Life) became other, and valid, primary motives for entering Religious Life, and celibacy in such cases was undertaken as part of the lifeform rather than the specific charism of the individual.

This means that within most congregations there will be Religious whose primary focus is on the contemplative or unitive dimension of the life, others for whom community life in its affective and interactive dimensions is primary, and others for whom ministry is the predominant concern. And all three motivations can be found in both stabile contemplative communities and in mobile ministerial ones. This diversity of primary motivation has caused considerable tension, especially in mobile ministerial communities, as various groups have tried to establish the priority of their concern, subordinating ministry to the demand for community presence and participation, or prayer to ministerial demands, or ministry and community to the fostering of the contemplative dimension of the life.

In my opinion this tension can and should be resolved (not in the sense of being permanently abrogated but in the sense of being brought into a life-giving moving equilibrium) through mutual recognition of the variety of primary motivations operative in different members of the community and a sincere seeking of ways to validate all of them while providing scope for each. They are mutually enriching approaches to Religious Life. The most actively ministerial not only keep the more contemplative attuned to the needs of Church and world but are themselves drawn back to the one thing necessary that is at the heart of all Religious Life, the exclusive and primary God-quest. Those whose need for community in its most experiential form could become narcissistic or neurotically demanding are challenged to find their affective center in Christ and to broaden their concern to the entire Church community even as they keep the centrifugal forces of diverse ministerial commitments from dissipating the community and the centripetal forces of the contemplative dynamic from privatization and selfishness. And the contemplative focus helps prevent ministry from becoming purely humanitarian activism and community from becoming an affective substitute for family or a form of long-term group therapy. Religious Life is, first and last, a lifeform devoted to the single-hearted quest for God through union with Christ. But as a Christian lifeform it is necessarily communitarian and ministerial. Perhaps part of its witness value today lies in its continual struggle to integrate these three dimensions of Christian life in a celibate incarnation as they must also be integrated in the other form of consecrated life in the Church, matrimony. In any case, it is my conviction that this form of life is a gift to the Church and should continue as long as there are people called to consecrated celibacy as the constitutive feature and form of their self-gift to God in Christ and that it should remain open to development through interaction with its ecclesial and cultural context.

CHAPTER FIVE

CELIBACY AS WOMEN'S REALITY

I. Introduction

The previous chapter was devoted to a consideration of consecrated celibacy from the standpoint of theology and spirituality. However, this charism is not an acultural platonic ideal
realized with minor modifications in diverse circumstances.
Its understanding and practice are profoundly affected by the
historical-cultural context in which it is lived. Without doubt
the two most significant contextual developments of the past
half century that bear directly on the issue of celibacy are the
sexual revolution of the 1960s and the raising of feminist consciousness among Religious, especially women.

The sexual revolution ended any pretense of Victorian
propriety in the areas of sexual information, experimentation, and practice. Words never heard in public (and rarely
in private) became commonplace in films, on television, and
in popular publications easily accessible to the young as well
as adults. Sex education was pushed lower and lower on
the educational scale because children were becoming
informed, well or badly, at an ever earlier age. People whose
sexual orientation and/or practices were not the norm,
including homosexual, bisexual, and transsexual persons,
began a painful but determined process of "coming out,"
demanding equal participation and rights in society.
Practices previously condemned as bizarre, unnatural, or
neurotic (or at least unspeakable in public even if widely

160

practiced) came to be regarded as objects of general curiosity and even of legitimate experimentation. All aspects of sex and reproduction became a matter of public debate in both society and Church, reopening previously "closed" discussions of contraception, abortion, sex and pregnancy among the unmarried (including homosexual people as individuals or couples), and premarital or extramarital sex (as preparation for or alternative to marriage).[1] There was a general reevaluation (even among Catholics whose Church has had for centuries a clear and rigorous sexual morality according to which any sexual activity except that within heterosexual marriage and open to procreation is intrinsically immoral) of such issues as masturbation and homogenital activity. Sexually freighted issues, for example, mandatory singleness of the clergy and remarriage of divorced people, reemerged. The explosion of the AIDS epidemic opened up frank discussion of homosexual sex, of "safe sex" practices, especially the use of condoms (which made a strange connection between the issue of homosexuality and that of contraception), which were definitely not limited to abstinence, and the role of openly practicing homosexual persons in the faith community, including in its ordained ministry. Finally, as the wall of secrecy protecting clerical sexual abusers, especially pedophiles, from exposure and prosecution collapsed, any delusions that the rhetoric of priestly celibacy might have sustained were fatally undermined.[2]

In short, virtually every aspect of human life related in any way to sexuality or genitality was opened to public discussion, and the basic trend was toward not only greater explicitness of public discourse on the subject but also increased permissiveness in practice for people of all ages. Probably no one (except the most naïvely euphoric libertarians) would regard the sexual revolution as an unmixed blessing, and many regard it as the ultimate degeneracy of the dying first-world empire. However, certain features of the revolution might be seen as positive. The dispersion of the Victorian obscurantism that shrouded so much of this area in confusion for young people and hypocritical denial for adults is a blessing. The exposure of the tight collusion among patriarchical social structures in the sexual and social victimization of women and children on the one hand and the oppression of sexual minorities on the other was long overdue. And it is perhaps a good thing, in the long run, that the case for sexual responsibility and morality now must be made on rational, humanistic, and spiritual grounds rather than through psychological or religious terror tactics.

The effects of the sexual revolution on a life whose central and distinguishing charism is consecrated celibacy involving lifelong genital abstinence are bound to be profound. One effect is the gradually increasing openness among Religious about problematic issues that were simply not discussed in pre—sexual revolution days and which, like any unacknowledged "elephant in the living room," seriously distorted communication and generated potentially explosive tensions. Especially in some men's congregations discussion of sexual orientation, the advisability of admitting homosexually oriented and/or HIV-positive candidates, the morality of sexual acting out and alternative strategies for dealing with sexual needs has led to real growth in individuals and communities. Male congregations have also been forced to deal extensively with the public fallout from sexual abuse cases involving their members and institutions. Both male and female Religious are being offered psychological, spiritual, and legal instruction (often mandatory) on personal and professional boundaries and avoidance of workplace sexual harassment. The case has been made by some, although it has not received much affirmation, for some kind of "third way" that would allow Religious to justify certain kinds of sexual relationships provided they were "responsible and faithful" and did not involve marriage or children. Among women Religious especially there has been extensive discussion of and experimentation with new forms of membership, and for some people part of the agenda in this discussion is the admission to full membership of married people and sexually active lesbians.

These issues were not caused by the sexual revolution, but their articulation and the attempt to deal with them could hardly have occurred forty years ago.

Other implications of the sexual revolution affect especially new candidates and formation. As already discussed in chapter 2 in relation to formation, few new candidates for Religious Life will arrive without some, if not a great deal, of sexual experience, both positive and negative, and the integration of that experience as well as preparation for a life of consecrated celibacy, including sexual abstinence, will have to be a major factor in Religious formation. Among the difficult topics that we now know have to be broached and dealt with in formation is the incest that so many young women have suffered as children[3] and the homosexual abuse, especially by clerics and Religious, of many young boys who later follow their tormenters into Religious Life. Religious Life cannot be validly chosen as a refuge from such abuse or a place where it will never have to be named and faced. Another issue is that of sexual identity and orientation. If such topics could once be wrapped in silence provided the person never "got in trouble" (meaning got caught in some flagrant offense), they cannot be today. These topics, whatever the person's gender and orientation issues might be, need to be an explicit focus of discernment before a person makes a perpetual commitment to celibacy. A third implication for formation is that sexual morality, at the theoretical and the practical level, cannot be presumed. Formation programs will have to make provision for sexual moral education of new members as well as for some older Religious who have awakened to sexuality as a much more complex reality than it was for them when they made profession.

Another implication of the sexual revolution touches all Religious but especially those who spent the first decades of their Religious lives in quasi-cloistered environments. All Religious have to learn to function not only in a two-sex universe (from which preconciliar Religious were largely insulated) but in a highly sexualized, hedonistic, and amoral cultural situation in which there is, unfortunately, no general assumption even among Catholics either that Religious are sexually "off limits" or that Religious themselves (especially men) are to be trusted. No doubt there are other implications, but I list these only by way of suggesting that the effects of the sexual revolution on the commitment to consecrated celibacy are profound and extensive and that we cannot afford to ignore them.

My primary concern in this chapter, however, is the effect of feminist consciousness on Religious, especially women, in their self-understanding as celibates and in their actual living of this charism. By feminist consciousness I mean the effective interiorization of feminism as theory and practice that leads the person to experience, analyze, and respond to the whole of her lived reality in feminist terms. Obviously, different Religious are at different stages of development in feminist consciousness. Some, for various reasons, have actively repudiated any involvement with feminism. In some it is barely emerging; in others it is sporadically active; for others, an increasing number, it is a fundamental orientation that affects every area of life. It is the last with whom this chapter is primarily concerned.

Elsewhere, I have defined feminism as "a comprehensive ideology which is rooted in women's experience of sexual oppression, engages in a critique of patriarchy as an essentially dysfunctional system, embraces an alternative vision for humanity and the earth, and actively seeks to bring this vision to realization."[4] In what follows I am assuming that most Religious, especially women, no longer require a basic introduction to the meaning and implications of feminism but, for those who do, such introduction is readily available from numerous publications. The remainder of this chapter will be organized around two concerns: appropriating an understanding of consecrated celibacy from the standpoint of women's experience of sexuality; understanding the dynamics of women Religious' experience of consecrated celibacy, especially in its unitive dimension, in the context of a patriarchal Church.

II. Consecrated Celibacy in the Context of Women's Experience of Sexuality

One of the most obvious and massively important realizations inherent to feminist consciousness is that women's experience is irreducibly different from men's. The debate about whether this results from nature or nurture is important, and on this subject the jury is still out. However, whatever the source of the difference it is clear that the virtually universal assumption, until quite recently, that women's experience was simply a deficient version of men's and therefore that men understood (by way of eminence and/or extrapolation from their own experience) whatever pertained to women is no longer considered valid. When most Religious alive today entered the novitiate they read the books on Religious Life written by men, listened to retreat conferences given by men, went to confession and received spiritual direction from men, listened to homilies and sermons by men, and studied theology constructed by men and taught by men on the basis of male experience. It was assumed by all concerned that men knew whatever women needed to learn, even about themselves as women, and that they were competent advisers and legislators for women's lives. (This was true not only for Religious but in some ways even more painfully for married women.)

Few areas of life are more deeply affected by the diverse personal experience of women and men than sexuality, which is, of course, central to the understanding of celibacy. The assumption that male experience was universal and normative, indeed simply equivalent to human experience, conspired with the abstract natural-law universalism of preconciliar Catholic sexual morality to prevent any influence (read: intrusion or interference) of women's experience of their sexuality into the overall theory of sexuality and celibacy that women Religious were taught. In light of feminist sensibilities this situation appears today as not only absurd but violent. Nevertheless, little has been done to redress it *in radice* despite piecemeal arguments with one or another conclusion from the male synthesis.

A. A Significant Hint from History

Until relatively recently most histories of Religious Life began with the exodus to the desert of (mostly male) ascetics in the fourth century, which was partially occasioned by the accommodation of the Church as official religion in the Constantinian Empire to secular culture. Actually, the earliest form of Religious Life was that of consecrated virginity (mostly female) that arose in the urban Christian communities of the first century. It is highly significant, it seems to me, that the characteristically male form of Religious Life was radical asceticism, within which celibate chastity functioned primarily as a form of self-control (often called continence), while the characteristically female form of the life was consecrated virginity, understood explicitly as "marriage to Christ," which entailed sexual abstinence as the outward expression of spousal fidelity.

In other words, though there were some male consecrated virgins and some female desert hermits in the beginning, the characteristic approach to Religious Life in general and to celibacy in particular differed significantly between the sexes. Typically, for men the life was a Christian form of the pursuit of the highest wisdom, that is, holiness, through contemplation,[5] and celibacy functioned essentially as an ascetical practice. In other words, its role was instrumental. For women, however, the life of consecrated virginity was one of self-donation to the person of Christ, and virginity was essentially unitive, that is, integral to the end itself. I think this tells us something very important about the diversity of the experience of both sexuality and celibacy in the life of women and men Religious. It is this difference I want to explore within the context of feminist consciousness.

B. Contrasting Experiences of Sexuality

Let me begin with a disclaimer. Obviously, nothing can be said absolutely or universally about men or about women beyond the recognition of certain biological facts of anatomy and physiology. In most areas there seems to be as much diversity within each gender as between the two. However, there do seem to be patterns of ideas, behaviors, sensibilities, and interests that surface repeatedly in literature and films, studies and surveys, and even in ordinary conversation ("women are from Venus and men are from Mars") that make some generalizations useful.

1. *Male experience of sexuality:* A fair amount of literature has appeared in recent decades attempting to analyze the phallic-centered approach of men to sexuality in contrast to the experience of sexuality of women.[6] The phallus is physically at the very center of a man's body and symbolically at the crossroads of his experience. Importantly, it is external both in location and in orientation, making it manipulable both by the man himself and by others. It is thus both a potential instrument (of pleasure or of aggression) and a point of extreme vulnerability (either through pleasure or attack). Furthermore, the phallus has a certain "life of its own" in that a man does not have absolute control over its responses. It can announce its presence and demand total attention at inopportune times and places and disturb sleep as well as waking activity. The urgency of male sexual desire may well be overstated as justification for a lack of self-control, but it is undeniably real and powerful. Finally, this quasi-autonomy and externality of the male genitalia leads naturally to a tendency toward "compartmentalization" of sex from other aspects of the self, including intellection, feeling, social interaction, and work. Women are often amazed and baffled by this capacity of men to disconnect sex from the rest of life.

The male experience of sexuality has been the context in which Catholic sexual morality as well as the theology and spirituality of celibacy have developed. Given the nature of male experience, it is understandable that a major concern for men is sexual control. In relation to themselves the issue is self-control. But since that control is easily threatened by the presence and attractiveness of women, men also have an interest in controlling women. Resisting the charms of women, who can evoke

unwanted sexual response, means not only prudence in necessary contacts with them but, in some cases, avoidance of contact
with them altogether. This is most easily managed by confining
the women in one way or another or at least by excluding them
from male precincts. Male concern with habiting, veiling, and
cloistering women is as characteristic of conservative Islam and
Judaism as it is of Christianity. And a major form of confine-
ment is pregnancy, which men have traditionally claimed the
right to control, and child rearing, which they have assigned
almost exclusively to women. The exclusion of women from
schools, gymnasiums and playing fields, political life, liturgical
activity, board rooms, and the military, in short, from any place
where men gather for any purpose other than sex, has provided
the agenda for much of the women's liberation movement.
Feminist analysis has convinced women that the male preoccupation with control and exclusion of women has as much or
more to do with male fear of their own sexuality as it has with
the protection of women's virtue.

Also important in the male configuration of sexual morality
is the valuation of the "seed," which men, for centuries, regarded
as the real source of life, women providing only the incubation
chamber for the "little man" (or the "misbegotten man," i.e., a
female), generated by the male. Thus masturbation, nocturnal
emission, or interrupted coitus in which the seed was "wasted"
were matters of grave concern in moral theology. Any act that
deliberately caused such waste was considered an act against
nature that was intrinsically gravely sinful. In elaborating the "no
paucity of matter" approach to sexual sins the theologians were
apparently oblivious of the fact that the whole discussion was
irrelevant to half the race. However, as Margaret Miles pointed
out in her intriguing feminist analysis of Augustine's conversion
struggle to achieve continence,[7] this concern deeply affects the
male understanding of chastity as a Christian ideal. In intercourse a man "loses" his seed, disperses himself, goes "outside"
of himself in search of happiness. Chastity is a way of preserving
himself, maintaining his integrity, finding his satisfaction within.
There is a certain self-absorption in this approach to celibacy

because the primary concern is to avoid "giving oneself away." This may well be in the service of maintaining concentration for prayer or reserving energy for charitable, artistic, intellectual, or even athletic and military activity, but it retains a certain aura of self-concern. Chastity is in the service of self-transcendence, not a form of self-transcendence.

Finally, the male concern with homosexuality has long been an unspoken but powerful feature of the moral discourse on sexuality that directly affects the theology and spirituality of Religious celibacy. The oblique discussions of "particular friendships" (as if there were such a thing as "general friendship"!) that often baffled young women Religious were not so much about divided hearts or communities as about forbidden sexual liaisons between members of the same community. It seems to be the case that active homosexuality has always been a fairly common problem and a focus of intense conflict among male Religious. Homoerotic attraction and homophobic revulsion, collusion and condemnation, have apparently been much more endemic to men's Religious Life than to women's. Many regulations in women's Religious rules that resisted any sensible explanation in terms of women's experience can be traced fairly directly to male concerns with preventing homosexual behavior.

In summary, the spirituality of Religious celibacy bears the marks of the exclusively male experience that generated Catholic moral theology in general. The Church's moral discourse is disproportionately fixated on sexual issues.[8] The male obsession with control has led, in the area of celibacy, to a focus on renunciation and asceticism. The externality and compartmentalization of male sexual experience has promoted an "act-centered" or physicalist sexual morality rather than a personalist morality that takes adequate account of the immensely complex reality of human sexuality as integral to relational life.[9] Thus celibacy was often presented as more concerned with an asceticism of avoidance and suppression (if not repression) than with relationship to Christ. Sexual morality in general and the spirituality of celibacy in particular, like education and other spheres of human experience that have been mono-gendered in their development, appeared almost exclusively as an arena of battle, of heroic exploits and disgraceful failures, of conquest and humiliation.[10]

2. *Women's experience of sexuality:* In retrospect it seems amazing that women's approach to consecrated celibacy, to which a rich tradition of mystical literature bears eloquent testimony, has played virtually no significant role in the official treatment of this reality. But, given that the theology and spirituality of celibacy is, in fact, male centered, it is very understandable that many women Religious today, as their feminist consciousness develops, have become suspicious about celibacy as a positive dimension of their own vocation. In what follows I am inspired primarily by the tradition of women's mystical literature in which the relationship to Christ is absolutely central to the understanding of celibacy.[11] I will begin, however, with some observations about female sexuality parallel to those above about male sexuality since how women understand celibacy is based, at least to some extent, on how they experience themselves as sexual subjects.

The most obvious difference between women and men in the area of genitality is that a woman's sexual center is interior to her body. Even the organ of greatest sexual pleasure is hidden. Consequently, female sexual arousal can be easily masked if a woman so chooses, giving the whole experience of sexuality a certain mysterious, intimate, and private character. Because women's experience of sexuality is not exclusively localized in a particular organ that either is or is not excited at any particular moment, women's experience of sexuality is more pervasive and wholistic, engaging their emotions and feelings, their intelligence and language, their spirits as well as their bodies. Women are more likely to experience themselves, rather than a part of themselves, as sexual and thus as relational rather than simply aroused.

Women Religious, from the beginning, spoke of their life choice as virginity rather than chastity. Virginity, like marriage, was a state of life, a self-disposition that involved the whole person, not a moral virtue that one practiced. Chastity, of course, was as essential to the understanding of virginity as it was to the understanding of marriage. There was, however, a subtle but very significant difference between a feminine understanding of chastity and the masculine. Male chastity was primarily about self-control on the one hand and self-preservation for "higher" things on the other. Chastity for women Religious was, likewise, about self-preservation. But women's concern was not to preserve themselves *from* self-dispersion and the resulting "weakness" but *for* a relationship that was experienced as calling for the totality of their being, body and soul. Virginity required an autonomy, a self-possession, that permitted a free disposition of oneself in relation to Christ. Chastity was implied in the totality of that self-gift, but chastity was primarily fidelity to a relationship rather than self-control.

There also seems to be a significant difference between women and men in the area of sexual identity and orientation. Statistically, far fewer women than men seem to be conflicted about their sexual identity, to entertain suspicions that they are not fully and securely rooted in their biological sex.[12] Proportionately fewer women than men seem to need constant reassurance about their gender identity, either from others or by means of sexual "acting out."

Although statistics about sexual orientation among Religious are extremely difficult to obtain and not especially reliable, it does seem to be the case that, whether or not there are as many homosexually oriented women as men in the general population,[13] the proportion of homosexually to heterosexually oriented women in Religious Life is lower than the corresponding proportion in men's orders.[14] It is very difficult to draw causal connections in this area, but women Religious seem to be less conflicted about friendship among themselves than are male Religious. This may reflect higher social tolerance of friendship among women as well as less fear that all same-sex friendship is evidence of homosexual inclinations. The male fear that love and tenderness are evidence of effeminacy is, of course, not a concern for women. One has to wonder whether, if homophobic guilt and anxiety had not been infused into women's Religious life by male founders, confessors, and spiritual guides, women would have had half the problems they did in regard to relationships. In any case, one of the immediate results of the lifting of certain strictures in this area during the conciliar reform was the surfacing of intimate friendships that had survived and developed through decades of official repression,[15] testifying eloquently to the subversion in practice of a theory about and attitude toward friendship and intimacy that were foreign to many women's actual experience.

In short, women's experience of sexuality grounds a very different attitude toward consecrated celibacy than does male sexuality. Women are less fixated on sex as a biological organ and/or a physiological event, less motivated by a control agenda either in relationship to themselves or to others, and thus less focused on celibacy as chastity, that is, as an ascetical practice or a moral virtue aimed at regulating behavior. Female celibacy throughout the history of spirituality does not exhibit (with relatively rare exceptions) the agonistic quality that marks male celibacy. It is neither warfare with the self nor athletic contest with others and is not about heroic exploits or disgraceful defeats. Women are generally not out to "prove something" (to God, others, or themselves) by the practice of celibate chastity, but to express a personal commitment. Although women Religious, following the lead and legislation of males, vowed "chastity" for many centuries and Canon Law as well as male congregations continue to prefer this terminology, it is significant that women Religious from the beginning preferred the terminology of virginity and today seem to prefer consecrated celibacy.[16] This linguistic difference is, in my opinion, highly evocative. Both "virginity" and "consecrated celibacy" are ways of referring to a state of life, not to the practice of a moral virtue or even an arena of ascetical combat.

An important implication of this approach to consecrated celibacy is that contemplative or unitive prayer is absolutely central to the celibate life. We will return to this point briefly below and at greater length in volume 3.

III. Consecrated Celibacy and Feminism

A very important result of the raising of feminist consciousness among women (and some men) Religious is the realization of the extent and depth of patriarchy in the institutional Church. Feminist Religious are no longer in any doubt that the patriarchal agenda that has controlled the history of the Western world to the disadvantage of women has been and continues to be operative in the Church despite lofty rhetoric in official documents about the dignity of women. If a convincing case is to be made for consecrated celibacy as a spiritually liberating and enriching reality in the life of Religious today, it is imperative to take utterly seriously the feminist critique and challenge. If the following description and analysis of the oppression of women in society and Church seems unduly grim, it is because I want to face squarely the enormity of the problem, which cannot be handled by trying to ignore it or minimize its seriousness.

The primary symbol and instrument of male control of women is men's appropriation of women's reproductive capacity and therefore of their sexuality. In a patriarchal system women are seen as possessions, resources for male purposes. Women are the producers of those who will augment the family's wealth, carry on the family name, and eventually inherit the ancestral property. Men, therefore, have had a vested interest in assuring that their women were virginal before they acquired them and monogamous afterward, not only because the men, for reasons of personal pride, did not want "damaged goods" but especially because they needed to be absolutely certain that offspring were theirs and that there were no rival claimants to family property.

Because men considered themselves not only the initiators but also the proprietors of the reproductive process, contraception and abortion were abhorrent, both symbolically

(because women thereby challenged the male claim to possession by asserting some control over their own reproductive
capacities) and practically (because they thereby deprived
men of a crucial economic and social resource, i.e., descendents). Female genital mutilation in Africa, foot binding in the
East, and medieval chastity belts all belong to the same ideology of male control of female sexuality.

Rape is another form of male control of females through
sexuality. We now know that rape has little if anything to do
with sexual satisfaction and everything to do with the exercise
of power through sex. Rape has been, from time immemorial,
a way that males punished and gloated over vanquished enemies, dishonoring them through the violation of their female
property and plundering their source of pleasure and progeny.
Many people were horrified to learn the role systematic rape of
the enemy's women played in the recent local wars in Rwanda,
Kuwait, and Kosovo. But, in fact, the history of European males
in their conquest of the "New World" and American males in
overseas wars bespeaks the same patriarchal evaluation of
women as "booty." Many women and men, Catholic and non-
Catholic alike, were outraged at the Vatican decree against the
use of pre- or post-rape methods to prevent pregnancy by
women caught in these violent situations. It spoke clearly to
them not of "respect for life" but of the collusion of patriarchal
systems, military and ecclesiastical, in the claim to ownership
of females through their sexuality. Even a potential pregnancy,
even one initiated by male violence, had absolute priority over
the actual well-being of a real woman.

Finally, the male fear of female power to cause sexual reac-
tions in themselves, especially when this might weaken their
resolve in war or athletic competition or distract them from
other "serious business" requiring nonrelational objectivity,
has led to a consistent practice throughout the world of confining women so that they might not exercise such influence
except when it suited male purposes. Combined with the
desire to protect their female property from other males, this
has led to male control of what women must wear (long skirts

and sleeves, habits, veils), to whom they may speak (to relatives when spoken to or to those permitted by their fathers, brothers, husbands), where they may appear (not alone in public), and what roles they may fulfill (none that imply authority over men or give access to the public forum).

In short, despite a rhetoric of respect and protection (and there is no denying that at least some men were at least partially motivated by such concerns), patriarchy as a form of social organization is very much about male ownership and control of women. What is important for our purposes here is that women whose consciousness is raised recognize all of the traits of this pattern in ecclesiastical attitudes toward and legislation about women. They see this pattern in numerous areas which have, in recent years, become arenas of struggle between women and official Church policy.

The refusal to ordain women or to allow them to preach in the liturgical context is seen by many women (and men) as being much more about keeping women out of positions of religious and ecclesiastical power than about God's will or Church order. Prior to the 1960s women were not even allowed to study, much less teach, theology, and recent efforts to curtail the presence and influence of women in seminaries and schools of theology suggest that, while some discriminatory practices may have changed, there has been no deep conversion on the subject of women's legitimate participation in the teaching mission of the Church.

In the area of morality women have repeatedly pointed out that the official polemic against abortion and contraception is not matched in frequency, absoluteness, or actual penalties by official attitudes toward murder, war, indiscriminate bombing of civilians, capital punishment, destruction of the environment, voracious greed which impoverishes millions, political corruption in state and Church, or the marital or clerical abuse of women and children, all of which are overwhelmingly male behaviors. They note that rape (male initiation of an unwanted pregnancy), while considered a sin, does not merit the automatic excommunication reserved for abortion (female termination of it). Wife battering (which women, for centuries, were urged to "offer up" or even to accept as God's will and man's right) has only in very recent times merited occasional expressions of official disapproval and admission of the woman's right to separate from the batterer, though not her right to remarry even when the good of her children warrants it.

In the political arena the concern of the Church to keep women out of the public workforce and the military, as well as its adamant opposition to abortion and contraception, has led to strong ecclesiastical opposition to the Equal Rights Amendment in the United States, which says nothing about any of these issues but would merely establish the right of women to equality before the law. To many women the message is that massive actual injustice against women is preferable to even the possibility of jeopardizing some element of the male agenda. This same agenda has also led to sporadic opposition to the international pressure for the advancement of women, most flagrantly expressed in the Cairo conference on population control[17] that caused an unprecedented protest by men as well as women, non-Catholics as well as Catholics.

Obviously, there is more than one possible interpretation of some of this data, but the feminist interpretation outlined above gives some idea of why feminist women are often very suspicious of anything in the area of sexuality that is approved of or promoted by the institutional Church, for example, celibacy. The Church, of course, did not invent patriarchy, and there is certainly some truth in the contention that Christianity, at least in certain respects, raised the status of women by the very fact of baptizing them and regarding them as fully (if inferiorly) human. Official Church attitudes and legislation have been, to a large degree, culturally determined. Feminist analysis, however, has exposed the evidence that the institutional Church, as a hierarchical power structure, has the same vested interest in the subordination and control of women as other patriarchal institutions in society and that the focus and locus of that control is women's reproductive power, that is, their sexuality.

This feminist analysis of patriarchy in the Church leads to a hermeneutics of deep suspicion about matters once taken for granted among Religious. When the Code of Canon Law was being revised in the early 1970s and '80s, the Leadership Conference of Women Religious, among many other objections and suggestions to the early drafts, raised serious questions about the glaring inequalities of Church law as it applied respectively to women and to men.[18] In 1917, when the previous version of Canon Law was promulgated, women would not have been consulted at all and would probably not have found such inequalities problematic. The validity of the LCWR observations, however, is actually recognized in the revised Code of Canon Law: "Whatever is determined about institutes of consecrated life and their members applies equally to either sex, unless the contrary is apparent from the context of the wording or the nature of the matter."[19] Although this provision begs the question since only men were involved in creating the final "wording" and determining the "nature of the matter," there is at least a preliminary recognition that equality has not been the norm and that it should be.[20]

The feminist hermeneutics of suspicion has, for all the reasons given above, been focused by both married women and women Religious in the area of sexuality. Religious have begun to question whether the idealistic rhetoric about virginity in the early Church and especially the use of the nuptial metaphor to articulate that ideal was not motivated by a desire to assimilate even women who did not marry to the patriarchal marriage structures that subordinated women to men. Was the veiling and habiting of women Religious really a matter of religious symbolism or an exercise of male control over women's behavior?[21] Were the imposition of male superiors on women's communities, insistence on male approval of women's rules, appointment of male confessors and spiritual directors for women who were obliged to submit in both the internal and external forums, and especially the extreme rigidity of cloister, an expression of generous pastoral solicitude for the integrity of Religious Life or various expressions of and ways of implementing patriarchal domination?[22]

This context of feminist suspicion of the patriarchal agenda necessarily frames the question I want to raise at this point about the use of the nuptial metaphor for the unitive/mystical dimension of Religious celibacy. For purposes of brevity I will use the term *virginity* when referring to this unitive aspect of consecrated celibacy not only because it was the original term women chose to talk about this experience, but also because it is less likely to focus the imagination on genital activity or renunciation thereof and is more inclusive of the whole person in a state of life. This is also suggested by the rehabilitation since the Council of consecrated virginity as a state of life undertaken by women who make Religious profession outside the context of an approved Institute.[23] However, I am using it within the framework of all the disclaimers given in the previous chapter, especially these two: that the primary and essential reference of the term *virginity* is to the total self-gift to Christ to the exclusion of other primary life commitments rather than to physical intactness; that not all Religious (and I would suspect that this is true among nuns in stabile contemplative communities as well as among mobile ministerial Religious) experience consecrated celibacy in a way that suggests the nuptial metaphor or are enlightened by it.

That being acknowledged, many years of dealing with Religious have convinced me that the unitive/mystical understanding both of Religious Life itself and especially of the role within it of consecrated celibacy is far more common than the general silence on the subject would suggest. For decades there has been a reticence on the part of Religious to speak of this dimension of their life. Feminist sensitivity, distaste for the flowery sentimentality of nineteenth-century piety, recognition of the romanticism and repressed eroticism associated with the nuptial theme in some spiritual literature as well as in the paraliturgical practices of some orders, and the legitimate reserve of many mature people in speaking publicly about the most intimate aspects of their lives[24] have made it much more acceptable and certainly easier for Religious, in talking about the meaning of their life, to focus on their ministries or community rather than on their direct relationship to God.

Despite this general reticence I have been surprised and touched by the affirmation, sometimes accompanied by tears of relief as if a dam of unnatural silence had been broken, that has greeted my references in writing and lectures to the unitive motivation and character of Religious Life, and it is certainly a recurring preoccupation of Religious in retreats and spiritual direction.[25] Consequently, at risk of precipitating serious misunderstanding, I am going to attempt to rehabilitate public discourse on the nuptial metaphor with the intention of suggesting language for those whose experience verifies it and of reclaiming for women a precious resource of liberation that, despite its appropriation by men for patriarchal purposes, is not thereby vitiated or invalidated and should not be simply surrendered by those women for whom it is deeply meaningful.

A. Background Considerations

Before discussing the theological and spirituality implications of the nuptial metaphor, I want to briefly treat three preliminary topics that condition that discussion.

1. Metaphor and symbol: First, *metaphor* and *symbol* need to be defined rather carefully in this context, both in their distinction and their relationship. A metaphor is a purely linguistic phenomenon, and it does not denote a physical, biological, or even psychological or social reality. It is a tensive way of using language to evoke meaning that cannot be expressed by literal or denotative language. A metaphor is tensive because it involves, simultaneously, an "is" and an "is not" that do not simply contradict or cancel each other out but mutually relativize, enrich, and fulfill each other.[26] For example, the statement that God is our Father is a metaphor. God *is* in some (nonliteral) way parental in relation to humans and therefore can be spoken of as father or mother but God *is not* literally a male who copulated with a female to produce humans as biological offspring. If we negate the "is" in the metaphor we lose

an important relational and affective dimension of our relationship to God, namely, that we are not merely objects created by God but somehow made in the image and likeness of
God as children are made human through generation by
human parents. If we negate the "is not" we fall into idolatry,
that is, making God in the image and likeness of the human
male, which leads directly into the divinization of the male
and the sacralization of patriarchy.[27]

Marriage, when evoked to describe the relationship
between Israel and Yahweh, between the Church and Christ,
or between the Religious and Jesus, is a metaphor. No matter
how vivid and erotic the language used by the mystics in
describing their relationship with Christ, none of them ever
suggested that she (or he) contracted a relation with Christ
that reserved him exclusively to her (as a husband is to his
wife), that they engaged in genital sexual intercourse, or that
they produced biological children.

Metaphors, however, are deeply rooted in symbols that are
not purely linguistic but that, as Paul Ricoeur so well
explained, operate on the frontier between extralinguistic
reality and language.[28] The symbol has one foot in each world,
as it were, and therefore mediates between that which transcends the symbol but is somehow embodied in it and those
who relate to the transcendent through and in the symbol.
The transcendent touches the world through the symbol and
the world reaches toward the transcendent through the symbol. Symbol is the mediational nexus between the finite and
the transcendent. For example, when ancient people wor-
shiped the sun they were experiencing the sun as symbol of
the Creator's power in the universe. The sun, which actually
gives the warmth and light that enables life, is not the Creator
pure and simple (i.e., God) but so participates in and mediates
the life-giving action of God in relation to the people that in
worshiping the sun they are actually worshiping God who
transcends both the sun and the people. The best example we
have of symbol in this strong sense is our own bodies. We are
not reducible to our bodies, but the reality of the persons we

are is mediated not only to others but even to ourselves through our bodies and it is only through our bodies (and their extensions in action, language, etc.) that we can interact with reality that is not ourselves.

Symbols give rise to metaphors, to the tensive language that evokes meaning beyond what literal language can express. When I embrace someone I am engaging in symbolic behavior, using the symbol of bodily contact to express the kind and degree of union with the other that I feel. Love poetry calls upon a vast repertoire of metaphors for embracing to evoke the reality of unitive love. In short, the reality (love) is experienced in the symbol (embracing), which is expressed in metaphors (*embrace* itself is a metaphor).

The *reality* that comes to expression in the *metaphor* of marriage to Jesus is union with God in faith through the glorified humanity of Christ. The *symbol,* the mediating reality that has one foot in the realm of human experience and the other in the humanity of Christ, and that gives rise to the nuptial metaphor, is virginity or sexual exclusivity for religious reasons. Marriage to Christ is a metaphor built on the analogy of virginity to monogamously faithful human marriage. Analogy is based on a perceived likeness in dissimilarity. In marriage the union of the spouses in love is symbolized by their sexual union in which the body-person of each is given to the spouse and, by monogamous fidelity, reserved from all others. In consecrated virginity the spousal union with Christ in love, which is realized in unitive prayer, is symbolized by the sexual reserve of the virgin's body-person from all others. The exclusivity of spousal love, in both cases, is not an exclusion of others from one's life or one's love—indeed it should open a person to more universal love—but an exclusion of others from that total access to one's self that sexual union symbolically achieves and expresses. I will explore below, in some detail, the richness of the nuptial metaphor of the symbol of virginity, but the point here is that the nuptial language is metaphorical. It is not the only way to express this experience though it is the most natural and adequate. The symbol, however, of sexual exclusivity or virginity is directly related to, arises out of, the reality of a particular experience of union with Christ.

 2. *Virginity as challenge to patriarchy:* Second, it is important to note the *protofeminist* character of virginity within Religious Life and the role of the marital metaphor in legitimating and expressing this character. Because marriage has been, from long before the birth of Christianity, a patriarchal institution and since virtually all of the treatises on Christian virginity were authored by males writing predominantly about women, feminists have been highly suspicious that a dominative agenda lurks in male interpretation of female religious experience in marital terms. This concern is certainly logical on the basis of feminist experience, but I think it is, in this case, actually mistaken.

 When virginity, virtually unknown as a personal choice in the Empire of the first century,[29] was embraced, for explicitly religious reasons, by first- and second-generation Christian women, their choice was seen as a dangerous challenge to patriarchal social structures of both family and state.[30] Women who declared themselves unavailable as reproductive agents to carry on the family name, seal interfamily alliances, or provide the future citizens of the Empire because they were "married to Christ" were refusing not only their species role but also their assigned social role as property of men and state. So radical was their action in the eyes of men that many women paid for it with their lives. Feminists have often objected to the designation of early Christian women saints as "virgin and martyr," but this bears reexamination.[31] The large number of heroic women who gave their lives for their faith during the early persecutions (and thus share with men the glorious title of martyr) included the married as well as the unmarried.[32] But some of the latter were not simply unmarried; they were virgins by profession. And their offense against the state was not only that they professed Christ (and refused to worship the emperor or observe the rituals of the state religion) but also that they refused to marry and bear children. Thus they are not simply "virgin martyrs," that is, martyrs who happened to be unmarried at the time they were executed, but women who had chosen an exclusive relationship with Christ and whose physical intactness was therefore the social symbol of the integrity of their faith which grounded such a relationship. The nuptial metaphor was an apt linguistic expression of this reality. *Virginity,* in other words, was not a negative term or privative condition, much less a denigration of the marriages of their sisters in the faith. It was a positive state of life which these women embraced with such passion that they were ready to die rather than renounce it.

The choice of virginity was so radical partly because it signified an assumption of personal autonomy by women that was extremely rare in the sociocultural world of the early Christian movement.[33] These women (and men) reserved their persons, symbolized by the reserving of their sexuality, from the ownership and control of patriarchal power. They withdrew from the control of their fathers, refused to become the property of husbands, and denied to the state their reproductive potential. While it seems historically unlikely that these women were thinking in terms of establishing personal autonomy in relation to men, much less subverting patriarchy as a social system (which is why I call it protofeminist rather than feminist, which I think would be anachronistic), they were in fact giving absolute priority to their own spiritual agenda in the face of overwhelming pressure to the contrary. They were abundantly clear, through the use of the nuptial metaphor, about their motivation. These virgins refused to marry because, in their experience, they were already married—to Christ. And marriage was by nature lifelong and exclusive. For one called to consecrated virginity to accept a human husband was, purely and simply, infidelity to Christ.

It is also important to recall, as we saw earlier, that the institutional Church has, from the very beginning with St. Paul, refused any attempt to suggest that baptism implied, much less required, virginity. Marriage was always regarded, at least among orthodox teachers of the faith, as perfectly compatible with the ideal of Christian belonging to Christ, although this theological position has not always been honored in the literature of spirituality or the attitudes of pastors.[34] In other words, the women who chose virginity as a state of life were not forced into it. It was a freely chosen path in response to what some Christians experienced as a personal vocation. Men as well as women chose virginity but, as far as we can tell from the extant literature, it was a predominantly feminine phenomenon.[35] This may be due more to the unusualness of women taking such initiative in the disposition of their own lives than to the actual proportion of women to men.[36] However, given that women Religious have continued throughout most of Christian history to outnumber men Religious there is some reason to suspect that virginity has some particular attraction for women. The subjective experience of virginity as symbolic marriage to Christ, a symbol much more natural for women than for men,[37] might have something to do with this phenomenon. In any case, my point here is that the marital metaphor as well as the unitive experience symbolically mediated by the choice of virginity is not only not the patriarchal imposition of men but is a powerful example of female autonomy and self-possession.

3. Scriptural basis of the nuptial metaphor for virginity: Third, and finally, the discourse on Christian virginity in nuptial terms is not an invention of an erotically overheated romantic imagination but is *scripturally based* in the Song of Songs of the Hebrew Bible and the continuation of the covenantal theme in the New Testament. The Song of Songs is a remarkable Old Testament book, the only one (with the exception of Esther in Hebrew) in which the name of God does not occur. There is relative scholarly consensus that the book's material was originally a collection of secular love songs, and for centuries Jewish scholars debated whether it belonged in the Bible at all. However, when its canonical place in the Bible was finally secured, Rabbi Aquiba (c. 135 C.E.) declared that the Song of Songs was the "holy of holies" of Scripture. It was admitted into the canon precisely because it was interpreted, which in rabbinic hermeneutical theory meant recognized as, the "love song" of the covenant union between Yahweh and Israel.[38] It is remarkable that this text, which was not originally about God or even about marriage, should become the canonical scriptural locus of discourse about the deep mystery of the union of God and humanity. Human love in all its ecstatic intensity, sensual bodiliness, and self-transcending dynamism is the symbol of that union, and the language of human love is its metaphorical expression.

Throughout the history of Christian interpretation of the Song of Songs, beginning with Origen's commentary around 240 C.E., it has been regarded as the love song of human-divine intimacy. Phyllis Trible in her feminist exploration of the rhetoric of sexuality in the Old Testament[39] traces the trajectory of the understanding of sexuality from the story of the creation in equality of male and female in the Garden of Eden and their fall into the pattern of domination/subordination by sin, through the patriarchal ups and downs of Israel's life and legislation, to its culmination in mutuality restored celebrated in the Song of Songs. It is no wonder that the mystics of the Christian tradition, those most developed lovers of God, have found in it the scriptural description of their own experience and the linguistic repertoire for voicing it. Although it was men, notably Origen, Bernard, and John of the Cross, who wrote the treatises, homilies, and commentaries on the Song of Songs, women mystics recognized it as their own biblical homeland. The writings of the women mystics (e.g., Gertrude of Helfta, Catherine of Siena, Teresa of Avila) are filled with references to and quotations from the Song. This recourse to the Song of Songs, like the preference among the mystics for the Gospel of John with its strong background music from it,[40] is not fortuitous. Certain biblical texts are gold mines of expression for certain spiritual experiences. Luther's reliance on Paul, liberation theology's recourse to Exodus and the Prophets, and the Roman Church's preference for Matthew are testimony to the diversity of spiritual experience. My point here is that the role of the nuptial metaphor in the discourse on virginity is not the personal idiosyncrasy of some individual writers or the unconscious overflow of the repressed sexuality of cloistered females. It is not, in the first instance, a tool of patriarchal oppression (although it has been used for this purpose). It is a biblically based discourse about what is most central to the experience of consecrated virginity, the unitive relationship with Christ to the exclusion of all other primary life commitments.

Two characteristics of the Song of Songs, to which we will return in greater detail in the next section, need to be pointed out here. First, in the Song the voices of the male and female lovers when they are exalting each other and expressing their love are sometimes even difficult to distinguish.[41] They use nearly identical terms of praise, longing, endearment, satiety, and rest in relation to each other. Usually the circumstances, reference to another person, form of address, or evocation of some social convention or geographical detail, as well as the gender in Hebrew, alerts the reader to the gender of the speaker. But in their intimate exchanges they are so one that the patriarchal markers of domination and subordination that usually distinguish male and female discourse respectively have vanished.[42] In fact, as Trible points out, "Of the three speakers, the woman is the most prominent. She opens and closes the entire Song, her voice dominant throughout. By this structural emphasis her equality and mutuality with the man is illuminated."[43]

Second, although the language is intensely erotic and certainly suggests the physical union of the lovers as well as an indestructible commitment that implies marriage, there is actually no unmistakable mention of marriage or of children even though translators and commentators often supply headings indicating that the female lover is the "bride" or even that the male lover is "spouse." The language of husband and wife, redolent of patriarchal marriage, is absent from the text. This is a love in which society's requirements, economic and political interests, and even the practicalities of family agenda play no intrinsic role. It is love for love's sake,[44] not so much a social contract as a passionate union of hearts that is its own reason for being:

> Set me as a seal on your heart,
>   as a seal on your arm;
> For stern as death is love,
>   relentless as the nether world is devotion;
>   its flames are a blazing fire.
> Deep waters cannot quench love,
>   nor floods sweep it away.
> Were one to offer all he [sic] owns to purchase love,
>   he would be roundly mocked. (Song of Songs 8:6–7)[45]

The nuptial metaphor for the union of the People with God in the Song of Songs is repeatedly taken up in the New Testament (e.g., Mt 9:15; 25:1–13; Jn 3:29 and elsewhere; 2 Cor 11:2; Eph 5:23–32; Rev 19:7 ff. and 21:9 ff.) where it is applied especially to the relation of Christ to the new People of God, the Church. It was thus a natural biblical locus for those individuals in the community who gave themselves exclusively to Christ in consecrated virginity. It became the primary scriptural referent for the great treatises on virginity of the fourth and fifth centuries.[46] Therefore, in trying to rehabilitate this metaphor to speak of the unitive/mystical motivation for consecrated celibacy today I am not breaking new ground but attempting to restore to Religious the primary scriptural resource for understanding and articulating this vocation. In doing so, however, we must be extremely sensitive to the underside of that tradition, namely its use in the context of patriarchal marriage and Church structures to sacralize the subordination of women by and to men.[47]

B. The Nuptial Metaphor as Resource

In what follows I do not intend to suggest that all Religious *do* or *should* experience their vocation or their celibacy in terms of consecrated virginity articulated by the nuptial metaphor. I want to explore in some depth what that metaphor contributes, or can contribute, to the self-understanding of Religious who do experience it that way. My primary resource is the self-revelation of mystics who used this metaphor extensively and Scripture which validates that use.

1. Totality and exclusivity: The nuptial metaphor as it functions in the ancient treatises on virginity and in mystical literature is almost always used of the relation of the person not to God but to Christ, emphasizing the deeply human character of the relationship. The person (often spoken of, especially by male writers, as "the soul") experiences herself in an intimate relationship with the glorified human being, Jesus. The relationship is qualified by an absolute totality of self-gift going both ways. A frequently invoked scriptural text is Song 6:3, "My lover belongs to me and I to him." Sometimes the genders are reversed and the text is addressed by Jesus to his human lover. Her life revolves around this relationship from which everything else derives and to which everything is directed.

The passion of the personal attachment to Jesus, which relativizes even such important aspects of Religious commitment as ministry and community, has the character of spousal love, which is indeed a form of friendship but has a particular quality to it that other friendships do not. Only to the spouse does one say, unequivocally and unconditionally, in merismatic extremes that are intended to encompass all that can be foreseen and all that is hidden in the mysterious future, "For better or for worse, in riches and in poverty, in sickness and in health" I belong to you as you to me.

The totality of the marital self-gift is expressed in the bodily symbol of sexual exclusivity. No one else has the access to the body-person of the spouse that is reserved for the Beloved. Although it is experientially clear what this means it is difficult to express it in such a way that it is not misunderstood. As already noted, the deepest and healthiest human loves turn both partners outward in ever-widening circles of inclusion. Marital love that totally absorbs both partners in their unique "twosome" is neurotic and ultimately growth-stunting, as is a "Jesus and I" spirituality that does not embrace the whole Christ and indeed the whole world. In fact, one of the most consistent and powerful motifs in the mystical literature is the insistent call of the mystic from contemplative solitude with Jesus into the service of Christ in his members.

Catherine of Siena, of whom one author wrote, "Her life was a miracle of inclusion" and her confessor Raymond of Capua said, "Catherine carried the whole church in her heart," is perhaps the paradigm of this feature of nuptial spirituality.[48] After three years of intense solitary prayer, during which she experienced herself mystically espoused to Christ who placed an invisible ring on her finger, Catherine saw Jesus one day not within her cell but just outside the door telling her to come out. His famous revelation to her, "The service you cannot do to me you must render your neighbors," initiated the youthful Religious (Catherine was a Third Order or active Dominican) who had just turned twenty into thirteen years of the most intense ministry in the fields of spiritual direction, social work and nursing, the reform of the clergy, and ecclesiastical and civil politics.

The exclusivity of the spousal relationship is the very source of its active fertility. Mystics often use the analogy of conception and childbirth to speak of this (pro)creative dimension of their marital relationship with Christ. The nuptial metaphor well expresses this feature of fruitfulness in exclusivity. Both married people in relation to their spouses and virgins in relation to Christ express outwardly the exclusivity of the relationship by reserving to the Beloved their creative capacity in the symbol of sexual fidelity.

The totality of the spousal relationship is also expressed and symbolized by its perpetuity. As the body itself is a zone of totality, the physical boundary of the self, so is the time span of one's life. It is all the life one has, whether it is the twenty-four years of Thérèse of Lisieux or the sixty-seven of Teresa of Avila. To give all of the life/time one has is, symbolically (i.e., really), to give the whole of oneself. Only to the spouse does one say, unequivocally and unconditionally, "until death," or "for the rest of my life." Just as sexual exclusivity is not a legal obligation but is an expression of marital fidelity, so perpetuity is not an external requirement but an internal exigency. It is inconceivable, even to one who is realistic about her own and the spouse's limitations and the vicissitudes of life, to set a temporal limit to the gift of self in marriage. For the person called to virginity, as for the person engaged to her fiancé, the longing to say "forever" is intrinsic to the call itself.

2. *Equality and Mutuality:* Feminist consciousness, as we have already noted, engenders a realistic suspicion about the use of the nuptial metaphor, especially by women in relation to a male Christ, because it evokes patriarchal marriage involving the possession and subordination of a woman for male purposes. Obviously, not all marriages are patriarchal, but patriarchal marriage is still the normative pattern in our society. It was virtually the only pattern throughout the many centuries during which the literature of nuptial spirituality developed.

The metaphor of marriage to Christ, like that of the fatherhood of God, is a two-edged sword. If the metaphor is literalized (i.e., if the "is not" is suppressed) one does indeed import into one's relationship with Christ or with God the patriarchal divinization of maleness and the sacralization of oppression. But if the linguistic tension of the metaphor is sustained (i.e., if the "is not" is kept active) the spiritual reality of divine partnership or parenthood becomes a powerful critique, subverting the patriarchal human reality and drawing a person into the divine ideal to which the human relationship is oriented. It is striking that women who have renounced marriage in response to a call from Christ have so often spontaneously seen that call as a marriage proposal by him. They were not instructed or forced to use this metaphor; it was the one that fit their experience. And it spoke to them of nobility and dignity, not of subordination. This is a highly suggestive witness to the possibility that a nonpatriarchal understanding of marriage itself is divinely normative, and the patriarchal human pattern is the deformation of the "original design." This is precisely what feminist exegesis of the creation account in Genesis suggests: that female subordination in marriage is not the expression of the divine will but the result of human sin.[49]

True marriage is a special, in fact a unique, kind of friendship and the *conditio sine qua non* of friendship, according to most philosophers who have written on the subject as well as the poets who have hymned it, is equality. As Aristotle explained, if the two friends are not equal by natural circumstances then the one better endowed must render the "inferior" equal by sharing all with the friend.[50] Sharing, in fact, of everything one possesses is the mark of friendship. Aelred of Rievaulx, following Cicero, defined spiritual friendship as "agreement on both human and divine affairs, combined with good will and mutual esteem."[51] What is unique about the friendship that is marriage is that the sharing is not limited to the areas in which the friendship operates but embraces the entire life of both partners, their material resources, their decisions and choices, their futures, even their bodies and the process and results of reproduction.

This would seem to render the nuptial metaphor for the union of the virgin and Christ a bit of pious make-believe because, in starkest terms, Jesus is divine and the virgin is human. There is an ontological inequality that can never be "remedied." It is greater than that which made Aristotle doubt the possibility of perfect friendship between a man and a woman because her natural inferiority to him makes complete mutuality impossible.[52] However, this is one of the real contributions of nuptial spirituality to Christian revelation, namely, its "unpacking" in the experience of the mystic of Jesus' amazing overcoming of this inequality.[53]

Jesus says to his disciples, on the very eve of giving his life for them, "I no longer call you slaves [inferiors]....I have called you friends [equals], because I have told you all that I have heard from my Father. It was not you who chose me, but I who chose you...." (Jn 15:15–16). In John's Gospel Jesus' "seeing and hearing" in the bosom of God (cf. Jn 1:18) is precisely what distinguishes him from all other humans. He alone came forth from God and he knows where he came from; he speaks and does only what he hears and sees in God (cf. Jn 8:28–30). Consequently, when Jesus tells his disciples that he has told them "all" that he has heard from his Father he is saying that he shares with them all that he has received from God, all that he is, all that makes him ontologically their "master and lord," which they correctly recognize him to be (cf. Jn 13:13). Jesus remains the vine and his disciples the branches (cf. Jn 15:1–10), but the distinction is reduced from one of superiority and separation to one of origin, of giving rise in them by the gift of his own Spirit to what is uniquely his by nature. Jesus' disciples are now born of God, born from above, as Jesus is (cf. Jn 1:12–13; 3:5–8; 17:16; 20:17). He has made those who are his ontological "inferiors" his equals, his sisters and brothers, his friends.[54]

One of the most striking, not to say startling, features of the literature of nuptial spirituality is the sense of equality with Jesus that the mystics express. John of the Cross is perhaps the supreme theologian of this equality, but his theological precision gives way to lyricism, especially in *The Living Flame of Love*. For example, John says, in 3, 6, that the divine Bridegroom

> loves you with supreme humility and esteem and makes you his equal, gladly revealing himself to you in these ways of knowledge, in this his countenance filled with graces, and telling you in this his union, not without great rejoicing: "I am yours and for you [note the variation on and reversal of the gender roles of Song 6:3] and delighted to be what I am so as to be yours and give myself to you."

Later in section 8, he writes:

> All that can be said of this stanza [he is commenting on the poem, *The Living Flame of Love*] is less than the reality, for the transformation of the soul in God is indescribable. Everything can be expressed in this statement: The soul becomes God from God through participation in him and in his attributes, which it terms the "lamps of fire."[55]

Some of the most delightful examples of this equality and mutuality occur in Teresa of Avila, who structured her great spiritual masterpiece, *The Interior Castle,* on the nuptial metaphor, the soul's progress from courtship to betrothal to marriage. The theme of mutuality emerged charmingly in her famous complaint to Christ about the hardships of one of her journeys in connection with her foundations. Jesus replied that that was how he treated his real friends. Teresa replied, "Then it's no wonder you have so few of them!"[56] But one of the most beautiful expressions of the parallel growth of intimacy and mutuality is Teresa's progressive name changes. When she entered Carmel she kept her family name "de Ahumada," her title to "honor" as an upper-class Spaniard. After her second conversion, when she began the reform of the Order, she changed her name to "Teresa of Jesus." Toward the end of her life she heard her Beloved, one afternoon, ask her, "Who are you?" and she replied "I am Teresa of Jesus, and who are you?" She heard the reply, "I am Jesus—of Teresa."[57]

Equally tender and powerful examples can be found in Gertrude of Helfta who frequently addresses Jesus as "dearest," and hears him reply to her with the same address.[58] In one of her revelatory experiences Gertrude says to Christ, "from east to west, from south to north, I know that there is nothing which could please me and refresh both body and soul apart from you" and he replies, "in virtue of my divinity, I assure you that I have no desire to find delight in any creature apart from you."[59] Not only does the nuptial metaphor not sacralize patriarchal inequality; it encourages the appropriation of a remarkable equality and mutuality with Christ in love and in ministry.

3. Historicity in relationship: In the 1950s, at the height of the biblical theology movement, a French scholar wrote a significant article on the theme of the covenant between Yahweh and Israel and its metaphorical vehicle, marriage.[60] Feminist scholars had not yet fully developed the critique, which has since become so important, namely, that the marital metaphor for the covenant is based on patriarchal marriage and demonizes women and women's sexuality.[61] In the Old Testament God is always the male spouse, Israel the female spouse. The initiative in the Covenant, of course, is God's. God sets the terms that Israel must accept if she is to live. God is ever faithful, Israel constantly going astray. And her sinfulness, her idolatry, is cast as adultery. All of this reflects, and attributes to God, the superiority and impunity of husbands in a patriarchal society while equating Israel, who is a favorite "son" when "he" is faithful (cf. Hos 11!), with a "harlot" when "she" is unfaithful.

Adultery, then as now, was far more characteristic of husbands than of wives, but only wives paid for it with their lives, which is graphically reflected in the story of the woman taken in adultery in John 7:53–8:11.[62] Male adultery, even if reprehensible, was not equated with idolatry, but idolatry was equated with female adultery. The use of the marital metaphor is sometimes achingly beautiful, as in Hosea where the aggrieved husband does not repudiate his unfaithful wife (which was his right under the Law) but yearns for her, calls her back, rehabilitates her, and revives the love of their youth (cf. Hos 3). But it has to be admitted that the social context in which this metaphor developed hardly permitted it to express the kind of equality and mutuality that we find in the mystics' use of it.

Néher correctly pointed out in his article that the inequality and subordinationist complementarity that is the subtext in the Old Testament use of the metaphor and that feminists rightly highlight (as we must the latent and overt anti-Judaism in the New Testament text or the condoning of slavery or war in both testaments) is not intrinsic to the idea or the ideal of marriage, however much it has perverted it from time immemorial. But the most significant contribution of his article was his reflection on why the marriage metaphor was uniquely apt for expressing the covenant reality.

Néher pointed out that, unlike other friendships, marriage has a unique "historical" dimension that is intrinsic to and conditioning of the relationship. It is a relationship freely entered, unlike, for example, that between parent and child. And no matter what eventually happens, marriage is forever in the intention of the spouses at its inception. It is a relationship that must develop over time. Normal ups and downs, tragic failures and soaring self-transcendence, conflicts and passionate love, are built into the fabric of this relationship. It is worked out bit by bit as the spouses learn to know each other in every possible way through deliberate self-revelation and the unintended revelation of shared daily life. The intention of perpetuity creates a context, a climate, in which simply walking away when things become difficult or the rewards seem to go one way and the responsibilities the other, is not even a theoretical possibility. No other relationship, even though all friendships intend permanence, has this historicity built into it by expressed exchange of vows or oaths.

This feature has also been very influential in the nuptial understanding of Religious virginity. Until modern times the solemn vow of virginity, like Christian marriage, which admitted of no divorce, was considered intrinsically incapable of dispensation. This intransigence has wreaked a certain amount of vocational havoc, as has the absolute indissolubility of marriage, but my focus here is on the unique contribution of the historical factor to the spiritual growth of people consecrated to Christ in virginity. As already discussed in chapter 3, many people who have lived together without marrying have discovered there is an instability woven into the very fabric of a commitment that will not speak its name in the public forum. Each problem is potentially a crisis. It raises the question, for one partner or the other, of whether this is the point beyond which one cannot go, the time to abandon a relationship that is not working and to which one is not actually bound, or whether they can, at least one more time, find a way. For the married person who takes her or his vows seriously it is a foregone conclusion that they will find a way, not just one more time but as many times as they have to, because walking away is not part of the relationship's repertoire of strategies.

There is, in my opinion, a qualitative difference between the nuptial experience of Religious virginity and the permanent commitment to celibacy made for the sake of ministry or community on precisely this point. In the former case abandoning the commitment to virginity is not a real possibility, whether or not membership in one's congregation remains viable or one's ministerial commitment continues to be meaningful or even possible. Religious profession, for the person who experiences it in nuptial terms, is not primarily a commitment to a group or to a ministry or even to a way of life. It is the inauguration of a state of life constituted by a personal relationship with Christ that is, finally, independent of all the conditions that qualify it and contextualize it or flow from it.

Sometimes people ask Religious how they persevere in a state of life within a Church whose institutional corruption is so clear to them and in which they may even be the objects of unjust persecution. Whatever answer they give, often the real reason is that Religious Life is not, for them, a commitment to an institution but a relationship with Christ that, in the final analysis, no authority can touch. There is a stunning passage in Gertrude of Helfta's mystical treatise, *The Herald of Divine Love*, that illustrates this point.[63] Her monastery had been placed under interdict by ecclesiastical authorities trying to force the community into submission on a financial matter, so the nuns were deprived of Communion. Gertrude prays:

> How are you going to console us, most gracious Lord, in our present trial? The Lord replied, "I shall increase my pleasure in you. Just as the bridegroom can take more pleasure in the bride in private than in public, so likewise your sighs and desolation will be my pleasure. The love you have for me will be increased in you, just as pent-up fire burns more extensively."

And a bit later in the same chapter Gertrude prays:

> Shall you, most loving Lord, suffer us, your members, to be cut off from you by the excommunication which those who are trying to rob us of our goods inflict on us? To which the Lord said: "If anyone is able to take from me the very marrow of my bones—for so closely do you cleave to me—let him cut you off from me. This excommunication which has been imposed on you will do you no more harm than would someone trying to cut you with a wooden knife, which cannot penetrate at all, but only leave some slight impression made by its blade."

This calm inward assurance of her union with Christ being basically untouched, no matter how much suffering the institutional Church imposed on her, is echoed in other writers and has been experienced by mystics, male and female, down through the ages. It is not a contempt for the Church as institution but a realistic, and very strengthening, evaluation of the relativity of the human element in the Church. Paradoxically, by not being overly influenced by the institution the mystics are able to sustain a profound love for the Church as the body of Christ, which they do not confuse with its caretakers, and even a compassion for the authorities whose exaggerated self-importance is causing the suffering. The historical dimension of the nuptial experience of virginity makes fidelity both very practical and at the same time transcendent, enabling the virgin, although hurt by persecution, to be undeflected from Christ's concerns.

4. *Contemplative prayer:* Consecrated virginity lives from contemplative prayer the way any marriage does from the communication between the spouses. All friendships depend on mutual sharing and friends long to be together. But in some friendships the form of communication may be primarily in the sharing of commitments, projects, or interests and in others in the group context in which the friendship was born and is nourished. A marriage, however, no matter how important shared concerns including the raising of the couple's children may be, depends ultimately on the quality of direct, self-revelatory interchange between the spouses, which may take many forms from the verbal to the sexual. The Religious who experiences her vocation primarily in terms of the nuptial metaphor has a need for regular and prolonged prayer beyond the liturgical and community prayer that may be part of her congregational lifestyle.

In preconciliar times this posed particular problems for Religious in mobile ministerial congregations. Members of such congregations put in a more-than-eight-hour workday, usually at least six and often six and a half days a week, and also followed a full monastic horarium of office, meditation, Mass, *Lectio Divina,* examen, adoration of the Blessed Sacrament, common meals and community recreation, as well as mandatory devotions such as rosary and stations of the cross and community vocal prayers. They also took full care of their convents (and

sometimes partial care of their institutions), which seldom had
even a cook and virtually never a housekeeper. Vacations, if they
existed at all, were brief and infrequent and often involved only
partial mitigation of the horarium.

Hungry for unregulated, silent, personal prayer, many Religious lived for retreats, days of recollection, and liturgical
feasts (all of which were themselves highly regulated), which
provided some time for solitude and contemplative prayer.
The daily silence in most Religious houses offered at least the
possibility of recollection during work and meals, and a surprising number of Religious could be found in chapel before
common prayer in the morning and after night prayers in the
evening or during their lunchtime or break periods.

This situation has changed enormously and in the right
direction in the wake of the Council. With great relief, most
congregations put aside the monastic prayer pattern, modified or suppressed the common horarium, gave much greater
latitude to individuals in the choice of their prayer styles and
times, encouraged members to make the kinds of retreats that
they found helpful, and promoted education and renewal in
the spiritual life. Although Religious, like their secular counterparts in the first world, still often work too much and too
hard, there is serious encouragement in many congregations
of a more balanced lifestyle, with adequate provision for rest,
vacation, educational renewal, and especially cultivation of
the spiritual life. Retreats and spiritual direction are expected
to be part of the lifestyle of all Religious.

Not all of the tensions around prayer that have emerged from
the individualization of the spiritual life of Religious have been
resolved. Some people need much more common prayer,
others more solitary prayer, and for some praying is a constant
struggle that arises primarily out of ministerial involvement. But
for the Religious whose spirituality is best articulated in nuptial
terms, solitude and contemplative prayer are as essential as air.
Her vocation cannot survive without it any more than a marriage can survive without quality time for the spouses to be with
each other. Deprived of contemplative prayer, her interior life

flattens out, her ministry becomes enervating and exhausting, and community participation can seem pointless.

These Religious might be less likely to express their need for or experience in prayer precisely because of the intimacy of the topic. But just as a happy married person witnesses to the quality of the marital relationship not by talking directly about it but by the energy and commitment that flow from the relationship into the rest of life, so joy, energy, ministerial effectiveness, and a capacity for deep relationships with others testify to the quality of prayer the Religious experiences. Prayer is the locus of that affectively fulfilling union with God in Christ that is the substance of her life.

Just as it is clearly not the case that all Religious experience their relationship to Christ in nuptial terms it is also the case that nothing that has been said in this section on the nuptial spirituality of virginity is exclusive to Religious. Catherine of Genoa, a married woman, gave powerful expression to her mystical experience in nuptial terms.[64] The themes of union, including transformation in Christ, participation in the divine nature, becoming a member of the Body of Christ, living as a branch in Christ the vine, being Jesus' sister or brother through participating in Jesus' filiation, apply to all the baptized. All are called to union with Christ that involves a deep sharing of life with him. What the mystics contribute to our understanding of this profound reality is the working out in their own experience, at the level of feeling as well as faith, of the implications of this calling. And as they do so they appeal again and again to the only metaphor that seems to embrace simultaneously all the aspects of that relationship, namely, the nuptial metaphor. While there is evidently a particular affinity between the choice of consecrated celibacy for the sake of the Reign of God and the type of spirituality I have been describing, and the literature of the history of spirituality seems to witness to that affinity, this claim in no way limits the experience to Religious. St. Paul even says to the whole Church at Corinth, "I have betrothed you to one husband to present you as a chaste virgin to Christ" (2 Cor 11:2), referring not so much to the union of love as to the exclusivity of their faith, which he felt was being threatened by some interlopers who were subverting Paul's message. The point is that the nuptial metaphor carries certain distinctive features of the God-human relationship and in the case of some people, notably many Religious who have vowed perpetual celibacy, expresses their spirituality in a vivid and powerful way.

CHAPTER SIX
CELIBACY AND "FAMILY"

I. Introduction

In the previous two chapters we have been concerned with consecrated celibacy in itself, that is, as the distinctive charismatic feature of Religious Life, and with its recontextualization, that is, its relation to the feminist consciousness of contemporary culture and the repercussions of this new situation on the spirituality of celibacy. In these two chapters I want to engage two aspects of celibacy that are both most obvious and least discussed (a virtual definition of the "elephant in the living room"!) among Religious. I suspect the topics will be highly controversial but, as in relation to other topics broached in this volume and its predecessor, it is part of my agenda to raise the questions about Religious Life that have become apparent only since, and because of, the breakdown of the insulating total institution context and the resultant interaction of Religious Life with mainstream cultural developments.

I would hypothesize that for most Religious who are women the primary personal and psychological impact of lifelong commitment to consecrated celibacy is experienced not in terms of genital abstinence as such but in terms of the renunciation and sublimation of the entire affective complex that I am subsuming under the rubrics of "family" and "home." I have placed the terms in quotation marks (which I will not continue to do unless the context could be confusing) in order to emphasize that I am not talking merely, nor even primarily, of biological kinship relationships or physical location but of a whole complex of relational realities connected to the human experience of "family" and "home." These experiences begin by birth into a biological family and unfold in some physical location. Therefore, in some ways family continues to function as a normative metaphor for whatever affective arrangements structure adult life and home as the metaphor for the context of these relationships. Although the two topics are intimately interrelated, for the purpose of clarity the primary focus of reflection in this chapter will be family and of the next chapter home.

II. The Problematic of "Family" in Relation to Religious Life

A. The Renunciation of Primary and Secondary Family

The parameters of the problematic can be sketched in terms of what sociologists call primary and secondary family. The primary family is the family of origin, the family into which one is born. The secondary family is the family one founds through marriage and/or reproduction. Obviously, both terms are problematized today by cultural reconfigurations of kinship relationships. What constitutes the primary family of a child abandoned or given for adoption at birth? Or of a child whose parents are divorced, especially if they are remarried? Or of a child raised by grandparents or others who may be related but are not the parents? Is the primary family the extended group or the nuclear unit? What role does blood relationship play in establishing the primary family, especially if the blood kin are estranged for some reason or even entirely unknown? And the same complexities, mutatis mutandis, attend the notion of secondary family. Suspension or cessation of parental rights, foster parenting and adoption, donor pregnancy and surrogate motherhood, in vitro fertilization, blended families, and other situations make the seemingly straightforward definition of secondary family as those related by marriage and/or through generation much less clear or even useful than it might have been in primal societies or on the American frontier.

But, prescinding for the moment from these complexities, it is safe to say that everyone who finally enters Religious Life grew up in some affective context, whether positive or negative, blood-related or otherwise constructed. A person comes from some relational background which, for the moment, may be considered a primary family or family of origin. Entering Religious Life involves separation from that context, that is, leaving home. This was very clear and often very traumatic in preconciliar times. Many orders insisted on a radical severing of family connections by proscribing any revisiting of the family home. Even parents and siblings could be seen only in a semipublic setting on convent grounds. Religious often could not take part in family baptisms, weddings, graduations, anniversaries, birthdays, or holidays, and correspondence, written or telephonic, was rare and censored. The desperate homesickness of some new candidates was often dealt with only by denial, distraction, or exhortations to sacrificial self-transcendence. And the sense of humiliation and alienation of parents who found themselves suddenly cast in the role of "temptations" in relation to their own children whose vocations they had nurtured and blessed was, in general, ignored.

Because Religious were expected not to dwell, even imaginatively, on the families they had left behind for the sake of Christ and often were forbidden even to talk about them, many primary family issues were never dealt with and continued to play the dysfunctional role of unresolved personal conflict in the relational life of the adult Religious. Furthermore, especially in the era of greatest numerical expansion (the 1930s to 1960s) the prevailing myth about the primary family of the "typical" nun aggravated this situation. Vocation literature suggested that every candidate came from a highly functional, loving, two-parent, practicing Catholic family that prayed the rosary together every evening. The future nun was a good-looking, highly popular, intelligent, socially well-adapted, fun-loving high school student who had no real problems, personal or social. Church law and the particular law of many congregations closed admission to children born out of wedlock or into families marked by alcoholism or mental illness as well as to those who were adopted, physically challenged, or academically slow. In other words, everyone was encouraged to romanticize her family of origin or at least to deny, to herself and others, the dysfunctionality that was as much a part of the families of many Religious as it was of those of other members of society. The number of Religious women who were sexually, emotionally, and physically abused as children has only begun to emerge. Trying to deal with such repressed experience in adulthood, especially after compensatory dynamics have had decades to solidify, is a major personal and spiritual challenge for many Religious.

Today, as we will have occasion to discuss later, the problem is almost the reverse. Some candidates never really leave home even though they enter Religious Life, and some professed Religious have returned home without juridically leaving their congregations. In other words, the primary family, however defined or delimited, has remained or become again the primary affective context and horizon of their relational life. I will suggest below that, for a number of reasons, this is highly problematic for people who have made a lifelong commitment in consecrated celibacy.

The secondary family is the family one founds. If it was ever true that marriage constituted the only license for morally and/or socially acceptable sex, that is certainly no longer the case. While pre- or extramarital sex may be problematic for other reasons, its general acceptance in contemporary society does help establish that the compelling reasons for marrying have at least as much to do with relationships as with sex.

For most people, marriage is the primary locus of their generativity, which is the distinctive marker of adulthood.[1] In most cases this generativity takes the form of biological or adoptive parenthood. By founding a family and raising children a person builds her- or himself into the flow of history through descendents who carry on the family name and/or bloodline. In the secondary family one has the chance to replicate the good parenting one received or to do a better job of raising the next generation than one's family of origin did in one's own case.

Marriage is societally perceived as the definitive boundary between childhood and adulthood, which is why, at least in Western societies, there is an age requirement for lawful marriage. A person has to be capable of assuming adult responsibilities for oneself and one's offspring (which, of course, cannot be guaranteed by age) before one can legally marry. Until a person marries, her or his family status is that of being the offspring, that is, the child (biologically or legally) of someone else. The child is the end of the previous generation. By marrying the couple become the beginning of the next generation. At least in first-world culture married couples are generally not expected to live permanently with the parents of either partner but to establish their own home as soon as possible, to make their own decisions about reproduction, and to raise their children as they see fit (within the limits of the law).

Marriage, however, as Vatican II finally realized, is not uniquely or primarily about reproduction (although this is one of its vital purposes) but also and equally about the relationship between the spouses. For the vast majority of people marriage is the primary relationship of their adult lives. When it succeeds in being the unique form of friendship that mirrors the relationship of Christ and the Church (cf. Eph 5:33–34), it is a privileged path to holiness, a singular contribution to the life of the ecclesial community, a rich context for the nurture of children and/or others who come within the influence of the couple, and a powerful, sustaining source of effective commitment to the coming of the Reign of God. Above all it is a source of the deepest joy available to human beings, the sharing with another person of a truly faithful love that encompasses the whole of one's life not only temporally but emotionally, physically, and spiritually. Even a marriage that falls far short of the ideal will often be the best experience of true love that a person will have in this life.

The need of the human heart for this kind of love, this incentive to and sustaining of generativity, this accession to adult status in society, is very powerful, and renouncing it is an extremely serious choice, perhaps much more serious than the sacrifice of genital sexual expression which, after all, derives its deepest meaning and joy from the marital relationship rather than the other way around. Although understandable in view of the age of most preconciliar candidates, it was unfortunate that their preparation for this choice to forego the secondary family was often less thorough than the processing of separation from the primary family. Religious certainly knew that they were committing themselves to not getting married and therefore to not having sex or children. But for many, especially women, they discovered much later and had to face with little help the real psychological and spiritual meaning and the ramifications of the choice they made with minimal reflection in their teens. Sexual awakening often came much later in life for women and sometimes it occurred with frightening suddenness when they fell in love with a companion at university, in a renewal program, or in ministry. For some Religious it was only when they had had time to grow up themselves that they began to realize how deeply they longed for parenthood, to hold and nurture their own child. But since both falling in love and parenthood had presumably been definitively dealt with by making a vow of celibacy, Religious experiencing for the first time the surging emotional attraction to the founding of a family often felt isolated with these issues, which were simply not supposed to arise.

All of us are suspended between the reality of primary family (even if that means primarily not having had the experience of such a family) and the reality of secondary family (whether the one we found or the one we never found). No matter how ideal the former may have been, all of us carry into adulthood some negativity that will eventually require attention, and many carry enormous burdens. All of us must somehow deal with the responsibility of the family we found or the fact that we have not undertaken our "species role" as progenitors of the next generation. We are all built into history, and build history, by our participation in the relational network we call "family." The fact that this aspect of the vocation to celibacy has never received much explicit attention is perhaps astonishing, but it is more than time to redress the lack. People entering Religious Life today are not teenagers, are often sexually experienced, and are usually fairly sophisticated and articulate about the influence of family of origin. Some are hungry for the family they never had as they were passed among kin and nonkin as children and alienated as young adults. Others are ricocheting from failed experiments in relationship. And they come from a society that is preoccupied with the problem of family, a topic to which we will return shortly.

B. The Ambiguous Legacy of Preconciliar Religious Life Regarding Family

Certainly Religious Life was no more remiss in handling the theoretical and practical issues of family than American culture in general. The post–World War II years saw a widespread social conspiracy to romanticize the American family in such TV series as *Leave It to Beaver* and *Ozzie and Harriet.* But that does not diminish the need today to recognize the ambiguity of the legacy of this period within Religious Life. Three areas in particular, it seems to me, require attention.

First, as has been mentioned, the unintended but real violence of the separation of candidates from the primary family and the continued stringent repression of family relationships even beyond the time of formation had obvious advantages but some unrecognized disadvantages. Among the advantages was the fact that candidates were forced, immediately, to face the idealism of the life they were embracing, which would make other painful demands in the future, such as leaving beloved missions and communities. A young woman who walked out of her family home never to return, knowing that she might never again have a truly private conversation with her parents, that she would miss the weddings of her siblings, the baptisms of her nieces and nephews, and all the other significant events in the life of her family including, in many cases, the funerals of her parents, was experiencing an emotional baptism by fire that left her in no doubt about the seriousness of her vocation.

The clean break with primary family freed the candidate to undertake her new life with wholehearted attention. Ideally, she was not receiving conflicting messages from family on the one hand and formation personnel on the other. And since she was definitively separated from her biological family she had considerable motivation to forge strong ties with her new Religious "family." Later, when ministry called her to distant locations, she was not hampered by habits of spending vacations with her family or having to consider how her absence would affect the care of aging parents or the sensibilities of other family members. Psychologically, the serious Religious "left home," a transition that was emotional as well as physical and that, in our culture, is almost a prerequisite for adulthood.

Needless to say, not all Religious managed this transition and many found loopholes through which to avoid some of the implications of entrance. Some simply went into muted mourning from which they never really emerged and that found expression in romanticizing their ancestry or childhood parish or school (if not their actual family), narcissistic immaturity, or seeking parent-figures among superiors. But judging from the overall maturity level of Religious they did as well with the issues as their married counterparts. There was a wisdom in the tradition, traceable at least as far back as the desert movement in the fourth century, which took seriously the gospel injunction to leave home and family if one wanted to truly follow Christ, a subject we will revisit below.

On the other hand, the radical separation from the primary family was, in some respects, problematic. It was a kind of emotional "death" (well expressed in some reception or profession ceremonies by a symbolic burial ritual) that was supposed to occasion only supernatural joy and allowed no genuine grieving of the loss. Today we recognize that such repression is not healthy.

For those who entered from dysfunctional families there was no inquiry into possible escape motifs in their vocations or encouragement to face and deal with their painful history. Again, today we know that such experiences do not simply "fade away," but stay operative in unhealthy ways until they are faced and resolved. Problems with authority, anger, addiction, unhealthy relationships, and so on were often rooted in unresolved primary family dynamics.

Residual guilt at abandoning parents or very young siblings, sometimes abetted by parental reproaches, continued to haunt some Religious throughout their lives and in some cases, when renewed family contact was possible after the Council, led to obsessive overinvolvement in the primary family to the neglect of responsibilities in ministry and community.

Second, Religious congregations, especially at the local community level, took over many of the functions of the primary family. Even the social structure mimicked the family, with one superior, a "mother," who was charged with the maternal care of her subjects, and a group of "sisters" whose affective relationships were understood as those of siblings.[2] In a certain sense, there was one adult in each community presiding over a group of children. Only the superior made decisions about intracommunity affairs or exercised agency without permission. Immature "sibling rivalries" for the superior's attention and affection as well as for positions of trust or influence in ministry often surfaced in these situations.

Life in the community had many of the characteristics of a primary family. In some ways this was a boon, providing a relational context in which people could feel "at home" and expect understanding and support. But in a number of other ways it created an unrealistic world that suddenly collapsed in the aftermath of the Council, leaving many Religious unprepared for the real challenges of community life among adults who had renounced family in the ordinary sense of the word.[3]

The approval or disapproval of the superior, a quasi-parent in preconciliar convent communities, carried disproportionate weight and often impeded the development of a mature adult conscience as well as initiative and responsibility in community and ministry. All members were expected at all meals, prayers, and other functions, so that, effectively, no one had a private life, personal friends, or activities in which the whole "family" was not involved, a situation characteristic of small children but increasingly resisted by healthy adolescents and finally suspended by young adults. The celebration of liturgical and congregational feasts as well as the name days of members often took on a childhood character with emphasis on trifling gifts from "mother," excessive indulgence in candy or entertainment, and "surprises" or "treats" hardly normal among adults.

Much of this dropped away of its own accord when the regimentation of the life was abrogated during the conciliar renewal. But what became evident was that the pseudo-primary family convent culture had masked, in many ways, the real character of the free sacrifice of family, both primary and secondary, that Religious Life involves. Some Religious, probably with minimal reflection, quickly began to compensate for the loss with which they had never really dealt because it had been cloaked by the experience of the community as substitute "family." Now, there was no longer this pseudo-family to nurture and care for these Religious who, in many cases, had little experience of building community among adults. Some quickly "returned home," spending every weekend and holiday with their primary family. Others sought out families among those to whom they ministered within which to play the role of surrogate child or favored aunt. Others became engulfed in a kind of loneliness and disconnection that made them psychologically "abandoned children."

Third, the pseudo-family culture itself promoted a kind of infantilization at home that was in stark contrast to the generative maturity of most Religious in their ministries. The CEO of a hospital or the president of a college became, in the convent, a child asking for a tube of toothpaste or being "scolded" for being late for dinner. Or, even more confusing, the administrator of the ministry was also the superior in the convent and the members of the community were, therefore, colleagues and coworkers in ministry with someone who had virtually absolute quasi-parental authority over their lives in the convent.[4] The healthy distinction between professional and personal life that should help adults maintain perspective on both, to say nothing of healthy boundaries, was largely nonexistent. Many highly professional Religious experienced, on a day-to-day basis, the disorientation other adults do when they visit their parents and discover that the latter still consider them children who need to be told when to wear their mittens.

In short, the nonrecognition of the issue of family in society in general was aggravated in Religious Life by the unnatural and even violent break with the primary family, the disguising of the reality of the sacrifice of family by a convent culture that imitated, sometimes in unhealthy ways, the primary family, and the conflict-laden assigning to adult Religious of the roles of minors in the convent family and adult professionals in ministry.

C. The Spiritual and Prophetic Challenge of Consecrated Celibacy in a New Cultural Context

In the following two sections I want to propose a consideration of family in relation to consecrated celibacy from two perspectives, that of the spirituality of Religious themselves and that of the prophetic witness which the celibate approach to family, lived consciously in a fully adult manner, might offer in contemporary first-world culture.

1. The spiritual challenge of the renunciation of family: Throughout this chapter and the next I will be using the term *homelessness* to talk about the situation of those committed in consecrated celibacy. In this chapter my primary focus will be on the relationships themselves ("family") and in the next on the place or locale or context of intimate relationships ("home"). By *homelessness* I do not mean, of course, that Religious are physically "on the street," much less rootless or unrelated, unloved or unloving. Family and home, as I am using it here, is a place of definitive belonging, the physical and psychological place that is a child's by right of birth and an adult's by right of title (marriage, reproduction, purchase of property, etc.). The term has connotations of permanence, affective identification with the others in the household whether or not the household is located in a specific material place, and established right to live there. Thus, no matter how welcome a guest might be, that is, affectively related to the host, the guest is, by definition, not at home but precisely in the home of another. The person is not there by right and the stay, however long, is not definitive. Likewise, an inmate serving a life sentence is not at home in the prison even though he or she is there definitively because there is no affective identification with the place or the people and being there is not the free exercise of a right. A prison population, in other words, is not a family or community. Finally, even if a person is affectively related with the members of the family unit and all involved hope the person's presence will be permanent, if the person has no real right to be there (as might be the case with an unadopted child for whom the family is caring) the person is not really at home. Jesus made the distinction between the slave and the son, both of whom were permanent parts of the ancient household but only one of whom, the son, had a right to be there permanently (cf. Jn 8:35). I am going to suggest that Religious are no longer children, either of their primary family or of their congregation, and that they have freely renounced the establishment of a secondary family, that is, the creation of a family and home of their own. In this sense, Religious are "homeless" both in terms of relationships and of permanent, physical affective context.

Like Jesus, who seems to have had a home base in Capernaum and who obviously had a marvelous capacity to be at home, in the psychological sense, with intimate friends as well as with recent acquaintances, but who nevertheless said of himself, "The Son of Man has nowhere to lay his head" (Mt 8:20; Lk 9:58), Religious are called to be at home in many places but, in fact, to have no "home and family of their own."

Again, I am not suggesting that a healthy community is not a positive affective setting for its members. Community members should indeed feel at home among their fellow Religious and/or others with whom they live. But, in fact, there is a real difference between the bonds that unite Religious in community and those that unite a primary or secondary family. This difference, I will argue, is theologically and spiritually very significant both for Religious themselves and for the prophetic witness Religious Life can give in the tangled societal situation of first-world culture.

A little reflection bears out the observation that Religious Life is neither a primary nor a secondary family, that is, a home in the normal sense of that term. First, Religious do not enter a congregation through or in response to the desire of other members as a child (ideally) is desired and brought into existence in the family by its parents. Second, Religious do not choose their community companions as spouses or members of other committed intentional households choose each other. Rather, they find themselves with others who, like themselves, have chosen Religious Life in the congregation and with whom they share the task of building community. And third, although a Religious community might be "multigenerational" in the sense that members might belong to different sociological cohorts (Depression era, World War II, baby boomers, or Generation X) it is actually composed completely of adults. There are no grandparents, parents, or children.

No one enters the community because of me and I do not enter because of anyone else. No matter how deep the bonds that are forged among community members may be (and it is to be hoped they will be deep and enduring), no member of the community is (or should be) the primary love of another, her reason for being in the community or for leaving it. Furthermore, the formation of any kind of primary and/or exclusive love relationship between two members, a relationship comparable to that of a married couple (whether or not it becomes genital), is contrary to the vow of consecrated celibacy. Religious community should give rise to deep and abiding friendships (which, as we will see, is a theologically important aspect of its prophetic function and crucial to genuine gospel community), but it is not the context for life partnerships in which the human relationship becomes the primary affective horizon of the partners. The primary love of each member, in the "exclusive" sense already discussed a number of times, is Jesus Christ. At the core of Religious Life is a radical and irreducible solitude, a virginity of the heart, which finds its outward expression in celibacy that involves the kind of "homelessness" I am discussing here.

Finally, the vow of consecrated celibacy unites with that of poverty to preclude even the physical context of "home and family," that is, ownership of a property that could be considered one's private home. Vowed Religious, even if permission to do so were mistakenly granted, may not own property, including real estate, in their own name or have a relative or friend establish such ownership for them. Providing any kind of privately owned and controlled "nest egg" for the future, whether pension or insurance or real estate, directly or indirectly, is contrary to the vow as well as the virtue of poverty. A Religious moving into a community-owned property cannot take possession of it in the sense of being immovable if the congregation wants to put it to some other use. Nor can the people living in such a dwelling undertake major modifications on their own initiative, sell it or lease it, or otherwise dispose of it as their own home. In other words, individual Religious may not own a "home of their own." Symbolically, this situation expresses the essential mobility of ministerial Religious who do not settle down in perpetuity but remain open to the call of mission, but it also underscores the continual reconfiguration of relationships that is characteristic of a community that is not a family. Even stabile monastic communities retain the right to move their members about within the monastery—some do so in principle at regular intervals in order to emphasize the detachment from place to which celibacy calls all Religious—and no member can make independent decisions about modifications of the house, the presence of nonmembers within it, or who may or may not enter the community.

The question this first perspective raises is the role of this "homelessness" in the spirituality of Religious themselves. Specifically, what does the Gospel say about home, family, and the Reign of God? What did Jesus have to say about these subjects and what do his own life choices in relation to family reveal? If the renunciation of family is to have real significance in the day-to-day spiritual life of Religious, it must derive from the Gospel and conduce to holiness. Given the rhetoric of the religious right in North America attempting to connect an agenda of "family values" with biblical revelation, it will be very enlightening to look, in the next major section of this chapter, at what the New Testament actually seems to say on this subject and to tease out the implications of that data for Religious spirituality and witness.

2. *The prophetic focus of the renunciation of family:* In chapters 9 and 10 of volume 1 I discussed the prophetic vocation and potential of Religious Life, stressing the fact that prophecy is the mediation of a three-way conversation among God, the believing community, and the culture in which that community lives. In other words, prophecy is not "generic," a thundering of timeless truths applicable to all in any situation. It is culturally specific. Perhaps no sphere of concern is more agitated and agitating in contemporary first-world culture than that of family. The replacement of extended family, which provided backup systems in the stressful demands of conjugal and parental life, with the model of the often isolated nuclear family as normative has preceded (and perhaps contributed to) a heretofore unknown epidemic of family breakdowns. Americans of all or no denomination divorce at record rates,[5] often several times over a lifespan. Children must cope with single-parent upbringing and more than one "home and family" among which they are shuttled, numerous sets of grandparents who come and go in their lives, aunts and uncles who are and then no longer are related, live-in lovers of no longer married parents, homosexual couples as parents, and other

relational complexities, any one of which would put a healthy adult into therapy.

In the richest country in the world, one in five children lives in poverty.[6] Even a booming economy apparently cannot (in fact, will not) provide a secure home, adequate food, insurance, basic health care, decent schooling, and physical safety for its youngest and most vulnerable members. An enormous number of children are cycled endlessly through so-called child services that place them in temporary shelters, foster care, or orphanages until they are dumped on the street at eighteen, often to take up the only occupations open to them, stealing and prostitution, staying drugged against the shame and pain until they are deposited in the penal system.[7] If they are black or Hispanic they are especially likely to stay in that system until they die or are executed.[8] The number of children in our society without minimally competent caretakers, to say nothing of genuine nurturers, is by any measure a national disgrace, and such children have few really committed advocates.[9]

The basic reason for this lamentable situation is no mystery. Since, at least in the white middle-class segment of society, children are no longer the only economic resource of poor parents, there is simply no reason to care for children except altruistic love. Children do not augment the family economy as they once did as workers in the family enterprise; instead, they drain the family resources of time, energy, and money. Children are unlikely to carry on the family business and provide home and support for their parents into old age; they are more likely to leave home and establish their own families whose demands will make care of the elderly difficult if not impossible. If families have little incentive to care for children from whom they can expect little of a material nature and upon whom they must expend a great deal, the government has less incentive. Until they become legal adults, children are worthless to the power brokers. They do not vote or pay taxes or fill the ranks of the army. The manipulators of the economy, on the other hand, have discovered that children are a ripe target for manufactured needs, which is good business for

the companies who do not have to care for their young cus-
tomers. This strategy produces even more stress for parents,
who must go well beyond providing food and shelter if their
children are to be able to compete on the playground with the
latest in brand-name clothes, toys, and electronics.

The problems besetting the first-world family go well
beyond the crisis in material and spiritual resources. The
deep-rooted patriarchy that still structures first-world nuclear
families and through them societal structures in general is the
source of widespread abuse of women and children. Incest,
long a taboo subject whose secrecy protected the perpetrators
and blamed the victims, has finally been exposed. It is generally estimated that one in three girls and one in seven boys are
sexually abused before the age of thirteen, almost always by
adult males in their own homes, ministers in their churches,
teachers, coaches, or youth workers in their recreational settings.[10] Physical and emotional abuse, meted out by both male
and female parents, cripples innumerable children before
they are in any position to defend themselves. Domestic violence against women is rampant and still underreported. Until
very recently police did not arrest, courts did not convict, and
judges did not appropriately sentence the abusers, who, again,
are mostly adult males attacking those within their own families.[11] The license of adult males to prey on the members of
"their" families is indigenous to patriarchy.

The emergence into the public view, especially since the
1960s, of homosexual persons who have, as a group,
renounced their enforced closeting and claimed their rights to
equal treatment as human beings and citizens is another area
of family-related stress in first-world culture. Beyond the obvious issues of parental acceptance of gay and lesbian children,[12]
protection of the civil rights and bodily integrity of homosexual people, and the special health issues raised by the AIDS
epidemic, there are deeper issues that are theological in substance. Is homosexuality a normal, God-ordained mode of
human being or some kind of "objective disorder"? If it is the
former, do not homosexually oriented people have the same

need and right to found secondary families that heterosexual people do? If it is the latter, what are the implications for the affective and sexual life of homosexual people? Is the recognition of permanent unions among gays and lesbians a threat to marriage and family or an encouragement to responsibility and commitment? Or, conversely, is making gay and lesbian unions equivalent to marriage placing restrictions on them that are inappropriate? To what are homosexually oriented people called by God, and how can the culture and the Church facilitate their response? The deepest questions in this area are about family: love, sexuality, children, permanent commitment, interpersonal fidelity, and societal responsibility.

Finally (in a representative, not an exhaustive, sense) we have the effect on the notion and the reality of family of increasing racial mixing and worldwide immigration and emigration. Cultural homogeneity has historically played a major role in setting standards and providing social control and support for the family. Parents in culturally homogenous environments knew what society expected of them; children's social developmental cycle was societally prescribed; cultural agencies supported and guided the family, however defined, as the basic unit of society; common feasts and celebrations articulated community self-understanding and values and initiated young people into their roles in the society while honoring elders and supporting current leaders. In every society there have been problems within families, but the clarity about the norms and even the ideals that a culturally homogeneous society offered prevented the kind of familial chaos that marks first-world culture, where the meaning of family can be, and in a way must be, reinvented by each domestic unit.

Today first-generation Asian youth are caught between the ancestor-oriented culture of their parents and the "now" culture of American adolescence. Black youth are growing up largely in female-dominant households without male role modeling. Each parent in many families may bring into their common life several background cultures and often more than one language. Often parents not only do not share a common ancestral culture but they represent diverse (or no) religious traditions and different political affiliations. As travel and emigration increase there will undoubtedly be more rather than less racial, cultural, religious, linguistic, and political diversity within families. Again, even though this diversity is broadening and enriching in many ways, it puts tremendous strain on the family, which cannot assume anything in any of these areas as normative, commonly accepted, nonnegotiable. Not only must everything be treated relatively since nothing is unchallenged but the relativistic atmosphere this generates flows over into moral standards, values, goals, and behaviors. Every expectation, even of young children, must be rationally defended (or at least defensible) or else enforced by sheer power. Almost nothing is simply imbibed as intrinsically justified and supported by a shared sociology of knowledge to provide a foundation for the young person's self-development as a moral agent.

Although the foregoing paragraphs do not provide a comprehensive description of the cultural situation in regard to family, they should suffice to suggest that first-world culture is in crisis around this subject. The isolation and the breakdown of the nuclear family and the resulting plight of children, patriarchal violence against women and children, the questions surrounding the emergence of homosexuality as a public social phenomenon, and the complexities arising from the multiculturalism, worldwide movements of peoples, and religious, cultural, and ethnic intermarriage combine to defeat most of the traditional bases and safeguards of what continues to be regarded as the basic unit of society. Attention to these issues is being brought to bear from a number of different directions.

The religious right in this country has been busily promoting a version of the Gospel in relation to family that, in my view, is highly problematic.[13] "Family values" is code for the support or restoration of patriarchal dominance in the isolated nuclear family. Men contribute to "family values" by asserting their God-given headship within the family and women by willing subordination, if not sacrifice, of their persons and their destinies,[14] while children revert to parental ownership to be handled by force if necessary. The state, or any other agency outside the narrow confines of the nuclear family, is barred from "interference" in the God-given right and responsibility of the father to run his household as he sees fit, unless it is clear that the children are in physical danger.

However destructive such an approach might be, there is not a great deal more help to be derived from a laissez-faire liberalism which, in effect, demands nothing sacrificial or self-transcending of anyone and regards family relationships and behavior as private affairs in which state and Church have no business interfering. If indeed it takes a village to raise a child, there has to be some way to reflect on these issues that is neither the rationalization of patriarchy nor the abandonment of responsibility to the exaggerations of privacy claims.

Meanwhile, the official Catholic institution offers, among some helpful premarital programs and important family social services, a list of threats, condemnations, and penalties that seem to convert no one but to alienate increasing numbers of people who should be able to look to the Church for pastoral care in this area: a refusal of sacramental marriage to young people living together before marriage; a humiliating process of annulment as the only escape with a future from a definitively broken marriage; the refusal of release from celibacy for many resigned clergy who choose to marry; a demand for perpetual singleness and sexual abstinence on the part of even very young divorcées who themselves need companionship and who have children in need of support and a second parent; exclusion from the Eucharist of the divorced and remarried; refusal of absolution to those conscientiously practicing birth control; excommunication of those involved in an abortion; and an insistence that a homosexual orientation is "objectively disordered" and all sexual activity of homosexuals, regardless of context, is "intrinsically evil." Although not all pastors enforce all of these policies and many nonclerical ministers work hard to mitigate them, they are all on the books and increasingly large numbers of Catholics have begun to ignore the Church as a source of moral guidance and support for family life. In short, there is little in the right wing, extreme liberal, or institutional Catholic agendas that provides positive resources for a Christian engagement with the problems of family in our time.

Certainly this is a prime area for the engagement of Catholics, especially spouses and parents, whose experience and competence make them, rather than celibate clergy or Religious, the experts. Vatican II called lay Catholics in a special way to ministerial responsibility in such areas.[15] However, the free choice of celibacy by Religious is the assumption of a particular stance in regard to sexuality, relationships, and especially the family. What does this choice have to contribute to the Christian struggle in this area? If the choice not to marry is to be something more than an irresponsible flight from the burdens of family and child raising, more than a haven for eternal boys and girls who are incapable of mature affective commitments, it must have something to say in the specifically Christian engagement of this subject. I think that if Religious reflect deeply on their choice of consecrated celibacy in light of the Gospel they will indeed discover the prophetic valence of their vocation for this turbulent and critical area.

III. Jesus and Family

In what follows I want to look at the Gospel presentation of Jesus' life, teaching, and practice in relation to family, sex and sexuality, and community in order to discern some patterns that may throw some light on both the significance for Religious' own spirituality of their choice to renounce family and on the prophetic potential of their "homeless" form of life in relation to the societal conundrums discussed above. In the next section I will suggest that celibacy, freely embraced for the "sake of the Reign of God," is directly relevant not only to the God-quest of Religious themselves but also to engagement with some of these issues, because the Reign of God is the eschatological community that is forming "in our midst" and celibacy witnesses in a particular way to the shape and dynamics of that community.

A preliminary observation is that Jesus says very little about sex or sexual morality in the Gospel. He reiterated the Decalogue's proscription of adultery (cf. Mt 19:18) and intensified it by extending it from actual behavior to lust itself (cf. Mt 5:27–28), but he says nothing on his own about masturbation, homosexual activity, contraception, or abortion. Even in his strengthening of the requirement of fidelity in marriage (cf. Mt 19:1–11) the emphasis is on the divinely established relationship that must not be violated by husband or wife rather than on sex. Jesus has a great deal to say about love of neighbor and right relations, but sex as such does not seem to have been central to his concerns. Consequently, in inquiring into Jesus' teaching and example in the area of family we are well advised to follow his lead, focusing not on sex but on relationships.

A. Jesus' Early Life

Jesus was born into a family, and this is the root of his solidarity with humanity. But from the very beginning in his family of origin, Jesus' relationship to biological sex and family was different. The Gospel suggests that his human father did not beget him (cf. Mt 1:18–20) and his mother was a virgin at least until after his birth (cf. Lk 1:34 and 2:7). Whatever actual biological facts this theologoumenon does or does not enshrine, the intent of the Gospel is clear: Jesus was truly human, born of a woman, raised in a family; but Jesus was not totally biologically determined because he was, even in his human origin, first and always a child of God. The first thing we learn about Jesus that is instructive for all humans is that his parents do not own him. He was not born without their cooperation but he is not entirely a product of their intention or actions. He is the first of those who are born, not of purely natural generation, nor entirely as the result of human decision or male initiative, but of God (cf. Jn 1:13). Even in his conception and birth Jesus begins to relativize any absolute claims on himself as a human being based on family or blood.[16]

The Gospels give us only one story of Jesus' youth, Luke 2:41–52, which tells of the visit to Jerusalem of the twelve-year-old boy with his parents for the feast of Passover. Although he goes up to the holy city with them and at the end of the episode goes down with them to Nazareth where he was "obedient to them" as he "advanced in wisdom and age and favor before God and humans," Jesus' behavior again relativizes parental claims to his person and activity. He remained behind when his parents started home from the feast and when, anxiously returning to Jerusalem, they found him in the Temple listening to and questioning the teachers of the Law, he rebuffed his mother's understandable reproach with "Why were you looking for me? Did you not know that I must be in my Father's house?"

This early Lukan vignette anticipates the scene in John at the wedding feast in Cana (Jn 2:1–11). At the very beginning of his public life in the Fourth Gospel Jesus attends a wedding to which his mother has been invited. When she implicitly appeals to Jesus to avert the embarrassment of the new couple by doing something about the failure of the wine supply, he rejects the request with an almost shocking, "Woman, what is this to me and to you? My hour has not yet come." Jesus will begin his signs only when God indicates that his time has come.

The message about family that the very few texts about Jesus' birth and early life seem to deliver is that Jesus, while being biologically laced into the human race through birth and into a particular ethnic/racial/religious group through family ties, is not absolutely biologically determined in either his being or his action. He is, before all else, a child of God, and his life unfolds in response to God's initiative. Family belonging and obligations are honored but relativized.

B. Jesus' Vocation

The Gospels tell us that Jesus was about thirty years old when he began his public ministry (cf. Lk 3:23) and that prior to that he worked (as a carpenter according to Mk 6:3) with his (adoptive) father, Joseph, whose ancestry Luke traces straight back to Adam, "the son of God" (Lk 3:23–38). But after this long and hidden apprenticeship, under the influence of the Holy Spirit, he set out on a vocation that was unusual. He sought initial purification from John the Baptist (cf. Lk 3:21–22), went out into the desert for a prolonged fast, during which he discerned the true character of his messianic call from God, and returned in the power of the Spirit to begin a brief ministry of preaching and healing (cf. Lk 4:14).

Two features of that vocation are pertinent to our concerns here. First, Jesus apparently chose not to marry. In his culture celibacy was not an honorable or ordinary option. Men were expected to marry, beget children, and thus assure the future of their own family and tribe as well as that of Israel. The "eunuch" passage (Mt 19:11–12) suggests that Jesus was taunted by his enemies as unfit for membership in the Community of Yahweh because he must have been a eunuch (cf. Dt 23:1). But Jesus replies that renouncing marriage "for the sake of the kingdom of heaven" (which could be necessitated by a Christian's divorce given Jesus' prohibition of remarriage, which is the context of this text) is a legitimate choice.[17] "Whoever can accept this ought to accept it." By remaining celibate Jesus definitively relativized both the imperious human need for sex and the absolute claim of family and people on the individual. Humans have a natural orientation toward sexual union and thus toward procreation, which is foundational to the continuation of the species, but it is not an absolute or coercive orientation that must be lived out by every individual person. Neither family nor society can lay an absolute biological claim on the person.[18]

By not marrying Jesus also removed himself from the patriarchal dynamics of family. He did not take a wife or beget children over whom he would exercise the authoritative dominion (if not domination) accorded by right to the male head of household. Not being a householder, he did not have servants or own slaves. As an adult, Jesus left home, thus removing himself from parental authority in his primary family, and he did not found a secondary family in which he would exercise such a role toward others. Jesus stands before us as a person, whole in himself, autonomous, relating freely and equally to men, women, children, outcasts, sinners, foreigners, the sick and even the dead. His very social identity as a celibate, made so by his own initiative for the sake of the Reign of God, called into question biologically based patriarchy. Neither sex nor family, according to Jesus, was the ultimate determiner of social status or relationships.

Second (and this will be taken up in greater detail in the next chapter but needs to be mentioned here), Jesus apparently chose a life of "homelessness." Although Mark (cf. 2:1) implies that Jesus had a home base in Capernaum, perhaps in the house of Simon and Andrew, where Jesus cured Simon's mother-in-law (cf. Mk 1:29–31), the Gospels present him as leading an itinerant life, moving constantly from place to place preaching and healing. But the most important datum on this subject is Jesus' own response to a person who wanted to become his disciple, declaring that he would follow Jesus anywhere: "Foxes have dens and birds of the sky have nests, but the Son of Man has nowhere to rest his head" (Mt 8:20; Lk 9:58). The context and the content of the logion make it clear that the subject is dwelling, home, a place of one's own. Jesus not only did not found a family; he had no real home. Among Jesus' disciples are those who had homes, such as Martha and Mary (cf. Lk 10:38–42) and, presumably, the wife of Clopas (cf. Jn 19:25), who is perhaps the unnamed member of the couple, one of whom is named Cleopas, on the road to Emmaus (cf. Lk 24:13–35), but Jesus had another kind of disciple, one who accompanied him on a full-time basis to the exclusion of all other primary commitments, and these were required to adopt his lifestyle of homeless itinerancy. Jesus' affective bonds were close and strong, but they were not based on biological family and they were not lived in the private context of a home of his own. Once again, Jesus' own choices relativized, without denying, the natural bases and contexts of human relationships.

C. Jesus' Ministry of Teaching and Healing

Unlike sex, which did not seem to be a major topic of Jesus' preaching, family was such a focus. Jesus began his ministry by leaving home, not just physically as Luke implies but psychologically and spiritually as the scene at Cana suggests. This was a challenge to the social structures of his society in which a male was a minor until he founded his own family. Jesus declared himself an autonomous adult, not by establishing his patriarchal dominion over a household of his own but by "leaving home" and ending any dependence on or subjection to his parents. Indeed, the relation between the unmarried Jesus and his family of origin was unusual enough to have given rise to some startling texts in the New Testament, especially in regard to his mother. The question of his relationship to his family, positive or negative, apparently came up repeatedly during his ministry, and every instance reinforces the same impression.

In a remarkable scene in Luke 11:27–28 in which a woman in the crowd praised Jesus through his mother in the words, "Blessed is the womb that carried you and the breasts at which you nursed," Jesus relativized the implication, suggested to the woman no doubt by Genesis 3:16, which says that a woman's relationship with God is based on and defined by her reproductive role. Jesus replied "Rather, blessed are those [women as well as men] who hear the word of God and observe it." Biology for women is not destiny. Women, like men, are called to respond to the word of God as autonomous and free persons.

On one occasion when Jesus was "at home," clearly not that of his primary family but probably his home base in Capernaum, he was preaching to a crowd so large and importunate that he did not even have time to eat. His family decided that he was out of his mind and came determined to take charge of him, perhaps to preempt action by the religious authorities who thought he was possessed by the devil. When his mother and other relatives arrived they sent word through the crowd to summon Jesus, but he replied, "'Who are my mother and my brothers?' And looking around at those seated in the circle he said, 'Here are my mother and my brothers. Whoever does the will of God is my brother and sister and mother'" (Mk 3:20–35). In this passage and its parallels (Mt 12:46–50; Lk 8:19–21), especially in Luke, which emphasizes characteristically that hearing the word of God is the prerequisite for doing it and doing it is the guarantee that one has truly heard, Jesus not only relativizes the claims of biological family on himself but also stipulates what constitutes any person a part of his new fictive family,[19] namely, sharing in his attachment to the word and will of God. It is striking, as Elisabeth Schüssler Fiorenza has pointed out, that the new family Jesus describes includes his siblings and mother but names no father.[20] Jesus does not establish a "spiritual family" of which he is head, but includes himself in a transcendent family of which God alone is the head. Jesus is redefining family, creating a new kinship that is not biologically determined by primary family, created or ruled over by a male, nor based on blood or on law but on faith.

From a different perspective the Gospel of John presents the same message as the Synoptic Gospels. The claim of Jesus' adversaries that they are free by birth, in no need of Jesus' message or saving work because they are children of Abraham, biological members of God's chosen people, is relativized by Jesus. He does not say that Jewish ancestry is unimportant[21] but that it is insufficient. Only those who bring their natural identity by birth as Jews to spiritual maturity by faith [in Jesus], that is, acceptance of his word, and doing the works of truth, are truly children of Abraham and of God (cf. Jn 8:31–59).[22]

Not only did Jesus relativize the claims of family on himself and preach about a new family not based on blood or ancestry but he actually formed such a family. We are told that Jesus had both women and men disciples who went about with him and others whom he visited, many of whom were not related to anyone else in the group even though some others were. Jesus does not say that being related by blood, either to other disciples or to himself, is necessarily an obstacle to discipleship, but neither is it a prerequisite or even a desideratum. Peter and Andrew were brothers as were James and John. Martha and Mary were sisters and Lazarus was their brother.

Jesus' own mother was present with him on Calvary. And after the resurrection James, the brother of the Lord, was apparently the leader of the Church in Jerusalem (cf. Acts 15:13–21). Jesus insists, however, that blood relationship is finally irrelevant to discipleship, whether that be relationship to another Christian or to Jesus himself.

Although this fact is more discreetly presented in the Gospel, the seeds of Christian universalism were also sown by Jesus himself in his ministry. Jesus apparently began his ministry convinced that he was sent, like the prophets before him, only to Israel (cf. Mt 15:24; 10:6) but his experience of God-given faith among people outside the Covenant community, such as the Roman centurion (Jn 4:46–54) and the Syro-Phoenician woman (Mk 8:24–30), amazed him and led to a broadening of his own understanding of God's plan of salvation. In Luke's Gospel Jesus used a Samaritan as an example of true practice of the Law to members of the Jewish hierarchy (Lk 10:29–37) and reminded his hearers of God's preference for the foreigners, the widow of Zarephath and the Syrian leper (Lk 4:25–27). Not only was the immediate family not the limit of Jesus' kinship but even the community of Israel could not contain God's salvific concern. Faith, not blood, is the criterion of membership in the family of God.

More difficult, but important for our purposes here, are the passages in which Jesus not only relativizes family blood ties but actually seems to mount a polemic against family. There are too many such texts to dismiss this aspect of Jesus' teaching as incidental. Jesus called his disciples to leave their parents to follow him (cf. Mk 1:20) and promised a reward to those who give up house, wife,[23] siblings, parents, children, and lands for his name's sake and that of the Gospel (cf. Mk 10:30; Lk 18:29).[24] He even rejected the request of a potential disciple to return home to bury his father (a serious requirement of filial piety in Jesus' society) and another's to say farewell to family (cf. Lk 9:59–62), declared that unless one "hates" parents, children, siblings, and one's own life[25] one cannot be his disciple (cf. Lk 14:26), and claimed that he had come to set the members of a family against each other (cf. Lk 12:49–53).[26]

The number and vehemence of these sayings suggest both that their content, if not always their actual formulation, comes from Jesus and that they were important in the early Church.[27] Becoming a Christian often involved rupture with one's family, one's religion, and one's status in society. Choosing to follow Jesus meant willingness to renounce, if necessary, the most intimate bonds of relationship in order to become part of the new family of faith Jesus initiated. In a real sense many of the first Christians (and some later ones even to our own time) had to renounce family and home in order to follow Jesus.[28]

D. The Paschal Mystery and the New Family

In John's Gospel the scene of the mother of Jesus and the disciple whom Jesus loved at the foot of the Cross (cf. Jn 19:25–27) brings the gospel trajectory from biological family to spiritual family to its summit and conclusion. From the cross Jesus explicitly forms a new family in which his own mother becomes mother of the disciple(s) and the disciple takes the place of Jesus in relation to Jesus' mother. Mary thus assumes a special place in the Christian community, and all the disciples, male and female, become brothers and sisters.[29]

This new relationship is sealed in the Resurrection scene in the garden when Jesus tells Mary Magdalene to "go to my brothers and sisters"[30] with the message that his Father is now their Father (cf. Jn 20:17). This is the first time in John's Gospel that Jesus' disciples are actually called his siblings and children of Jesus' Father. Only through the paschal mystery is Jesus' work brought to completion: He came "to give the power to become children of God to those who believe in his name" (Jn 1:12). But this new family of siblings of Jesus, children of God, is explicitly not a biological family. It is made up of those "who were born not by natural generation nor by human choice nor by a man's decision but of God" (Jn 1:13).

E. Conclusions

This too rapid scan of the remarkably extensive gospel data on family relationships suggests some unavoidable conclusions that have been suppressed, to a large extent, by Christian tradition which, at least in modern times, has placed disproportionate stress on the importance of the biological, indeed nuclear, family. Without doubt the Christian family should be an *ecclesiola,* a Church in miniature. But rather than meaning either that the structures of the patriarchal family should be "writ large" in the Church or that the nuclear family should be absolutized as the only image of the Church or the only context for Christian identity, it means that the gospel values that should structure the life of the Church should also be realized in the family. And those gospel values are not those promoted by either right-wing fundamentalists or patriarchal ecclesiology.

The first conclusion from a review of the gospel material on the family is that biological (and a fortiori, nuclear) *family is relative.* The family, either as ancestral or as biological, is not absolute and cannot make absolute claims on the person. While this might strike some people as alienating, as depriving a person of the primary source of identity and relationship, it is in fact liberating. No one chooses the family into which one is born. Blood relationship, by its nature, is "fate," a bearer of necessity rather than freedom. It is that from which there is, in one sense, no escape. Even the person who was abandoned at birth and never discovers his or her biological parents carries the genes of those parents, is psychologically marked by the abandonment itself, has a "family" somewhere who may, at some point, appear and make claims. And those who grow up in a family are also determined physically and in many ways socially and psychologically by their family of origin.

Jesus teaches that this conditioning, though real, is not definitive. Like death, which is the fate of every human but not our true destiny, family is not the final determiner of identity or destiny. No matter into which sex, into what economic or social class, in what condition of servitude or economic privilege, in what nation or ethnic group, into what race one is

born, one is called to a destiny that transcends all these qualifications, namely salvific participation in the paschal mystery
of Jesus. In the last analysis, every person is autonomous
before God, fundamentally equal in relation to every other
person, a child of God free to choose to hear the word of God
and do it, destined for eternal life. Rather than being determined absolutely by our family of origin, fated to replicate its
dysfunctional patterns or carry out its ambitions, we are
empowered to relate to that family freely, as believers, to be
grateful for what it has given us and to forgive what it has done
to us, but finally to choose our own path.

Second, the *absolutizing of sex is called into question* by the relativizing of biological family. Faith, not sex, is the foundation
of Christian identity. Sex can be absolutized in a variety of
ways. The hedonistic "if it feels good, do it" philosophy promoted by mass media in first-world culture absolutizes sex as
the ultimate pleasure, the need for which cannot and should
not be denied or even subordinated to values such as fidelity
or morality. Sex can also be absolutized by a physicalist
approach to morality that isolates sexual acts from their personal context and permits or prohibits them as intrinsically
good or evil in themselves rather than seeing sex as a language
that takes its meaning from intention and relationship, from
what is said and meant, as well as from the expression, the act
itself.[31] Sex can also be absolutized as "nature" determining
roles, rights, and limitations in family, society, and Church,
which usually means gender-based privilege for males and
inferiority and exclusion for women. None of these forms of
absolutizing promotes the kind of personal commitment and
self-transcending relationality that Jesus preached.

Third, the relativizing of biological family *subverts the hierarchical claim* to be the natural and necessary, and therefore the
paradigmatic form, of human relationship.[32] It is true that
every child is born dependent and that the family is, in that
sense, "naturally" hierarchical since the parents precede and
have responsibility for the child. But the Gospel calls believers
forward from family into a new pattern of relationships. It is

precisely because we are called to a community not based on blood relationships, not founded on the original hierarchy of parent/child, that we can envision a Church in which ontologized hierarchy is replaced by gospel equality.

Fourth, *voluntary community*, not biological family, is the ideal Jesus offers. The Church of Jesus is a community of siblings in faith, a community without fathers, and even more deeply, it is a community of friends.[33] The principle of cohesion in this community is shared faith in and commitment to God in Christ, not blood or obligation. Its unity is sustained by love, not by coercion or even, finally, by authority.

In short, Jesus, who left his primary family and did not found a secondary family, transcended the necessity, the fatefulness, of ancestry and biology. He modeled a free personal autonomy that found expression in interdependent, faithful friendship with those who shared his vision. He called his followers to join him in a new "kinship" that is a voluntary community of friends. This community, which later called itself "Church," was to be the seed, the realization in this world, of a whole new order that Jesus called the Reign of God.

IV. The Changed Problematic of Renunciation of Family in Postconciliar Religious Life

A. The Sociocultural Revolution in Relation to Family

As we have repeatedly noted, the global effect of the Council on Religious Life was the dismantling of the total institution that had enclosed Religious in a self-contained world with its own lifestyle that was to a large extent physically separated and culturally distinct from (if not incoherent with and antagonistic to) the modern world. The result of the demise of the total institution was the immersion of Religious in contemporary culture, which has had a profound effect on virtually every aspect of Religious Life, including the issue of "family." In this section I want to explore how the dissolution of the total institution has affected Religious in this area and how they have tried to cope with the challenge in order to suggest what needs to be done if the spiritual potential and the prophetic witness of this aspect of Religious Life is to be realized in our changed cultural context.

In preconciliar times Religious' living of their renunciation of family was both less and more of a problem than it is today. The absolute break with primary family was so dramatic that, whether it was viewed as heroism or cruelty by others, no one could doubt that it was a fact. And since all Religious lived, by virtue of an assignment on which they had no influence, in fairly large groups structured as quasi-primary families of parent and siblings, the question of compromise regarding renunciation of secondary family seldom arose. In one sense, the total institution handled the issue of family in a way that did not involve any choices on the part of the Religious themselves beyond that of entering the life in the first place. (As I will propose later, this noninvolvement of Religious in the problematic of family as it affected their lives may be responsible for some of the problems in this area that we are seeing today.)

The witness value of Religious homelessness, however, was seriously compromised by the way the life was structured. Religious lived the pseudo-primary family reality with an intensity that few real families could ever attain. Although they were a group of adult professionals they ate every meal together, did all their recreating together, worked together, prayed together, and everyone was "home" every night of the week. No one really had a network of personal friends or professional colleagues who were not shared with the whole community since they could not be engaged anywhere but in the convent parlor. All feasts, both liturgical and personal, were celebrated together in the house. There was never a moment when the "mother" figure did not know the exact whereabouts and activities of every member of the "family." She chose the community's doctors, dentists, and other service personnel and gave permission for consulting them, controlled the finances, and assigned all professional tasks in the apostolate as well as all domestic duties in the house.

This intensified primary family structure and dynamics helped create the fallacious but very tenacious impression that Religious, especially women, were naïve children who were easily amused into innocent giggling by childish pleasures and could be taken, as a group, to picnics and ball games and amusement parks like denizens of an orphanage being provided an outing. Parish adults often took it upon themselves to find ways to mitigate what they perceived as the excessive rigor of the life by providing "treats" such as candy or special food. They also often made, with the pastor, decisions about the kind of housing that would be provided for the "good sisters" and how it would be furnished, when and how it would be repaired, and so on. Since members of many congregations were not allowed to drive cars, lay adults often shuttled the sisters about as parents do their preteen children.

It has already been pointed out that this situation tended to obscure, even for Religious themselves, the radicality of their choice of celibacy in relation to family by replacing the parental home with an intensified replica in the convent. This certainly encouraged in some Religious an immaturity and irresponsibility, at least in regard to their personal lives, that fed the misperception by the laity that Religious women were perpetual little girls who combined a rarified "Bells of St. Mary's" faith with a wide-eyed naïveté that was often parlayed into a delightful outmaneuvering of the worldly wise. But, apart from the fact that this stereotype was far from the truth about the lives of most Religious, which were serious adult enterprises both spiritually and apostolically, it blunted the witness of gospel homelessness. Religious were perceived as having given up their family home in order to become even more totally enmeshed in their "convent home." Perceived as perpetual minors, they were seldom seen as adult participants in the work of the Reign of God even though, in fact, they did most of the Church's apostolic work. Rather than being seen as initiators and leaders (which they were) they were often regarded as "Father's helpers," more like children doing assigned chores.

The shock many laypeople experienced when Religious, in the wake of the conciliar reforms, became active in political life, social justice work, and Church reform, testified eloquently to the fact that Religious had been seen as "the good sisters" doing wonderful work in protected settings but not as autonomous adult women capable of initiative, risk taking, and leadership. It has taken a few decades for most of the Church to realize that the women who are representing the oppressed in NGOs at the United Nations, serving as poverty lawyers and prison chaplains, running parishes and serving as diocesan chancellors, providing housing for the poor, shelters for battered women, and compassionate care for people with AIDS, writing controversial articles and books, giving retreats, settling refugees, and even serving time in prison and being martyred for their work with the poor and oppressed are the same "good nuns" who filed silently with downcast eyes into the first pew for daily Mass and never ate in public. The politically motivated martyrdom of the Church women in El Salvador and the film *Dead Man Walking* gave many people their first realistic images of contemporary women Religious.

The emerging perception of Religious as adults is a function, to a large extent, of the dissolution of the total institution and the sociology of Religious Life it generated. In our society people are not perceived as adults until they have "left home." In many cases, however, Religious in the conciliar era did not so much leave their convent home as experience that the convent home had left them. While this precipitated a widespread and rapid assumption of personal responsibility for themselves, their spirituality, and their ministries on the part of many Religious, which had the potential to offer a much more challenging gospel witness in the Church, it also precipitated some real problems with which Religious, as individuals and groups, are struggling. In my opinion, the demise of the pseudo-family form of Religious Life has generated a genuine

crisis, a situation of danger and opportunity, which has not yet
been addressed by many congregations.

With virtually no preparation many Religious found themselves, for the first time since they had left their parents' home
as teenagers, without a convent home and family provided for
them by their community. In some cases this resulted from
sudden congregational losses of institutional ministries, which
left Religious "jobless." They had to find a ministry and relocate to undertake it, often to areas in which few or no other
members of their congregation lived or worked. In other
cases, Religious finished educations undertaken to prepare
them for positions in their order's institutions and saw those
institutions disappear or be turned over to others just as they
were ready to assume responsibility in them. They had to find
a ministerial setting in which to exercise their newly acquired
competencies that often was not connected to their own congregations. In still other cases, ministerial discernment led
Religious, in continuity with the pioneering charism of their
founders, to begin to address needs that no one else was meeting and that their congregations had not yet corporately
addressed. They went off singly or in twos or threes to
Appalachia, to Latin America, to the inner city, to jails and
shelters, to special schools.

Another factor in the dispersion of previously concentrated
communities was postconciliar reflection on community itself,
a topic we will take up in more detail in part 3 on community
life. Many Religious began to question the healthiness of the
type of convent life they had led. They questioned the abnor-
mal restrictions, collective lifestyle, infantilizing dependency
patterns, and deep-level anonymity that the sheer size of many
local communities fostered. Many wanted to experiment with
much smaller groups in which a more intense relational life
and sharing of faith might be possible. Others wanted to form
intentional communities organized around shared ministerial
commitments to social justice or spiritual renewal. Whatever
the reasons, and they were usually some combination of necessity and well-motivated desires, Religious were scattered from

their secure and insulated private convents into apartments and houses in ordinary neighborhoods where they lived in very small groups and often singly. As the total institution became, for the most part, a thing of the past the "convent home" disappeared and with it the pseudo-primary family.

But with the rigidity and collectivism also went the structure, the orderly horarium, the guaranteed silence, the prayer routine, the regularly provided meals, the access to services of all kinds, the communal celebration of feasts, the day-to-day companionship of others, some of whom were always in the house. Many Religious gave a sigh of relief at being able to set the alarm a little later after a strenuous evening meeting, relished the freedom of being able to decide what to eat for dinner, or the sheer delight of going out to lunch alone with a friend. But many soon found themselves in very isolated or lonely situations. They oscillated between ministry settings in which they interacted professionally primarily with clergy and laity rather than their own sisters and a dwelling in which they were alone most of the time, either because they lived singly or because the schedules of everyone in the house were different and they seldom found themselves home at the same time even for meals or prayer.

Many Religious have coped creatively and well with this intensified experience of being without a ready-made "family." Unprotected by inviolate convent routines or necessary permissions, they experience the intensity of ministry that leaves them, like Jesus, sometimes with "no time even to eat" (Mk 3:20). They are often far more available to others than they were when they were buffered by bells and rules. And, like Jesus withdrawing alone to the mountain to pray, they relish the few hours of solitude and silence in morning or evening in which to recenter themselves in the One to whom they have given their lives. They struggle to balance their ministerial involvement and need for solitude with truly life-giving contact with community and other friends rather than routine presence. But they do not deny the loneliness involved in the fact that they are not really part of either a biological family or the pseudo-family of preconciliar Religious Life. Rather they strive, in prayer, retreat, and spiritual direction, to transform their celibate solitariness into genuine solitude, that aloneness which is not isolation but the quest of the one thing necessary that is the ultimate motivation of Religious Life.

A variety of new forms of community have emerged in the wake of the renewal. Many are smaller and more intimate. Intercongregational arrangements have proved life-giving for some people. The fostering of community through intermediate level structures such as area groups, mission units, or regional communities that bring together in intentional ways Religious living at some distance from one another, or the grouping of individuals who live within relative proximity on a weekly or biweekly basis, and the growing use of electronic means of frequent communication are all ways of struggling with the problems of social fragmentation and loneliness. These will be discussed later in the chapters on community. The point here is that the demise of the convent as total institution does not mean necessarily the end of community in its deepest sense but it does raise challenges with which Religious Life has not adequately dealt.

There is no denying that not all Religious have succeeded in negotiating the transition from pre- to postconciliar Religious Life in a healthy manner. Many who entered early in the renewal period were still too young and too unformed in the spiritual life when they suddenly found themselves without the supports of traditional common life. Some, especially older Religious who had never lived outside a family structure in their lives, lacked the basic skills necessary for a more independent life, for example, experience in shopping and cooking, driving, house maintenance, handling their finances, or dealing independently with doctors and car insurance and personal travel. Conversely, more mature new candidates who entered in the '80s and '90s had plenty of experience of independent living but had a real need for a more structured and daily mentored initiation into Religious Life as a full-time and shared lifeform, and that experience was simply not available. Some Religious, especially energetic middle-aged Religious who were naturally more gregarious, found prolonged solitude onerous if not dangerous. Perhaps most poignantly, the emergence of more self-selected living patterns made no provision for those chronically ill-adapted individuals with whom no one would choose to live but who, in the days of placement by superiors, were absorbed into the large communities to which they were assigned. While for some of these people their difficulty finding a place to live was a wake-up call to begin to deal with their problems, for others it led only to forced isolation, estrangement, and even alienation from community. We will return to these issues in the chapters on community, but here our concern is with the problematic relational coping mechanisms that emerged as enclosed common life with its primary family structures and dynamics ceased to be the normative form of community for many Religious. Insecurity, loneliness, and isolation spawned a number of choices, probably not fully understood or articulated, that require serious reflection and perhaps some intentional revision today.

B. Problematic Responses to the Changed Situation

1. Return to the primary family: One way of dealing with the situation was for a Religious to simply "return home," that is, for all intents and purposes to become again a member of her primary family. She began to spend evenings and weekends and then holidays and virtually all vacation time with parents and siblings. These were the people to whom she looked for extra money, clothes, vacations, or whatever she did not want to request from or felt she would not be given by the community. She turned to primary family members to discuss her problems and help her make decisions about education, ministry, or relationships. Without reflection, perhaps, she had concluded that the only people who were truly concerned about her, accepted and loved her unconditionally, and therefore could be really trusted were her blood relatives.

It became unthinkable that she would consider any ministry that would take her far enough away from her family that she could not be with them on a day-to-day or weekly basis. She took on more and more responsibility in the biological family and gradually family events and obligations took precedence over community affairs. For all practical purposes she had returned "home," but home now meant, not the community in which she was a vowed member, but her parents' or siblings' home, which she had once left. She now lived with her primary family and visited the community.

2. *Establishing a secondary family:* Another way of dealing with felt isolation and especially with the insecurity and fear of unfamiliar responsibility for oneself was what might be called "coupling."[34] Two Religious, often friends of long standing, might find a ministry in the same area and decide to live together. Often they chose the least expensive housing available, a small two-bedroom apartment or house that had no room for a third person or a guest. Sheer space limitation at home, often exacerbated by age-related limits on energy for travel, led to their being nearly always alone together. Years of such experience created a virtually exclusive relationship in which they took their vacations together, recreated together, cultivated the same friends and contacts, shared their finances, their television tastes, in short, became as much a social unit as any married couple. No one would think of inviting one of them to something to which the other was not invited, nor would either of them choose to accept such an invitation. It would be as unthinkable for a third person to enter their "community" as for a third person to enter a marriage.

Often the two became so emotionally and physically dependent on one another that neither would consider a ministry that would break up their household. Where one went the other went, and the ministry was less important than living together. With or without appropriate training, for example, a college professor might become an accountant, a nurse become a secretary in a rectory, or a scientist become a spiritual director in order to keep the couple intact. Neither really belonged any longer primarily to the congregation or Religious Life but to each other and their life together.

Although often suspected of sexual involvement, most such couples probably are not genitally involved with each other. As Jeannine Gramick has pointed out in her study of lesbianism in Religious congregations, most women Religious (unlike men Religious) who discover that they are homosexual and are attracted to living out that orientation in a permanent partnership leave Religious Life.[35] The couples described in the last paragraph are emotionally and psychologically "married" rather than necessarily genitally involved.

Like the return to the primary family of origin, this arrangement supplants the physical and social security that preconciliar convent family life provided with a quasi-secondary family. The person is never alone, on her own in unfamiliar territory, without a backup system in the ordinary and not so ordinary challenges of life. There is someone in whose life one holds first place and who holds first place in one's own life, someone who cares, who supports, who is there when one comes home at night, and with whom one can share all significant events. The two provide for each other what spouses do and what common life once did in a very different way. But once again, one has to raise a serious question about whether such a relationship is, in fact, a truly celibate form of life. Or has the solitude of the heart been sacrificed even if physical intactness has not been violated? Has a celibate witness to gospel "homelessness" become the victim of the need for security?

3. Adoption of a single lifestyle: A third, and perhaps more disturbing, coping mechanism has been gradual estrangement from the congregation by the Religious who effectively resumes a single lifestyle organized around her profession. The Religious who have gone this route are often highly independent personalities, well-educated and respected professionals who, had they not entered Religious Life, might well have remained unmarried and found their identity primarily in their work. These people do not need a parental home, a life partner, or a community. They cope very well with the realities of independent secular life, which is an increasingly widespread lifestyle in contemporary America, especially for talented women. Their professional involvements are stimulating and within that context they develop significant friendships and colleague relations. Being "in the convent," that is, being a Religious, becomes a quaint fringe factor in their life that they do not often mention, and community events are seldom allowed to compete with professional or social commitments. Some of these people have not been seen at a congregational meeting or celebration in many years, have only occasional and superficial contacts with congregational leaders, and move ahead in their career without much attention to its ministerial character or any real discernment with the congregation about its relationship to corporate mission or commitments. If the first group of Religious "returned home" to their family of origin and the second "got married," this group has "left Religious Life" without juridically terminating their membership. Most renewed communities have agonized over their "fringe members," unwilling to precipitate a confrontation that would drive them out, but aware that, for all practical purposes, they are simply carrying membership cards that have long since expired.

C. The Challenge of the Current Situation

Religious as individuals and congregations are aware of and increasingly uneasy about the situation I have just described even if it involves only a small minority of community members. Usually the concern is raised as an issue of community life and/or corporate mission. It certainly affects both, as we will have reason to discuss later, but it is, in my opinion, most radically an issue of celibacy. It is a question of the heart, of relationships, and specifically of how relationships do or should function in the spirituality of the consecrated celibate and in the prophetic witness of Religious Life in the Church and world.

A puzzling inconsistency is that most serious Religious figured out relatively rapidly how to protect and nurture their prayer lives when the safeguards of horarium, prescribed prayers, silence in the house, and common annual retreats suddenly disappeared, whereas many have had a much more difficult time adjusting constructively to the dismantling of the relational context once constituted by common life. It has been suggested that Religious have succumbed to the individualism, materialism, and hedonism of American liberal culture, but I doubt that this is an accurate analysis or adequate explanation.

Although prayer was highly routinized and regulated in preconciliar convent life, it was also highly interiorized as the primary value of the life itself. Religious learned from the day of entrance that the primary end of their life was sanctification, personal holiness or union with God, and that the primary means to that end was regular, frequent (indeed continuous), authentic prayer. The routine may have supported or impeded Religious in their prayer life, but for serious and mature Religious it never substituted for it.

The area of human relationships was quite different. The basic message about relationships was negative. Religious Life began with the renunciation of primary family and the ideal was emotional detachment from relatives, from fellow Religious, from colleagues, from those to whom one ministered. The good Religious was ready to pull up stakes at a moment's notice to undertake a mission in any place assigned. She was taken out of or inserted into different communities often and was expected not to show (indeed not even to feel) the emotional wrenching such separations or challenges to belonging caused. She was not to maintain contact with children or others in a previous mission situation. So-called particular friendships, which really meant any kind of deep relationship with another community member that made the normal demands for some leisure time together and some privacy of communication and which would endure beyond a common ministry assignment, were forbidden and often violently ruptured by transfers or proscriptions of contact.

Although charity in community was highly prized, it was understood to mean a nonemotional, general acceptance of and benign affection for all other members among whom, ideally, no distinctions were to be made. A sister perceived as deliberately choosing to sit next to or walk with a preferred companion would normally be immediately corrected. A true "community woman" was responsible in carrying her share of common work and generous in serving others. She never expressed anger, gossiped or made unkind remarks about or to another, or deliberately hurt another's feelings and if she did so she apologized promptly. Community life was usually (and conflictually) presented as both ideally a warm and loving family in which the Religious was a dutiful and happy child and as a primary source of adult ascetical practice through the patient and cheerful bearing of the friction, misunderstandings, and even deliberate hurts one encountered in group life.

In short, unlike the life of prayer that was deeply interiorized and personalized from the very beginning of Religious Life, relationships were discouraged, often mutilated if not perverted, burdened with guilt and shame, often cloaked in secrecy. Because Religious were expected to express emotions they did not feel and feel emotions they did not experience, their access to their own relational capacities, their insight into their own dynamics and those of others, as well as their social skills were sometimes seriously underdeveloped if not deformed. The truly amazing thing is that wonderful friendships among Religious did form and survive and many if not most Religious matured as social and professional persons. Their generosity, ability to control negative emotions, responsibility for the group, concern for inclusion of the less popular, and capacity to delay gratification have made many Religious engaging and positive participants in a widening network of friends and coministers. But there is little doubt that the relational artificiality of the detached pseudo-family kept many preconciliar Religious from engaging in depth the spiritual issue of family in relation to a celibate commitment. It should not come as a surprise that the dissolution of the total institution which involved the breakup of the "convent home" and the dispersion of the "family" that dwelt in it left many Religious stripped of the only relationships they had and ill prepared to reconstruct them on a different basis.

It is not good for human beings, celibate or not, to be alone. Relationships are crucial for health and happiness. The issue is not whether a healthy celibate should have relationships but with whom, how, and to what end. The Religious who returned to her primary family, coupled with an available friend, or immersed herself in the relational network of professional life or ministry was simply using the resources that seemed most available to fill a void that was indeed intolerable. The most tragic cases are the isolated individuals who float vaguely in community and ministry without significant connections of any kind. But none of these arrangements is an adequate approach to celibate relationality.

Religious, for the sake of their own spirituality, need the kind of community that Jesus formed among his disciples, including strong, particular personal friendships both within and outside the congregation, colleagues in ministry, and those toward whom they exercise the spiritual generativity Jesus encouraged in his followers. Their unique vocation in the Church entails living and witnessing to the mystery of God's abundant sufficiency as the exclusive primary love of a human heart and that this primary love, like that of a faithful spouse, does not constrict one's relational capacity but expands, enriches, and purifies it. The characteristic form of affectivity of the consecrated celibate is friendship. Friendship is freely chosen, nonexclusive, altruistic, developmental, faithful. Friends care not only about one another but about the causes and commitments they share. The "family" Jesus founded was neither a primary nor a secondary sociological family nor a corporation but a community of friends. Friendship, however, is as much a developed human capacity as is prayer. Religious Life should be as much a school of friendship and altruistic relationship as it is of prayer, which is the first friendship in the life of the celibate.

Religious Life is also, ideally, a primary prophetic witness in the Church to the kind of community Jesus intended. The "family" he founded was not only a group of friends but a mutually responsible community in mission and shared ministry. It included some people related by blood but most were not so related. It included, as we will see in the next chapter, both itinerants and householders. Some members lived together and others lived apart. But what they had in common was their faith in and love for Jesus, their commitment to his Reign, and their willingness to lay down their lives for those they loved as Jesus had loved them.

This witness, it seems to me, is both crucially important and very hope-filled for contemporary society. In the United States only about one-fourth of households is a traditional nuclear family of husband and wife and their biological children.[36] Many households are composed of single parents or grandparents raising their own children's or other peoples' children, unrelated adults in voluntary groupings such as retirement residences or young people involved in study or various projects, single people living alone by necessity or by choice, or nonmarried couples related by friendship or homosexual commitment. The Church often presents all types of householding except the intact, heterosexual nuclear family as exceptions or aberrations that should be corrected into nuclear families or patiently borne as necessary misfortunes. One seldom hears mention, in the homily on Holy Family Sunday, of all the types of "families" that do not reflect the supposed ideal, or even a reference to the fact that Jesus' family of origin was certainly not "traditional," that he did not found a secondary family of any type, and that the family he proposed for his followers was not based on biological relationships. Religious Life can and should witness to a unique kind of "family" that is usually single-sex, composed entirely of adults who are unrelated by blood, inclusive from the standpoint of race and ethnicity, brought together by faith and love and common commitment to the Gospel. In other words, Religious Life is, or should be, a prophetic witness to the transcendent "family" Jesus called into being.

The challenge in this area facing congregations today, it seems to me, is how to promote among their members the kind of relational lives that a mature and committed celibate spirituality should and must entail and how to integrate those lives into the kind of corporate witness that will make a genuine prophetic contribution to the complex, confused, and highly dysfunctional social situation of contemporary first-world society. These challenges are intimately related to issues of community and ministry. But I suggest that they are most fundamentally related to consecrated celibacy. By professing celibacy Religious have given a particular shape and direction to that most significant dimension of their human existence in this world, their capacity for relationship. By choosing not to live that capacity through sexually based family but through participation in a transcendent and inclusive community of friends in mission they have accepted the challenge to work out what that means, personally and communally, and to find the appropriate way of embodying it in a public lifestyle that will be prophetically powerful for the Church and world. If, in times past, the structure of traditional convent life was such a lifestyle, it is so no longer for most Religious, especially those in mobile ministerial congregations. Recognizing the true nature of the challenge as an issue of celibacy, its roots in an underdeveloped approach to relationships in times past, and its potential for the spirituality of Religious themselves as well as for the Church in which they witness and serve should be the incentive not to discouragement or resignation to loneliness on the one hand or unhealthy compensations on the other, but to a concentrated and corporate effort to create a type of relationality and community inspired by the Gospel and appropriate for our cultural situation.

CHAPTER SEVEN
CELIBACY AND "HOME"

I. Introduction and Transition

The premise expressed at the beginning of the previous chapter, that the renunciation of family and home are at least as important as the renunciation of sex itself in the living of consecrated celibacy, also governs this chapter, in which I want to turn from the discussion of family to that of "home." Family and home are closely related and intertwined realities, but they are not identical nor coterminous. The notion of family places the emphasis on relationships whereas that of home emphasizes the "place" or context of one's life, especially of one's relational life. Many people in our society, for example, those who are single by choice or circumstances, do not live with family but do maintain a home. On the other hand, a distressing number of families in our society do not have a physical home. Some of these would maintain that they do have a home, that is, a psychological "place" constituted by the close relationship of their members, but simply lack a house in which to place it. Such a statement illustrates both the relationship between family and home and the more-than-physical connotations of "home."

In the previous chapter I talked about "homelessness" in terms of relationships. Religious live out their commitment to Christ as the exclusive primary focus of their lives by leaving their primary family and not founding a secondary family. This situation is supremely important for their personal spirituality, for the character of their community life, and for the prophetic witness to the kind of community Jesus founded, which is not biologically based but rooted in shared faith and love sealed in baptism and celebrated in Eucharist. In this chapter I will be talking about "homelessness" in terms of gospel itinerancy and its role in the personal spirituality, community life, and prophetic witness of Religious. Religious are those who not only have left all things (especially family) but those who follow Jesus in his itinerant lifestyle (including especially not having a home of their own).

II. The New Testament and Early Church on Itinerancy and Householding

A. Jesus and Home

Jesus, as the Gospels present him, lived approximately the first thirty years of his life at home, with his parents in Nazareth. He apparently shared his father's occupation of carpentry (cf. Mk 6:3). The only indication of how he lived that life is the note in Luke 2:51–52: "He went down with them [his parents] and came to Nazareth, and was obedient to them....And Jesus advanced in wisdom and age and favor before God and man [sic]." He then left home and began a very short period of life, one to three years depending on which Gospel one reads and how one calculates the time indications in it,[1] which ended with his death by crucifixion at the hands of the Roman governor Pontius Pilate who was provoked to execute Jesus by some of the Jewish authorities.

Jesus, in other words, lived successively two very diverse lifestyles. He lived a stabile, domestic, private or hidden life in the home of his parents for a long period of time. He then undertook a short public life of continuous mobility or itinerancy in which he had no permanent abode or stabile family context. He described his public lifestyle for a prospective disciple as follows: "Foxes have dens and birds of the sky have nests, but the Son of Man has nowhere to rest his head" (Lk 9:58).

In the course of his public life Jesus also had two quite distinct types of disciples. He called some people, both women and men, to go about with him sharing his itinerant or homeless lifestyle. The Gospels recount the calls of some of the individuals who made up the group of itinerant disciples and notes the presence in the group of others whose calls are not described. Some we recognize as members of the "twelve" (e.g., Simon Peter and Matthew); other named disciples were not among the twelve (e.g., Nathanael, the Beloved Disciple, Mary Magdalene, Joanna, and Susanna); still others are unnamed (e.g., the seventy [cf. Lk 10:1–20] who were sent to prepare his way, some of whom were probably men and women traveling in pairs for safety).[2]

Not everyone Jesus wished to include in this itinerant group accepted the invitation and not everyone who wished to be part of this group was accepted into it by Jesus. The story of the "rich young man" in Mark 10:17–22 tells of a virtuous individual, one who had kept the commandments all his life and earnestly desired to do even more in the service of God, who goes away sad when Jesus invites him to what the "more" entailed: "Go, sell what you have, and give to the poor...then come, follow me." The Gospel tells us the invitee demurred because "he had many possessions," and the story is followed by Jesus' disquisition on the danger of riches. But what exactly constitutes this danger? Is it simply the possession of goods, or is it the fact that extensive holdings make both detachment and itinerancy, the lifestyle to which Jesus called this man, extremely difficult or even impossible?

Jesus often connects having little with being able to travel in service of the Gospel, for example, "Take nothing for the journey, neither walking stick, nor sack, nor food, nor money, and let no one take a second tunic" (Lk 9:3). However, while all disciples are called to take up their cross and follow Jesus, being willing even to lay down their lives for him if necessary (cf. Lk 9:23–27), not all, apparently, are called to the voluntary poverty and itinerancy that stymied the rich young man. Martha and Mary, good friends and disciples of Jesus, apparently were fairly well off (cf. Lk 10:38–42) and maintained their home in Bethany. Jesus did not object to the wealth of the tax collector Zacchaeus (cf. Lk 19:2–10) or the Pharisee, Simon, whose dinner invitation he accepted (cf. Lk 7:36–50). The issue was not possession of property but how they acquired and handled their wealth. Voluntary poverty seems connected only to the call to itinerate discipleship.

On the other hand, there were those who wished to join the itinerant band whom Jesus did not call to that life. Luke describes several such people in 9:57–62. Each is held back, significantly, not by material possessions but by the issue of home and family. These episodes suggest some fault on the part of the persons, or at least an attachment that Jesus deems an impediment. But there is one episode in which no fault or attachment is implied or suggested, namely, the story of the Gerasene demoniac (Mk 5:1–20). After Jesus had exorcised the man and sent the legion of expelled unclean spirits into the herd of swine, the man pleaded with the departing Jesus to be accepted into his company, "to remain with him. But he [Jesus] would not permit him but told him instead, 'Go home to your family and announce to them all that the Lord in his pity has done for you.'" We are then told that the man "went off and began to proclaim in the Decapolis what Jesus had done for him" (Mk 5:18–20).

Apparently, both the personal example of Jesus and his practice in the calling of followers legitimate two quite different lifestyles of discipleship, one the stabile lifestyle of the householder and one the mobile lifestyle of itinerant ministry. Jesus himself led both a hidden life and a public life, and he had disciples who were householders and others who shared his homelessness in the service of the Gospel.

B. Itinerancy and Householding in the Early Church

The early Church experienced considerable tension over the implications of this data for those Christians who desired not only to live the Gospel, that is, to take up their cross and follow Jesus, but to minister full-time in the Church and/or to embrace a life of consecrated virginity. The Third Letter of John, for example, presents a situation in which a resident ecclesiastical leader, Gaius, is commended by the writer for receiving itinerant preachers such as Demetrius who "have set out for the sake of the Name" and should be helped on their way so that the stabile community "may be coworkers [with them] in the truth" (cf. 3 Jn 5–8). But the writer also excoriates Diotrephes, apparently another resident official, who "will not receive the [itinerant] brothers, hindering those who wish to do so and expelling them from the church" (3 Jn 9–10), because Diotrephes fears the insinuation of false teaching by traveling strangers.

Paul was perhaps the most widely traveled preacher of the Gospel in the first generation, and he maintained vehemently that he was not called to resident pastoral ministry but to preaching the Gospel, moving continually at the behest of the Spirit to new venues where the Gospel had not yet been implanted. However, he founded communities within which he established or which he encouraged to establish stabile ministries with resident ministers who would build upon the foundations he had laid (cf. 1 Cor 3) so that together itinerant apostle and resident minister might collaborate in the building up of the body of the Church. The so-called pastoral epistles (1 and 2 Timothy and Titus), whether or not actually written by Paul, invoked Paul's authority in counseling pastors about their duties to those they are called to shepherd. In this choice of personal itinerancy and encouragement of others to resident ministry Paul mirrored the decision of the Twelve in Jerusalem to hand over the work of pastoral maintenance to chosen assistants so that they could be free for the "ministry of the word" (cf. Acts 6:1–7) with its evident requirement of travel. In the Epistle to the Ephesians, possibly written in Paul's name after the latter's death, we are given a carefully constructed apostolic ecclesiology in which ministry is described as multifarious and unified by God's design, including both itinerant apostles, prophets, and evangelists and resident pastors and teachers, working together "to equip the holy ones for the work of ministry, for building up the body of Christ, until we all attain to the unity of faith and knowledge of the Son of God,...to the full stature of Christ" (Eph 4:11–13). Paul, insofar as he ranks the charismatic functions in the Church, gives first place to the itinerant ministries of apostleship and prophecy by which the faith is implanted but follows them immediately with such resident pastoral ministries as teaching, healing, and administration, by which the implanted faith is nurtured (cf. 1 Cor 11:27–31).

One of the earliest nonbiblical documents of the Church, the *Didache*,[3] bears eloquent witness to the ambivalence of the early Church around the issues of itinerancy and stability or householding. In the early community of householders from which this document arose, charismatic prophets are accorded the privilege, evidently borne of the high esteem in which they were held for both theological competence and personal holiness as well as their call from the Spirit, of impromptu "eucharistizing," that is, of not being bound by local formulae when they guest-presided at Eucharist.[4] On the other hand, criteria are given for judging the authenticity of these visitors and identifying and expelling frauds. Prophets are to remain no more than two days as guests, after which time they are to move on or begin to work for a living in the community.[5] Prophets who are seeking personal financial gain are judged false, but especially the prophet whose personal life does not both match his or her teaching and mirror the radical life of Jesus is to be repudiated.[6] The householders felt called to listen to the itinerant prophets and to take instruction from their radical lifestyle but not necessarily to imitate them.

The dialectic between the two lifestyles, that is, itinerancy and householding, in the early Church appeared also in regard to the life of consecrated celibacy that arose within the first eighty years of the Church's life. The issue continues into our own time. The earliest Religious, the consecrated virgins, lived in the local Church communities, often in their own homes, and subject to the local bishop. But as the Church itself, freed of persecution by the Constantinian Edict in the early fourth century, became over-accommodated to secular life, too "rooted" in the world, Religious moved to the desert, where they lived precariously in solitary huts or caves, moving frequently and settling nowhere definitively. However, the "unanchored" life of the early monks was often conducive to spiritual instability, which was counteracted not only by the insistent admonition of the elders to remain in the cell at all times but also by the emergence of cenobitic monasticism among the desert dwellers.

Benedict, the father of Western monasticism, made stability a foundational element in his Rule. "Vagrant" or wandering monastics (*gyrovagi* rather than *monachi peregrini,* who were legitimate itinerant ascetics) who avoided the discipline and accountability of the life by moving on whenever the demands exceeded their vague commitment were excoriated by Benedict who, following earlier monastic tradition, made a perpetual vow of stability in the monastery of profession a structural feature of monastic life.[7]

While the mendicant orders of the Middle Ages retained the monastic commitment to conventual life they reemphasized the itinerant aspect of Religious Life by both begging and preaching. The mendicants were part of the widespread "Vita Apostolica" movement of the Middle Ages, the commitment of hundreds of thousands of Christians, secular and Religious, women and men, to following Christ even to an attempt to literally replicate his itinerant lifestyle to the extent possible. The desire to literally "sell all" and follow Christ in absolute poverty, preaching the Gospel to all creatures, was integral to the vision of Francis of Assisi and Dominic Guzman and other founders of male mendicant orders but also to women like Clare of Assisi who, though necessarily cloistered, saw her life and that of her Sisters as intrinsically apostolic, a sharing by prayer and vision, but also by absolute poverty and insecurity, in the itinerant life of the male Franciscans.[8] Tertiaries in the mendicant orders, like the Dominican Catherine of Siena, evaded cloister by not making solemn vows so that, like the men, they could go where they were needed, preaching the Gospel by word and deed.

The struggle of women throughout the immediate pre- and postrevolutionary eras in Europe and colonial America to found Religious orders and congregations that would be noncloistered and ministerially active has been described in volume 1, chapters 9 and 10.[9] Although repudiating the absolute stability of papal cloister and affirming their vocation to mobility and ministry, these "apostolic Religious" also valued and maintained a form of common life that replicated in many respects that of their cloistered Sisters. The struggle continues today as the reaffirmation in renewed congregations of the essentially ministerial character of their lives raises questions about the possibility and significance of residential community life. At the same time, traditionally cloistered contemplative Religious are increasingly resisting the absolutist understanding of stability as total enclosure.

C. Conclusions from History about Gospel Homelessness

As John Dominic Crossan in his provocative article on itinerants and householders in the early Church points out, the two types of life should not be compared hierarchically but seen as equal and complementary.[10] Both itinerancy and householding are not only legitimate paths of discipleship, able to appeal for legitimacy to the example of Jesus himself, but also necessary for the ongoing life of the Church. Each has its own gift to offer and each presents characteristic challenges to fidelity. The itinerant is the bearer of the Gospel beyond the safe boundaries of the like-minded community, and the householder is the anchor of community stability, nurturing the faith on a day-to-day basis. If householding exposes one to the risks of attachment to material goods and security, to settling down spiritually as well as physically, and to narrowness of vision, itinerancy can tempt one to irresponsibility in ministry, idiosyncrasy if not heresy in teaching, manipulation of others for livelihood, elitism and entitlement, and carelessness and nonaccountability in personal practice. Like matrimony and consecrated celibacy as states of life, itinerancy and householding, as lifestyles, need each other for balance, mutual criticism, and support.

There has always been a tendency in the Church to privilege literal continuity between Christian status and practice and the actual historical details of the life of Jesus. This tendency virtually always leads to real mischief. Its most egregious instance is surely the privileging of men over women in the Christian community because of the former's physical/biological likeness to Jesus as male. But regarding the itinerant lifestyle as a "closer following of Jesus" makes no more sense than regarding carpentry as superior to farming or disparaging intellectual labor in favor of manual work. The point of what follows is not to vaunt itinerancy or homelessness as a superior lifestyle for the Christian, as a better or "closer" way to follow Jesus, but to explore its spiritual significance for those who are called to it, specifically ministerial Religious. Furthermore, as I will suggest later, both itinerancy and stability contribute to the life of all followers of Christ, though in different degrees and proportions. The themes of journey and homecoming, of pilgrimage and dwelling, of the importance of both roots and wings are part of the spiritual life for everyone, including Religious, but different aspects are more characteristic of certain lifeforms. It seems that matrimony, especially when children are involved, more characteristically gives rise to a householder lifestyle, and consecrated celibacy, especially that of ministerial Religious, to an itinerant lifestyle, although there is nothing absolute about this and it should not be regarded as prescriptive or even normative.

III. Gospel Homelessness in Relation to the Vows, Community, and Prophetic Witness

Two preliminary remarks will introduce us into considerations of the significance of itinerancy in the spirituality and lifestyle of Religious. First, I will use the terms *itinerancy* and *homelessness* interchangeably even though at times the emphasis will be on the lack of a place of one's own and at other times on the mobility of ministerial Religious Life. In other words, the lifestyle of Religious, whether or not they are actually traveling or moving about from place to place at any given time, is one of being nonattached to any particular place, of being always disposed to move in response to gospel incentives. Second, I am considering this topic in the context of consecrated celibacy because I regard celibate commitment as the root of evangelical homelessness. However, as we will see, it is intimately involved in all the vows, as well as with community, ministry, and prophetic witness. We will look at all of these dimensions in themselves, remaining aware of the interconnections among them, and most of them will be further discussed in subsequent chapters and in volume 3.

A. The Vows and Homelessness

I am presuming in this section all that has been said previously about the vows as global self-disposition in relation to persons, possessions, and power through the poetic and prophetic performative language of profession rather than as literal language about juridical obligations. All three of these structural dimensions of human life, that is, relationships, material goods, and power, are affected by the basic lifestyle of either householding or itinerant homelessness.

1. Consecrated celibacy: As we discussed in the previous chapter, the decision to leave home in the sense of separation from the primary family of origin and to renounce marriage or the founding of a secondary family creates a unique affective life-situation that colors everything else in the life of the Religious. While the Religious community supplies many of the affective resources mature people need to live healthy and productive lives, it is not a family or a family substitute. One effect of the fact that the Religious is "family-less" is, or should be, a predisposition to itinerancy, to being able and willing to move in response to gospel needs. The Religious does not have and is not responsible for a family that will be affected by her decision to move. However wrenching her leaving of kin, friends, colleagues in ministry, and community members may be for her personally (and it would not be a good sign if she did not feel such separations deeply), she is not uprooting a spouse from job, children from school, or the family itself from its support network and community involvements. Consecrated celibacy is a major condition of possibility of lifelong itinerancy.

The meaning of celibacy, as we have stressed repeatedly, is not primarily that one is not sexually active. It is that one's whole heart is invested in the relationship with Jesus Christ in a way that excludes any other primary life commitment. The only "place" that is nonnegotiable for the Religious is union with Christ. And that makes the fostering of the Reign of God her only real work. No particular place or ministry, however deeply invested she may be in it, is absolutely necessary for the Religious. In times past this reality was dramatically acted out in both the re-missioning of Religious to new places and communities without preparation or consultation and in the extraordinary pioneering of Religious into foreign settings, which often separated them, sometimes for the rest of their lives, from their place of origin and all that was familiar. The stories of missionaries setting out for foreign lands without even the language of the new culture to facilitate their work is matched by the stories of Religious, even in their own culture or country, moving from urban to rural, from settled to frontier, from financially established to utterly destitute situations with little more than the clothes on their backs. Religious today are much more involved in the discernment of their ministries and thus of their location. But the fundamental disposition to go where the Gospel calls is integral to the homelessness of consecrated celibacy.

2. *Poverty:* Religious Life involves a basic renunciation of personal or private ownership of material goods. Perhaps nothing in our culture is as symbolic of self-sufficiency as "owning one's own home." It is a way of describing someone who is financially secure and independent. John Dominic Crossan, commenting on the itinerancy of Jesus, says that in first-century Palestine peasants who owned at least a small parcel of land, a homestead, were poor, but the person who was landless was destitute. Jesus left home and did not establish a home of his own. Economically, he would be classed as destitute, but destitution is not the impression one gets from the

Gospel, and herein lies the originality of Jesus' choice. Jesus, whose gift to his contemporaries was the "Good News," seems to have been sustained himself by sharing the well-being of friends (such as Martha and Mary), the resources of affluent disciples (such as the women disciples who accompanied him), or the family assets of other disciples (such as Peter, in whose house at Capernaum Jesus seems to have had a kind of operational base). Homelessness for Jesus does not seem to have entailed destitution but it did entail insecurity, dependence on others, and sharing.

When Jesus sent out his disciples, the twelve or the seventy, to participate in his ministry he specified that they were to take no backup supplies such as food, a second outfit, or even a knapsack. Particularly interesting is the prohibition of a bag. A bag could either carry one's own provisions or be used to collect alms. In either case, it was the receptacle for the goods one needed. But Jesus says, in effect, that his emissaries are neither to provide for themselves nor to beg. Rather, they were to approach those to whom they were sent and, if accepted in Jesus' name, expect to share in whatever the receivers had. If they were not accepted, they were to move on, attempting to prepare the way elsewhere.

This is a very enlightening version of poverty. It is not a romantic glorification of destitution nor a euphemistic end-run around real economic insecurity. It is a challenge to solidarity and mutuality in a totally ministerial community. Jesus tells his emissaries to share openly with those to whom they are sent by offering freely the good news of the Reign of God and to accept their livelihood from those whom they serve (cf. Mt 10:8). Crossan calls the result a "community of mutual empowerment."[11]

While this picture is obviously a model, a presentation of the ideal structure of itinerant ministry that cannot be worked out in detail in every setting, it does suggest the connection between homelessness and poverty on the one hand and between itinerancy and householding on the other. To be homeless is to be without resources, vulnerable to the elements (whether physical, economic, political, or social). Whether or not one has what one needs in any given instance, this lack of ownership makes one insecure, vulnerable, dependent. The dependence, however, is not meant to be a source of crippling anxiety or debilitating destitution, much less subservience to the wealthy, but rather a source of solidarity through the sharing between itinerant and householder, between the Religious and the community, both the one to which they belong and the one they serve.

In times past this structure was usually quite evident. Religious often ministered without remuneration and lived from what was provided by the parish, the surrounding community, the families and individuals whom they served. Sometimes this was actually an in-kind contribution of food, help in the house, transportation, or professional services. But the point is that whether or not Religious earn a living wage, they do not, because of their vow of poverty, own anything as private possession. In a way the congregation is a kind of householder, a resource for all the members that keeps them solvent for the sake of the mission, but the individual Religious, if she is actually living a vow of poverty, has no personal bulwark against destitution. She does not own her own home or car. Her salary belongs to the congregation. Her budget and expenditures require approval and accountability. She has no independent access to health care or retirement resources. The vow of poverty is a global declaration of embracing the kind of detachment, insecurity, vulnerability, dependence—in short, the homelessness—that Jesus asked of his itinerant disciples. And it is, paradoxically, also a primary source of the interdependence of the Religious within a congregation and of the interdependence between Religious and the rest of the Church community.

3. Obedience: Obedience is the vow that requires the most careful nuancing today because of the evident historical mayhem to which blind obedience has given rise. We will return to this issue in volume 3. Here the issue is the surrender of independence in life and ministry that the vow entails. No matter how fully involved in the discernment of her ministry and living situation a Religious might be (and that involvement, normally, should be extensive), the final decision about how the Religious will participate in the corporate ministry that expresses the mission of the congregation rests with the congregation and not with the individual Religious. This is expressed in most congregations by some type of formal missioning by the competent leaders at intervals specified by the particular law of the congregation. Significant revisions of the arrangements specified must be negotiated with congregational leaders in whatever manner the constitutions specify. In other words, the life and ministry of all the members of the congregation are coordinated and "made corporate" by the vow of obedience lived by all the members according to the constitutions.

The disposition of Religious to "go wherever one is sent," to respond to needs wherever they are discerned and especially to those to which other agencies are not responding, is in direct continuity with the ministry of Jesus who did all things in obedience to the One who sent him (cf. Jn 5:30). Jesus himself discerned what needed his attention, but he discerned this, the Gospels tell us, in the context of sustained prayer to the One he called his Father (cf. Jn 11:41–42; Lk 6:12–13) and under the impulse of the Spirit driving him to teach, heal, and serve (cf. Lk 4:18–19).

The homelessness of Jesus the itinerant, according to Crossan's interesting analysis, was directly related to his vision of his mission.[12] Unlike the Jewish authorities, who set up their permanent site in the Jerusalem Temple and implicitly required the people to come to them for religious services, Jesus went about, seeking the lost sheep of the house of Israel (cf. Mt 10:6). Crossan suggests that hierarchy of place symbolizes and masks hierarchy of persons. The established sacred place, with the established religious mediators, who dispense the established religious benefits for the established price institutes what Crossan calls a "brokerage" of the Reign of God. The goods of salvation are mediated from the patron-God to the client-people by the religious brokers who both take their "cut" from what they collect in God's name (like the Jewish tax collectors for the Romans) and lord it over the powerless clients in God's name. The religious "business" they set up and to which others must go for salvation is the location of the hierarchical operation, which supposedly benefits God and surely benefits the brokers but at the expense of the people.

Whether or not one accepts Crossan's analysis of first-century religious institutionalism, it is not hard to recognize what he describes from the Gospel itself. When Jesus cleansed the temple, which he claimed the religious authorities had made into a "den of thieves," he was clearly objecting to religion as business, as brokerage of the Reign of God (cf. Jn 2:16). But what alternative does he offer? Jesus went about freely offering the goods of salvation, teaching about God and God's Reign, healing, exorcizing, giving life, symbolized and effected in open-table fellowship in which status and wealth were irrelevant, without asking any payment or claiming any authority based on office or hierarchical position. How often his adversaries asked, "by what authority" he did all this (e.g., Jn 2:18). His only authority was the self-evident goodness of what he was doing. If God is good and what Jesus does is good, who can raise an objection? Jesus established no "place" in which he was the power figure, no religious equipment by which to operate, no prescribed rituals, no "entrance requirements" (ritual, monetary, or personal) to God's presence. He simply went about doing good and he did all things well (cf. Mk 7:37).

The ministerial obedience of Religious,[13] like Jesus' obedience to God, is in the service of those to whom they are sent, not of an institution, even the Church. Religious are not clergy, that is, officials or agents of the religious institution. Historically Religious congregations have struggled to develop ways, such as canonical "exemption," to retain their freedom to move among and beyond ecclesiastical jurisdictions, to respond to needs not being met by others, to "do good" wherever it needed to be done. There is no question that Religious, as congregations and as individuals, have often been domesticated by ecclesiastical authority, subsumed into the localized religious business, and have colluded in their own domestication. In our own time the widespread parochialization of Religious, both men and women, is cause for serious concern for precisely this reason. The obedience that Religious vow is not an enlistment in the ranks of Church workers, much less qualification as "brokers" of salvation who dispense their services to the deserving who qualify by keeping the rules. Religious are, like Jesus, "homeless." They are sent to the marginalized, the "law breakers," like the sinful woman, the people whom the Pharisees referred to as "those people" (the *am ha'aretz*) who know nothing about the Law, the people who despair of their own capacity to do good, like the publican in the Temple, who are outside the pale because they are diseased or belong to the wrong ethnic group or religion. Even when they minister to the financially well established or the educated, Religious should be sowing the subversive seeds of antielitism, antihierarchicalism, solidarity with the poor and oppressed, open acceptance of all at the table of salvation. Homelessness, not having a fixed abode and the vested interests that go with it, is integral to this mission of opening wide the gates of divine love to the hedgerow dwellers, the unclean, and the desperate as well as to the rich young seekers and the compassionate "Samaritans."

B. Community and Homelessness

In one sense community would seem to be the opposite of homelessness, and the intense desire for community among many seeking Religious Life today brings this very issue to the fore and demands careful discernment. The ambiguity, even paradox, of a community of itinerants, is actually rooted in the Gospel itself. Jesus came to call people together, to make enemies friends, to unite rich and poor, educated and ignorant, insiders and outsiders, the pure and the defiled in a community that is rooted in and modeled on his own union with God. On the other hand, he subverted all the natural boundaries that ground and mark off natural human communities. Blood relationship was relativized. Ethnic and religious affiliation was subordinated to faith. Class

and gender conferred no titles or authority. All were welcome at the table, welcome in the community of friendship
and empowerment Jesus was forming.

The Religious community is also a highly original type of
community. It is not a natural family. No one belongs to it by
birth or marriage, that is, by right. Although the community
exercises prudent discernment about who enters, no one is
excluded (or at least no one should be excluded) who has the
vocation, desire, capacity, and willingness to undertake fully
and to live the life. Everyone in the community is responsible
to make a place at the table for whoever enters, regardless of
personal tastes. People who have been cherished members
may leave definitively, but no one leaves with them or because
of them, and the community itself does not disintegrate as a
family does when partners divorce. And even among those
who enter and stay, there is a continuous reconfiguration of
immediate community as individual members in local groups
come and go in response to the needs of the congregation and
the calls of ministry. No one has the right to demand the presence of any particular member even though all have the right
to expect the support of the community.

In short, Religious community is a voluntary relationship of
people motivated by faith in and love for Jesus and the call to
serve his members. At the deepest level they do not come
together to be together, to meet one another's affective needs,
to solve their shared economic problems, to wield collective
political influence, to experience feminist solidarity, or even
to carry out some social or intellectual project even though
they may also do all or many of these things. Like Jesus' first
disciples, they respond to his call to leave all and follow him,
and they find themselves in the company of others who have
experienced the same vocation, others whom they are called
to learn to love, others with whom they will share faith and life
but who will never "belong" to them and to whom they will
never "belong" in the natural bonds of family.

A symbol of the call to gospel homelessness of Religious that
is especially eloquent in our society is the fact that no Religious

has a house of her own. In most cases the congregation owns real estate[14] that is used by the members, or it approves the rental of such property. The congregation is thus a corporate "householder" in relation to the individual itinerant members. Not owning one's own home, in our society, puts a person in a state of financial precariousness since nonowners are always vulnerable to all kinds of vicissitudes from rent hikes to eviction. But there are other, more subtle but even more demanding, aspects to not owning real estate.

It is not necessarily the case in first-world societies, as it was in the Palestine of Jesus' day, that not owning land is tantamount to destitution. But it is the case that, until a person owns a home, has the proverbial "castle" in which one's own decisions are final, one is seen as in transition from childhood (when one lived in one's parents' home) to adulthood (when one has one's own home). Because where she lives is not her own, the Religious does not control absolutely who may share her dwelling, how long she will live there, or even how it is to be furnished. Religious surrender the societal title to adulthood and the independence that comes with home ownership, as Jesus did in not founding a family of his own in a home of his own. The only earthly "home" of the Religious is the congregation itself, as her only human "family" is the community, and in neither case is this a simple substitution of one natural arrangement for another. Neither home nor family mean the same thing for Religious that they would have meant had she established her own home and founded her own family. This raises the question of what home and family do mean for the disciple who follows the One who had nowhere to lay his head.

C. Prophetic Witness and Homelessness

1. Homelessness and ecojustice: Traditionally, the state of celibacy, including its renunciation of family and a home of one's own, has been seen as an eloquent proclamation in the Church and to the world that "the People of God has here no lasting city but seeks the city which is to come" (*L.G.* VI, 44).

The attitude was often that we are in exile, traveling toward our true home, which awaits us in heaven. At best, this world is an inert support system for humans and at worst a tawdry distraction from our true business of seeking salvation. Today we are only too aware of the ambiguous fallout from such an attitude. People who think they are just "passing through" a locale do not feel responsible for it, may even disdain it or at least treat it as a mere commodity. On the contrary, people who regard a place as home love, protect, and care for it because it is their native context and the primary resource for their own survival and that of the generations who will follow them.

In the last few decades the Judaeo-Christian biblical tradition in general and Christianity in particular have come under increasingly serious criticism by ecologists for the mischief they have promoted by their species-centered domination ethic in relation to nonhuman creation and its world-denying spiritualities. Although some of this criticism is less than well founded, there is no denying that Christianity as a tradition, despite notable exceptions like Franciscan nature spirituality, has been far less cosmically invested than primal religions in general and many Eastern traditions. The ingrained sense that we are the owners of a soulless world that exists for our benefit has led to enormous advances in agriculture, manufacturing, and technology. But it has also spawned massive ecological destruction the scope of which we are only beginning to realize. There is no question that the human race, and especially the first world, is called to deep conversion from a stance of ownership, exploitation, irresponsibility for consequences, and contempt for nonhuman creation to ecological commitment.[15]

Religious are in an interesting position on this subject. On the one hand, Religious "leave the world" (in the sense discussed in volume 1, especially chapter 4), renouncing participation for their own profit in the economic, political, and social dynamics of culture and maintaining a certain prophetic distance or marginality in regard to secular society. Such a stance certainly has world-despising potential, a potential that has unfortunately been too often actualized. On the other hand, the nonproprietary stance of Religious toward material goods has discouraged the greed and rapacity that are so natural to human nature. The Rules of Religious orders have always encouraged frugality and respect in the use of material goods,[16] careful stewardship of resources, community sharing, and reverence for creation as manifestation and gift of God. It is not surprising that Religious, especially women, have been in the forefront of the ecological movement as it has begun to influence Catholicism. There is a kind of natural affinity between the attitudes and values encouraged by Religious Life, especially in regard to poverty and community, and ecological sensibility.

It seems to me that the homelessness of Religious has the potential for a particular kind of prophetic witness in regard to the Christian's place in the world at this juncture in history. First, we are being challenged, as humans and as Christians, to renegotiate our world-consciousness in relationship to biblical revelation.[17] On the one hand, we are indeed "exiles" in this world, not because we are on our way to some extraterrestrial homeland so superior to this world as to make the latter comparatively worthless, but because the way life on this planet is organized is so profoundly antagonistic to what Jesus called the Reign of God (God's will done on earth as it is in heaven) that, in many respects, it has driven out the truly human. Religious' "world renunciation" is not cosmic estrangement, much less contempt, but a prophetic critique of human lordship that calls humanity to recognize God's authorship of all creation and its destiny in God. The God-infused character of all creation, not just of humanity, grounds its claim to reverence, care, partnership, responsibility. Precisely because Religious want to live in a nonowning, noncontrolling mode, they are in a position to witness in a special way to a nondominative stance toward all creation, human and nonhuman.

In a paradoxical way homelessness grounds a kind of universality. Because no place is our "home" in the sense that we own it, control it, and can exclude others from participating in it, we can treasure every place in which we are with the kind of "caring and not caring," the kind of detached solicitude that can use things, without exploiting them, for the ends for which they are made. Religious are called to be citizens of whatever place they inhabit, children of the cosmos who do not recognize any absolute claims except those of God and hence can transcend the artificial boundaries humans have introduced to divide up land, resources, peoples, and even religion itself. Deep reflection on the kind of homelessness that Religious embrace in imitation of Jesus the itinerant messenger of God could lead to grounding ecological consciousness and commitment as well as global citizenship in Religious profession itself. Such a commitment could foster alliance with a similar sensibility arising in other movements (such as ecofeminism) and religions (such as Buddhism), bringing our particular spiritual heritage to the conversation even as we learn from the traditions of others. Needless to say, this topic must be taken up again in relation to poverty, but here we are concerned with the particular potential of celibate homelessness to foster an ecological spirituality.

2. *Homelessness and evangelical equality:* A second area in which gospel homelessness can offer prophetic witness is that of equality. Householding has an inveterate tendency to encourage hierarchy because social organization tends to require offices and offices require authority and authority tends to power. But itinerancy, life "on the road," tends to encourage *equality among those who share the ministry.* Without stores of resources or ready access to outside support the survival of the itinerants and the accomplishment of their objectives require everyone to contribute what she or he can and to rely realistically on the others for everything else. A functional equality arises from the homelessness itself. Since Vatican II many ministerial Religious have discovered through experience that there is no real need to duplicate the authority structures of the congregation at the local level. A group of Religious on mission probably does not need a local superior or even a local financial officer. They can negotiate their mutual service in community, whether they live together in

one house or congregate periodically from a variety of locations, without setting up a hierarchy of life or ministry.

Religious, especially women who are not part of the clerical system but who frequently work with men, both ordained and lay, often experience *an equality with men* that cannot be explained by the developmental stage of Western society. Crossan offers the fascinating hypothesis, which cannot be proved or disproved, that the seventy disciples Jesus sent on mission in pairs (cf. Lk 10:1ff.) as well as the couples to whom Paul refers in 1 Corinthians 9:5 composed of an apostle and a "sister wife" (ἀδελφὴν γυναῖκα)[18] were male-female (usually not married) pairs of equal missionaries. He proposes

> that a sister wife means exactly what it says: a female missionary who travels with a male missionary as if, for the world at large, she were his wife. The obvious function of such a tactic would be to furnish the best social protection for the traveling female missionary in a world of male power and violence. Was that the original purpose and focus of the "in pairs" practice—namely to allow for and incorporate safely the possibility of female itinerants?[19]

Whether or not this hypothesis is correct, it does point out something that is verified in the experience of many Religious, namely, that celibacy fosters equality and solidarity not only among women but between women and the men with whom they share ministry.[20] Women publicly vowed to consecrated celibacy, while certainly not immune from the dangers all women face in a patriarchal society, nevertheless have a certain protection, especially when working with Christian men in ministerial situations, against the sexually predatory assumptions of that society. Religious are simultaneously not "already taken" as spouses of another man (which would make them socially off-limits) and "not available" because of their celibate commitment (which makes them, nevertheless, actually off-limits). They are not, actually or metaphorically, "in their own home," but they are also not "on the street" in the sexual sense of that term. The equality and immunity of such women, in other words, are both the fruit of their ministerial homelessness and the facilitator of it.

As has already been said, itinerancy promotes another kind of equality, namely, *equality between ministers and those to whom they minister.* This witness has, unintentionally but unfortunately, been seriously obscured in eras in which Religious have become too institutionally entrenched. Crossan invites his readers to

> [i]magine...that Jesus had settled down with his family at Nazareth or with Peter at Capernaum and sent out disciples to bring or send back to him those in need of healing or teaching. That would have symbolized a God of domination and a Kingdom of control and mastery....he would have to be understood as promoting domination, kinder and gentler to be sure than Caesar's, but still domination and not empowerment.[21]

As already said, hierarchy of place can symbolize and therefore effect hierarchy of persons. The ensconced minister interacts with the beneficiaries she chooses, according to her schedule, on her terms, and at her price. The itinerant, on the contrary, has no more leverage than the beneficiary. The only condition for service is the generosity, the compassion of the minister. When Jesus asked the leper what he wanted, the man replied, "If you wish [want to], you can make me clean," and Jesus replied "I do will it. Be made clean" (Mk 1:40–41). Jesus does what he can, on the spot, in response to the faith-grounded request of the petitioner. He was not an agent of a patron-God or a patron religious institution but a fellow human being who wanted to do whatever he could do for anyone who needed his service.

After the Council many Religious congregations experienced a strong desire to divest themselves of institutional holdings, especially large schools, hospitals, agencies, and even motherhouses or other centers of government. The motive was primarily to jettison some of the "baggage" they felt impeded them from discerning and responding to new needs. Vested interests buttressed by historical attachments and the nonnegotiable commitments of their financial resources and personnel had made them maintainers and managers rather than risk-taking missionaries. While some of the divestment may have been too hasty and perhaps ill planned, the basic instinct was, it seems to me, very sound. It reflected a realization that itinerancy, not householding, is fundamental to ministerial Religious Life. No doubt some realistic balance has to be achieved between the congregation as householder for the community (perhaps like Peter's home or the Bethany family for Jesus and his disciples) and the Religious themselves as itinerant missionaries. And a spirituality that not only cherishes the congregation, including its physical homestead if that is part of the tradition, but also sees homelessness, being "on mission," as the normal situation of professed Religious needs to be developed. This topic will be taken up again in relation to community, but the point here is that celibate homelessness grounds a prophetic witness to a kind of equality that is rooted not in secular democracy but in the Gospel itself and the example of Jesus.

IV. Celibate Homelessness and Friendship

In the previous chapters devoted to consecrated celibacy I have spoken a great deal about both the unitive dimension of celibacy and its relativizing of ordinary human relationships. But, like poverty and obedience, consecrated celibacy has communitarian and ministerial dimensions as well as its preeminently unitive one. And although it relativizes all other relationships, especially those to primary and secondary family, and incorporates the Religious into the particular kind of following of Jesus characteristic of his itinerant disciples, it also raises to prominence in the life of the celibate a particular type of human relationship, namely, friendship. This was the relationship Jesus developed with his followers and encouraged them to develop among themselves.[22]

In one sense the logical context for an extended discussion of friendship in the life of Religious is celibacy since this is the distinctive and characteristic qualification of relationships in the Religious lifeform. The problem with a sequential treatment of issues in Religious Life is that because the latter is an organic lifeform rather than a collection of separable elements, every aspect implicates every other aspect, making it difficult to discuss any aspect or dimension of the life without discussing everything else. So, in the interests of avoiding unnecessary repetition and devoting adequate attention to each facet, some fairly arbitrary decisions have to be made about where to place certain discussions.

I am going to reserve discussion of friendship in the life of Religious to part 3 on community. This is not, however, a purely utilitarian decision. Like all human beings, Religious live in a context of human relationships that are constitutive of their life. The community that Religious form is neither an intentional community in the usual sociological sense of that term, that is, one that comes together to meet the common needs of the members, nor a network of associates whose contacts, casual or intense, are dictated by occasion, necessity, or mutual convenience. Less obviously, Religious community is also not a bureaucracy set up to handle individual and corporate affairs of people engaged in a common enterprise.[23] I am going to propose that Religious community is essentially a community of friends. Friendship will be explored not only as a basic human relationship, perhaps the most noble and enduring of all such relationships, but also as a reality that was transformed by Jesus into a participation in the life of the Trinity and a prophetic witness to Jesus' own understanding of the Reign of God. The community of friends that Jesus inaugurated is, of course, the pattern for the whole Church, but in the lives of Religious it is the primary and distinctive form of their relational life. Because it is not conditioned by primary or secondary familial contexts, it has a particular clarity and therefore witness value in the Church at large.

Such a proposal requires reflection in depth in the context of community. Here, suffice it to say that the renunciation of family and gospel homelessness do not, in a healthy Religious life, result in lifelong loneliness, isolation, narcissism, or a "lone ranger" approach to life or ministry. Although celibate and itinerant, Religious are not nonrelational monads tangentially brushing or occasionally colliding with other monads. Nor are they a corps of workers on the march with eyes so fixed on the goal that they do not see one another or the people to whom they are sent. Religious Life is, or should be, richly relational on many levels radiating outward from the primary relationship with Christ in which originate numerous other types of relationship. Among the latter, friendship holds pride of place, and its potential for enriching the affective life of the individual Religious, nourishing ministry, uniting a community, grounding its care for its own and their relatives, and incarnating a prophetic witness to the Reign of God is enormous.

V. Conclusion

In this final chapter on consecrated celibacy I have explored the particular type of discipleship, namely, that of following Jesus in his itinerant ministerial lifestyle, which is particularly characteristic of Religious in mobile, ministerial congregations. Not all Jesus' disciples are called to this "homeless" lifestyle, and it is not definitive of discipleship as such nor more perfect than the stabile lifestyle of the householder. Discipleship consists in taking up one's cross and following Jesus. The lifestyle within which one follows Jesus on the way is a response to one's own vocation, neither superior nor inferior to other vocations.

Those called to this lifestyle choose to share in Jesus' homelessness, basing their lifestyle primarily on his itinerant ministry rather than on his hidden life in Nazareth. Although no lifeform or lifestyle in the Church can witness equally to all the aspects and dimensions of the mystery of Christ, this particular lifestyle is especially enhanced by and expressed in the vows of consecrated celibacy, evangelical poverty, and obedience. It creates a particular kind of community that is distinct from that of family life or householding. And it has a special prophetic contribution to make in two areas of concern to contemporary spirituality: ecojustice and gospel equality in ministry.

Although the discussion of friendship is deferred to the next chapter, it was important to note that the renunciation of home and family is not a repudiation of human relationships but does grant a pride of place to a particular type of relationship, namely, friendship.

Finally, it needs to be said, as it was in volume 1 apropos of stabile monastic and mobile ministerial Religious Life, that both itinerancy and householding, both homelessness and homemaking, are dimensions of the life of every disciple of Jesus. Because they are materially dialectical they cannot assume the same public face in the same life at the same time. While Jesus lived in Nazareth he was not an itinerant missionary. During his public life he did not live at home nor establish a home. But unless the homeless missionary has truly found her heart's home in God, her itinerancy will degenerate into aimless wandering, the kind Benedict excoriated as vagabondage. One who is not truly at home in God may move about from place to place but will not have that life-giving capacity that Jesus had to be "at home" wherever he was, enhancing the relationships of all involved and bringing the peace the world cannot give. Unless the householder maintains an evangelically restless heart, a continuous thirst for the coming of the Reign of God that will not let her "settle down" either in relation to her own spiritual life or in her zeal for the neighbor's well-being, she will become a spiritual "domestic." We are all basically homeless, our hearts, like Augustine's, restless until they finally come home to God. Journey and home, mobility and stability, ministry and contemplation are, or should be, at least interiorly, in a dialogical rather than dialectical relationship. All Religious (indeed all Christians) are called to both, but how they are realized in each individual's life is determined by vocation and charism and the response to that vocation is a gift to the Church as a whole.

PART THREE

Community

CHAPTER EIGHT

RELIGIOUS COMMUNITY: BIBLICAL AND THEOLOGICAL FOUNDATIONS

I. Introduction and Transition

The decision to place the unit on consecrated celibacy before this unit on community expresses my conviction about the priority of celibacy in the constitution and specifying of Religious Life as a distinctive lifeform in the Church. The central relationship around which this life is constructed is the relationship to God in Jesus to the exclusion of all other primary life commitments. Community is the relational context in which that life of total, loving self-gift is lived. Contexts can be either extrinsic or intrinsic, simply part of the environment or constitutive of the very meaning of a reality. The family, for example, is the context of the marital relationship. It is generated by that relationship, integral to it, and powerfully determinative of it. Community, as the context of Religious Life, is similarly intrinsically related to the relationship with Jesus Christ that is at the heart of the life. The conviction that community is not only important to Religious Life but integral and essential to it is a presupposition of these three chapters.

However, it is important to begin by recognizing that Religious Life is communitarian not because it is Religious but because it is *Christian*. Religious community is indeed a distinctive kind of community precisely because it is the community life of consecrated celibates, just as family is distinctive because it is the community life of a couple committed to each other for life and of the children who are nurtured by that relationship. In other words, the fact that Religious Life is communitarian arises from what Religious share with all the baptized, and this is theologically prior to what distinguishes it from other forms of Christian community.

In this chapter, therefore, I will consider community first as a constitutive dimension of Religious Life as *Christian.* Against that theological background we can explore the distinctive features of Christian community life among people who have made perpetual profession of consecrated celibacy within the same Religious congregation. I will be focusing specifically on the community life of cenobitic and ministerial Religious in contemporary congregations in the first world, hoping that what I say will also be helpful for stabile monastic Religious and Religious in other cultural contexts as well as for laity.

Integral to the discussion of celibate community life is the question of what type of affective bonds unite the members of such a community. I suggested in the last two chapters that family, whether primary or secondary, is not an appropriate model. Religious are called to participate in the itinerant or homeless life of Jesus, who initiated a new kind of kinship that is not based on natural family. In this chapter I will propose, as an appropriate model for understanding the distinctive type of community relationships among Religious, the relationship that Jesus established with his immediate followers, namely, evangelical (i.e., gospel) friendship.

Such a relationship has implications, which will be briefly indicated, for the spirituality of Religious themselves, for the Church, and for the world. But the primary purpose of exploring the nature and dynamics of evangelical friendship as the distinctive form of Religious community life at this point is to lay a foundation upon which to engage anew the questions of the next two chapters: How can the theological reality of Religious community be sociologically embodied today, both in the life of the individual and as a dimension of the corporate reality of the congregation; how do the various possible sociological embodiments express and affect the spirituality lived by Religious; and how can the witness of embodied Religious community life function within the Church in its postmodern context?

II. Religious Community as Christian

A. Community as Foundational to Christian Life

The entire Christian tradition, grounded in Scripture and lived throughout history, testifies to the fact that as humans and as believers we are called to community. The first creation account in Genesis (1:1–30) tells us that humanity was created in God's image "male and female," that is, as a community, from the very beginning. Even the second account (Gn 2:4b–25), much more anthropomorphic than the first, which recounts the creation of an individual human "earth creature" *[ha'adam]* (2:7), immediately suggests that the earth creature was not happy even in the Garden of Eden because it was solitary. God decides that it is not good for the creature to be alone (2:18) and transforms this first being into a pair, two who share human nature as woman and man (2:23–24). The first human community comes into being as a family, woman and man united first for their own well-being but also to procreate their species and to care for the earth.

When the Creator, according to Scripture, called some human beings into a special covenantal relationship in order to reveal Godself to the nations, God chose not an individual but a people (cf. Gn 17:3–8). Abraham and Sarah were to be the parents of "many nations" beginning with a people that was taken into slavery in Egypt but rescued by God through the leadership of Moses with his sister Miriam and brother Aaron as collaborators. It was with the Hebrews as a people, as a community, that God made an everlasting covenant at Sinai (Ex 24).

In the fullness of time God sent Jesus as savior of the world. Jesus did not emerge from God like Athena from the mind of

Zeus as a fully formed adult, but was born as an infant into a human family that was part of the community of Israel. He grew up in a human community, internalized its worldview and values, was shaped by its spirituality, and shared in its longings for freedom and life. And when Jesus was anointed by God through the descent of the Holy Spirit to preach the nearness and the inbreaking of the Reign of God, he formed around himself a community of men and women upon whom he breathed that same Spirit (cf. Jn 20:22) and whom he commissioned to share that new life with the whole world. The result of their preaching is what we call the Church, a vast, unbelievably diverse community that has lasted over two thousand years and continues to attract God seekers in our own time.

In short, no matter how scholars deal with the mythological and anthropomorphic material in the Old Testament or the kerygmatic reshaping of the Jesus story and its aftermath in the New Testament, the basic message is very clear and in no way attenuated by historical criticism of the biblical texts. Humanity is communitarian by nature and by divine vocation. Jesus redeemed the whole human race. The Church is a community called by God, first for the salvation of its own members and through them for the salvation of the world. Creation, redemption, Church, and ministry are intrinsically and essentially communitarian.

Religious Life, then, is not a uniquely communitarian venture in a basically individualistic world and Church. It is communitarian because it is human and Christian. Unfortunately, especially in the Tridentine period, Religious congregations often appeared not only as a distinct form of community within the Church but as a separate form of Christian life over against the mainstream of the Church. This separation was never absolute, of course, because Religious lived the sacramental life common to all in the Church. But private Mass, confession, and last rites in the convent, to which no one else was admitted, separate seats even when Religious attended Mass in a parish Church, a virtually completely enclosed life, as well as the undisguised conviction that association with "seculars" was a threat to the spiritual life of the Religious created a sense that Religious alone lived a real "community life" in the Church. Even the family, the first community created by God, was viewed as both inferior to the Religious community and a danger to its own members who became Religious.

Today, fortunately, this separatism seems to be a thing of the past. Religious not only minister with secular Christians as equals but share liturgy with the rest of Church, both by participating in parish community and welcoming others to their own celebrations. They share life and spirituality with lay associates, have friends outside their own communities, and participate in the lives of their own and other families. Although this situation is undeniably healthier and more in accord with the divine plan discerned in Scripture, it also creates an entirely new set of issues around community with which Religious, as individuals and as congregations, must deal.

B. Implications for Religious Life

The reappropriation of the fact that Religious community is not a substitute for, much less a competitor to, Christian community but rather a particular way of realizing and living the common Christian vocation to community both absolutizes and relativizes community as a dimension of Religious Life, although in different respects.

First, it *absolutizes* community as essential and necessary to the life, not because it is Religious but because it is Christian. Whether one lives Religious Life as a hermit in the Egyptian desert or as a member of an enclosed monastic community or as part of a highly mobile ministerial congregation whose members are scattered across the globe, community is a constitutive dimension of the life itself. How it is lived is another matter, but that it is lived is nonnegotiable. I will reserve most of the questions about "how" to the next two chapters, concerning myself here with the theological and biblical foundations of Religious community.

Second, the Christian character of community also *relativizes* the community life of Religious institutes. This is particularly important today when some, if not many, people considering Religious Life for themselves are particularly attracted to the life as a way of living community. Although this is certainly a valid aspect of motivation for Religious Life, it requires considerable discernment. If a prospective member sees Religious Life as the only place or way of life in which spiritually motivated Christian community is available or possible, she is not only projecting unrealistic expectations on the Religious community in question but is also setting herself up for inevitable disappointment. Furthermore, she is misconstruing the theology of Christian community that is basic to Religious community life.

Given the concern with community of many currently thinking about Religious Life, it seems to me that congregations need to pay particular attention to the community background of prospective candidates. Ideally, a person should come to Religious Life not as a social isolate, an areligious or denominationally unaffiliated "seeker,"[1] or as a virtual "catechumen," but as a mature and experienced Catholic Christian seeking to shape an already deep commitment to Christ in the Church in a particular way. Of course, a best case scenario would include an upbringing in the "ecclesiola" of a Christian family, in which participation in the life of the Church has inculcated a Catholic Christian culture of personal prayer, liturgical celebration, and service to neighbor, and at least a brief experience of active adult membership in the local Church. In preconciliar times one requirement for application to a Religious congregation was a letter of recommendation from the applicant's pastor, the point of which was to ensure that the person was already an active and responsible participant in the Christian community. In reality, many candidates for Religious Life today come from backgrounds that not only did not include a practicing Christian family life within an active local Church community but may not even have included anything that could be called a healthy family life. Some candidates are adult converts to the Catholic Church who may or may not have entered the Church through an effective RCIA program. And many who are nominally Catholic are devoid of any systematic religious education.[2]

In my opinion, it is very risky to admit a person to a Religious congregation who has not had a fairly extensive and active experience in a normal Catholic community such as a parish, whether geographical, university, or nonterritorial. Not only is the local Church community the place to develop a basic Catholic culture, to learn something about the recent and longer history of the Catholic Christian community, and to integrate regular liturgical and sacramental participation and active involvement in ministerial outreach into one's personal spirituality, but it is also the proper place to learn how to accept and deal with the imperfections in leadership and membership so glaringly apparent to the newcomer to any community, to face the issues of authority and power that are endemic to ministerial involvement today, and to see the "Catholic thing" in action with all its promise and poverty.[3] Leap-frogging over this normal experience of Catholic community directly into the highly distinctive and specialized form of Catholic community that is characteristic of Religious Life, especially by very recent converts with an idealized conception of their new spiritual home or Catholics who have been estranged from the faith of their childhood for many years and have missed much of the postconciliar experience, is to court serious conflict if not failure. I am not suggesting that such applicants be rejected but that their candidacy be extended, perhaps to several years, and that it be spent in a context in which participation in the local Church is the norm, not the exception.

In other words, people should not enter Religious Life "for community" as if this were the only place in the Church in which community is or can be lived, or even worse, as if it is the best or ideal form of community life in the Church. Religious community, as we will see shortly, is a unique kind of Christian community, in different ways both more and less intense than most other forms. Community is a constitutive dimension of Religious Life, the context of shared celibate commitment, but it is not its exclusive prerogative, not its raison d'être, and certainly not its totality. It is also not the place to acquire one's first experience of what community means or how to live it. Religious community life offers many gifts and makes many demands, and anyone who lives it seriously will learn a great deal about herself, others, and life together. But the chances of this happening are greatly enhanced if the candidate is already a "communitarian" Christian with varied experiences, realistic expectations, and developed social coping skills upon which the specific experience of Religious community life can build.

III. The Specific Character of Religious Community as Celibate

What distinguishes Religious community life from other forms of Christian community such as the family, the parish, communities of solidarity and resistance, lay missionary communities, and so on is the fact that its members are consecrated celibates, usually of the same sex. This entails three features of Religious community that give it a unique character.

A. Religious Community Is Not "Natural," Necessary, or Intentional

First, unlike a natural family, a Religious community is not bound together by blood or marriage relationships. In this sense it is not a "natural" community. Not only is no one born into it, but no one must be accepted because of her or his relationship to someone who is already a member "by nature" as in-laws, stepchildren, or half-siblings become members of a blended family.

Second, Religious Life is not a requirement for salvation, for first-class membership in the Church, or for participation in ministry. The congregation is not under obligation to accept any particular applicant. In other words, membership is not necessary, either from the standpoint of the potential member or from that of the community. Membership in a Religious congregation, and therefore in the Religious community, is purely voluntary on both sides.

Finally, no one enters, stays, or leaves a Religious community because of another member. There is no guarantee that anyone who is a member when one enters will remain so or, at least in ministerial congregations, that one will share local or immediate community with any particular member or group within the community. No one has a "right" to be in immediate community with any other particular member(s) and, although few renewed congregations make arbitrary or non-consultative decisions about constituting or breaking up local communities or about moving members from one local community to another, there is no question that the good of the congregation and the effectiveness of its mission have a real priority over the self-selection of community configurations. In this sense, Religious community is not intentional in any absolute or nonnegotiable sense.

B. Religious Community Is Typically Monosexual

Although there have been experiments, both in the past and in emerging contemporary communities, with male-female Religious community, the vast majority of Religious congregations are one-sex communities, and experience suggests that attempts at two-sex community, unless the community aspect is rather strictly regulated (as it was, for example, among the Shakers or in medieval double monasteries), are not highly successful.[4] There is no question that the one-sex or homosocial characteristic of Religious community marks it off from virtually all other forms of community inside and outside the Church. Families, parishes, intentional communities of all sorts, social action communities, volunteer communities, even school or university communities are virtually always composed of males and females. Monosexual groups such as single-sex high schools, military academies, or Scout troops are transitory homosocial environments constructed for some particular purpose and not intended to last into adulthood much less to be permanent.

Both women and men today, often for very different reasons, can find single-sex community highly attractive. Although statistics are hard to obtain, experience and the reports from reliable sources suggest that male Religious life attracts a significantly higher proportion of homosexual men than there are gay men in society at large, suggesting that monosexual community is part of the attraction to the life.[5] While this disproportion seems to be much less characteristic of women's Religious Life, many women, hetero- as well as homosexual in orientation, especially committed feminists whose tolerance of patriarchy in society and Church is wearing increasingly thin, find the possibility of living and ministering with other committed women in an all-woman environment highly attractive.[6]

Needless to say, the one-sex character of Religious Life also presents unique challenges, whether a person is heterosexual or homosexual, feminist or not. For the homosexual man or woman the one-sex environment can be particularly sexually stimulating, making it difficult to maintain, without undue tension, a genitally abstinent celibacy and nonexclusive relationships with fellow community members. For the heterosexual woman or man the absence of the natural stimulation that is generated by a two-sex environment can drive the person to seek such stimulation outside the community and to form relationships with people of the other sex that become exclusive, genitally active, or so involving that they interfere with community life or ministry.

In other words, the person who enters a Religious congregation is not simply opting for community life. She is joining a unique form of community that requires a high degree of psychosexual integration and maturity if it is to be lived in a healthy, relatively relaxed, and growth-producing way. Only a person truly called to consecrated celibacy, who finds both psychological and spiritual fulfillment in her commitment to Jesus Christ in himself and in his members, is likely to find this one-sex environment a naturally supportive matrix for her own affective development. This is not to say that only such a person can successfully live the life of celibate community, but it does suggest that a person who does not feel personally called to consecrated celibacy is highly likely to find this type of community stressful if not frustrating and, if she lives it faithfully, probably less than affectively fulfilling. Research, especially among diocesan clergy, suggests that achieving healthy, genitally abstinent, sexual integration is a relatively rare achievement among those who do not feel called to consecrated celibacy.[7]

C. The Bonds and Permanence of Celibate Community Are Unique

Most intentional communities in the course of history have begun in fervent enthusiasm about some cause, lifestyle, or project but have unraveled relatively soon.[8] This usually happens in contemporary communes as members marry and begin to raise their own families, finish their educations and begin to function as professionals, relocate in response to career demands, develop different attitudes toward money or politics, or simply lose interest in the original project. Some intentional communities, for example, the Catholic Worker, have developed mechanisms for the continuance of the community through change of membership, but most communes, especially those without foundations in shared faith commitments, have dissipated sooner rather than later. Often the only way to hold such communities of unrelated members together has been by authoritarian leadership and the development of coercive and even punitive rules of life. The unhealthy nature and destructive dynamics of such cults have been explored extensively in the last few decades.[9]

Religious communities, as we will see in greater detail in the next chapter, are not "intentional communities" in the sense that communes, communities of solidarity or resistance, or cults are. This means that the members do not belong to the community in order to satisfy their own or one another's emotional or affective needs, however legitimate these may be. Nor do they belong in order to maximize economic or political power, even for the sake of service to the poor and oppressed. The members of a Religious community are drawn together by the love of Christ and commitment to the Reign of God. Because they share this love and commitment they bond together in community. In the next section I am going to suggest that the bond that unites them to one another in community is evangelical friendship, which is not peculiar to Religious Life but that takes on a particular tonality in the celibate community.

History testifies that, paradoxically and amazingly, Catholic Religious community is one of most stabile and long-lasting forms of voluntary community in the history of the Western world, even though it lacks a sexual, blood, economic, or political base and is not created with community itself as its objective.[10] Perhaps community, like friendship and happiness, is something most likely to happen when not sought in and for itself. In any case, this history suggests that people looking at Religious Life today should seriously question and be questioned about whether they are primarily seeking God or seeking community. If it is not the former, as St. Benedict said fifteen centuries ago,[11] they are well advised to look elsewhere.

IV. Evangelical Friendship:
The Bond of Religious Community Life

Having started by saying what Religious community is not, namely, a natural or necessary grouping based on blood or relationship, an intentional community based on economic, political, or other shared objectives, a substitute family, or simply an emotional home base for people seeking refuge from postmodern alienation, it is now necessary to try to say what Religious community is. What unites these very diverse people who enter a community that preexists them, made up of members they may not know at all prior to entrance and some of whom they may never like in any natural sense of the word, but within which they will make a lifelong commitment to share a life of consecrated celibacy and full-time ministry?

In previous writings I have suggested that the familial model often suggested for Religious Life presents more problems than resources for understanding Religious community.[12] As already discussed in chapter 6, Religious community is not a primary family of parents and children nor a secondary family of freely chosen partners. If neither family nor the military nor the business world supply the model, what can enlighten our understanding of the unique community that characterizes Religious Life?

Perhaps because of the extraordinary diversification of human living arrangements and relationships in the second half of the twentieth century, which has relativized the apparently self-evident normativity of the nuclear family,[13] a good deal of attention has been focused of late, not only among social and cultural analysts but especially among theologians and biblical scholars, on the category of friendship. From being a minor or trivial category, as in "She's just a friend" (meaning nothing serious is going on between us), friendship has become the preferred category within which to understand many of the most significant relationships among human beings. Friendship is the category I find most useful for talking about the bonds of Religious community.

In recent years a number of studies have appeared that focus on friendship in the Fourth Gospel.[14] One of them, Sharon Ringe's *Wisdom's Friends,* deals with this subject in a manner very close to what I will propose, and I acknowledge in advance my debt to her for some new insights but especially for help in organizing a vast amount of data into a manageable section for this chapter.

The Gospel of John, more than any of the other Gospels, develops the theme of relationship: God's relationship to the world (epitomized in Jn 3:16); Jesus' relationship to God (Jn 1:1–18 and passim); Jesus' relationship to his disciples and theirs to him (esp. Jn 15:1–12); the relationship of the disciples among themselves (esp. Jn 15:12–17); the relationship of Jesus and his disciples to the world (e.g., Jn 16:1–3 and esp. 9–19); and finally the continuation of the relationship between Jesus and his disciples through the gift of the "other Paraclete" after his glorification (Jn 14:16–18, 26; 15:26; 16:7–11 and esp. 12–15). Central to this intricate and expansive exploration of relationship is the category of friendship, which has a rich history in classical Greek and Roman literature that predates Christianity but especially, for our purposes, in the Wisdom literature of the Old Testament. The exploration of this literature is beyond the scope of this chapter but it will be utilized in what follows.[15]

Unique to the Fourth Gospel is its identification of Jesus in the Prologue, which is a thematic overture to the Gospel as a whole (Jn 1:1–18), as the λόγος (logos) or Word of God made flesh. Logos (a masculine noun in Greek) seems to be the masculinization, perhaps in deference to Jesus' biological sex, of the feminine gestalt of God in the Old Testament, σοφία (sophia) in Greek and חָכְמָה (hokmāh) in Hebrew, which are both feminine in gender.[16] Whatever the history of the logos terminology in the Prologue of the Gospel, it is clear from the Gospel as a whole that the evangelist intends to identify Jesus as the Wisdom of God incarnate.

Wisdom, who appears in several books of the Old Testament (esp. Proverbs, Sirach, and Wisdom of Solomon), is the high point of the development of the history and theology of the Word of God that begins with God's creation through the Word in Genesis 1, continues in the divine gift of Torah on Sinai, through the prophets who are the special bearers and defenders of the Word of God, to the sages who reflect on Wisdom's role in history and daily life. So, when the Fourth Evangelist identifies Jesus as the Word of God, Holy Wisdom incarnate, the reader has a rich context within which to understand what is being said about Jesus.

Wisdom in the Old Testament is God's very self as creative love who, after bringing into being all that exists, wanders about in her creation seeking a dwelling place among humans, a home on this earth.[17] She is often rejected by the foolish, but to those who receive her she grants the inestimable gift of taking up her dwelling among and within them and making them friends of God and prophets (cf. Wis 7:27).[18] Anyone familiar with the Fourth Gospel will immediately recognize in this description of the Word of God/Holy Wisdom, the God who became flesh in Jesus. This is the Word in whom all things were made, who came unto his own who received him not but who gave to those who did receive him the power to become children of God, among and within whom he took up his abode, and whom he finally called his friends.[19]

John's Gospel offers us a detailed meditation on the meaning of this friendship. Jesus both demonstrates what friendship means and explains it in words. To be a friend is to share life in continuous companionship (the theme of indwelling in John, esp. 14:20), to accompany (the theme of following and being where Jesus is, 12:26, and esp. 14:2–3), to care for (like the model Shepherd caring for the sheep, esp. 10:1–6), and even to lay down one's life for one's friends, (esp. 10:15–18 and 15:13–15). The central passage about friendship (15:1–17) occurs in the context of Jesus' last meal with his friends in which Jesus offers the image of the vine to explain the intimate life-giving relationship between himself and them. He then goes on to explain the interlocking of his relationship to them, their relationship to God through him, and their relationship to one another in him. Central to this development are verses 15–16: "I no longer call you slaves, because a slave does not know what his master is doing. I have called you friends, because I have told you everything I have heard from my Father. It was not you who chose me, but I who chose you." The relational life that Jesus inaugurates with and among his disciples has three interrelated phases or moments: filiation, fraternity/sorority, and friendship.

A. The Relation of Jesus and His Disciples and Their Relationship to One Another

1. Filiation: According to the Prologue of John's Gospel, those who receive the Word made flesh in faith become "children of God" (cf. Jn 1:12). It is significant that, in this Gospel, there is no reference to divine adoption. Jesus' disciples are not adopted children of God (τεκνία θεοῦ) but are really children of God, "born from above" as Jesus is (τέκνα θεοῦ). The extraordinary image of the vine and the branches (Jn 15:1–10) underlines this sharing of nature between Jesus the only Son and God's children in him. The relation between a vine and its branches is one of identity and distinction, like the relation between God and the Word who is "with God and is God" (cf. Jn 1:1). A vine and its branches do not differ in nature but only in origin in that the vine is the source of the branches, which derive their nature and power from the vine. Without the vine the branches can neither exist nor bear fruit, but astonishingly, the vine, which can exist without these branches or indeed any branches, can bear no fruit without branches! The intimacy of the union between Jesus and his disciples is one of shared nature and distinction of relation to the source. They share his identity as children of God even while remaining distinct from the only Son, and they, like Jesus, bear fruit to the glory of God (cf. 15:8).

The filiation that his disciples share with Jesus, their being really God's children, is the basis of both their union with him and their union with one another. As we saw in chapters 6 and 7, the replacement, within the context of faith, of biological family determinant of identity and destiny with the family of faith is a theme in all four Gospels, focused in a special way in the transformation of the relationship of Jesus with his mother from a natural bond of maternity to that of those "who hear the Word of God and do it." (Lk 8:21).[20] In John's Gospel the two passages in which the Mother of Jesus appears (Jn 2:1–11 and 19:25–27) underscore this common theme and bring it to culmination.

This theme of the replacement of natural family with the family of faith, which forms a major inclusio[21] in John's Gospel through the figure of the Mother of Jesus, is enclosed within an even more comprehensive inclusio on the theme of divine filiation. In the Prologue, at the very beginning of the Gospel, we learn that the purpose of Jesus' coming into the world, of the Word becoming flesh, is to give the power to become children of God to those who believe in him (Jn 1:12). At the end of the Gospel, when the paschal mystery or the "hour" of Jesus is finished, he commits the Easter kerygma to Mary Magdalene, telling her to announce to the disciples that they are now sharers in his divine filiation, that his Father is now their Father (Jn 20:17).[22]

2. *Fraternity/sorority:* Children of the same parents are siblings, sisters and brothers. Nowhere in John's Gospel, prior to the completion of the paschal mystery, does Jesus refer to his disciples as either his siblings or siblings of one another. But once glorified, he tells Mary Magdalene to "Go to my brothers and sisters [ἀδελφοί, like English "brethren," is masculine in form but inclusive in meaning when the subject includes both genders], and tell them...." And Mary obviously understands this to mean, "Go to my disciples" because we are told that "Mary of Magdala went and announced to the disciples" (Jn 20:18), a group that, in John, is clearly inclusive of both women and men. The implication of shared filiation is bondedness in shared fraternity and sorority, not only with Jesus the Son of God but with all the daughters and sons of God typified in John's Gospel especially by Mary Magdalene and the Beloved Disciple.

3. *Friendship:* Divine filiation and the resulting sisterhood and brotherhood creates a spiritually "necessary" bond. One does not choose one's siblings. One is born into the family that includes the other children of one's parents. The major difference, of course, between the human analogue and the spiritual "family" used as metaphor for the relationship among Jesus' disciples is that one must indeed choose to be born into the spiritual family. Only by coming to believe in Jesus is one born of the Spirit into the new family in which Jesus is the firstborn and his disciples are truly children of God. Thus the "necessity" is not natural but freely chosen. However, the metaphor of siblinghood is important because it stresses the fact that neither our relationship with God nor our relationship with Jesus, however intimate and personal they are, is solitary or private. To be

a child of God, to be a sister or brother of Jesus, means to be related by the blood of the Lamb to all the others who share this covenant relationship, that is, to all those whose God is the God of Jesus (cf. Jn 20:17).

As everyone knows from experience, being members of the same family, no matter how permanent and unavoidable it is, does not necessarily entail a positive relationship. Perhaps no feuds are as bitter and intractable as those among relatives. Sibling relationships, if they are to be lasting and life-giving, must develop as the children mature into friendship. In John's Gospel friendship is the ultimate description of our relationship with Jesus and the model he proposes for our relationships among ourselves. Jesus closely links our friendship with him with our friendship among ourselves. "This is my commandment: love one another as I love you" (Jn 15:12). He then goes on to say how he loves us: "No one has greater love than this, to lay down one's life for one's friends. I no longer call you slaves....I have called you friends" (Jn 15:13–14). And Jesus himself makes the connection between his friendship with us and ours with one another: "You are my friends if you do what I command you," namely, love one another as he loves us, unto death.

The relational life described in such detail in John's Gospel is the model for all relationships in the Church. Finally, it is well known that any human relationship, whether between parents and children, among siblings, or between spouses or other life partners, only reaches its ultimate point of development if the persons involved become friends. Each of these friendships retains, however, its own unique features. Adult children who become truly friends of their parents do not usually abandon the filial form of address, signifying that this is a particular kind of friendship. Siblings have a relationship based in shared history and biological relationship that is different from the other friendships of each sibling. The friendship between spouses includes an element of sexual intimacy and exclusivity that no other friendship does. And friendship without any biological basis, what we might call archetypal friendship, has characteristics, which we will explore below, that make such friendship unique.

B. Evangelical Friendship

In what follows I want to explore what evangelical friendship unto the laying down of one's life involves and suggest that it is precisely this relationship that should be the characteristic bond among Religious in community.

1. Intrinsic features: Friendship that is not based in biology but is freely chosen has some features that shed light on the community bonds of Religious Life. First, friendship is a relationship that is *mutual* and *egalitarian.* Much has been written about the reflection of the classical Greek and Roman philosophers, especially Plato and Aristotle, Cicero and Seneca, on this aspect of true friendship.[23] The important point, clearly exemplified in John's Gospel, is that friendship requires the leveling of inequalities. Jesus, even though he is by nature Lord and Master in relation to his disciples, does not consider them slaves or servants but equals, friends. And he demonstrates this by rendering to them the service slaves would render their masters (cf. the foot washing, Jn 13:1–20). Friends can mutually render any and all services to one another without any implication of humiliation, dependence, or condescension because equality renders such categories irrelevant. One of the most immediate changes effected in women's Religious congregations after the Council was the abolition of distinctions, historically understandable perhaps but fundamentally contrary to the meaning of Religious community, between choir and lay members, between the servers and the served.

Second, as we saw in relationship to marital friendship in chapter 5, friendship is *historical and developmental.* It begins in some mysterious fashion as two people get to know each other, and it grows, through ups and downs, conflict and reconciliation, communication and challenge to whatever depth it is destined to attain. In other words, it is not a "given" as is biological relationship. Whether or not one loves one's parents or siblings, one continues to be related to them, and that relationship has some influence on one's life. The relationship can stagnate, deteriorate, and even end in total estrangement. But it remains a relationship. Friendship, by contrast, must either continue to grow and deepen or it will die. Friendships are not sustained by blood or genes but only by love freely shared. This makes them both more vulnerable and ultimately stronger than any other kind of relationship. A true friendship actually can call a person to lay down her life for her friend. The laying down of one's life in such a case is not a sacrifice for "another" but a sharing of life with one who has become one's "other self." In Religious community this sharing of life is expressed in many ways, but perhaps the most powerful is the mutual commitment of all one's resources, economic, intellectual, professional, personal, and social, to the shared life through the vows of poverty and obedience. No one in the Religious community sustains her own life out of her private means but freely puts her resources at the disposal of all and becomes completely dependent on the community for life in all its dimensions. We will consider this in more detail in volume 3 under the heading of poverty and obedience as the vows of community life.

Third, friendship is *particular and individual.* While there is certainly such a thing as general benevolence, "love of humankind," there is no general friendship. One says "friend" only to a particular person with whom one has a relationship that is not identical to any other relationship in the life of either person. This characteristic can help explain "degrees" of friendship as well as specificity. Friendship runs the gamut from willed benevolence, even that which is contrary to our natural inclinations, to the most intimate and fulfilling relationship of which humans are capable. In a Religious community the members choose to relate to one another as friends. The community is not an anonymous "them" but individuals to whom one is related specifically and individually, to whom one is committed for life, even if some of these members are less naturally congenial than others. Some members will always challenge one's capacity to love, but each is committed to not allowing the relationship to die, to not crossing the person off and consigning her to the category of "general benevolence." When all is said and done the member of one's community who is least naturally congenial has a claim on one that is irrevocable and even ultimate. And at the same time, there is room within the community for truly intimate friendships that, nevertheless, never exclude any other member of the community from one's love and concern.

The entire history of Religious Life bears witness by exhortations, conferences, legislation, and all manner of behavioral manifestations to the sense Religious have had of the challenge to live as a community of friends. This material is often found under the heading of charity, forbearance, patience, common life, "fraternal" love, or just community. But when carefully analyzed it is always about the specific and individual love of each member for each other member that takes precedence over all other relationships, even those of natural family.

2. Implications for community: The type of relationship among the members that is characteristic of and fundamental to Religious community, namely, evangelical friendship, has implications for the structure and function of community life. The first two implications, mutual sharing and egalitarian government, are actually the subject of particular vows, poverty and obedience respectively, and I will reserve discussion of them for volume 3. Here it will suffice to point out that holding all things in common is a feature of community life that seemed, even to the early Church, to flow directly from baptismal incorporation. The ideal Christian community described in Acts is characterized by the unity that arises from and is expressed by *mutual sharing:*

> All who believed were together and had all things in common; they would sell their property and possessions and divide them among all according to each one's need. (Acts 2:44–45)

> The community of believers was of one heart and mind, and no one claimed that any of his [or her] possessions was his [or her] own, but they had everything in common....There was no needy person among them, for

those who owned property or houses would sell them,
bring the proceeds of the sale, and put them at the feet of
the apostles, and they were distributed to each according
to need. (Acts 4:32–35)

The story of Ananias and Sapphira, which immediately follows
this text, makes it clear that this communal approach to material goods was voluntary, not required (see Acts 5:4), and in the
course of Christian history voluntary donations for the poor
and tithing have replaced the totally communal life, if indeed
such a life ever existed in the ecclesial community as such.
Putting all things in common so that no one has more than she
needs and no one less became the characteristic approach to
evangelical poverty of Religious communities, and it remains
so today. Friendship requires equality and mutuality and, especially in the first-world setting where money is the measure of
everything from physical well-being to social status and private
wealth is virtually idolized the sharing of all resources is a striking testimony to the practical power of the Gospel and the
unique character of Religious community.

Friendship is also incompatible with a social structure of
domination/subordination. *Equality* is intrinsic to friendship,
and a community of friends, no matter how it structures itself
for purposes of good order and efficiency, cannot be based on
ontological inequality among the members. The deleterious
and divisive effects of hierarchy in the Religious community
are often seen in clerical orders in which the ordained are
defined as ontologically different from and superior to lay
members.[24] Even the inequality between choir and lay Religious, which may have begun as a simple recognition of different gifts but developed into a class system of servants and
served, if not nobility and peasants, was genuinely inimical to
Religious community, and its abandonment after the Council
was an important step toward the reappropriation of the communitarian nature of Religious Life.[25]

It may well be that the present generation of Religious is the
first to have the resources to unfold the radical implications of
gospel friendship for Religious community, especially the

implications of intrinsic equality among all the members. Prior to the French and American Revolutions, the understanding of the basic equality of humans beings as such was not part of the intellectual repertoire of Western people who thought that blood lineage actually made some people, for example, royalty, intrinsically superior. And even after it was recognized that "all men are created equal" it took more than a century to begin to see the implications of this realization for people of color, women, the poor, and others who had been considered intrinsically inferior and who are not, to this day, fully equal in society. The rhetoric of equality notwithstanding, the reality that superiority and inferiority among human beings is a pernicious human invention and not a divine institution is clearly not yet incarnated in the legislation and practice even of so-called "developed" nations. And the institutional Church continues to maintain that the Church itself, a communion of intrinsically equal members baptized into Christ's one body (see, e.g., Gal 3:28), is by divine institution hierarchical (see, e.g., *L.G.* II, 10 and III). Religious Life is a lifeform in the Church that is in a position to explore and promote the reality of equality in its concrete daily life even as the institutional Church resists the implications of baptismal equality, the Council's challenge to dialogue and collegiality, and the power of "People of God" as a governing metaphor for the Church. Since the Council, women's congregations and nonclerical men's orders have moved rapidly, in practice as well as in rhetoric, toward the dehierarchicalization of their life. The language of superiors and subjects, blind obedience, and the use of parent-child and military metaphors for relationships have been largely retired. Class distinctions among members have been abolished, and patterns of government have moved toward collegiality, wide participation in corporate decision making, and mutual discernment about decisions affecting individual members. Not all of these developments have been enthusiastically endorsed by the Vatican, but their evident rightness is clear to Religious themselves, who are convinced that there can be no turning back.

3. Implications for ministry: The biblical link between Wisdom and friendship also has important implications for the ministerial involvement of Religious in the postmodern world. Wisdom is God's creative and salvific engagement with all that God has made. In Jesus, the Wisdom of God made flesh, this engagement manifests itself as friendship, the quintessential form of right relationship. Friendship with God in Jesus achieves its clearest manifestation among humans but, like God's concern for all that is, human love and concern should also extend to all creation. If Religious community is a particular realization of the universal friendship rooted in Jesus who is the Wisdom of God incarnate, then ecological concern and a prophetic mission of salvific presence and inclusive community are logical ministerial implications of the particular type of community realized in Religious Life.

Ecology has become a burning issue among aware people since the concern for the degradation of the environment emerged in the scientific community of the late twentieth century. As already noted in chapter 7, Christians in particular have been confronted with the negative contribution of the Judaeo-Christian tradition to the ecological problem through its anthropocentric theology justifying, often through an appeal to the first creation account in Genesis (1:28), humanity's domination of nonhuman creation.[26] Although the discussion about responsibility has become considerably more nuanced in recent years and the positive contributions of biblical religions to concern for the earth have been highlighted, it can hardly be denied that regions of the world in which Christianity is the predominant religious tradition have tended to lack the reverence for and sense of interdependence within nature that has characterized other cultures, notably those of primal and Asian peoples. The deep ecology and ecofeminist movements have made considerable progress among first-world Christians, and Religious congregations have been especially attuned to these developments.[27] At this point, most Religious do not need to be convinced of the urgency of the environmental crisis nor the rightness, from a human point of view, of ecological sensitivity and commitment. What may still need to be made explicit is the intimate relationship between ecology and Religious community, that is, between the ideal of universal friendship rooted in Jesus, the Wisdom of God incarnate, and the well-being and flourishing of all creation. If Religious community incarnates Wisdom's presence and work in the world, then concern and active care for all creation, which came to be through the Word, are implicit in the commitment to community itself, which cannot be limited to human beings. In other words, community that begins in the congregation among those who have vowed to share life together in Christ must radiate outward to include not only all people but non-human creation as well. The network of friendship that transcends bonds of blood or even common self-interest must include all that is within the web of life and being. In short, ecological commitment, for Religious, is deeply rooted in the community dimension of their life, which is itself deeply rooted in their exclusive God-quest in Jesus.

Ecological concern for the cosmos and our relationship to all creation, therefore, is not an extracurricular activity or the personal project of some people that makes no necessary claim on the congregation as a whole. It belongs to the very fabric of Religious Life. The fact that this realization seems new should not make us think it is invented for our time or is some kind of New-Age fad. In fact, it is not altogether new. In certain forms of Religious Life in the past, for example, in the monastery of Hildegard of Bingen in the twelfth century and the Franciscan movement, which dates from the thirteenth century, the theological basis of a nature-affirming spirituality was well developed. And the gradual unfolding, under new and different historical circumstances, of its implications for the present is part of the dynamic of revelation, which is not a dead letter of the past but God's living Word in the present.

A second ministerial implication of the Wisdom/friendship understanding of Religious community arises in the area of *missiology*. In the increasingly pluralistic postmodern world the traditional theology of mission is under considerable strain. No matter how historically understandable it might be, the conception of Christianity as the one true religion commissioned and empowered by God to stamp out all other religious traditions and incorporate all humanity into the Roman Catholic Church by baptism appears to most enlightened people as simply indefensible. Somehow a valid theology of mission has to simultaneously affirm *both* that the riches brought to the human family in Jesus are meant to be shared by all *and* that religious traditions which know nothing of Jesus but which have proved their efficacy in bringing people to spiritual maturity and fulfillment are genuine paths to salvation not meant for extinction. Grounding this development in missiology is dependent upon developments in the theology of religions, which is still far from full development.[28] In the meantime, Christian ministers, including Religious, must map a course of action in the arena of evangelization that is both committed to the unique revelation of God in Jesus and open not only to dialogue with but even to evangelization by non-Christian religious and spiritual traditions.

The Wisdom christology of John's Gospel and especially its implications for community may be a resource for engaging this conundrum. In John's Gospel the final missionary commission of the glorified Jesus differs significantly from that of the Synoptics. The Great Commission in Matthew 28:18–20 reads:

> "All authority [or power] in heaven and on earth has been given to me. Go, therefore, and make disciples of all nations, baptizing them in the name of the Father, and of the Son, and of the Holy Spirit, and teaching them to observe all that I have commanded you."

This commission, especially amplified by the version of it in the Markan appendix (cf. Mk 16:15–16) has, rightly or wrongly, undergirded a missiology of conquest. The commission in John 20:21–23 is strikingly different:

> "Peace be with you. As the Father has sent me, so I send you." And when he had said this, he breathed on them and said to them, "Receive the Holy Spirit. If you forgive

the sins of any, they are forgiven them; and those whom
you hold fast are held fast."[29]

This version of the commission would seem to supply the
rationale for a different kind of missionary program that may
be more compatible with a contemporary approach to non-
Christian cultures.

First, the basis of the commission in John is not Jesus' power
or authority [ἐξουσία] conferred on his disciples but his shalom
breathed into them. Second, the task is not to succeed Jesus by
making disciples, baptizing in the name of the Trinity, and
teaching Jesus' message, but to carry on Jesus' own mission as
the Lamb of God who takes away the sin of the world (cf. Jn
1:29) by forgiving sins and holding fast in communion those
who are thus reconciled with God. The narrative description of
how this mission is to be enacted in ministry is found in John
13:1–20, the account of the foot washing. Jesus ministers to his
disciples as friends and tells them that they are to do the same
to one another, thus manifesting a love that is truly that of the
personal God. The mutual love of friends, the community life
of his disciples, will reveal to the world not only that they are
Jesus' disciples (cf. Jn 13:35) but that God has sent Jesus for the
world's salvation: "I pray not only for these [his earthly disci-
ples], but also for those who will believe in me through their
word, so that they may all be one, as you, Father, are in me and I
in you, that they also may be in us, *that the world may believe that
you sent me"* (Jn 17:20–21, emphasis added).

In John, mission is primarily a matter of living the community life of friends in equality and mutual service, which will
draw others to seek the source of that life and to desire to
share in it. Jesus' disciples are to respond to that desire by sharing Jesus' word and offering the reconciliation that Jesus has
offered them, thus drawing them into community life which,
according to this Gospel, is Jesus' own life shared in the Spirit.
In short, one of the models of mission and ministry in the
New Testament, that of the Fourth Gospel, places little emphasis on going out to conquer the nonbeliever for Christ but
rather emphasizes a ministry of presence rooted in the kind of

community that can only derive from the inner life of the Trinity itself. It is a preaching by being, being together in friendship, reaching out in friendship. Friendship is not about changing the other but about accepting the other as other. In the end, probably nothing changes people as profoundly and permanently as the experience of friendship, but the change comes from within in response to the love offered, not from without by argument, much less by force.

Not only does this model of mission and ministry as lived community suggest the importance of the quality of community life among Religious themselves, but it helps explain and justify the choice by Religious (throughout history and today) to go, as Jesus did, among the most marginalized and abandoned, the "sinners" excluded by society and even by the Church, and to choose to serve them without condemning their "sins," trying to "convert" them, or even insisting on personal reform. There is, or should be, no moral or religious price tag on the ministry of Religious. It is primarily an extension to others of the love that binds the community itself, the love of Jesus, the Wisdom of God, who makes them friends of God and prophets.

A third ministerial implication of understanding community in this way might be the light it can shed on the divisive issue of membership (discussed at length in volume 1, chapter 2) and the problem of *inclusivity*. The Religious congregation as a life-form, that is, as an organic system that exists as a specific reality and relates to its environment without being absorbed in or by it, has and must have boundaries. A living system can have very porous boundaries, and the more mature it is the more porous its boundaries can be without threatening the identity of the system. But the community, which subsists in the congregation, can go well beyond the boundaries of the congregation itself. Many congregations are experiencing the mutual enrichment of extended community that involves not only vowed members of the congregation but also associates, volunteers, resident oblates, secular order members, confraternity members, and coministers, as well as friends and benefactors of the congregation who do not formalize their relationship with the congregation but remain attached to it by bonds of friendship.[30] Evangelical community is essentially diffusive of itself. Therefore, it is inclusive in its attractive power and its capacity to accept the other as other without attempting to change, convert, or otherwise dominate and without any need to absorb those who relate with it.

V. Conclusion:
The Role of The Spirit/Paraclete

According to the Fourth Gospel Jesus did not merely leave his disciples, the community of friends he had formed around himself, an historical example or a platonic ideal. He assured them that his going away in the flesh at the end of his earthly career was simultaneously a return to them in a new mode of interior indwelling (cf. Jn 14:28). By the gift of the Holy Spirit, the "other Paraclete," Jesus and the One who sent him would take up their abode within his disciples, empowering them to love one another as he had loved them and to do not only what he had done but "even greater works" no longer limited to one historical time or place.[31] He promised that the Spirit/Paraclete would lead them into all truth as they gradually, through historical experience, became able to handle more of the infinite reality of Jesus and the love of God for the world that Jesus came to reveal (cf. Jn 3:16 and 16:12–15).

Consequently, the effort of Religious to live the mystery of celibate community, the life of evangelical friendship, with all its implications of equality, mutuality, service, ecological commitment, nonimperialistic mission, ministry to the most abandoned, and inclusive love is not some human ideal invented by utopian visionaries. It is the Christian life itself, undertaken in the Spirit of Jesus and embodied in a particular lifeform within the Church.

All Christians are called to the kind of community Jesus inaugurated. But not all are called to live it in lifelong celibate commitment in an intergenerational, monosexual community of people brought together by a vocation to seek God in Christ to the exclusion of all other primary life commitments. Religious community, therefore, is both common to and unique among forms of community life in the Church (as is family life and other specific forms). It faces particular challenges and offers a particular witness. It cannot incarnate or express all that needs to be manifested in the Church or the world about evangelical community, but it says something that only it can say, and this is both a privilege and a responsibility.

CHAPTER NINE
EMBODYING RELIGIOUS COMMUNITY I: THE INDIVIDUAL PERSPECTIVE

I. Introduction and Transition

If community is theologically intrinsic and essential to Religious Life as a Christian lifeform and gospel friendship is the characteristic bond among the members of the celibate, single-sex community, it becomes crucial to inquire into how this unique kind of community is embodied in everyday life. In other words, what kind of social and institutional incarnation will enable and foster the theological reality of Religious community? This is a critical question today, the discussion of which neither theology, sociology, psychology, spirituality, nor canonical legislation alone can mediate. The topic is so tangled that many congregations hesitate to discuss it openly at all for fear that even naming the issues will hopelessly split the community.[1] Those who experienced the repressive and infantilizing uniformity of some preconciliar forms of common life are afraid that discussion of community will inaugurate a return to "the bad old days" from which they have so recently emerged. And those Religious who have been victimized by the excessive individualism of postconciliar developments, as well as newer members who have no experience of "the bad old days" and long for real community in an anonymous culture of alienation, may be seeking an unrealistic form of togetherness that is out of touch with contemporary developments. Very recently some courageous leaders have begun to suggest that the time is ripe for a renewal of the discussion and that it is imperative to get beyond stereotypes and fears.[2]

In this chapter I want to discuss Religious community on the personal or individual level, that is, from the perspective of the Religious herself rather than of the congregation as a whole. First, I will offer an hypothesis about the type of community appropriate to mobile ministerial Religious Life in order to shed some liberating light on the guilt-producing dilemma of the presumed normativity of classical "common life." Second, I will try to describe and analyze the various ways of embodying community life in ministerial congregations that are actually being practiced by Religious today: congregational group living in its contemporary form and three types of individual living, two of which I will propose as valid embodiments of Religious community and one of which is, in my opinion, a lamentable aberration that should not be confused or equated with the other two. Finally, and by way of transition to the next chapter in which I will take up the corporate dimension of community life, I will draw some conclusions about the various embodiments of community analyzed in this chapter.

II. Community in Mobile Ministerial Religious Congregations

In what follows I will use the term *common life* to designate that sociological form of community that was virtually universal among Religious congregations prior to the Council, namely, one in which all members of the congregation lived in groups composed exclusively of members of their own congregation, under an elected or appointed superior. They shared daily prayer, meals, work, and recreation, all of which were mandatory, virtually exclusively with each other. Members were rarely out of the house except when engaged in the ministry in which all members worked together, and when they were out, always with explicit permission of the superior and her knowledge of their whereabouts, they traveled in a group of at least two—that is, they took the community with them.

Despite official hierarchical lamentation and occasional threats, this form of community has largely ceased to exist among renewed congregations. Even in those that favor group living arrangements, the horarium is much less rigid, and members are rarely all home at the same time. Members travel frequently and alone or with nonmembers of the local community. Permissions are not required for most ordinary activities. Ministerial commitments are diverse, occasioning differences in schedules, relationships, and activities.

The question with which many Religious, as individuals and as congregations, are struggling concerns this de facto dissolution of common life. Lurking in the background of most discussions are two contradictory, and largely unexamined, premises. First is the assumption, fostered by tradition, Canon Law, Vatican literature, and the rhetoric of even revised rules, that common life, mitigated perhaps by certain necessities but essentially intact, is the normative form of community from which any deviation is an (ideally temporary) "exception." In other words, if it were possible (which, most would admit, it is not), all members of the congregation should and would be living a perhaps updated but basically traditional version of common life. Second is the gut-level conviction of most Religious that returning to common life would be personally and ministerially counterproductive, and so, whatever lip service is given to the "ideal," they have no desire or intention of doing so. In other words, there is a fundamental contradiction for many Religious between what they claim to believe and what they actually believe about community life. The first premise requires theological examination and the second requires sociological, psychological, and organizational examination, in terms of both spirituality and ministry.

A. Is Common Life the Theologically Ideal Form for Religious Community?

Historically, common life was, in fact, the virtually universal form of Religious community life for women from about the third century until Vatican II.[3] While it was heavily theologized in terms of Acts 4 and the second great commandment of the Law, neither of which was actually any more applicable to Religious than to other members of the Christian community, and promoted as the primary form of asceticism and the sure path to holiness of life, I would suggest that the primary reason for the universality of common life was historical, sociological, and canonical rather than theological. This is especially true in America where ministerial Religious Life developed primarily on the frontier.

Prior to the last third of the twentieth century, a single woman needed to live in a group if she were not to be sexually vulnerable in a society that regarded unmarried women not living in the house of a male relative as "loose" and therefore available. Furthermore, in an economy that largely excluded women from paid employment and in which money, even if and when available, did not provide access to many of the goods and services necessary for life, group living in relatively economically self-sufficient units was virtually the only context that could assure physical well-being or even survival. In days when travel was not only inconvenient but often virtually impossible, staying in one abode was normative. And when communication with any but one's immediate companions was an expensive and time-consuming process, people's relationships tended to be restricted to those with whom they lived and near neighbors.

On the American frontier all of these historical and sociological factors were intensified. Most Religious communities were economic units that provided for the physical and social needs of their members, protected them from harm, and created the sociological context for pursuing an intensely Catholic spiritual life that was in marked contrast to most of what went on around them in a militantly Protestant environment. Emerging historical records testify to the rapid spread of Religious congregations from their point of arrival on the Catholic scene in the new nation, but new foundations were always made by small groups sent from the original foundation, not by individuals.[4]

History and Church law reinforced this sociological necessity, suggesting that it was theologically necessary. Most Religious congregations came to America as missions from European congregations that were effectively cloistered. Although, as was discussed in volume 1, chapter 9, there was from the 1600s onward a gradual erosion of the enforcement of canonical enclosure among European women's orders engaged in active ministry, official recognition of noncloistered women's congregations as Religious did not come until 1900. Well before this official recognition, the American branches of some of these orders had begun to lead a much less cloistered life in response to the demands of the immigrant Church and the conditions on the frontier, which, in many cases, led to a juridical separation of the American branch from the parent order. But, historically, common life was the only form of community of which these Religious had any experience, and even when they abandoned rigorous enclosure for the sake of ministry their working model of community was that of the cloister, namely, absolute common life. Furthermore, this semienclosed model was required by the Vatican for recognition as Religious of even approved apostolic congregations, and such recognition was extremely important to most of them. Consequently, there was an assumption that strict common life, a form of social cloister adapted slightly for the sake of ministry, was intrinsic to Religious Life as such.

Today, physical and sociological survival does not require common life. Indeed, common life in large groups seems to many both unnecessarily physically demanding and psychologically stressful. And, in fact, ministry, which previously required a common effort of several Religious working together in a shared enterprise, often neither requires nor even permits Religious to function in groups. Thus, the burden of legitimating, or even requiring, common life for all Religious falls on canonical legislation appealing to history. The argument that because Religious Life has "always" been lived in common (which is, of course, not true) it must be lived that way today is not persuasive with Religious who have seen virtually everything in secular and ecclesiastical culture change within their own lifetime.

In short, unless common life can be shown to be theologically necessary in and of itself as the only valid embodiment of gospel community for Religious, there is no argument for its mandatory universality. It may, in fact, be the best or most functional version of community or be preferred by a particular congregation, but such a choice is not the only possible valid decision.

I want to suggest at this point that common life—not to be equated with community life or even with what I will call congregational group living—belongs naturally, and perhaps intrinsically,[5] to the monastic lifestyle of the stabile contemplative form of Religious Life but not to the mobile ministerial form. From the beginning, all communal Religious Life for women was stabile and monastic in lifestyle. When the ministerial form of the life finally emerged and was recognized, such monastic lifestyle elements as habit, horarium, and common life were retained both in order to foster the life itself and as evidence that it was genuine Religious Life. The first element of the monastic lifestyle to be modified and finally abandoned by ministerial Religious congregations was enclosure. Only after a century and a half of experience with nonenclosed Religious Life, and under the impetus of the Council, did ministerial congregations begin to question the compatibility with their own lifeform of other monastic lifestyle elements such as habit and horarium. Common life is only now beginning to be seriously examined.

A major difference between stabile monastic life and mobile ministerial life is that in the former the monastic community is, in fact, the congregation or order one enters. Monastics make a vow of stability within the local community or undertake an analogous obligation in other ways when they enter Religious Life. In intention (there are always exceptions) the community they enter is the one in which they will live until death. Thus a person becoming a Benedictine or a Carmelite not only chooses the Order but a specific monastery. Monasteries are at least relatively autonomous even within an order. They have their own history, ethos, and customs. Monastics do not normally move about from monastery to monastery. Consequently, and especially when combined with enclosure, monastic profession binds the Religious to the local community within which he or she will live out the entirety of his or her Religious Life.

Nevertheless, any acquaintance with monastic communities makes one aware of the enormous variety in the living of community life. Camaldolese monks, who are Benedictine, live a combination of the eremitical and the cenobitic life, occupying separate hermitage cells and coming together for liturgy and some meals. Cistercians (including those known as Trappists), by contrast, who also follow the Rule of St. Benedict, live a completely common-life form of cenobitic life.[6] Some women Benedictines live a strictly monastic common life, sharing the same dwelling even when numbers are large, while others function much like ministerial congregations even though all members remain attached to the one monastery of profession and the monasteries do not exchange personnel or become financially interdependent. Carmelite women's monasteries, although sharing a common Rule and belonging to the same Order, are extremely individual in their spirit and lifestyle and have only recently begun to have somewhat more frequent communications among themselves.

In other words, although the way in which common life is realized may differ widely from one monastery to another, and a modified eremitic lifestyle may be mingled with the generally cenobitic lifestyle, common life itself tends to be the outward expression of monastic stability. Monastic life consists primarily of personal prayer, liturgical celebration of Eucharist and Divine Office, and shared, usually intramural, work that supports the community itself. Any ministry undertaken, whether of prayer or service, is usually done within the monastery rather than by going out to those in need. Living, praying, and working together in a common and shared rhythm is monastic life in action.

Ministerial Religious Life is not monastic in lifestyle. The person who enters the Sisters of Mercy, the St. Joseph Sisters, or the Sisters of Charity does not enter a particular house or a particular local community. She enters the congregation. In preconciliar times this distinctive feature was clear. The Religious, once her initial formation was complete, was sent out "on mission." And she was changed from mission to mission throughout her ministerial life. Each mission, far from developing its own "personality" like a monastery, replicated as closely as possible the horarium, practices, and customs of the central congregational house, that is, the motherhouse or provincial house. The mission was a local realization of the congregation, not an independent entity in its own right. The fact that no one entered the local community, the frequent reassignment of members, the limited term of office and frequent changes of superiors, and their dependence on central congregational authority for the exercise of their office made it virtually impossible for a local community to develop any sense of itself as autonomous, any distinctive corporate personality, any ethos of its own, any financial independence in relation to the congregation. And this was precisely the structure and organization that served well the purposes of ministerial congregations. In such congregations community is intimately entwined with ministry, and while it is not completely instrumental it is also not the whole of the life of the members.

However, the combining of this ministerial centralization and mobility with the rhetoric of monastic common life created some serious tensions for ministerial Religious. The Religious was expected to invest herself deeply in the local community and its ministry but not to express (or even, ideally, to feel) any sense of loss, much less violation, when she was suddenly removed from the mission without any opportunity for ritualized leave-taking or appropriate grieving. She was to have the kind of confidence in and openness toward the local superior that would make sense if the superior, like the monastic prioress, were in office for an extended period, but she was not to continue her confidential relationship with that superior once the latter was out of office or the Religious herself had been reassigned. In that case, she was expected to start over with a new superior, whom she had no role in selecting, and to invest in her the same confidence that she had built up with the predecessor. (Needless to say, most learned to protect themselves spiritually from the dangers of such a situation.) Local superiors were temporary officeholders who had little real authority (they often could not give permission for a trip of more than a few miles or an emergency home visit)—although they often had too much power—but who, because of their investment with many of the marks of veneration characteristic of monastic abbots and abbesses, were very difficult to reassimilate into "the ranks" once they were out of office.

In short, ministerial congregations were caught in a double bind between their congregation-based ministerial identity and the common life expectations of a monastic lifestyle. As ministry took center stage during the conciliar renewal and congregations reappropriated the charism of their foundations, the incompatibility of the two lifeforms became increasingly evident. Ministries diversified rapidly and many Religious found themselves in situations in which there was no local community group with whom to live or one in which they could not live because of the nature of their ministry. They were "on mission" in a much more radical sense, out where ministry called them without the supporting structure or the restrictions of common life. But even when group living was possible, the uniformity of classical "common life" was not possible for or desirable to most. Traditional common life, despite official exhortations, chapter directives, and constitutional requirements, was in the process of disappearing.

As already discussed in chapter 6, for some this meant loneliness and even isolation, a sense of disaffiliation from their congregations that led to the formation of other primary relationships that eventually took priority over congregational membership, whether or not they eventually left. For many others it brought a welcome sense of liberation from burdensome restraints, a reduction of internal contradictions in their life, a chance to organize their personal spiritual life in function of their ministry rather than trying to fit their ministry into the crevices between the demands of the common life or "get their prayers in" between the duties of full-time ministry. They found themselves more committed to and strengthened by their individualized spirituality as well as more focused in their ministries.

The conclusion I would draw from the foregoing considerations is that, whatever is the case for stabile monastic communities, classical common life is not, theologically, the necessary or ideal embodiment of community for mobile ministerial Religious. If common life is not theologically mandatory, then it has to be examined for its possible contribution to the spirituality, psychological well-being, and ministry of the members of the congregation as well as to the sociological stability and ministerial effectiveness of the congregation itself. It may be the case that a congregation would choose this lifestyle for most or all of its members, would decide that it is actually inappropriate in view of its charism and current commitments, or would find that it is desirable or even necessary for some members or for most members at some times in their lives. In other words, common life is an aspect of the monastic lifestyle, like enclosure, habit, horarium, choral recitation of the Office, etcetera, which may or may not be helpful for ministerial Religious under some circumstances, but there is no foregone conclusion that, if possible, it should always be the first choice, much less that any other embodiment of community is deficient or inferior.

B. Is Congregational Group Life Conducive to Ministerial Religious Life?

Once liberated from an unexamined (and, in my opinion, erroneous) conviction that common life is the ideal or theologically necessary embodiment of community for all Religious, and the guilt that this conviction sometimes generates in those not living common life, ministerial congregations might feel more free to discuss honestly the pros and cons of some renewed form of congregational group life. Such discussion could result in a shared vision of community that could generate some concrete experiments and arrangements designed to realize an appropriate form of group living of community that is chosen and coherent and thus able to offer (probably in tandem with other forms) a prophetic witness in our individualistic and fragmented society.

1. Describing congregational group life: The reader will have noted by now that I am consistently distinguishing community or community life (the biblically based theological reality discussed in the preceding chapter that is essential to and constitutive of Religious Life) from lifeforms (monastic; ministerial), and such lifeforms from lifestyles (group living, including both common life and other more contemporary types; individual living, of which there are several types). The discussion that I am proposing would probably be facilitated by abandoning the term *common life* because of the historical baggage it carries, especially its negative connotations of total institution, uniformity, and authoritarianism, as well as its positive connection with the monastic lifeform. Perhaps a term such as *congregational group living* could better express what is being discussed in what follows. Such a term would denote several (usually more than two) members of the same congregation living together in the same dwelling and sharing life as members of the congregation. Each of these characteristics bears reflection.

First, a congregational group would normally be more than two. It would not be, ordinarily, a couple or dyad, for reasons discussed in chapter 6. Second, the core group would be members of the same congregation. This would not necessarily mean that no one else ever lived with them but that the community would be a St. Joseph community or Mercy community rather than a common dwelling for Religious of a variety of congregations such as a house of studies at a university or a convent shared by a variety of congregations ministering in the same school or hospital might be. Third, the members of the group would intend to share life, to make the community the present "home" of its members, and not simply a hotel in which they sleep and keep their belongings. Finally, they would share life as members of the specific Religious congregation, not simply as people who find it convenient to share expenses or happen to find themselves in the same neighborhood.

This last characteristic would entail, positively, corporate participation in congregational affairs; openness in hospitality, temporarily or permanently, to other members of the congregation; celebration of congregational feasts and events; a presence to one another in terms of prayer and respect for the spiritual needs and desires of each other; and a centering of community life on the Religious commitment that they share. Negatively, it would mean that the group does not become an enclosed and self-sufficient entity that is a law unto itself within the congregation, which pressures members to stay when ministry or other considerations call them elsewhere, which sets up covert ideological "entrance requirements" or social acceptability criteria for possible new members, or which creates an expectation of psychological intimacy that is unrealistic in a group whose members are not married to one another or committed to life together in this small group forever.

In terms of organization such a congregational group would select its own patterns of leadership within congregational guidelines, apportion responsibilities among its members, establish its internal accountability requirements, generate its mechanisms for fostering shared life such as times for meeting, prayer, meals, and so on. In other words, it would not be a "clone" of the motherhouse or central headquarters as missions once were, nor would it be an autonomous and self-contained society such as a monastery. And it certainly would not be a clique within the congregation. It would be characterized by the openness and flexibility appropriate to a community in mission but would have sufficient sense of its own identity to develop its own distinctive life and to contribute its own originality to the congregation.

2. *Advantages of congregational group life:* Against the background recognition that congregational group life is not theologically mandatory, that it is also not simply a resuscitation of the uniform, common life lifestyle of the total institution of the past, and that affirming or denying its value or desirability does not mean that all members of the congregation must therefore either live or not live this way, we can perhaps consider with some freedom of spirit what such a style of Religious community might have to offer and the challenges it raises.

It will probably always be the case that some Religious at least at some times in their lives will not be able to live in a congregational group even though they might desire it. Historically, this has often been the case, as with Damien on Molokai or Francis Xavier in China. Ministry, periods of study or renewal, family emergencies, or special projects can place a Religious where there are no other members of her congregation. But often it is possible for members to form a congregational group if they really want to do so. Our question is, why might they so choose? Or why might the congregation encourage them to consider this possibility?

a. *Advantages:* There are obvious *economic* advantages to group living. Everything from furniture to newspaper subscriptions to food and utilities is likely to be less expensive, and less wasteful, if shared. Religious poverty is not primarily about saving money but it does suggest prudent and ecologically sensitive use of resources as well as simplicity of lifestyle. Paradoxically, the economy that scale introduces can make it feasible to beautify a shared dwelling in ways that would be exorbitant for an individual. Aesthetic surroundings can be both economically functional and psychologically and spiritually nourishing.

Modern life is *psychologically* both hectic and stressful, and living with others can often, at least for many people, reduce this stress. A group can share household maintenance, shopping and cooking, financial management, dealing with service people, airport transportation, hospitality, and numerous other daily tasks that can be nearly overwhelming for an individual who has to handle all of them alone in the midst of full-time ministry. Psychologically, coming home at least a few times a week to a prepared meal with companions, or taking time to creatively prepare for the group a meal one would rarely take time to prepare for oneself, leaving for a business trip without having to foresee and take care of everything from newspaper and mail delivery to watering the plants, returning from a busy day to people who understand and respect one's commitment and its demands, and the simple pleasure of being able to share spontaneously a television program or a film without advance planning can be strengthening and calming. In emergencies and crises the presence and availability of trusted companions can be an inestimable gift. The sharing of one another's friends and colleagues can be a stimulating enrichment of life just as communication with one another about diverse ministries and interests can broaden one's horizons. Interesting spontaneous conversation with non-work-related people is one of group life's unprogrammed joys.

Living with others can also be a positive factor in *spiritual growth.* For many people shared prayer is a major support for their spirituality, and prayer is much more likely to be a regular part of such a person's life if she has daily companions. Faith sharing is not only conducive to depth in community life but a strong incentive to and affirmation of one's own faith development. Occasionally celebrating a nonsexist, participative liturgy with companions can be a relief and encouragement for Religious whose parish experience often ranges from dull to grim. Seeing one's companions at personal prayer, knowing that they are faithful to spiritual reading because of what they share, or being aware of their choices for spiritual direction, retreats, and days of reflection can support one's own spiritual discipline, especially in times of stress or weakness. In a supportive and affectionate community group younger (and older!) Religious can be mentored into responsibility and generosity and helped to grow out of behavior patterns they would not even notice if they were not interacting on a daily basis with other Religious. And living with others, none of whom is perfect, is an opportunity to serve, to be patient, to grow in compassion, and to courageously deal with difficulties even as one experiences the love and long-suffering with one's own problems offered by others.

Living with a group can also be a support in *ministry*. Movie-goers got a glimpse of this dimension of Religious Life in the film *Dead Man Walking* as Sister Helen Prejean was affirmed and relieved in her demanding prison ministry by the timely support and even the humor of her local community. Some-times companions can come to one's aid in ministerial emer-gencies without the need for planning that enlisting the help of outsiders entails. But most of all they affirm by their own commitment in ministry, one's efforts, which are often taken for granted or even denigrated in the public forum. The life of faith, whether in the arena of prayer or of ministry, is difficult to sustain without the stimulus and the credibility lent to it by others who share it, and having such support on a daily basis from people who are habitually, physically present is a gift.

The *organizational* advantages to the congregation of having some of its members living in groups are increasingly evident. As numbers of new members increase (as seems to be the case in the last five to ten years), so does the need for communities in which they can live at least the first several years of professed life. Newer members want and need such community environments, which cannot be invented or constructed on the spur of the moment. People thinking about Religious Life will get a much clearer and more authentic picture of the life if they can visit with, or even spend some months with, a vibrant local commu-nity while they are discerning their own call. Hospitality to other members of the congregation can be offered by a community group much more easily than it can be by an individual, if only because of the practical details of space and scheduling that hav-ing a guest entails. Although it is a highly sensitive issue and not something that should be taken for granted, a local community's willingness to accept, for a time, a difficult member or someone recovering from illness or addiction, or in transition from a traumatic situation can be an invaluable contribution to the congregation as well as the individual.

Finally, there is unquestionably a potential for *witness* that a happy and vibrant congregational group has to offer. A group is much more visible than an individual, able to invite neighbors or prospective candidates into its midst, likely to know and be involved in its surroundings in a way that brings gospel values into the social, political, and even the personal lives of a neighborhood. In a fragmented and anonymous society the ability of an intergenerational group to live together, to support and care for one another, to be politically and economically active and responsible, to be ecologically committed, and to live the Gospel's challenge to universal friendship in simple relationships with its neighbors, can be a powerful evangelical witness.

b. Challenges: At least two challenges faced by congregational groups have become evident in the past three decades of experimentation with new ways of living community at the local level. The first, the fuller discussion of which I will defer to the next chapter, is that of *inclusiveness.* Whether one refers to "intentional community" (a term that is, as we will see, problematic for a number of reasons), or "self-selection," the issue of how a local congregational group is, or should be, constituted is highly problematic. The renewal era reaction against the unintentionally violent practice of simply assigning Religious to local houses with the expectation that they would form community is certainly understandable. Somehow it was expected that holy obedience to one's assignment would solve all the sociological problems attendant on one or two new members entering an already constituted group, melding of diverse ages and experiences without any process to facilitate mutual understanding, or a change of leadership in which the members did not participate in any way. It was also expected to solve the psychological problems of sudden loss of loved companions without appropriate rituals of separation, personality conflicts that were not even admitted much less dealt with, relating to problem individuals whose problems were not acknowledged, and numerous unhealthy limitations on the development of friendships with close companions. The fact that Religious were simply put together in local communities without much if any attention to the interpersonal or group dynamics involved made most Religious very eager to experiment with some more humanly sensitive alternative.

The alternative was, in most cases, that individual Religious constructed self-selected groups based on common views of Religious Life and especially renewal, shared spiritual tastes, common ministerial interests, personal friendships, and the like. While this certainly had advantages in terms of the quality of community life that it made possible, at least in theory and hope, since it provided a natural substrate for the union of minds and hearts that was the goal, it also had some disadvantages that sometimes took some time to surface.

The most painful effect of self-selection was the de facto exclusion of certain members of the congregation from membership in a local community. Since members could no longer be simply assigned to a group that was obliged to accept them, individuals found themselves having to seek admission to a group. Some people were simply less personally attractive; some had personal problems that made including them in a highly committed group risky; some were "mavericks" who did not subscribe to any consistent ideology of renewal or ministry and so simply did not "fit in." Others were too timid to risk rejection and waited for an invitation to join that just never came. In short, many Religious ended up living singly even though they would have much preferred to live in a congregational group. This problem is still with us and needs more explicit attention than it has yet received. I will return to it at the end of this section.

The second challenge to which experimentation with congregational group living has given rise is that of *congregational integration*. The emotional expectations of self-selected groups who came together in enthusiastic shared commitment to intensive faith sharing in community, renewed spirituality, a particular approach to or focus in ministry, more radical simplicity of lifestyle, or some combination of these, were sometimes unrealistically high, and the resulting tensions could become intense. The unspoken commitment to fidelity to the founding ideal of the small group could militate against growth, producing friction and self-criticism as well as impeding movement of original members out of the group or new members into it. Such local communities sometimes became, in effect, cliques or exclusive subgroups that were not only closed to other members of the congregation but sometimes resisted the legitimate requirements of congregational leadership, refusing to abide by financial or other community policies.

Unfortunately, the Vatican often encouraged such groups, especially if they were conservative in orientation and preconciliar in their understanding of Religious Life, to become autonomous provinces or even to break off from their congregations. Some traumatic splintering occurred as a result of this divisive policy. On the other end of the ideological spectrum, more radical approaches to renewal also led to insular developments within congregations and painful frictions and distrust among members. Those in the in-group implicitly or explicitly denigrated the larger community for its lack of social consciousness, or its middle-class lifestyle, or its failure to identify with the poor, or its noncommitment to real community, while the members of the larger community nurtured increasing resentment against the judgmentalism and separatism of the in-group.

We will return to these issues in the next chapter, on the corporate dimensions of community. There I will suggest that neither Religious congregations nor local congregational groups are or should be "intentional communities" in the sociological sense of that word. While it certainly seems advisable that members of local congregational groups have much more agency than was once the case in the formation and organization of the groups in which they live on a daily basis, a certain commitment to inclusivity in regard to all members of the congregation and an openness toward the congregation itself have to be worked into the formula so that the congregation does not become a collection of hermetically sealed cliques around which float lonely monads.

In short, congregational group life does not necessarily provide all or even any of the advantages discussed above. People can live in the same house for years without meaningful contact, insulated by defensiveness and isolated by unresolved conflict or indifference as was too often the case in assigned groupings in preconciliar times. Groups can also be inbred and isolated from the rest of the congregation, hostile to "outsiders," and indifferent to their surroundings. Individuals can take advantage of group living, especially in large local communities, to avoid personal responsibility, evade contribution to the shared life of the group, indulge in a lazy, consumerist, or even hedonistic lifestyle, or "hide out" in spiritual individualism. Anyone who had much experience of preconciliar common life knows that simply being in the same dwelling does not automatically produce community or even civility to say nothing of expansive commitment. And anyone who has followed the fortunes of group experiments since the Council knows that having a choice about community does not necessarily produce healthy community for everyone in the congregation. But perhaps that very experience can make contemporary Religious more capable of planning and creating group embodiments of community life that are life-giving.

c. Planning for congregational group living: Nancy Schreck, in the article referred to in note 2, suggests that one of the forces pushing contemporary Religious away from congregational group living of community is "drift." I would like to pick up that suggestion and specify it because I think it may indicate a desirable line of action in regard to contemporary community life. Schreck speaks of increasing numbers of Religious moving into individual living without really giving much thought to whether it is preferable simply because it is the easier thing to do even though they might prefer to live in a group or the congregation prefer group living arrangements for economic and other reasons.

I suspect that, for the reasons given above as advantages, many if not most Religious would choose a congregational group living situation if it were possible. But *possible* means at least two things: That a livable group situation is available in the area in which her ministry or other obligations place her; that the physical arrangement in the local community is such that a reasonable degree of privacy is assured.

To start with the second, the issue of *privacy,* one of the problems occasioned by the closure of large congregational institutions and the divestiture of extensive property in the wake of the Council was that many Religious had to find housing that the congregation did not own and did not want to acquire since it was not at all certain that members of the congregation would live in that area for more than a few years. In practice this meant that many individuals or small groups rented apartments or small houses near their places of ministry. In the effort to minimize expenses they often chose the simplest and smallest accommodations available.

Necessary and well-intentioned as these moves were, they almost inevitably entailed real problems. Two or three people living in a very small apartment in which there was no physical space outside one's bedroom except a small living-dining area meant that the Religious were literally always within a few feet of each other. There was no possibility of having an overnight guest. The degree of exclusive "togetherness" involved in such an arrangement was calculated to encourage either the kind of tight-knit quasi-marital dependency relations described in chapter 6 or to foster absenteeism as each person sought a little personal space. A reasonable degree of privacy is, for most first-world adults in Western society, a felt necessity. No one wants to spend all her personal time in her bedroom, but if the only alternative is sitting in one of the two or three chairs in the only other room in the house, she might be driven to reclusiveness or escapism.

It might be the case that some of the "drift" toward living singly is due to the sheer need for some space, both physical and psychological, that is not available in small dwellings that have no extra room. One person living singly in a one-bed-room apartment can at least make or receive a phone call that is not overheard, entertain a visitor privately, or just relax with the newspaper and a cup of coffee without being observed or addressed. No matter how much she may long for the companionship of fellow Religious, her need for ordinary privacy may be greater.

Availability may be a second factor in the "drift" toward living singly. When a Religious changed ministry and had to relocate, it was often on fairly short notice and she had little time to find out who else was living nearby or to investigate the possibilities of shared living. It was unlikely that these others, if there were some, had any extra room (for reasons just given) and asking even one or two people to join in the search for a new house and to relocate often seemed like too much of an imposition, especially if the newcomer did not know the others well. Furthermore, there was no certainty that the people involved would find life together sufficiently sustaining to justify such expenditure of time and effort, to say nothing of the expense involved in moving. The point of the person's move was to take up her ministry in the new locale, and where she lived was seen as secondary to that goal. It was easier by far to find a place to live, move, start one's new ministry, and then make contact with others in the area. Occasionally this led eventually to exploration of the possibilities of living together, but most often the magnitude of such a move was prohibitive and no one wanted to initiate it.

It seems to me that if many Religious, after sufficient experimentation with various options, are coming to the conclusion that they really want to live with other members of their communities and congregations really want to encourage group living among their members, that the resources of the congregation have to be put into motion to facilitate it. A number of strategies might be explored and experimentation begun.

For example, those in congregational leadership who deal directly with members in their discernment about ministry might raise the issue of community life early in the process.

Some Religious are in ministries that are not easily transferable, for example, administrators of hospitals or tenured university faculty. Others, for example, high school teachers or psychological counselors, or those just beginning their ministerial lives, might be more able to consider various locations before looking for a new position. The latter might be put in touch with the former to see if persons who are moving might be able to relocate close to those less able to move with the aim of bringing members together in close enough proximity to make shared living feasible.

A community might establish a housing office that would act as a clearinghouse for members in transition or looking for a group-living situation. Information about available housing or about people seeking others for shared living could be made available regularly and meetings of prospective group members facilitated so that they could come together on neutral ground to explore their hopes and expectations prior to making commitments that would be difficult to reverse.

At least in some locations where a certain concentration of members develops, the congregation might consider buying or leasing housing that provides enough space for community members to be together with sufficient privacy and for the community to welcome visitors, candidates, or new members for shorter or longer stays. The very existence of available housing is a strong encouragement for members to come together to create a community living situation.

Some congregations already have central stores of furnishings relinquished by their previous users available to members setting up new households. Perhaps the principle of facilitating sharing of goods through information and encouragement to make use of what is available could be applied to the issue of real estate. If rented housing, rather than being relinquished when a local community disbands, could remain in the control of the congregation so that it would be available for another group, it would be much easier for a new group to risk an experiment in living together since the only requirement would be moving in rather than finding, renting, and furnishing a place prior to any experience of life together. This might mean that the congregation would pay rental or leasing fees for a few months between occupations of the property, but if congregational group living is really a value, incurring such expense might be a very good investment.

No doubt there are other ways in which a congregation could facilitate group living if members and leadership were really committed to developing this type of life among themselves. The past three decades have probably given many people the kinds of maturing experiences, both personal and social, that will make group living more possible, even among very dissimilar personalities. And frank community discussions could help a congregation to develop some principles that all could espouse, for example, that any congregational group should be open to any member unless there were some really serious impediment to her inclusion; that everyone in the congregation has a right to inquire about joining a local community and thus that such an inquiry is not an intrusion or imposition; that local communities with room would invite others to consider joining them; that members in transition would normally look for new ministries in locations in which there are other members of the congregation unless there were compelling ministerial reasons for going into a more isolated situation; that members are encouraged to join with other members in the establishment of new ministries; that community dwellings should be sufficiently spacious to provide the members of the community with adequate privacy and the possibility of hospitality and that the congregation is committed to facilitating this, and so on. Different congregations might have different priorities and establish different mutual understandings, but it seems that some common ground has to be established if a contemporary version of congregational group living is to be more than a vague desideratum that no one knows how to implement. Some aspects of life, especially in a relatively large organization, are too complex to be handled by each person acting individually, and it would seem that the construction of local communities is one of these.

Finally, I would reiterate that placing a priority on facilitating congregational group living or even the numerical preponderance of members of a congregation living in such groups does not necessarily imply that this is the normative (much less only legitimate) form of community life. It is a recognition that most people, other things being equal, probably find living with others more congenial, more conducive to personal well-being, spiritual growth, and ministerial effectiveness than living individually. If this is the case it should be made possible, indeed be facilitated, just as opportunities for an annual retreat, vacation, or education for a new ministry are made available. Not everyone needs the same thing at the same time but certain supports of spiritual and ministerial life should be readily available in any congregation and the opportunity for local community living would seem to be one of them.

C. Is Individual Living a Valid Form of Religious Community Life?

It is a fact that many Religious today do not live in congregational groups. Often they are described as "living alone." But just as it is by no means accurate to describe all congregational group living as "common life," so it is not accurate or helpful for analysis to lump together all those who do not live in groups under the (often pejorative) term "living alone." In what follows I want to distinguish living singly, living alone, and solitary living because they are qualitatively different and pose different challenges for discernment and decision making for individual Religious and congregations.

1. Living singly: As already mentioned, there are all kinds of personal, educational, and ministerial reasons why congregational group living is not always possible even when it is preferred by the individual Religious and/or considered desirable by the congregation. In other words, the fact of belonging to a mobile ministerial congregation will sometimes require a Religious to live singly unless she chooses to live with the local group of some other congregation, with her relatives, or with lay contacts (none of which is self-evidently a better choice).

Like congregational group living, living singly can be life-giving or an occasion for personal or spiritual shipwreck. Which it becomes depends to some degree on a realistic assessment of the opportunities and challenges it offers, the personal resources of the individual, and the integration of this lifestyle into the congregation's community life both juridically and sociologically.

A. ADVANTAGES: Living singly, especially for the first time, can be a very maturing experience. Many people entering Religious Life today will have had that experience in their young adulthood prior to entrance, but many active Religious who entered in the 1950s and 1960s did not. For both types it can be a significant challenge.

For active middle-aged and older Religious who have spent virtually their entire adult lives in institutional settings, it can be quite enlightening (to say nothing of terrifying!) to have to confront the ordinary realities of modern adulthood such as finding housing, making a rental contract, dealing with service people and neighbors without the automatic buffer of being "one of the sisters." For some, just overcoming the sense of insecurity or even fear of being alone in their dwelling at night, having only their own company when they come home from ministry or school, and waking up in the silence of a dwelling in which others are not moving about will force them to recognize not only the essential aloneness, the theologically "monastic" quality (see volume 1, chapter 1), of Religious Life and the centrality of the presence (or absence) of their sense of and reliance on God who is ultimately their only life companion, but also their own insecurities and inadequacies. If consecrated celibacy is a life that is singularly autonomous, in which the lifelong companionship of another particular human being is renounced, in which primary and secondary family have been truly surrendered in favor of transcendent universality of commitment, then finding oneself actually alone on a daily basis should be neither frightening nor depressing. If it is, one is offered a precious opportunity for reflection and deepening of one's life commitment.

Many Religious in recent decades have experienced and grown from the practical challenge that living singly presents. Mastering all the aspects of caring for a car; learning how to shop efficiently and economically and to create and maintain a balanced diet when one's meals are not prepared and served; learning how to handle finances, keep the checkbook balanced and the bills paid on time; how to keep an apartment clean, repaired, and secure when the responsibilities are not divided among several people, no one is "in charge," and there are no backup systems when one is out of town or indisposed are all valuable lessons in what living as an adult in the modern world involves. They can greatly increase one's empathy for parents, both those with small children and one's own elderly parents, and fellow workers juggling private life and job. Experiencing what it takes to handle modern life without daily institutional support can also make the Religious both more appreciative of the currently remote but very real institutional support the congregation provides and of the educational and professional advantages that enable her to cope when so many of our contemporaries are simply overwhelmed financially, domestically, or morally by the sheer complexity of modern life.

Newer members who learned to live on their own before entering Religious Life will face an entirely different set of challenges when, for the first time since entering, they find themselves again living singly. These people learned what Religious Life involves, developed their Religious spirituality and the discipline of a well-ordered spiritual practice, and cultivated the responsibility and accountability of community and ministerial involvement within the supportive and responsive environment of congregational group life. Finding themselves outside that environment, "on their own" again, can present a real challenge to either simply shed demanding disciplines or to let them slide in a barely noticeable way until they have slipped back into the kind of life they led prior to entrance.

They may find themselves bolting out of bed late with barely enough time to get to work, skipping prayer and spiritual reading with the rationale that they will make it up in the evening, and then sitting in front of the television with junk food and drinks replacing a meal they do not feel inclined to prepare, and getting to bed so late that the pattern starts all over the next day. They can easily drift away from congregational involvement and begin to build a social life that they find more relaxing, given the hectic pace of ministry on the one hand and the unexciting familiarity of congregational people and events on the other. Relationships can develop that are incompatible with either celibacy or congregational belonging and that can be too easily pursued because of having a place of one's own in which to entertain. Problems with financial accountability, mounting credit card debt, worldly (to use an older but still eloquent descriptive) choices about dress, transportation, travel, vacations, and so on can easily develop as the absence of daily support from congregational group living and its requirement of communal discernment turns occasional lapses into habits.

The advantage of such an experience, if it is not to end in disaster, is that it will force the person to examine her Religious commitment and to personally appropriate and internalize her Religious identity. She will see through her own experience that one can live *as* a Religious in a congregational setting, carried by the system and the relative impossibility of too much public deviation in a group situation, for many years without actually *becoming* a Religious from the heart out. She will grow in self-knowledge about the temptations to which she is particularly vulnerable, the situations in which she cannot afford to get involved if she does not want to be overwhelmed, and the discipline she needs to develop if she is to continue to be and to live as a Religious. Her prayer life, her responsibility and accountability to her congregation, her ministerial commitment, how she balances asceticism with healthy and appropriate relaxation, and how she integrates the living of the vows into her day-to-day life will have to become matters of personal discernment, continual examination, energetic practice, and incessant reappraisal, repentance, and recovery.

In short, living singly can foster the maturity of older Religious who went from the family home into the total institution of Religious Life without learning to function as adults in modern society, a skill they increasingly need for effective ministry and that is very conducive to the mental and physical competence and spiritual health that can make later life more vigorous. And it can turn well-behaved "performers" of Religious Life into real Religious who are now capable of living and ministering anywhere because they have appropriated and internalized their life commitment. These are the Religious who can model the life attractively and challengingly for their contemporaries, not by fitting indistinguishably, like social chameleons, into their environments but by living with integrity the alternative that is consecrated life in the midst of the world without the institutional buffers that can make it appear admirable but inimitable.

B. CHALLENGES: It is not necessary to dwell at length on the challenges of living singly that are fairly easily deduced from what has preceded. Obviously, the person living singly lacks the advantages (economic, psychological, spiritual, ministerial, and organizational) that congregational group living offers. For some people, living singly will involve the daily suffering of real loneliness, and at least at times, fear and insecurity. Many will find the challenge of taking care of all the details of daily living an onerous burden, more ascetical than observing a flexible horarium in a group setting.

The real possibility that, without the daily physical presence and support of fellow Religious, one's spiritual life will degenerate into routine practice or nonexistence is the greatest danger of living singly, and the number of disasters over the past three decades make us aware that this is not a hypothetical peril. Alcoholism, addictions to food, drugs, clothes, shopping, or mindless passive entertainment, the development of questionable relationships, estrangement from the congregation and loss of corporate identity, and a sense of isolation in mission are the occupational hazards of living singly.

C. CONCLUSIONS: As I am discussing it here, living singly (as distinguished from living alone or living in solitude to be discussed below) arises not as an object of choice among other possibilities but is the situation in which a Religious finds herself because of educational, ministerial, or personal responsibilities. I am suggesting that, rather than simply enduring it as a temporary sentence to loneliness or gleefully taking a psychological and spiritual "leave of absence" from her Religious Life during the time it is necessary to live singly, the person in this situation can make it a free choice and can grow and develop within it in ways that are much less possible in other circumstances. Just as being assigned to a difficult mission community in the past could be the occasion of growth or disaster, so can the necessity of living singly. The real issue for discernment, both on the part of congregational leaders and the individual in question, is under what circumstances it is wise and healthy for a Religious to undertake a project that will involve living singly for some time. Placing a person's Religious commitment in serious jeopardy is hardly justified by ministerial or educational need.

First, as has been said above, newer Religious, regardless of their age and previous life experience, ordinarily need to live for a relatively long time during and after initial formation in a healthy congregational group situation. This is necessary in order for them to imbibe the spirit of the congregation, learn to live a disciplined and regular Religious Life, learn the skills of community living (which many contemporary Religious did not have a chance to develop in either family or other committed relationships prior to entry), develop their own spirituality and ministerial gifts, and profit from the active mentoring in life and ministry of experienced Religious. Consequently, it would seem highly imprudent to put someone who has recently made profession into a situation requiring her to live singly.

This being recognized, however, the fear (or projection) of some people in authority that anyone not living in a group situation, that is, under the scrutiny of superiors and subject to social pressure toward conformity, will certainly slide into spiritual ruin needs to be called into question. Any growth situation involves risks. But it could be questioned whether the risk of nondevelopment in an anonymous group situation is any less acute than the risk of dissoluteness in an individual situation. Healthy living singly needs to be compared to healthy group living, rather than an unhealthy version of the former with a healthy version of the latter.

Part of my argument in this section is that community life, for ministerial Religious, can be embodied in a variety of lifestyles, each of which involves dangers and opportunities. None is fail-safe; none is predetermined to failure. Therefore, none is intrinsically superior or normative or preferable. The issue is what way of living community is best for this individual and the congregation at this time? If living singly is necessary or preferable because of educational, ministerial, or other responsibilities and the person seems (to herself, congregational leaders, and others involved in her discernment) sufficiently mature to deal with the challenges, the move into such a lifestyle may be the most creative choice for her. Many Religious know that a period of living singly, often during a year or more of sabbatical or continuing education, in a mission situation, or while caring for an elderly parent, was a decisive turning point in their spiritual development during which they consolidated their commitment to Christ within Religious Life and from which they emerged as more mature, compassionate, and committed members of their congregation and ministers to God's people. This development was not an accident, something that happened in spite of living in an anomalous and exceptional situation, but the outcome of a responsible choice to live community in a single situation.

2. *Living alone:* Although no one can control the development or use of language, I am proposing, for the sake of clarity in sorting out the issues around individual forms of community living in ministerial congregations, to reserve the term "living alone" for unhealthy and/or isolated living situations that are actually a deviation from community life rather than a form of it.[7] I am suggesting that "living alone" not be confused

with "living singly" (just discussed) or "living in solitude" (which will be discussed below), both of which can be legitimate and spiritually growthful ways of living the theological reality of community.

A. SELF-MARGINALIZATION: Since the Council, some Religious who chose not to leave their congregations juridically have done so in fact. Their lives are characterized by some or all of the following features. They have established themselves in a dwelling they share with no one and that often exceeds congregational standards of living or is even owned in their own or a relative's name and whose equity they use independently. They have virtually ceased active participation in congregational affairs and developed a social context that does not include other members of their own congregation or even other Religious, often because the latter cannot condone their lifestyle even if they refrain from openly challenging it. They often refuse financial accountability or observance of congregational financial policies, determine employment with minimal consultation (much less discernment) with congregational leadership and without reference to the congregation's corporate mission or ministerial guidelines, maintain individual investments or retirement accounts that they use independently, travel and vacation with wealthy lay acquaintances and maintain an extensive and expensive wardrobe for such recreation, maintain cars that exceed congregational standards, and so on. In some cases they have become involved in hetero- or homosexual relationships that may or may not be genital but that are contrary to the spirit and the virtue of consecrated celibacy and often scandalous to those who know that the person is a vowed Religious.

Living alone is crucial to maintaining this type of lifestyle. It keeps the person safe from the "interference" of congregational leaders who would question or even disallow some or all of these behaviors and from the glaring incompatibility of such a lifestyle with congregational expectations that would be obvious if she lived with other members. In other words, the purpose of living alone for such individuals is to avoid

accountability for a lifestyle that is in substantial violation of
one or more of the vows of Religious Life and the legitimate
congregational requirements of community life.

Most congregations have such "marginal" members who
continue to put the congregational letters after their name
when it is expedient but who admit little or no responsibility
or accountability to the group to which they nominally belong.
Leaders agonize over whether to confront such members,
demand the changes necessary, and thereby perhaps drive the
person out of Religious Life or to wait, invite, and try to per-
suade the person to reconsider the choices she has made and
reappropriate the life she has effectively abandoned.

Without presuming to have any wisdom on this prudential
dilemma of leaders I would make one point about such cases,
namely, that such living alone should not be confused with living singly or solitary living, and its motivations and aberrations
should not be projected, explicitly or by innuendo, onto faithful Religious who are living community integrally and seriously
in an individual situation. Laws, as we all know, should not be
made for the exceptions and the number of Religious living
alone in the sense described above is small and probably getting smaller. There is little stigma attached to leaving Religious
Life today, and a person who is living in opposition to most or
all of what she has vowed and has developed the financial and
other resources to live independently of the congregation can
avoid conflicts of conscience and procedural hurdles by simply
leaving. It may well be that most such individuals have already
left and leaders have sufficient experience at this point to prevent new cases. In any event, reflection on the issue of individual forms of community embodiment will be systematically
distorted if living alone in the sense just described is the
implicit background for discussion of it.

B. NONJURIDICAL EXCLAUSTRATION: Another version of isolated living alone, more tragic and pitiable than self-marginalization, is that of the person who has become such a problem
in community that no congregational group is able or willing
to absorb her, who is too young and/or active to be assigned

to a large institutional setting such as a central house or retirement center, and who has given no moral or canonical grounds for expulsion.

Actually, this is not an entirely new phenomenon. Enclosed monastic communities have always been able, at least in principle, to obtain an enforced exclaustration of a member whose presence in the community is so disruptive or even dangerous that she cannot be carried, even with the most charitable efforts, in a group living closely on a day-to-day basis. Some postconciliar Religious leaders of ministerial congregations have found themselves with no alternative to requiring such a problem member to get her own apartment. In other words, she is exclaustrated in practice though often not juridically.

No one, probably, thinks this is a good arrangement because such people are often incompetent to handle their own affairs, disruptive or scandalous in relation to neighbors, and sometimes a danger to themselves or others. They can compromise the congregation financially or legally, and sometimes their bizarre behavior reflects negatively on other members living in the area or on the congregation's ministries. They frequently deeply resent being "sentenced" to the loneliness of exclusion and vent their conviction of being persecuted to anyone who will listen, sometimes orchestrating elaborate and fantastic plots to remedy their situation. Again, my purpose in discussing this sad situation is not to suggest solutions (which may not exist and which I certainly do not have) but to try to prevent assimilation, overt or covert, of healthy forms of individual community living to unhealthy versions of living alone. All that the two actually have in common is the fact of a single person occupying a particular dwelling.

3. *Living in solitude:* In what follows I am going to propose an hypothesis based on experience of and discussion with a small but significant number of highly committed Religious who belong to ministerial congregations and have chosen to live individually, not because of educational, ministerial, or personal necessity or convenience but because they feel called to live a modified form of solitude. Because there has been, to

my knowledge, no public discussion of this matter and it seems to be disallowed by the basic assumption (which I have called into question) that community life is normatively embodied in congregational group living, I am venturing into uncharted waters at this point in hopes of stimulating some discussion of this matter. We have had three decades of experience with variations in community living, including some very successful experiments and some lamentable failures. Some aspects of this experience have been much discussed but this one has not. The time may be ripe for culling the experience of those who have lived and/or continue to live a modified solitary form of community in ministerial congregations.

A. PRESUPPOSITIONS: In order to clear the ground for undistorted discourse I will begin with some observations about the Religious I am discussing and their lifestyle. I am drawing this description from actual experience of such Religious and discussions with them and with congregational leaders who have some members living community this way, not from an imaginary ideal or hypothetical construction.

First, these Religious are not alienated or estranged from their congregations but deeply committed and actively involved, sometimes even holding office or serving on ongoing committees or councils or in special projects. They participate regularly in congregational assemblies and other events, in chapters, and in the intermediate governmental structures of their congregations such as living clusters, mission units, or governmental local groups. They visit and are visited by other community members, enjoy being with their fellow Religious, and have close friends in their own and other congregations.

Second, these Religious are fully accountable to congregational leadership in regard to finances, ministry, and personal lifestyle. They stay in touch with the leaders to whom they are responsible; live within congregational budgetary guidelines unless exempted for some reason and do not maintain private funds, accounts, or property, or withhold earnings; willingly discern ministerial commitments and changes with leadership; are appropriately open about their personal lives and relationships. In short, they live the vows of community life (poverty and obedience) according to the constitutions of their congregation.

Third, these Religious are not hermits or anchorites. They are ministerial Religious who are usually involved in very demanding full-time ministries. Usually, their ministries are evidently related to and expressions of the congregation's corporate mission. And often they serve as resources, from within their own ministerial competence, for the congregation itself, for example, as chapter facilitators or organizational consultants, as resources for the formation program, or as consultants for the congregation's health, retirement, or development programs.

Fourth, these Religious are actively committed to the justice agenda of contemporary Religious Life, both in society and in the Church. Often they are articulate feminists, committed ecological advocates, and/or peace and justice activists.

Finally, the personal lifestyle of these Religious is disciplined, ascetical, hospitable, and spiritually committed. They live simply in relation to dwelling, food, clothes, and recreation; are concerned about maintaining a healthy balance of prayer, work, and relaxation; are not suffering from addictions. They are faithful to prayer both on a daily basis and in terms of regular retreats, spiritual direction, and liturgical participation. They read widely and maintain an active and healthy intellectual life in relation to both their professional life and their spirituality. They have close friends whom they see frequently and with whom they can share intimately not only recreation but the spiritual life, ministerial concerns, congregational issues, justice commitments, and personal struggles and successes. But they are mature and discerning about the sexual dimension of relationships and act as consecrated celibates both in private and in public.

In other words, these Religious are comparable in virtually every way to zealous and committed Religious who live in congregational groups. They differ only in choosing to live individually rather than in a group. And, although they may have originally experienced living individually out of necessity, perhaps while doing graduate study or because of their ministry, they continue to choose to live this way and might well continue to do so even if the possibility of a group living situation arose.

B. ANALOGICAL RESOURCES FOR REFLECTION: I think this situation is somewhat analogous to that which ministerial congregations confronted in the 1960s and 1970s when the House of Prayer Movement began. A major concern of many congregations that were attracted to participation in this movement was that maintaining a house of prayer or spirituality center of some kind seemed incompatible with "active" apostolic life. After considerable reflection and experimentation most ministerial congregations seem to have concluded that ministry to the spirituality of people, especially to its contemplative dimension, was no less ministerial than teaching or nursing or social justice involvement. A house of prayer in a ministerial congregation was not a "monastery" in their midst, and the Religious who served in it did not become "enclosed" or isolated from the rest of the congregation. They did not embrace a different kind of spirituality from that of other members or a radically different lifestyle even though their ministry involved more formal prayer, liturgical planning and leadership, and one-to-one ministry in retreats and spiritual direction.

In other words, although ministry in the area of spirituality has tended to be associated with monastic orders, ministerial congregations discovered that they could exercise such ministries without subverting the ministerial character of their lifeform and that their members involved in such ministries could exercise them as fully participating members of their congregations. The question I am raising is whether we have something analogous in the case of ministerial Religious choosing to live community life in modified solitude.

Historically, the solitary living of Religious Life has tended to be associated with monastic life, specifically with the eremitical form. However, highly communal monastic orders, such as the Trappists, Camaldolese, and some Carmelites, have sometimes made provision for a more solitary lifestyle for some of their members. Thomas Merton, a Trappist in a monastery that placed an almost extreme emphasis on a group form of community living, felt strongly called to solitude and in his middle years was permitted to retire to a hermitage within the confines of the monastery enclosure. He continued to share in the liturgical life of the community and to participate in the work of formation of the younger monks as well as to write and pursue his ecumenical and interreligious ministry. Significantly, he was outside the monastery on a ministerial trip to an interreligious encounter when he died. But at home he lived in a small cabin where he took most of his meals, prayed, worked, and slept in solitude. In other words, he lived a modified form of solitude in the midst of, and as a way of participating in, the community life of the Trappist monastery.[8]

C. A PROPOSAL ABOUT SOLITARY LIVING IN A MINISTERIAL CONGREGATION: Spiritual solitude of heart is constitutive of the life of consecrated celibacy. All Religious are called to such solitude. They honor this call by the practice of personal prayer, by regular retreats, by the practice of silence in some form, and in the celibate quality of their relationships. The question is whether some Religious, whether in stabile monastic orders or mobile ministerial ones, might be called to a more material or physical realization of this call to solitude so that it becomes an aspect of their lifestyle itself. And if this is the case, can this call to a somewhat solitary lifestyle be integrated into a ministerial congregation? In other words, is such a call compatible with apostolic Religious Life or an aberration that cannot be tolerated?

It seems to me that there is no intrinsic contradiction between a modified form of solitude and full, authentic community life in a ministerial congregation. Let us defer for a moment the question of what such a call to solitude might mean, intentionally and in the concrete, and presuppose (on the basis of the evident presence of the solitary vocation in the history of Christian spirituality) that some people are called to solitude in a way that most people are not, that is, to a way of life in which a somewhat extensive physical solitude plays a public role in their lifestyle. How can living in such solitude be integrated into the active lifestyle and corporate lifeform of the ministerial Religious?

Ministerial Religious who have chosen a solitary form of individual living do not withdraw from ministry. Often it is the intensity of their active ministry that accentuates their need for solitude. They also do not withdraw from active congregational participation and community life. Finally, they do not, like hermits or anchorites, discontinue social relationships or participation in the ordinary activities, professional and recreational, of modern adults (although they may reduce the scope or frequency of such activities for the sake of deepened solitude). So, the solitude being discussed is not absolute or a determinant of all aspects of life as it is for a hermit. It consists in choosing not to live in a group but in a separate space of some kind.[9]

The modern history of apostolic congregations has ingrained the suspicion that community life is supposed to involve a continual abrasive contact with others that "polishes the rough edges of the personality" and provides the opportunity to practice self-abnegation and mortification as well as practical charity. Not experiencing the incessant interpersonal challenge of continually living in immediate contact with others is thought to promote selfishness, self-absorption, self-indulgence, and ultimately to subvert the development of the generous self-transcendence that real community requires.

I would suggest that committed full-time ministry, especially in combination with active participation in congregational life at all its levels, provides ample opportunity for the practice of such virtues. Group living, while perhaps more important as a school of charity for Religious who are not involved in active ministry on a daily basis, does not seem to be the only way to experience the challenge to be attentive to the needs of others and to put their needs ahead of one's own, to keep annoyance and even anger in check, to surrender one's opinions or preferences for the sake of the common good, to stay with seemingly futile processes until some progress is made, to patiently mentor the young and less experienced, to be responsible and accountable to others, to absorb without bitterness unmerited abuse and lack of appreciation, to forgive injuries, and so on. Any serious ministry presents such challenges on a daily, if not hourly, basis. The modified solitary lifestyle of the contemporary ministerial Religious living individually by choice does not seem to be an escape from the challenges of charity that, in the days of Religious Life as total institution, occurred much more continuously in the interchange of group living in the convent.

If living in modified solitude is compatible with congregational participation and ministerial commitment and does not impede the growth in charity that daily challenges to self-transcendence provide, it would seem that it is not intrinsically incompatible with ministerial Religious Life. If that is the case, two further questions must be asked. First, what is the motivation for and advantage of such a lifestyle choice? In other words, is there a legitimate and proportionate reason for a ministerial Religious to choose a lifestyle of modified solitude? Second, what practical and concrete considerations should play a role in discerning such a choice and undertaking it?

My experience and conversations with Religious who have chosen a solitary living situation suggests that the primary *motivation* is virtually always spiritual, closely intertwined with the psychological. Many of these Religious exercise intensive ministries. Often they have a very high public profile that requires a great deal of personal interaction and leadership in the public forum. Others exercise intensely interior ministries of spiritual accompaniment, psychological counseling, crisis intervention, formation, research and writing, or art. In many cases they are highly involved in both public and intra- or interpersonal types of ministry. In other words, they are often people whose outward energy flow is constant and qualitatively intense. And very often they are psychologically somewhat or very introverted and intuitive personalities. In other words, they are often people who experience a continuous deep need for spiritual resourcing and whose replenishment, both spiritual and psychological, does not happen through social interaction, which they find both stimulating and draining, but through recourse to interiority in silence, solitude, recollection, reflection, and prayer.[10]

Everyone, especially anyone leading a serious spiritual life, needs a certain amount of solitude and silence to foster interior growth. But many people find sufficient resources for their spiritual lives in more intermittent experiences of silence. They are spiritually refreshed rather than drained by social interaction and find liturgical or group prayer easier and more nourishing than solitary prayer. The person called to solitude thirsts for long periods of silence in which the tensions of the spirit, the continual readiness that incessant novelty demands, relax in the embrace of God. This tends to happen for them only when it is relatively certain that the silence and solitude will not be interrupted for at least a foreseeable space of time.

The choice of living in solitude, then, has a number of ramifications that such a Religious finds highly congenial or even necessary for her own spiritual development and psychological health. She may be in her solitary space only from the time she comes home from work in the evening until she leaves for work in the morning as well as on some weekends or during vacations. But the individual space provides real, uninterrupted, physical silence that is visual, auditory, and personal. Not having to fit her own activities around or into a shared schedule of prayers and meals at particular times, or to attend to the activities going on around her in a shared house, she is free, at least for a few hours each day, to establish a personal rhythm of prayer, *Lectio Divina*, reflection, intellectual or artistic work, and daily domestic duties contemplatively performed that maintains the silence and the inner attention from which she finds the continual interaction of group living a real distraction. Merton's descriptions of his days in the hermitage, which he found deeply centering in contrast to the monastic routine even though the latter was virtually entirely silent, illustrate this seemingly subtle but very real contribution of physical solitude.[11]

The differing psychological and spiritual profile of the Religious called to modified solitary living marks her neither as superior nor inferior to her more interactively inclined companions. Honoring the differences by permitting a variety of lifestyles as authentic embodiments of community life in the ministerial form of Religious Life is not a condescension to social incompetence or a canonization of the religiously gifted. It is simply a recognition that people differ from one another spiritually and psychologically as much as they do physically, intellectually, artistically, or socially. Maintaining the corporate identity and appropriate boundaries of Religious Life need not depend on an absolutely uniform pattern of group living. Provided that affective and effective integration into the community life of the congregation and active ministerial commitment are maintained, it would seem that considerable variety of personal lifestyles could be sustained without detriment to the life.

If such is the case, history can provide some *criteria of discernment* by which to decide who might be called to this lifestyle of modified solitude as well as a number of cautions by which to avoid the problems to which solitary living is particularly prone. First, solitary life, for the Christian and a fortiori for the Religious, is never absolute. If there were no other reason, liturgical participation requires the physical presence of other community members. Both spiritual and psychological health preclude absolute isolation. So, the solitude in question here is not reclusiveness or flight from relationship. It is the arrangement of a certain dimension of personal life, namely personal dwelling place, to maximize solitude and silence as more conducive to the interior life for some people.

Second, monastic wisdom has always maintained that the very young Religious or anyone who has not had a prolonged experience of basically successful group living of community life (regardless of age) should not be permitted to undertake a solitary lifestyle. In other words, solitude requires the spiritual and psychological skills of interpersonally honed maturity. The ability to sustain the temptations to boredom and discouragement (the classical temptation of the "noonday devil" of *acedia*, which is particularly active among solitaries) is developed through a fairly long period of initial and ongoing formation. One acquires the self-discipline necessary for a productive, ascetically restrained, and relatively undistracted idiorhythmic lifestyle, the self-knowledge to recognize incipient dangerous patterns before they develop into problems, the humility to be accountable for failures, and the inner fortitude to continually start over largely through the stimulus of encouragement from and admiration of others with whom one lives in community during the first several years of Religious Life. The person who has not learned to live group community life relatively gracefully needs the continued practice in charity and forbearance that comes from group living and should not be permitted to escape into "solitude."

Third, a person living individually, for whatever reason, has more need than most people of regular and competent spiritual direction. Without the kind of social support and even pressure to live Religious Life faithfully that is supplied by the shared routine and practice of group living, the solitary Religious needs the accountability, to herself above all, and the encouragement that regular discussion of her life with a wise director provides. Lack of self-knowledge and rationalization of failures is a real danger for the person living individually and can easily subvert any spiritual advantages of solitude.

Fourth, the Religious herself and the congregational leaders to whom she is responsible should be alert to signs that indicate a revision may be in order. Estrangement or marginalization in relation to the congregation, lack of accountability, antisocial attitudes, problems in ministry, secretiveness about relationships, and so on invite reexamination of the solitary lifestyle of the Religious. On the other hand, increasing energy, productivity, serenity, centeredness, generosity, flexibility, perseverance, ability to handle conflict, and vibrancy of faith and hope are good signs that the lifestyle is promoting the well-being of the Religious. Solitude, of itself, is neutral, but a good tree produces good fruit.

III. Conclusions about Group and Individual Embodiment of Community Life

In the preceding sections I have tried to survey the actual practice of individual Religious today in regard to personal living of Religious community as a constitutive dimension of ministerial Religious Life[12] in order to analyze it theologically and spiritually. I began by raising the question of whether classical "common life" is the theologically normative, ideal, or necessary embodiment of Religious community life. After suggesting historical, sociological, and psychological reasons for the development of this now canonically enshrined presupposition, I called it into question and argued that a variety of lifestyles might, at least theoretically, be equally compatible with the theological/spiritual reality of community life.

In the next section I discussed various aspects of a group lifestyle that might legitimately and effectively embody community for individual Religious and pointed out both how such a group lifestyle differs from classical common life and the advantages to the individual Religious and the congregation of at least some if not the majority of its members living this way. The witness value of the group lifestyle is also a compelling argument for its validity and value in contemporary society and Church.

Finally, I discussed the much more controversial subject of individual living as a possibly valid embodiment of community. I distinguished three different versions of individual living, two of which I think are entirely compatible with community life and one of which is not. The one that is truly an aberration and undesirable even when it is necessary is "living alone" or isolation from the congregation. "Living singly," a situation that arises from educational, ministerial, or personal necessity and is usually temporary, is discerned to be the best situation for the individual at the present time. Like group living, it offers challenges that can be either very growth producing or very dangerous, depending on how the individual handles them. But in any case, living singly is not a flight from community life or ministry in which, on the contrary, the individual continues to participate with commitment and energy. "Living in solitude" is a choice of an individual Religious, for spiritual and psychological reasons, to occupy a separate dwelling rather than living in a group. This is a modified form of solitude since the Religious remains fully involved in ministry, in the community life of the congregation, and in contemporary professional and social life. It is motivated by a need and desire for the kind of psychic and spiritual "space" some people find much more nourishing of their spirituality. It requires careful discernment and regular reevaluation, but if lived authentically it is fully compatible with, and a legitimate embodiment of, community life in a ministerial congregation.

What I have proposed is that community life, an intrinsic and constitutive dimension of ministerial Religious Life, is theologically necessary for all members of the congregation but that it can be embodied on the personal level in a plurality of lifestyles, both group and individual, which are related to each other as equally valid variations, not as legitimate to aberration, normative to exceptional, or superior to inferior. Just as the corporate mission of the congregation is not necessarily subverted by a plurality of ministries, so its community life is not necessarily threatened by a plurality of dwelling lifestyles. The challenge is to integrate these lifestyles in such a way that real community is promoted and nurtured in the congregation, which is the topic of the next chapter.

Finally, I think it is important to reflect that just as classical common life, in the past and in some cases today, offered a powerful witness in the local Church and neighborhood of people unrelated to one another by blood, from several generations and often more than one race, living together in faith and supporting one another in charity, that is, being local

Church on a day-to-day basis, so the pluralistic community life of contemporary Religious can speak powerfully to postmodern society.

Demographic data suggest that the fragmentation characteristic of postmodernity is especially evident in relationship patterns in American society. A minority of the population of the United States lives in a traditional family unit composed of two heterosexual parents and their biological children.[13] Even in such traditional families, daily meals together can be very rare, needing to be scheduled with care as parents and children operate within and interact increasingly with different groups, pursue incompatible projects and interests that take them in as many geographical and social directions as there are individuals in the family. Grown children rarely live at or even within visiting distance of the parental home. Adult siblings are often scattered across the country (or world) coming together when business trajectories intersect, family weddings or other celebrations occur, or at family reunions that have to be planned months if not years in advance. An increasing number of marriages are "long-distance," with spouses working most of the week in different cities or even states and commuting on weekends to be together. Many children spend a good deal of time shuttling between separated or divorced parents. No matter how one judges this situation, as a healthy sign of personal autonomy among people, a neutral datum of contemporary experience, or a tragic breakdown of community as we have known it, it remains a fact that, on the one hand, healthy human life demands community and that, on the other hand, the traditional coordinates of community, daily and prolonged shared space and time, have been largely subverted by the developments of the twentieth century.

In light of this situation, it may be that the witness to community that is most needed in our time is not a model of community as it was lived in rural settings or ethnic neighborhoods before the car, airplane, or internet became virtually universal features of everyday life. It may not even be the idealized commune model of the 1960s or '70s. Modeling a type of community living that, no matter how desirable it might be, is virtually impossible for the vast majority in urban American society may offer an ideal or criterion like the Jerusalem community in Acts 4, but it may not be the most useful resource for our contemporaries. Perhaps what is most needed in our times is the model offered by a concrete realization of the possibility of building real community among people who do not all live in the same place at the same time, do not work together in the common enterprise of either the family farm or shop or even the breadwinner/homemaker family unit, for whom real diversities in everything from personality to work necessitate and legitimate an irreducible plurality of lifestyles and yet who long for and need authentic relationships in life-giving community. Embodying community in such circumstances, and the witness it offers, will be the topic of the next chapter.

CHAPTER TEN
EMBODYING RELIGIOUS COMMUNITY II: THE CORPORATE PERSPECTIVE

I. Introduction and Transition

The previous chapter looked at community from the perspective of the individual Religious who incarnate the living of congregational community life in either group or individual lifestyles, in either of which they belong intimately to the congregation and participate actively in its life and mission. In this chapter I want to look at the same reality, Religious community, from the corporate perspective, that is, from the perspective of the congregation to which these members belong. From the beginning of this work I have consistently made two distinctions that must be kept operative in what follows.

The first is the distinction between the *autonomous monastic community* that is a permanent and selfsame group living together over a lifetime and does not normally exchange members or share resources or ministries with other monasteries even of the same Order, and the *ministerial congregation* whose members are sent on mission in continuously reconfigured groupings that all depend upon and are the local incarnation of the life of the congregation as a whole. This distinction is very important because the ministerial Religious belongs first and foremost, affectively and effectively, to the congregation as such even though her more immediate context may be a local group

353

(such as a mission community) or an intermediate grouping
(such as a cluster group or mission unit) that mediates her participation in the community life of the congregation. These
groupings change fairly frequently, and she moves about among
them. But her stabile locus and focus of community belonging
and identity is the congregation itself. In this sense, there is an
important way in which congregation and community are identical in a deeper, more radical way than local grouping and community. The local grouping is a transitory incarnation of the
congregational community, not an autonomous community
unto itself. This will have important ramifications for a number
of complex issues to be discussed below.

The second distinction is between the *congregation* and the
community. As I pointed out in part 1, in preconciliar experience
the institute (the Religious group as canonically constituted), the
congregation (the particular juridically constituted Religious
group), and the community (the same group as an affective and
effective relational and ministerial unit) were coterminous and
for most people synonymous. Today's reality demands greater
nuance, particularly in regard to the latter two terms.

The congregation is a juridical institution. It has recognizable boundaries, entrance requirements, a period of probation
for prospective members during which they participate in a
formation process by which they are progressively assimilated
to the life (not only Religious Life as such but the specific version of that life particular to this congregation), a formal ritual of induction (profession) that confers particular rights and
responsibilities that are legally binding such as active and passive voice, and a way of living prescribed by the constitutions.

The community is the group of people who have all
entered this particular congregation considered in their
affective and effective union of minds and hearts in life and
mission. Thus, there is a distinction, at least of point of
view, between the juridical institution of which all the professed are members and the relational solidarity that binds
them together in gospel friendship but, at this point, congregation and community are actually coterminous. All and

only professed members of the congregation are part of the community considered in this way.

However, in recent years congregations have become explicitly aware of all the types of informal affiliations they have with laypeople and clerics and even with non-Catholics and non-Christians. Furthermore, they have established various types of formal affiliation of nonmembers (associates, volunteers, resident oblates, etc.) with the congregation.[1] The term *community*, therefore, has necessarily been expanded in meaning and application precisely because all of these connections are primarily relational, that is, affective and effective. In other words, today the community as a relational entity is considerably broader than the congregation. Consequently, whatever is said below about community considered from the corporate perspective has to keep constantly in view the distinction between the congregation-community, that is, the community made up of the members of the congregation, and the wider community, which includes nonmembers in many degrees and kinds of relationship with the congregation.

In view of the purpose of this volume, which is to talk about the life of Religious themselves, when I use the term *community* without qualification (unless the qualification is implicit in the context) I will be referring to the congregation-community, that is, to the professed members (and those preparing for professed membership) in terms of their relationship to one another. This in no way minimizes the reality or the affective importance to the congregation of its wider connections but narrows the scope of the discussion for the sake of clarity in dealing with the issues at hand.

II. Light from the Sociology of Organizations

When Religious Life in the wake of the Council ceased to be the tightly ghettoized subculture of a total institution, it seemed to many to unravel as a sociological reality. Members no longer lived and worked as a unit, dressed identically, or avoided interaction with nonmembers. Thus they were no longer distinguished by their virtually total nonassimilation to the surrounding culture. This raised in sharp relief a question that had rarely been asked: What kind of social grouping does Religious Life involve? Although it was not always the case, today one can no more talk meaningfully about Religious community without some understanding of human group life than one can talk about sanctity without some theory of human nature.

Fortunately, in recent years sociologists have not only supplied nuanced theoretical frameworks for understanding groups in general but have specifically studied the remarkable social phenomenon of Catholic Religious community life. Unlike virtually all utopian communities in history, which tend to have relatively short life spans and usually leave no sociological progeny, Religious Life has a nearly two-thousand-year history. As such it has recently attracted considerable attention from sociologists, especially those interested in organizations.

Two types of sociological analysis, one of organizational life cycles and one of the structures and mechanisms of organizations, were applied to Religious congregations in the 1970s and '80s. The first was exemplified in the detailed study of the growth and decline of male Religious orders by Raymond Hostie[2] and the more popular application of the same data in the work of Lawrence Cada and his associates.[3] These studies helped generate in Religious an historical consciousness about their lifeform that has greatly facilitated thinking about change. The second type began with the disturbing assimilation of Religious Life, along with prisons and the military, into the category of "total institutions," exemplified in the work of Erving Goffman.[4] More recently a number of sociologists and historians, notably women, have undertaken studies of Catholic Religious Life focused on women's congregations. In what follows I will make extensive use of the work of Patricia Wittberg, a Sister of Charity of Cincinnati, who has produced an impressive body of sociological description and analysis of Religious congregations especially since the emergence of the ministerial form of the life among women. Although I will sometimes disagree with her implications or conclusions, I am enormously indebted, for my own reflections, to her fine sociological work.[5]

A. Three Models of Group Life and Relationships

Sociologists distinguish among intentional communities, bureaucratic organizations, and associations. The distinctions bear on how the groups are organized, the mechanisms of belonging or affiliation they utilize, and most importantly for our purposes, the kinds of relationships among their members that they generate and support. This typology can supply a conceptuality and a vocabulary for describing and analyzing some of the issues facing Religious congregations today as they struggle to free themselves from some of the oppressive aspects of Tridentine community life and appropriate in new ways the theological reality of community life for today.

1. Intentional community: Wittberg defines intentional community as "a group of persons living together on a more or less permanent basis, who voluntarily surrender control over some choices which are normally considered private for the sake of establishing a whole new way of life."[6] The archetypal form of intentional community is the "total institution" in which members live, work, and recreate together, and have little or no contact with persons or ideas from the outside world in order to preserve the beliefs and values of the group, which usually differ significantly from those of the surrounding society. Commitment in such communities is fostered by charismatic leadership, ideological commitment to the ideals and projects of the group, and intense, family-like (and sometimes cultlike) relational bonds among the members. Such mechanisms as intensive indoctrination, shaming or shunning of those who do not conform, common rituals and traditions, sharing of work and recreation, rigid boundary maintenance, the demand for heroic sacrifice, and mortification or stripping away of personal identity and its replacement by member-identity are powerful promoters of

belonging.[7] Members, in effect, have no private life apart
from or alongside their community life.

Religious who entered their communities prior to conciliar
renewal will recognize almost everything in this description
as characteristic of at least the external functioning of Tridentine Religious Life. And many people arguing for a return to
"real" Religious community life as well as some applicants
entering Religious Life "for community"[8] openly promote the
reinstating of the intentional community model. There is no
question that such intentionality fosters intense commitment,
a day-to-day sense that one is doing something different,
important, special and even superior with one's life, affective
involvement, and an invigorating sense of being called to self-
transcendence for a worthwhile cause. But there is also no
doubt that this type of community has many liabilities and
even dangers. In my opinion, it is potentially (and often actually) antithetical to certain important gospel values, to say
nothing of psychological maturity and mental health.

Although Religious community is voluntary in the sense
that becoming a Religious is not required for salvation and no
particular congregation is mandatory even for someone who
feels called to the life, I would suggest it should not be intentional in this sociological sense (i.e., as total institution) at
either the congregational or the local level. Religious community should be a zone of freedom, not of restriction and con-
straint, for its members. Their commitment to Christ, his
members, and the community itself should be rooted in personal religious conviction that does not need to be maintained
by isolation from the surrounding culture by rigid and exclu-
sionary boundaries, cognitive and affective inbreeding, and
punitive authoritarianism. Initial brainwashing, shaming techniques for maintaining group behavioral standards, encouragement of personality cults around leaders, arbitrary
suspension of freedom in work and relationships, and denial
of potentially "contaminating" cultural and educational
enrichment—no matter how willing or even eager recruits

might be to participate in such a system—should not be characteristic of a community of mature followers of Christ.

The total institution model of intentional community characteristic of Tridentine Religious congregations is historically understandable, and it was highly effective, at least in terms of membership maintenance and ministerial efficiency. However, the theological rethinking and experimentation of the conciliar renewal has made it clear to most Religious that total institution is not the only conceivable model of authentic Religious community life, that it is not only not mandated by the Gospel but, at a deep level, is potentially antithetical to gospel values, and that its cost in human dysfunctionality is much too high. Finding an alternative has not been easy. Indeed we do not yet seem to have found a universally affirmed viable alternative. But that does not justify a return to a type of community that is essentially ill suited to Religious Life both theologically and from the standpoint of spirituality. This being said, however, Religious can profitably look at what makes intentional community work and see what can be learned from its success in promoting belonging and cohesion. In what follows this typological description I will be evoking some of the features of each of the three models in discussing current experiments in Religious community.

2. Bureaucratic organizations: The Religious community to which the categories of *intentional* and *voluntary* apply is the people bound together by life commitment. But these people who, from one perspective, are community are also organized into an institution called the congregation. From this perspective the category of bureaucracy is relevant to the social reality of Religious Life. As Wittberg says, bureaucracy has a bad image and worse press.[9] To most people it suggests anonymity, rigidity of procedures, remoteness of personnel, narrow vision, the priority of maintenance over mission, administrative high-handedness, and in-house squabbling if not mutual subversion among isolated units vying for survival and prominence. The classic protest against bureaucracy is the plea of the depersonalized 1960s student: "Please, do not 'fold, staple, or spindle' me to fit into your procedures and pigeonholes."

Nevertheless, most operations in the modern world are highly bureaucratic. Bureaucracy is the characteristic form of organization in business, government, education, health care, charitable works, and even (or especially) the ecclesiastical institution. And probably most of us, if truth be told, actually want it this way despite our protests against the impersonality, buck-passing, and lack of commitment to good work and real service that bureaucracy promotes.

Wittberg gives four characteristics of bureaucracies: division of labor and hierarchy of authority; written rules and files; separation of office and incumbent; universality of treatment.[10] Actually, the very word *bureaucracy* is the clue to its distinctiveness. *Bureau* is the French word for "office," and in English *office* denotes both the emphatically unhomelike place in which business is conducted and the specific *role* in the hierarchy of authority that a person plays. In a bureaucracy office replaces person as locus of authority and official procedures replace interpersonal relationships as the preferred way of operating.

Bureaucratic organization, once it replaces communitarian forms, is almost never abandoned. In other words, the process from familial or communitarian to bureaucratic does not tend to reverse itself. There are reasons for this. Bureaucracy has advantages that cannot be as readily realized in more communitarian forms of organization, and some of these advantages, once experienced, will not be surrendered by modern people even though they may nostalgically long for the more informal and personal modes of operation they have surrendered. However, in the case of the Religious congregation there cannot be a definitive replacement of community with organization comparable to the replacement of the one-room village schoolhouse with the multicounty unified school district. The Religious social entity remains both a community as well as a congregation. If the exclusive priority of the former leads to organizational inefficiency if not chaos, the exclusive recourse to the latter leads to affective alienation and disaffiliation.

Religious congregations, especially since the 1950s, have become increasingly bureaucratized. To some extent this has been due to external pressures arising from ministry. Ministries carried out in the modern world have to conform to secular standards regarding credentialing of personnel, record keeping, fairness to employees, clear policies and procedures in running institutions and handling large sums of money, and so on. To some extent congregations have seen the advantages for their own internal operations of standardizing procedures, eliminating waste of time, money, and materials by unnecessary duplication, keeping accurate records, depersonalizing and limiting the power of officeholders, respecting the privacy of members, and building procedural justice into congregational processes.

Nevertheless, many Religious also lament the loss or at least the muting, through bureaucratization, of the bold and visionary risk taking that characterized their founding periods in which formidable women cut through red tape and bypassed chains of command in pursuit of gospel objectives. Energy was generated by the intensely personal and holistic mode of *cura personalis* (pastoral care of members) in which superiors treated an individual's life as a whole rather than as a collection of aspects, each of which could be handled by a separate office. The organic approach that made less rigid distinctions between community life and ministry, and the corporate élan that encouraged every member to feel responsible for the whole enterprise regardless of who was assigned to what task integrated life and clarified goals. The prebureaucratic ethos emphasized that Religious Life at its best is a lifeform, not a job; members of a congregation are a community, not a workforce; the congregation's schools and hospitals are ministries, not businesses. And Religious are stewards of whatever they have for the sake of God's people, not entrepreneurs intent on running profitable enterprises whose success is measured by the bottom line.

Despite the fact that congregations are not primarily or exclusively organizations and the evident dangers of bureaucracy, congregations are at least organizations, and bureaucracy is an efficient way to handle the public aspects of life in such a system.

There is much about Religious Life and ministry that falls, at least in part, into this public sphere. Congregations need to keep records of the education, health care, ministries, and locations of members. If congregational events are to take place and projects be accomplished, the congregation needs to plan and publish calendars, appoint committees, delegate responsibilities, require and evaluate reports, and establish uniform policies and procedures. Effective stewardship demands financial planning and responsible management that is open and accountable. A congregation needs to know where its cars are and who is driving them, what property it owns and rents and who is occupying it, what its insurance policies for personnel and property cover and how they are being handled. Members of the community have a right to be dealt with justly, not according to the favoritisms or whims of those in power. People in office should be accountable to the members according to expectations that are public, and members should have equitable access to congregational resources and to information that affects them as well as equal opportunity to influence decisions. All of this requires communications systems appropriate to the size of the congregation and its geographical distribution. While this list is not exhaustive it does suggest that there is much about contemporary Religious congregations that is best handled by the bureaucratic processes and procedures that have proven their worth in modern society.

The advantages of bureaucratic organization are clear, and it does not pose major theological problems. However, unlike a business that is essentially an organization that only rarely, and by way of exception, suspends its bureaucratic structure for a community-style event such as a Christmas party, the Religious congregation is not primarily an organization but a community that makes use of bureaucratic structures and functions to handle certain public aspects of its life and mission as a congregation. How to maintain corporate efficiency at the congregational level without sacrificing the priority of community requires a very discerning approach to the integration of bureaucratic elements and procedures into the congregation's life.

The first important feature of Religious Life that warns against wholesale bureaucratization is the fact that the *Religious are members of the community,* not club participants or even employees. They did not join an organization; they became Religious. The conundrum in secular society of the prenuptial agreement provides an enlightening analogue of the dilemma in Religious Life over bureaucratization. When one commits one's entire life in perpetuity to a great love that needs to say "forever," tying it up in qualifying red tape "just in case"—no matter how prudent that might seem in light of current divorce statistics—seems somehow crass and demeaning of the whole project. Religious Life is not a nine-to-five job but a gift of one's whole person, including all one's personal and material resources, twenty-four hours a day every day of one's life, to Christ and his members within the context of the community. The person who makes such a self-gift has a right and a need to be dealt with as a person, in her wholeness, with all her strengths and fragilities, in terms not only of her record of success and failure in the past but also of her potential and promise for the future, not only in terms of congregational needs but also of her spiritual good and growth. Her health cannot be bracketed when considering her ministry or education. Her family and her friendships are not irrelevant to her ministerial location. Even such mundane decisions as whether she may change living situations, have a car or computer, or go on a particular vacation cannot be made entirely "by the book" but have to take account of the person as a person, as a Religious, as a member of the community who is loved and cherished for who she is and not merely for what she does or earns.

Secondly, *Religious Life does not transpire exclusively in the public sphere* or through public interaction. The relationship between a provincial and a member of the province, between the Religious administrator of a ministerial institution and a Religious who is on the staff, among committee members designing a congregational project, or among members of a

local community may have public features that are best handled bureaucratically, but the Religious are also sisters (or
brothers) who have thrown in their lots, their very lives, with
one another and who will share community until death, long
after these public relationships and projects have become history. Just as a husband and wife might make out wills or make
legal arrangements to care for a disabled child, a congregation
may appropriately bureaucratize certain aspects of its relationship to its members, for example, power of attorney for health
care or financial arrangements for student members. Various
dimensions of the life of members, such as buying and insuring
cars, renting real estate, health insurance, educational decisions, and so on, will have to be handled by different offices
within the congregational organization. But the relationships
among community members, like those among family members, are far deeper, more extensive, and more complex than
can be formalized or totally compartmentalized. Reducing
community relationships to bureaucratic procedures is ultimately destructive of the union of minds and hearts in gospel
friendship that is the substance of Religious community life.

This means that while basic equity is a minimal requirement that can be bureaucratically protected and assured,
love, specifically the love of friendship, is the appropriate
global relationship of the members to one another, of the
members to the community, and vice versa. Love does not ask
primarily what is owed, what is deserved, what is obligatory,
what is demanded by the written policy, but what is for the
good of the member and of the community as a whole.
Bureaucratic divisions of labor can protect against chaos and
interference, but in a community of friends there is frequently overlap between areas of responsibility. Strict bureaucratic equality may supply a neutral starting point for
discernment, but it must be modified by love's desire to meet
the differing needs, private as well as public, of every member. Office and authority are in the service of good order and
effective leadership but, at the deepest level, all who have
made the same Religious profession within the community

are radically equal, and no one should be subordinated or sacrificed to the power agenda of another.

Just as it is clear that Religious Life should not be an "intentional community," that is, a total if not totalitarian social system in which the individual is completely subsumed in the collectivity, but that the emphasis on relational quality that is characteristic of intentional community is desirable in Religious Life, so it is also clear that Religious Life should not be reduced to a bureaucracy but that bureaucratic structures and functions can and should play at least some role in any modern congregation larger than a few people. How genuine community and bureaucratic elements and processes can be integrated is what is not clear. Once again, we will return to this question below.

3. *Associations:* Wittberg defines an association as "a group of persons who have invested a certain amount of their resources in the attainment of some common goal or objective, but who retain more personal autonomy and competing loyalties than would be possible in an intentional community."[11] The fundamental relational difference between the association and its contrary, the intentional community, is that the latter is bonded by what sociologists call "strong (or primary) ties" and the former by "weak (or secondary) ties."

Strong primary ties such as those in intentional communities (but which can be realized also in other voluntary communities) are relatively permanent, intimate in the sense that they involve many aspects of the persons' lives and at deep levels, and continuous in that members are in frequent contact over the entire time of membership in the community. A close-knit family, an intimate friendship, a small rural village, or a congregational local group or mission unit would be examples of communities with strong or primary ties. These relationships are not necessarily totally positive in affective tone but they are long-lasting, constant, face-to-face, and intimate. Strong ties in a community can tend to isolate the participants in enclaves and to restrict their contacts with outsiders, but this does not have to occur. When it does occur, as in intentional communities, members are highly interdependent in ways that meet their basic needs but usually have few outside resources upon which to call. The Shakers or the Amish might be good examples of such communities, illustrating both the advantages and disadvantages.[12] Most Religious congregations in the preconciliar era, at least at the local level, were characterized by strong ties.

Weak or secondary ties are less intense, intimate, and global. They tend to form bridges between an individual and groups of which the individual is not a full member (e.g., between a military spouse and the army), between diverse groups that might have only one or a few concerns in common (e.g., between Buddhists and Christians involved together in antiwar activism), or among pluralities of individuals who share some common interest but not life as a whole (e.g., feminists across many relational, occupational, and religious lines). Often, weak ties create networks or chains of influence or power even though not every member of the network knows every other member personally and not all are involved in all the concerns of the others. A large network of weak ties gives an individual access to much wider realms of information and influence, financial resources, leadership skills, and power connections and puts her or him in the position to mobilize resources, even on short notice, toward commonly espoused goals. Weak ties can hold together and facilitate relationships within a group that is too large or far-flung to be bonded by primary ties.

Although sociologists in the past, and probably the popular imagination today, tend to see strong ties as healthy, vibrant, and life-giving and weak ties as shallow and alienating, this is not necessarily the case. Although a person who lacked any primary ties in her life would probably have a fairly superficial affective life, most people in contemporary society seem to function best with a few strong ties and many weak ones.

Wittberg and some other sociologists seem to suggest that postconciliar Religious congregations have transformed themselves almost completely from intentional communities into associations or networks.[13] I am not convinced that this analysis, which seems sociologically persuasive, is entirely accurate.

There is little question that contemporary Religious congregations have become much more associational since the breakdown of the total institution. However, since I am persuaded that that breakdown was both necessary and essentially positive and that attempts to reconstruct Religious Life as exclusive intentional communities are mistaken, I am concerned to deepen the analysis of the associational trend. I want to suggest that contemporary Religious Life is, or can be, a healthy blend of strong primary ties in a voluntary community context, bureaucratic efficiency and procedural justice in a genuinely communitarian context, and wide networking both within and beyond congregational boundaries that enriches rather than enfeebles the primary bonds.

The essential problems with association as an exclusive model for Religious Life arise in three areas. First, an *association is not a lifeform* that engages a person in her totality with the community in its totality. An associate participates in a community on a voluntary basis to the extent that she or he finds personally meaningful. In other words, association allows for individually chosen levels of commitment and involvement. In a Religious congregation that has been reduced to an association this would mean that leadership could not require participation by members in community life, acceptance of or compliance with obligations of rule or vows, or self-sacrifice for the common good. Those who think that Religious congregations have, in fact, devolved into pure associations think that this is precisely the situation today, that is, that most members have redefined their relationship with their congregation as voluntary association rather than as membership in a lifeform. However, while contemporary congregational leaders tend to lead by persuasion rather than coercion, I doubt that either leaders or members would maintain that members actually have no real obligations in and to their congregation. They would probably not even deny that, if it were necessary, leaders could require participation or compliance and would have both the right and the authority to sanction refusal or noncompliance. In other words, while

some members may have receded to the fringes of their congregations and are behaving as if the congregation were
merely an association with which they had a loose networklike
relationship, I do not think that most congregations have
become associations.

Withdrawal from total participation in community life into
an associational relationship with one's congregation is often
expressed most clearly in the reversal of financial flow. The
member who has become associational in her relationship to
the congregation no longer sees herself as supported by the
congregation out of the common resources of the community
but rather as making voluntary, freewill financial contributions to the congregation from her personally earned and controlled funds the way one might send a contribution to a
favorite charity. Although this is a matter to be discussed theologically in volume 3 under the heading of evangelical
poverty, it has a direct effect on the quality of community
because total economic interdependence of the members is
the material substrate and a public expression of the communitarian lifeform as distinct from an association.

In short, association is a possible model for persons voluntarily sharing many concerns but not permanently committed
as members to the sharing of the totality of their lives. It is,
therefore, in my opinion, not a model for a community whose
members have each committed their whole person and life to
Jesus Christ through consecrated celibacy, that is, to the exclusion of any other primary life commitment, and have chosen
to live that commitment until death in community and shared
ministry with others who have made the same commitment.
Again, contemporary marriage offers an enlightening analogue in the dilemma some couples face over whether to establish a community of goods or to maintain individual control of
earnings and expenditures and whether to have a monogamous or an "open" sexual life.

The second problem with association as an exclusive model
for Religious Life arises from the fact that association, although
it offers many advantages in terms of contacts, relationships,

and influence, *cannot meet the human need for intimacy and security,* for the kind of deep, personal, perduring relationships that satisfy our longing to know and be known, to share our innermost selves with people we can trust, to know that there is someone there for us in joy and in crisis.

Wittberg describes very well the strategies for dealing with the loss of intimacy and security experienced by many Religious in congregations that have gone the route toward a more associational character without sufficient reflection.[14] They are precisely the ones I described in relation to consecrated celibacy and family in chapter 6. Some Religious have virtually returned to their families of origin; some have formed dyads or couples who cannot be separated and whom no one else can join; some have formed small subgroups with some other members and nonmembers that are equally impenetrable and from which, for a number of internal and external reasons, no one can easily depart. Others have cast their affective lot with friends outside the community. Aside from the problems already discussed in regard to consecrated celibacy that these arrangements involve, all of them make it difficult to provide a welcoming context for potential members, to facilitate belonging and rehabilitation for members trying to overcome various kinds of problems, to permit intergenerational sharing within the community, or to maintain the kind of flexibility and mobility in ministry that should be characteristic of Religious congregations. The point is that healthy human beings need primary relationships and if the Religious congregation/community has devolved into a purely associational network, members will have to find those relationships elsewhere. If they find them exclusively elsewhere they have, in fact, ceased to be members of the congregation. They are people whose primary affective base is outside the congregation and who occasionally visit the community to which they remain loosely networked.

Finally, a purely associational model of Religious Life *fosters not only relationship with, but assimilation to, the surrounding culture.* For most first-world Religious this means assimilation to the middle class, both economically and ideologically. Intentional communities isolate their members from "contaminating" contact with the "outside world." The totalitarian character of such communities tends to absorb all the time, resources, work, and affective energy of the members in intracommunity involvement. Consequently, the community and the individual members may be very countercultural in their relationship to their surroundings. Because the more associational structure of contemporary congregations allows for much more contact, cooperation, and networking between members and nonmembers, and members do not tend to live together in such a way that they are immediately recognized as a distinct group with life patterns and values they do not share with their neighbors, it is much easier for them to be assimilated, to become "invisible," to lose the capacity to resist values they have renounced or live according to countercultural values they have espoused. In other words, the corporate public witness of shared identity is characteristic of real communities, not of networks.

Again, I do not think Religious congregations, in general, have become associations. And I do not think wide associational relationships of members beyond congregational boundaries is unhealthy or dangerous. On the contrary, it is a major source of enrichment and can, if properly integrated into real community life, become a resource for ministry and witness. But Wittberg and others are right to caution us about the drift toward a reduction of Religious community to pure association, and congregations need to attend to the temptation and its manifestations, both individual and corporate.

B. The Challenge to Contemporary Religious Community: Its Sociological Uniqueness

Our concern in this chapter, as in the preceding two, is not with institutional organization as such but with the meaning and living of Religious community life. However, this chapter is particularly concerned with the embodiment of community looked at from the corporate perspective. Thus, the area of overlap between community and congregation, that is, between the Religious social entity as relational and as organizational, is extensive. It will be a challenge to maintain the focus on community itself while remembering that the organizational dimension is integral to the structure and function of the community as a modern corporate entity.

The foregoing typology suggests that Religious community is a unique reality that does not fit easily or exclusively into any of the available sociological categories. Although most congregations in their Tridentine period were, sociologically speaking, intentional communities, whether or not they knew anything about the theory of groups, most renewed congregations have abandoned this model as fundamentally unhealthy, and few are inclined to resuscitate it even though there is considerable pressure from ecclesiastical authority to do so. The coerciveness, authoritarianism, ideological rigidity and thought control, shaming and shunning techniques for formation and social control, and virtually total separation from persons and systems outside the congregation are fortunately a part of the past that seems definitively outgrown. In suggesting below that there are aspects of intentional community, especially in terms of primary relationships and affective commitment, that need to be fostered in contemporary congregations, I will be taking it for granted that the negative aspects have been recognized and repudiated.

Bureaucratic efficiency and procedural justice are clearly important to most Religious and have certainly facilitated the interrelationships between Religious Life and the culture in which it lives and works, but few healthy people want to commit their lives to a bureaucracy nor do they expect to find in it the affective depth and richness that should characterize a human, to say nothing of a spiritual, life. Again, Religious congregations will need to discern how to build the values of bureaucracy into their corporate life without transforming their community into a corporation.

Wide association with people outside the Religious congregation has greatly enriched the life and expanded the ministerial effectiveness of Religious. Furthermore, the myth of equal and

identical primary relationships among all members of the congregation has been exposed and repudiated as an unrealistic
and dangerous fiction. In other words, many relationships of
individual Religious, inside and outside the congregation, are
either basically associational or at least more secondary than primary. However, neither the purely voluntary character of associational participation nor the weak ties characteristic of such
relationships is sufficient to constitute the organic lifeform that
is Religious Life, much less to satisfy the relational needs of
mature people over a lifetime. Networks are communitarian at
times, but they are not communities, and for Religious who
renounce family, both primary and secondary, as the relational
context of their life, real community that is permanent, ongoing,
committed, and reliable is not a luxury but a psychological and
spiritual necessity. Part of the contemporary challenge for Religious congregations is to extend and deepen the network of relationships of the congregation/community as a whole and
support associational relationships of and among its individual
members without allowing membership to be attenuated into
association or the community to become a network of people
with only tangential, sporadic, or purely instrumental relationships to the congregation and to one another.

In short, it seems to me that if Religious Life is not only to
survive but flourish as a unique form of community life in the
Church it will have to find a way to combine the positive
aspects of all three sociological forms just discussed while minimizing or eliminating the aspects of each that would militate
against genuine community in the congregation. To do this it
will have to discriminate between the positive and the deleterious in function of its own distinctive core values, or what Margaret Wheatley, culling an analogy from contemporary physics,
called the "strange attractor of its corporate identity.[15] I have
suggested that the shared commitment in lifelong consecrated
celibacy, gospel friendship as the normative form of relationship among the members, a plurality of complementary
lifestyles in which this community relationship is embodied
and lived by the individual members, and corporate ministry

as the generative expression of celibate friendship in community constitute that identity in relation to the problematic of community. The challenge is how to realize the corporate character of this shared identity in the community life of the congregation as such.

III. Some Presuppositions for Discussion of Community Life from the Corporate Perspective

The current discussion of community in Religious Life is one of the most important and most fraught with anxiety of all the issues that have emerged from conciliar renewal and the consequent dissolution of the total institution. The discussion is impeded by factors from both the past and the future. Religious who entered before the renewal had an extensive experience of community life that, from different points of view, was both positive and negative but that was, in any case, the only experience they had. The unraveling of that tightly organized system, a version of the intentional community model, has left many with a sense that community life itself has unraveled. Without necessarily reflecting explicitly on the subject, they have equated community with preconciliar intentional community, which creates a dilemma. It can seem that they must choose between returning to the only model of community they know, which most are not inclined to do, or resigning themselves to the fact that they cannot look for real community within their congregations but will have to find some private way to meet their relational needs.

At the other end of the spectrum are newer members, especially those who entered (and often were born) after the Council. They frequently assert that they were attracted to, even entered Religious Life "for community," sometimes with the implicit reproach that they are not finding it and that this involves some kind of false advertising on the part of the congregation. This ambiguous expression, "entering for community," can hide

immature personal needs that no evolved congregation can or
wants to meet. But often it is a somewhat inarticulate way of saying that what they are seeking in Religious Life is not a new
organization to join or even a worthwhile service project to pursue but a real life to be lived. They want to share the whole of
their life with companions who are involved in the exclusive
God-quest that is the Religious Life to which they feel called.[16]
Consequently, they want real community life, whatever that
means. They do not want to be merely card-carrying operatives
of a remote corporation to which they periodically report but
which is not an integral part of their day-to-day experience, is not
a powerful factor in who they are and what they are trying to do
with their lives and for their Church and world. This is a perfectly legitimate, indeed a very healthy and potentially creative,
desire and a valid expectation to address to the congregation. I
suspect that only congregations that find a way to respond to it
are going to attract newer members.

This double challenge, the dilemma of members who have
implicitly identified community life itself with intentional community or what I described in the last chapter as "common life"
and the desire of newer members for real community within
their congregations, necessitates two presuppositions to an
attempt at constructive reflection on contemporary congregational community life.

First, we have to be honest in recognizing that the intentional community model most Religious experienced prior to
renewal, no matter how effective it was in many ways, did not
facilitate the kind of community Religious, whether experienced or new, are seeking today. Aside from the coercive and
collectivist features already mentioned and which can be recognized as unintentional perversions of the ideal, many of the
explicit objectives of Tridentine common life actually
impeded the development of the gospel friendship that should
characterize Religious community. Keeping people virtually
always in groups as well as prohibiting "particular friendships"
was intended, positively, to maintain a generalized benevolence in which all were loved equally by all with a charity

devoid of passion. No one, probably, actually realized that such an objective was not a realistic and holy ideal but was calculated, despite its lofty intentions, to prevent anyone from really loving anyone with the warm, human fullness of real friendship. Of course, this program did not work. Many wonderful friendships among Religious were formed and maintained.[17] But this happened more in spite of the system than because of it, and these relationships virtually always had a certain clandestine character and an aura of guilt associated with them.

The intentional community model was well suited to many of the objectives of Religious Life. The generalizing of relationships facilitated the detachment thought necessary for ministerial mobility. It assured that no one found herself without company and assistance when she needed it, whether at recreation or at a dentist appointment or on a home visit. It required the acceptance, at least behaviorly in the public forum, of the difficult as well as the congenial personalities in the congregation and assured that the former would always have a home and a job. There was never a lack of social contexts into which to place a newly professed member. Without doubt the community ethos fostered the working together, whether in summer canning bees or spring cleaning of large institutions or the staffing of schools and hospitals, which developed "community women," bound the congregation together, and made Religious such a formidable presence in the Church's ministry. The isolation of the members from outsiders and their constant close contact with one another built up a shared history, a trove of tales that wove a narrative context in which all participated, and an esprit de corps that generated real excitement about reunions and a felt sense of deep belonging. In short, the intentional community of the preconciliar period was a highly effective social form in terms of ministry and corporate life. But in terms of what Religious today are seeking, a faith community of shared life in gospel friendship, it fell far short.

Thus, my *first presupposition* is that we need not denigrate the preconciliar form of congregational community life or its real achievements in terms of corporate identity and effectiveness in order to say that, from today's perspective, it is simply deficient as an ideal of community or a model of community life. Therefore, developing community today does not mean returning to a preconciliar form of intentional community. Just as there is no 1950s ideal family that should serve as a model for the family of the twenty-first century, so there is no communitarian Garden of Eden in our Religious past to which we are called to return. If this is explicitly admitted, more experienced Religious need not fear that entering fully into the challenging effort to imagine and build community today will involve a resuscitation of the type of community life they are happy to have left behind. And newer members can espouse the challenge of helping to create a new model rather than insisting that the congregation provide community for them by reconstituting what they imagine existed in the past. The challenge today is to imagine and create something that has not previously existed in Religious Life, a form of community appropriate for ministerial Religious congregations that will both provide for the relational growth and development of the members and facilitate ministry.

My *second presupposition* is that there is no generic "community life" that is suitable for all forms of life in the Church or even among Religious lifeforms. It seems to me that any realistic attempt to engage the issue of community from the corporate perspective must start from a clear conception of the nature of ministerial Religious Life itself in contrast to other forms of life. Ministerial community cannot be modeled on monogamous marriage, with its lifetime commitment to daily shared life with the same person(s), or on the small, autonomous monastery in which the same people will live together, physically, over a lifetime. These two forms of community life have significant features in common, especially the formative influence on spirituality of the challenge to deal every day of one's life with the same people, who come to know one extremely well and vice versa, and with whom one must work out, rather than escape, the whole range of tensions arising from simple differences as well as real difficulties in personality.

The ministerial congregation, however, is a different type of social entity characterized by a certain economy of scale, fairly constant mobility of members, and a focus on extramural ministry. While challenges to spiritual development equivalent to those in monastic communities or marital relationships are present in this life, they are differently shaped, differently experienced, and differently negotiated. Ministerial Religious Life presents other challenges that are particular to it, such as frequent adjustment to new situations and persons, willing detachment from the familiar for the sake of mission, and acceptance of more institutional ways of dealing with such significant personal issues as health care and aging, because of the priority of ministry in the lives of one's companions.

The mobility intrinsic to ministerial Religious Life means that, except in a very small, geographically concentrated congregation in which virtually all members live and minister together (and which therefore approximates a stabile monastic community), most members will not live in the primary locus of corporate identity, that is, at the motherhouse or provincial house, after initial formation. Nor, today, will they live in local houses that are, in virtually all respects, clones of the motherhouse. They will live in very diverse circumstances, in small groups or individually, and may move fairly often from place to place. Therefore, conscious planning and strenuous effort will have to be expended if members are to come together and share their varied lives in really meaningful ways that generate corporate élan and esprit de corps and sustain corporate identity and ministerial commitment.

Congregational members "on mission," whether they live together in a group or individually, will be continuously moving in and out of community configurations. This will require vigorous efforts both to retain relationships already established with members from whom one is now physically separated and to establish relationships with new companions who come into the area or into whose area one moves. At times, when a Religious is the only member of her congregation in a particular place, she will have to do the traveling necessary for meaningful, ongoing participation in community at different levels of corporate organization. It seems to me that attempts to avoid the implications of ministerial mobility, whether for affective or apostolic reasons, by forming virtually permanent and self-enclosed quasi-intentional communities or subgroups that pressure members not to move into new congregational groupings or configurations or, even worse, create a separatist or antagonistic ethos in relation to the congregation as a whole actually militate against congregational unity. Ministerial congregations are not pseudo-families nor stabile autonomous monasteries. But neither are they collections of isolated individuals or of separate and autonomous subgroups.

These two features of ministerial Religious Life, namely, the fact that members leave the central congregational locus of identity to go on mission and that they remain mobile throughout their lives, have implications that are in constant tension with each other. On the one hand, the congregation is the primary relational context of every member. But, on the other hand, each member also must develop personal relationships, both to individuals and to smaller groups, inside and outside the congregation, which will not coincide exactly with the relational patterns of anyone else in the congregation. Relating these two dynamics is complex to say the least. While the congregation and its members retain a certain affective and effective priority in the life of each member, not all relationships within the congregation are equal nor will the congregation be able to meet all the relational needs of each member, as the intentional community of times past intended and claimed to do. The attempt to suppress or neutralize more intense friendships between members or between members and nonmembers, or to intensify all relationships within the congregation to the level of intimate friendship and total self-disclosure are both counterproductive projects. Somehow a moving equilibrium of extremely varied and interlocking relationships that sustain both individual members and the congregation as a whole has to be established within a framework that allows this variety to intensify identity and belonging without homogenizing relationships or isolating members.

IV. Resources from Recent Experience of Congregations

The first decade and a half of renewal saw the dissolution of the total institution and with it the breakdown of the intentional community model of common life. No one can deny that in many respects this has been a traumatic experience for individuals and communities, and some major mistakes have probably been made. The current sense of urgency around the question of community testifies to the sense many Religious have that we must find a way to embody (rather than simply to affirm) that unity of minds and hearts that is intrinsic to Religious Life but that this cannot be achieved by returning to a model of community that we abandoned because of its inability to mediate that very unity. Particularly during the second decade and a half of the postconciliar period, many Religious congregations have experimented with a variety of strategies of reintegration, some of which have been remarkably successful and most of which offer some useful data for the task in which we are involved. In this section I will consider four kinds of experiences that can provide resources for the task of reimaging and recreating community life in ministerial congregations from the corporate perspective.

A. Negative Experiences of Distance and Disintegration

As ministries diversified and some congregations divested themselves of the institutional properties necessary for large gatherings, Religious dispersed, singly, in dyads, or in small self-selected groups that shared an affinity for simplicity of lifestyle, intense faith sharing, or a particular ministry. For many this was an experience of blessed liberation from the oppressive and restrictive burdens of a collectivist "common life" that they had seldom found truly life-giving. For some it was an exciting adventure into new possibilities that had been closed off in single apostolate congregations in which every-one lived in large groups. For others, it was a frightening expe-rience of finding themselves suddenly "on their own." For the first time in their lives they had to find a place to live and a paying job, and the congregation was not in a position to sup-ply or guarantee either.

In many though certainly not all respects these experiences were negative in whole or in part. Those who rejoiced in a newfound liberty often enough disappeared, sometimes for years, from congregational life. Indeed, many who discovered that they were quite capable of life on their own and that min-istry did not require affiliation with a Religious congregation left. Others became rather permanently estranged from or peripheral to their congregations. Those who discovered their talents for new professions often became absorbed in acquir-ing the training and credentials for a "second career," and Religious Life receded from the center of their attention. Those who found themselves unable to cope well with their sudden responsibility for themselves were most likely to des-perately clutch at the first situation that offered survival but that was sometimes a dead end both ministerially and person-ally. In retrospect we can see how the geographical dispersal of personnel and the diversification of ministries coupled with the loss, by choice or necessity, of large corporate holdings led to a breakdown not only of the intentional community (which is what many members chose to leave behind) but of the cor-porate experience of community that is integral to Religious Life as such (and which they had no intention of renouncing).

Like many apparently negative experiences in life, these experiences have provided some valuable resources for the current task of reimaging and rebuilding community at the corporate level. The distance some members established between themselves and the congregation allowed time and space for the healing of some very painful community wounds. It allowed some members who had been estranged psychologically long before they could move out physically to realize that, in their focus on the negative dimensions of community life, they had not noticed or responded to some of its gifts, which came to look much more positive in hindsight. As they interacted with colleagues and friends who had no community obligation to tolerate their idiosyncrasies, they also realized that perhaps not all the problems they experienced in community were someone else's fault.

The discovery by many members of their real talents and desires, a discovery that had often not been possible when all members were simply assigned to roles in the congregation's already established works for which these people may have had little aptitude, allowed for remarkable personal growth and reenergizing of commitment. And, from the corporate perspective, the congregation in which everyone was a teacher or nurse, a school or hospital administrator, suddenly found itself with psychotherapists, lawyers, social activists and politicians, researchers, writers, social workers, pastoral workers, prison and hospital chaplains, retreat and spiritual directors, organizational consultants, financial experts, and numerous other types of specialists.

Even for those who became rather "lost souls," lonely and isolated and often mired in work that was more a job to pay the bills than a life-energizing ministry, the experience often yielded some fruit. Unable to hide in the collective anonymity of common life, these people had to stand up and speak up and often grow up in ways they had been able to defer when companions, material support, occupation, and a daily routine were provided without their input. Some of these people confronted their own arrested development and chose to do something about it.

In any case, many congregations that floated some tentative attempts at corporate gatherings of one kind or another in the 1980s had some interesting experiences when many of their members reconvened from disparate places. Everyone had changed, and many in positive ways. The changes were visible the way a child's growth, so incremental the family scarcely notices, is visible to someone who has not seen the child in a few years. Old prejudices needed to be reexamined. Stereotypes were challenged. A person who wanted the newness in her own life to be seen, respected, and taken seriously owed the same to her companions. Even those who had been at the motherhouse or in a geographical area of congregational concentration had often had broadening experiences and realized that some of the people they had not seen in quite awhile were quite different and not necessarily less interesting. These experiences were not entirely positive, as anyone who lived through them knows well. Ranging from the flamboyant "shocker" who, by appearance and manner, dared the more conservative to accept her new persona to the archconservative calling into question the faith and virtue of anyone not in a habit, these first group experiences were often very tense. But they supplied new data, infused fresh perspectives, and began to suggest the contours and scope of the challenge to community that was emerging.

B. Positive Experiences of Corporate Identity and Life

In the late 1980s and throughout the '90s many congregations had extraordinary corporate experiences that seem to have launched a new phase in their congregational community life. And these congregations shared their experiences and their resources so that the positive energy rippled outward to other congregations. Most often, these experiences took place in assemblies, chapters, or congregational days of some sort. They were planned and organized not by "superiors" operating in isolation but by committees of members who freely called upon the expertise of other members and did not hesitate to employ outside talent in the form of facilitators or consultants. And they were seldom command performances. Rather, members were invited and enticed to participate so that those who came were positively expectant and disposed to contribute and to be enriched.

Congregations that were successful in such events testify to the high levels of energy, esprit de corps, corporate élan, renewed sense of belonging, and even a tentative recommitment to recruitment (which had nearly come to a standstill in the identity confusion of the early years of renewal) that these events generated. Experience led to rapid improvement in the ability to put such events together. Committees realized the importance of engaging not only intelligence and decision-making competence but the aesthetic, the social, and the spiritual dimensions of participants. Dance and music enlivened ritual, visual arts beautified space, drama conveyed and mobilized corporate memory, trained facilitators guided productive group participation, and democratic processes involved everyone in formulating and owning the decisions made or the directions taken. Many congregations rediscovered the variety of talents in the community itself as they called on different people to handle everything from preregistration and local logistics to ritual and liturgy, political processes, and the inevitable evaluation and cleanup. Increasingly organizers realized how crucial it was to provide time both for personal and corporate prayer and reflection and for members to be together socially, to reconnect and to reminisce as well as to share current experiences and hopes for the future.

Once again, not everything in these events was positive, and occasionally real crises arose around liturgy, inclusive language, theological diversity, or membership issues. But the enthusiastic, sometimes ecstatic, reports emanating from one congregation after another suggested that something had begun to turn around. More and more members showed up for congregational events. People did not want to miss something that might be critical for the future, or even just fun and energizing. They were eager to see friends and classmates. They wanted to influence decisions. They had begun again to care about the congregation in ways they had in the Tridentine past but that had, in many cases, become inoperative in the years of dispersal.

Although little systematic reflection has been done on this cross-congregational experience it seems to me that it is supplying important resources for the reimaging and rebuilding of congregational community life. The difference between the mandatory, uniform, virtually entirely cerebral and moral, hierarchically controlled congregational meetings of preconciliar times and the vibrant, participatory, inclusive, and multi-dimensional successful events of the present is remarkable. What is emerging is the real possibility of members of a congregation, and in some circumstances those associated with them, being together and acting corporately in a very different way. The assumptions are different; the processes are different; and the outcomes are different. And most people would probably say they are more authentic, life-giving, and engaging. In any case, they are far more in tune with twenty-first-century sensibilities than the medieval procedures of preconciliar congregations.

C. Content Experiences

Although there is no clear-cut division between the corporate events just described and what I am here calling "content experiences"—and the two often coincide—there is some merit in attending specifically to a type of congregational experiment that arrived on the scene somewhat after the first successful assemblies, chapters, and other corporate events.

1. Reappropriation of corporate history: The Council charged Religious congregations to return to the spirit of their founders as inspiration for the work of renewal. This resulted in a good deal of somewhat frustrating, if not futile, wheel-spinning around the issue of charism that we looked at in volume 1, chapter 9. But it had the effect of engaging at least some people in many congregations with archival material that had not been examined in decades, if ever. This move from within congregations coincided in time with two forces from without: the growing interest of feminist historians, Catholic and non-Catholic alike, in the remarkable story of women Religious in America, and the emerging feminist critique of patriarchy in the Church.

As the researchers in congregational archives uncovered not only fascinating stories of the early days but sometimes disturbing, or even shocking, material that had been suppressed for reasons of ecclesiastical expediency, they began to tell the story of their beginnings and growth in new ways.

Most Religious were aware that their congregations survived harrowing early years in the new world because of the heroism and visionary commitment of remarkable women or men in their founding group. But most of the inside stories, especially of women Religious outsmarting, outmaneuvering, or just outrunning powerful ecclesiastical and civic patriarchs in order to provide health care for the poor, opportunity for blacks and Native Americans, education for girls and women, and even relative autonomy for their own congregations and development for their own members, were largely unknown. As this exciting material began to be exhumed, many congregations undertook various historical projects: writing feminist histories,[18] publishing archival newsletters, organizing meetings of archivists, setting up semipermanent or revolving historical displays, but most importantly beginning to incorporate some of this material into community events through drama, letter-readings, and the like.

The pride that Religious felt in their congregations in the past and that contributed enormously to the experienced esprit de corps was largely built on a conviction of superiority not only to the laity but often to neighboring Religious congregations. This corporate pride is being revived today on much sounder grounds as Religious become aware of their history, of the breadth and depth of their apostolic efficacy and the courage of their congregational forebears, and of the legacy of greatness that even small congregations possess. They are reclaiming their founders in new ways, tracing the continuity between these courageous men and women of their past and their members struggling today in the inner city, in third-world countries, among society's outcasts and rejects. History is beginning to function as a touchstone for discernment about which ministries should have priority today. Often history supplies justification for thinking the unthinkable in regard to inclusivity, challenge to Church and civic power, and roles of women in society. Identity, belonging to a tradition, and pride in corporate achievements are all resources for the nurturing of community solidarity.

2. *Corporate self-education:* Another area from which such resources are emerging is that of shared educational experiences. Many congregations have realized, since the Council, their need to continue the educational development of their members, which was undertaken so effectively at the time of the Sister Formation Movement in the 1950s and '60s. This need is even more pronounced when ministerial involvement is extremely diverse. Congregational study days around issues in psychology such as the Myers-Briggs personality typology and the Enneagram, issues of professional conduct, financial responsibility, phased retirement, care of elderly family members, conflict resolution, and numerous other topics occurred in most congregations in the postconciliar years.

More recently, a number of congregations have begun to realize that in the theological diversification that followed the Council many Religious had lost the moorings of their spirituality in solid, postconciliar theology. Brought up in the uniformity of scholastic Thomism, and reeducated in neo-Thomism in the years immediately before the Council, many Religious who read eagerly and widely at the time of Council had not been able to keep up with the theological explosion that followed. Some had simply given up, especially if they were not involved in ministries that required them to deal explicitly with theological issues. Others substituted social analysis or a personality science framework for a theological one in dealing with the issues of their own lives and those arising in ministry. Some put together for themselves eclectic New Age spiritualities whose elements often lacked any real theological content and did not cohere well with each other or with the Christian tradition but which were more serviceable than cognitively implausible medieval constructs. The effect within congregations was considerable tension and even conflict as different theological presuppositions came into play around issues of liturgy, the divinity and centrality of Christ, world religions and Christian exclusivity, eucharistic presence, papal infallibility and authority in the Church, issues in moral theology, the nature of Religious Life, and numerous other strictly theological issues that had major implications for life.

This situation raised the need for some kind of effort to reestablish the ability of a congregation's members to converse with one another about the deepest issues in their lives in a mutually comprehensible and respectful way. In 1994 the Sisters, Servants of the Immaculate Heart of Mary of Monroe, Michigan, developed a six-year theological education program for their own members, and a number of other congregations undertook similar projects using the IHM materials or developing their own. These programs are not typical "refresher courses" designed to provide the current answers to hot-button topics. They are attempts by congregations as a whole to engage the contemporary problematic of thinking and talking about God in a rapidly changing Church and world, to develop the capacity of nonspecialists to read and discuss contemporary theology in fruitful ways, to restimulate enthusiasm for study of the faith, and to illuminate the role in Religious Life of spirituality, ministry, and theology.

The processes used have tended to be interdisciplinary and multifaceted, bringing congregations and subgroups together to listen, study, discuss, reflect, and celebrate. In some cases the theological event has been a congregational event such as those described in part B above. The rebuilding of a shared theological foundation, even though it will be of necessity irreducibly pluralistic in ways that would have been unimaginable in times past, has enormous importance for any group of Religious whose shared life must be, at its deepest level, an expression of shared faith. Congregations that have pursued some kind of corporate engagement of theological issues in recent years have garnered indispensable resources for reimagining community as a gospel reality.

3. Spirituality: Finally, and perhaps most importantly, many congregations have begun to realize the importance of fostering sharing among their members in the area of spirituality. Perhaps the very fact that preconciliar common life involved praying together (or at least praying in the same place at the same time) several times every day and the fact that no one formally disavowed the value of prayer or changed the constitutional requirement of daily prayer created the impression that this area of Religious Life, at least, had retained its preconciliar centrality. Whatever the explanation, something kept many Religious congregations from realizing the significance of the massive change in the area of spirituality that resulted from the dissolution of the total institution. Not only was everyone in the congregation not saying the same prayers at the same time, but there were few common understandings about what the prayer life of the members was supposed to be or to involve.

However, a great deal of serious individual experimentation in the area of spirituality went on during the 1970–1990 period. In particular, individual directed retreats and personal spiritual direction became staples of the spiritual life of most serious Religious who were struggling to keep their own spirituality healthy and to make good decisions about matters that had formerly been handled by superiors, such as lifestyle and ministry. Many made extended renewal programs in which spirituality was a major focus. Exploring the interface of spiritual growth and psychological growth was high on the personal agenda of many Religious who availed themselves of lectures, workshops, and weekends of prayer and reflection to learn from an ever growing corps of resource people in the field of spirituality. The integration of spiritual discipline with social justice activism was a virtual second formation program for some. Experimentation with non-Christian spiritual practices such as yoga, zazen, Native American ritual, chanting, and various New Age systems was widespread. In small group living situations Religious tried many ways of praying together, from incessant variety to variations on the Divine Office. Those that succeeded were probably the minority among numerous failures and frustrations as different people in the group claimed their right to a type of prayer that nourished them. The once self-evident value of simply "showing up" and doing what was agreed upon, regardless of its personal appeal to the individual, was no longer generally affirmed. And struggles over language, imagery, and leadership, the increasing unavailability of clergy for Eucharist, and major difficulties in scheduling among people with very diverse ministries combined to make shared prayer, liturgical or paraliturgical, a very complicated matter.

A particularly painful situation for many congregations was their increasing inability to pray together liturgically even at major congregational events. The inappropriateness, to say nothing of the sheer affront, of having to introduce an outsider to preside at the most intimate community gatherings became increasingly evident. And for women it was exacerbated by the necessity of the outsider being male. The symbolic subordination and enforced sacramental dependence were galling to increasing numbers, and the struggle over language became, in many cases, acerbic. Many congregations simply substituted noneucharistic celebrations rather than liturgically polarize the congregation. But the bitter irony of the sacrament of unity functioning to divide the community was not lost on Religious whose love of and longing for Eucharist was still very much alive.

It is certainly not clear at this point how the reintegration of congregations in the area of spirituality is going to work itself out. However, I think we can recognize certain positive fruits of this stormy period. First, most who have stayed in Religious Life throughout the postconciliar period have constructed and appropriated a much more personalized spirituality than they had had a chance to develop in the days of rigid uniformity and routinized horaria. Their prayer lives have deepened and their repertoires have broadened. They have had to take responsibility for their spirituality, and many have done so in impressive ways and at great personal sacrifice. Praying people in the community are certainly the most important resource for a developing shared spirituality.

Second, congregations seem to be realizing that praying together is essential and central to the work of unity. Some congregations have organized corporate prayer days or retreats and made them a regular feature of congregational time together while calling all to observe special community feasts and fasts, or prayerfully support certain community endeavors by the use of distributed rituals or prayers, no matter where the members might be at the time. Most have increasingly framed congregational events in ritual, personal prayer, and exercises in discernment. And many have found ways to celebrate Eucharist, especially at professions, jubilees, missionings, and installation of leadership ceremonies, that minimize the most disturbing patriarchal aspects and maximize community leadership and participation. Faith sharing in smaller groups is becoming easier and more widespread, facilitated both by personal growth and by shared theological resources. And congregations are choosing to make use of their most spiritually talented and developed members as resources for congregational growth in spirituality.

Third, many newer members have come to Religious Life already habituated to a regular practice of prayer and/or hungering for growth in spirituality. If formation personnel are spiritually mature and experienced, they can foster this rich resource of creativity and power for the whole congregation.

In short, it is highly unlikely that ministerial congregations will reinstate a fixed horarium of regulation prayers, large mandatory retreats in common, or the choral recitation of the Office. But it seems very likely that the serious commitment to a vigorous personal spirituality that many Religious have developed over the last thirty years will be increasingly supported by a corporate expression of faith that will gradually reappropriate in new ways the distinctive character of different Religious congregations. Combined with increasing attention to congregational history and sharing of theological resources, it is certainly possible that such a distinctive congregational spirituality will be deeply rooted in the community's unique tradition and nurturing of its contemporary expression. It seems to be the case in many congregations that people are less defensive about the possibility of spiritual coercion, more willing to express their intimate faith convictions and spiritual desires as well as their doubts and hesitations, and more able to support one another in mutual trust and respect. The foregoing is conjecture, well founded I hope, but that shared spirituality is a sine qua non for Religious community life is certain.

D. Organizational Experiences

A fourth cluster of resources for the renewal of community life derives from the strenuous experimentation with new forms of governance and organization that has gone on in most renewing congregations. The enormous diversity and the broad scope of these experiments defy not only description but even cataloguing. However, I think at least three categories of experience can be usefully highlighted.

First, congregations seem to be getting beyond the reaction against the infantilizing overcontrol of the total institution acting through its sometimes authoritarian superiors and the resulting experimentation with both excessive individualism and various kinds of impersonal bureaucratization. There seems to be a growing realization of the importance, especially in large or geographically dispersed groups, of an individualized and personalized *pastoral care of members*. Even the most mature and autonomous individual who has no need of maternalistic hand-holding needs and wants to be known and treated as a person in the community to which she has committed herself for life.

Many aspects of daily life, from dispensing funds and furnishing transportation to keeping educational and health records up-to-date, can be handled by office personnel who may not even be members of the congregation. But it remains crucial that someone mediate between the individual member and the congregation as a whole, someone who knows the Religious as a person, authentically cares about her, believes in and respects her fundamental commitment to personal holiness and ministry, and is committed to her best interests, sometimes even in spite of the individual's immediate wishes.

It is important that this person have the congregational authority to underwrite decisions arrived at with the member and to mobilize community resources for their implementation. And it is important that this person also be an official representative of congregational concerns to the member so that absorption in her personal situation does not blind the individual to her corporate responsibilities. Whether the person charged with the pastoral care of members is a local coordinator, provincial or regional, mission councilor or president, or some other elected or appointed official, she needs to be someone with the personal gifts of attentiveness, discernment, affective availability, generosity of spirit, and decisiveness necessary to deal with the members as individual persons in the ordinary flow of life but especially in crisis situations affecting their personal lives, their families, or their ministries. She mediates to the member the affective and effective concern of the congregation for her as a person and she personalizes the concerns of the members to and within the congregation as an institution.

Second, there is increasing recognition in most congregations of the necessity of *intermediate structures* of some kind between the individual member and the congregation as a whole. Many Religious do not, and will not during some or most of their ministerial lives, live in large or even medium-sized groups comparable to local communities in preconciliar times. Although, as discussed above, congregations have been making strenuous efforts to bring their members together at least once or twice a year for major events such as assemblies and chapters, a real sense of belonging to something larger than oneself, being involved in a corporate enterprise with other individuals who share one's life commitment, requires more frequent, regular, and intimate contact than a large annual assembly of the whole, on the one hand, or, on the other hand, the daily contact with one or two companions in a small group, can provide.

In many congregations there are now structured provisions for such regular, relatively frequent, and hopefully somewhat intimate contact and sharing. The intermediate structures may be called local groups, area groups, clusters, affiliation groups, mission units, governmental units, or something else. But the expectation is that every member of the congregation belong to and participate faithfully in a group that meets regularly at sufficient length to both participate corporately in congregational business and, even more importantly, function as a support group for its members in faith and ministry. In different congregations these groups are of different sizes, are differently organized, and are differently related organizationally and governmentally to the central administration of the congregation. But the important thing is that every member of the congregation is rooted and based in a manageably sized group whose members know and care about each other and support one another. In other words, every member has a context in which to experience her community and herself in community.

In comparison with monastic-style local community life these groups or units constitute a distinctive innovation in Religious Life by ministerial congregations. The members do not live together, or at least not all the members live with all the other members. Sometimes people living together belong to different clusters, perhaps a particularly healthy choice for people living in a dyad or very small group situation. People usually choose the group to which they belong but cannot move about or change groups whenever the mood moves them. Virtually any group will have people who are more and others who are less congenial. Unless one's own abode is the place for a given meeting (which involves major preparation), everyone has to travel to get to meetings, and in some cases it involves a significant amount of time, effort, and money. Meetings do not happen casually at the breakfast table or in the corridor. They have to be planned and executed. And while at the meetings, and often between times, there is no way of avoiding contact and interchange with the other members. In other words, anonymity and routine are not options. Intentionality is built into the structure itself, which demands commitment, self-sacrifice, and generous service of the group. It remains to be seen if this type of face-to-face primary relationship within large congregations will be able to serve community as well as the day-to-day living together of monastic-style local community. But the quality of this experience is crucial, and many congregations are expending considerable energy and financial resources to nurture this feature of congregational life.

Third, the experience of congregations in attempting to renew their governmental structures has gradually surfaced a number of *principles* that most ministerial Religious congregations are beginning to own as constitutive of their self-understanding as groups. These principles bear directly on the fostering of community, especially in larger congregations.

The principles and processes of democratic and representative government have largely replaced the principles of divine-right monarchy that undergirded preconciliar Religious Life and still hold sway in the institutional Church. Implied in these principles is the need for extensive participation of members in congregational processes. Although the almost total involvement of every member in every decision that seemed to be the ideal in the first flush of renewal has given way to a much more realistic use of delegation and representation, most congregations now place a high priority on the involvement of everyone, directly or indirectly, in all important decisions that affect the congregation as a whole. It is generally recognized that anyone directly affected by a decision has a right be involved in its formulation. And despite Vatican legislation designed to thwart it, group or team leadership at the congregational level has, in practice, largely replaced monarchy as the preferred form.

Many congregations have instituted representative bodies, called Senates, Coordinating Councils, Representative Assemblies, or something similar. These bodies are, in effect, ongoing chapters of affairs, even though they may not have such status canonically. They are bodies of elected delegates that meet a few times a year to deliberate on the larger affairs of the congregation. Whether they are consultative to leadership or have decision-making authority, they collect congregational input on major matters, discern carefully, and set policy. It is hardly conceivable that leadership would bypass or ignore the considered conclusions of these groups.

Committees, task forces, and other team forms of organization for both planning and executing specific congregational tasks have replaced the "lone ranger" approach of the superior's appointee. Because of both the geographical dispersal of members and the increasing complexity of congregations' interactions with the surrounding culture, the number and significance of tasks to be undertaken have escalated. Religious work with one another in both ongoing and task-specific bodies. They serve on the boards of congregationally owned or sponsored institutions, on committees to formulate and revise congregational documents, on task forces to plan chapters and assemblies, organize regional meetings, plan and carry out elections, and do fund raising and vocation promotion. Committees participate in the admissions process and assist the formation team. They sit on internal grievance boards, serve on subsidy-granting committees, and participate in decisions about educational and sabbatical leaves for members. In short, few members of a contemporary ministerial congregation can avoid being involved in a variety of tasks within the congregation that require them to attend meetings, correspond and work closely with other members, and accept major responsibility for outcomes that affect the entire community.

Finally, it has become a working principle in most renewed congregations that competence rather than connections (much less cronyism) should determine who does what. The use of expertise, that of members if it is available or that of others employed by the congregation, is standard procedure. This has been extremely important in regard to congregational processes. Facilitators and organizational experts have played major roles in helping contemporary Religious learn how to relate to one another in honest, caring, and effective ways while minimizing the kinds of dysfunctional behavior that was not only tolerated but often even unintentionally promoted in assigned communities under appointed superiors. In short, the way in which members of congregations relate to one another in democratically functioning communities has gradually become much more mature and effective than was the quasi-familial modus operandi of preconciliar convent life.

My purpose in bringing to explicit articulation these four areas of recent experience in Religious congregations is to highlight the fact that, chaotic as the postconciliar period may have appeared (or actually has been and is) in regard to corporate community life, the courageous experimentation with almost completely new ways of being together has yielded a rich experience, both positive and negative, which is ripe for harvesting.

V. Facing a New Challenge with New Resources

A. Recognizing the Real Newness of the Situation

One of the most important insights to which ministerial Religious came at the time of the Council was the realization that what they had called "the apostolate" was intrinsic and central to their form of Religious Life. Ministry was not the "overflow" of a basically monastic form of Religious Life nor was service of the neighbor a "secondary end" of the congregation. Rather, as the Council affirmed, ministry was proper to their life and exercised in the name of the Church (*P.C.* 8). In other words, profession itself was the basis of their ministry and its specific nature derived from the charism of the congregation. If this is true, then community, like every other aspect of the life, has to be understood and structured to support and foster ministry.

Prior to the Council, the only real adjustment of the monastic lifestyle that ministerial congregations had made consisted in

the modification of enclosure to permit apostolic activity outside the convent. But even this modification was quite
restrained. Most ministries were carried out within walking distance, if not actually inside, the convent and, except for the time
spent at the place of ministry, the Religious lived a fairly strictly
cloistered life. During the immediate postconciliar period of
renewal, most congregations made further modifications of the
monastic lifestyle, specifically in terms of mission and ministry,
as they set aside habit, horarium, choral recitation of the
Office, and other practices that now appeared incompatible
with full ministerial commitment. In most cases the changes
were examined and justified, and Religious found ways to maintain the values, for example, a serious prayer life, enshrined in
the practices while changing the practices themselves.

The real exception to this process of reflective change was
community life. The changes in living situations necessitated
by intensified and diversified involvement in ministry effectively ended the kind of common life characteristic of Tridentine Religious Life. But the changes tended to be "fallout"
from other choices rather than reflectively examined choices
about community life. The really new challenge congregations
are facing today is how to understand, structure, and live community life in a way that is not only compatible with but fostering of ministry, not because ministry has priority over
community any more than community has priority over ministry but because the two must be integrated into a coherent
lifeform if both are to be accorded their appropriate role in
ministerial Religious Life. The growing concern among individual Religious and within congregations with the question
of community suggests to me that the time has come to face
this final challenge to the construction of a genuinely mobile
ministerial form of Religious Life.

Let me summarize the premises that these three chapters
have developed. First, community is intrinsic to Religious Life
as Christian life and thus not optional. Second, community is
not synonymous with "common life" either as it was practiced
in the preconciliar period or in modified form today. Third,

the kind of community appropriate to Religious Life is a unique phenomenon both spiritually and sociologically. Spiritually, it is a community of consecrated celibates joined together in gospel friendship and sharing the mobile lifestyle of Jesus' public life. Sociologically, it attempts to blend modified realizations of the affective quality of intentional community, the efficacy of bureaucratic organization, and the wide contacts and interlocking relationships of an associational network without the narrowness and coerciveness of the first, the impersonalism of the second, and the qualified commitment and purely secondary relational quality of the third. If these premises are theologically well founded, the challenge is to work out what it means to build community on such a foundation and to live it in the postmodern context of the first world.

B. Claiming the Resources

In the previous section I suggested that we are not bereft of resources for confronting this challenge. Like the challenge itself, the resources are new. For more than three decades ministerial Religious have been living and compiling a body of experience of community, both negative and positive, which no Religious before them have had the opportunity to gather. This experience has come both from the actual living of Religious Life in diversified situations outside the modified cloister of preconciliar convent life and from the attempts, aided by the social sciences and people who specialize in the theory and functioning of groups and organizations, to create new mechanisms of belonging and ways of fostering esprit de corps among members. Some very concrete progress has been made, especially in the development of new governmental structures that interlock intermediate and general levels of participation in ways that include all members. Undoubtedly, there is still a long way to go but, given the radical newness of the situation, the genuineness of the progress is more to be celebrated than its missteps bemoaned. If it took four hundred years to move from total enclosure to ministerial Religious

Life, we should not be surprised that reenvisioning every aspect of the life in terms of ministry has taken four decades.

VI. Conclusion: Testing the Spirits

If we assume that community life cannot be reduced to common life and that the criterion of genuine community is not how many people are together in one place at one time, the logical question is "What is the criterion by which to discern whether the reality of community is being lived by individuals and within the congregation-community as a whole?" This might be a very good question by which to inaugurate a fruitful discussion of community within a congregation. The issue is discernment, testing the spirits, distinguishing the valid from the invalid, and affirming the former while correcting the latter.

Without making any claim at all to exhaustiveness, or even adequacy, I will suggest by way of example some criteria that might be surfaced in such a discussion. Following the structure of the discussion in these three chapters on community, I will address the question first in regard to the individual Religious and then in relation to the congregation-community as a corporate entity.

A. Discerning the Reality of Community in the Life of the Individual

In deciding whether a Religious should live in a congregational group or individually (either by necessity or by choice), three questions would seem particularly important. The first is whether or not the living situation is conducive to her Religious Life as such. Is it the best, or at least a positive context for the development and living of a deeply contemplative life that is fully integrated into and nourished by her involvement in meaningful ministry? Most Religious could supply the touchstones in terms of prayer, self-discipline, relationships, and so on that would help in discerning the answer to this question.

The second question is whether her living situation is conducive to her living of her membership in the congregation. Does her lifestyle permit, encourage, and actually lead to her active involvement in the life of the congregation through active participation at the intermediate and the general level? This question is probably especially important for Religious who have become involved in parochial or diocesan ministries and whose lifestyle has been assimilated to that of the clergy. But it also admits of some fairly obvious material considerations, for example, how faithful the person is to participation in her cluster or mission group, how regularly she is present for congregational events, how responsible she is in regard to finances and accountability to congregational leadership.

The third question is whether her lifestyle is sufficiently personally nourishing for her. Does she have close friends in the congregation and beyond it? Does she experience sufficient support in her personal life and in her ministry? Loneliness is a reality in any adult life, especially in our society, but it should not be the predominant climate of the life of a Religious. And alienation or a sense of being unwanted or unimportant in the community is a serious countersign, as is any pattern of addiction or other ways of compensating for a persistent sense of worthlessness.

If the answer to these three questions is affirmative, that is, if the lifestyle of the Religious is conducive to prayer, ministry, congregational belonging, and personal health, it would seem that the real meaning of community is being lived by this person, both in terms of her contribution to community and the community's contribution to her. And it is entirely possible—indeed if we can give credence to the personal testimony of many Religious, it is the case—that Religious living in congregational groups, others living singly for reasons of education or ministry, and others living in modified solitude are, by these criteria, living community life in a real and healthy manner, not in spite of their living situation but because of it.

B. Discerning the Reality of Community in the Congregation

A congregation trying to discern whether it is making progress in developing a valid form of community life might examine some of the following indications. Some of them can be partially determined quantitatively and others require a more qualitative judgment.

A first question might be "What is the level of personal involvement of members with the congregation?" If most of the members of the congregation have some active role in its operation as officers, board members of institutions, committee members, volunteers for community functions, participants in processes, consultants or presenters for various community events, formation team consultants, assistants in development or in any of the innumerable other ways that congregations engage the expertise and generosity of their members, there is good reason to think that the sense of community is high. Especially today, when such involvement is not mandatory in most congregations, it is reasonable to conclude that people take part because the community is important to them. This is even more evident when people are carrying full-time ministries that could easily excuse them or are living at a distance from the center of congregational operations.

A second indication, it seems to me, of a high level of community belonging is the quality and quantity of people who make themselves available for leadership in the congregation. People seldom stand in line to take the helm of a sinking ship. And no one wants to spend all day every day caring for an enterprise in which she has little stake. Someone willing to assume leadership has to believe in Religious Life and in the congregation to the extent of being willing to put her own ministerial projects on hold for a term of office. Obviously, a minority of people in any congregation has the particular constellation of abilities necessary for leadership, but a healthy community produces good leadership.

A third question might be how the young and the old in the congregation feel about their place in it. Are the elderly valued, reverenced, cared for, not only in a professionally competent way but with the kind of loving concern that one offers a beloved sister, brother, friend? Is the effort made to include every elderly member to the extent she is able and wishes to be included in community events, or are those not earning a salary considered irrelevant? Is the community at large concerned about new members, ready to invite them to participate in ways that will expose them to the variety and richness of the community, and eager to listen to their insights and questions and to take them seriously? Or is the incorporation of new members regarded as the job of someone appointed and the opinions of the young dismissed as näive? A healthy community is marked by the members' sense of belonging to one another in well-being as well as in frailty, vulnerability, and inexperience.

Fourth, a congregation might examine itself on the intangible characteristic of group pride. Do the members consider being part of this community a privilege? Do they enjoy being together, even when the occasion for coming together is congregational business that might be less than entertaining? Do they rejoice and share proudly in one another's achievements rather than jealously undercutting one another or cloaking non-responsiveness in a concern for preserving another's humility? In a healthy community everyone's talents are valued, and their deficiencies supplied by others' abundance. It is not an ascetical duty but a spontaneous esprit de corps that makes one proud to be associated with those who are doing good.

Closely related to justified pride in one's community is a desire to make it available to others. Are members interested in promoting vocations, at ease in suggesting to eligible young women or men that they look at Religious Life as a challenging and worthwhile possibility for their own life? Do they radiate their own love for the life and for their congregation and their sense of fulfillment in this chosen vocation? Are they open to people who want to associate with the community as volunteers, oblates, or in some other way? Again, a clear sign of a healthy community is the happiness of its members and their desire to share their life with others.

Questions such as these might be a way of assessing the quality of community life in a congregation. No doubt every congregation will discover not only signs of its health but also indications of what still needs to be worked out. For example, in many congregations some members do not see the importance to the community, for generations to come, of keeping personal records and archives up to date. Others do not make the connection between personal response to requests for financial and personal data, including one's whereabouts and relationships, and the community's ability to care for its members. There are undoubtedly areas and topics that bear directly on community life that congregations need to discuss because, in the past, such matters were handled by superiors rather than individual members. My point here is that the reality of community life today is very different but not necessarily inferior to that of the past. What is required is articulation of the congregation's experience, affirmation of the signs of health, honest examination of areas or features that require attention, and corporate commitment to addressing what is still inchoate or unclear. Just as something new in Religious Life was born on the frontier in the eighteenth and nineteenth centuries, so something new is emerging today. Religious, in my experience, are convinced about the importance of community and committed to it. The challenge is to create the new forms it must take.

Several important aspects of this issue have not figured in these three chapters on community. The vows of community life, namely, poverty and obedience, and the distinctive expression of ministerial community life in corporate mission need to be situated within the framework of a theology and spirituality of mission and ministry and discussed in the context of the postmodern experience of economic life and personal freedom. The concentration in this volume on the theology and spirituality of community and its individual and corporate embodiment will supply a foundation for discussing these dimensions of Religious Life in volume 3.

CONCLUSION

In the conclusion of the first volume of *Religious Life in a New Millennium* I evoked, as a metaphor, the "uncertainty principle" formulated by the quantum physicist Werner Heisenberg. A colloquial version of the principle is that if one knows the location of a subatomic particle one cannot know what it is doing, and vice versa. In other words, one cannot attend to location and activity at the same time. Religious Life, of course, is not a subatomic particle, but in trying to organize the material that had to be included in any reasonably comprehensive treatment of the life, I found that, in fact, I could not attend simultaneously to its situation and to its inner nature. In volume 1 I was concerned with locating contemporary Religious Life in its postconciliar ecclesial and postmodern cultural context, and consequently it was necessary to put aside most of the questions about its inner dynamics. But trying to determine *where* the life is in relation to its contemporary context was a way of saying *what* it is and *why* it continues to be a life project eminently worth pursuing, a treasure for which some people, in their joy at finding it, will choose to exchange all they possess, even their very life.

In this volume I have presumed the location that was plotted in volume 1 and have turned to the life itself to explore its internal structure and dynamics. The leading question has been not "Where do we find it?" but "What is it all about?" The deceptively simple but absolutely fundamental answer to that question that I have tried to explore is love. Religious Life is about *whom* we are committed to and *how* we live those commitments. Without doubt, the ecclesial and cultural context, which profoundly

405

affects our understanding of ourselves, others, our world, and God, shapes and qualifies the commitments we undertake. We can only live and love in our own time and place. But in the final analysis every human life, no matter in what age or culture it is lived, is ultimately determined by what one most deeply desires and to whom or what one gives one's life, one's very self. Withholding that self-gift, trying to save our life, is surely in the end to lose it (cf. Mk 8:35 and Jn 12:24). The only real question is not whether to "sell all," to give ourselves in love, but for whom or for what will we choose to exchange our one and only life. In other words, the quality of life is determined by the relationships that constitute its dynamics.

Throughout this volume, I have been exploring the three intimately interwoven relationships that constitute Religious Life as a distinctive form of life in the Church and structure it from within: *commitment* through perpetual profession to Religious Life itself within a particular congregation; total and exclusive self-gift to God in Jesus Christ symbolized by lifelong *consecrated celibacy;* affective and effective integration into a specific *community* of persons in mission to the world. Each of these complex topics has been approached first from the perspective of the way each of them is newly problematized by the contemporary context in which Religious Life finds itself today. But the ultimate intention in respect to each topic and their interrelationship has been to interpret the constitutive relationships of Religious Life theologically in order to suggest the implications for spirituality, that is, for the actual living of Religious Life today.

The choice to relate consecrated celibacy first and foremost to perpetual commitment and community rather than, as is traditionally done, to the vows of evangelical poverty and obedience, is crucial to the interpretation of Religious Life that I have proposed. It expresses my conviction that fundamentally celibacy is the symbolic expression of the central and defining relationship of Religious Life, the unreserved self-gift to God in Jesus Christ to the exclusion of all other primary life commitments. And it is celibacy that distinguishes Religious community life from other equally valid and significant forms of

Christian community such as matrimony. In volume 3 I will resituate consecrated celibacy in relation to evangelical poverty and obedience, treating the three vows as the coordinates of community life, ministry, and witness.

I am under no illusion that what I have offered in this book will either answer definitively (if at all) many of the pressing questions about the inner dynamics of contemporary Religious Life or be met with unanimous agreement among those living this life today. My purpose in sharing these reflections has been not to close but to open discussion, to create a climate and supply resources for a renewed and ongoing engagement of Religious, as individuals and corporately, with the rich experience of our life that has emerged in the nearly four decades since Vatican II. I have dared to suggest some new terminology, to tentatively offer some definitions, and to propose possible reinterpretations of certain aspects of the life, not because I have some superior insight into how things actually are or should be, but in order to furnish some fresh starting points and renewed impetus for that ongoing engagement. If the text identifies some of the proverbial "elephants in the salon" and takes their measurements in ways that can help us coax them out of our way, clarifies the real issues at stake in some discussions that have repeatedly run aground, and facilitates that graced civil discourse that moves us forward in relation to what we most deeply believe as well as what most challenges us, but especially if it encourages Religious to affirm the validity of our experience, celebrate the beauty of our vocation, and commit ourselves anew to the Reign of God, it will have attained its objective.

NOTES

PREFACE

1. Sandra M. Schneiders, *New Wineskins: Re-Imagining Religious Life Today* (New York/Mahwah, N.J.: Paulist, 1986).

2. Throughout the work, unless the context clearly stipulates otherwise, I will use *lay* to refer to baptized Catholics who are not ordained or vowed members of Religious Institutes. This is not a pejorative designation, as I explained at length in volume 1, chapter 7, but a recognition of the fact that Religious have rights and obligations under Church law that other members of the laity (in the sense of the nonordained) do not. That means that they constitute a canonical category distinct in some ways from other nonclerics. *Laity* is, at least potentially, a positive term whereas *non-Religious* is a privative term and open to more negative connotations than *laity*.

3. In volume 1, chapter 9 I discussed the problematic character of these traditional designations, tried to discern the real differences and relationships between the two forms of Religious Life, and made some suggestions about more appropriate terminology.

CHAPTER ONE

1. I am using *founder* for both female and male initiators rather than *foundress* for females, both to reduce repetitions and to avoid the somewhat diminutive connotations that the "feminine" form carries and the presupposition that founding is a normatively male activity.

2. Canons 573–606, *CCL*, 1983.

3. Canons 607–709, *CCL*, 1983.

4. For a good explanation of social movements and social movement organizations see Patricia Wittberg, *Pathways to Re-Creating Religious Communities* (New York: Paulist, 1996), esp. 46–58.

5. I dealt with this question at some length in chapter 2 of *Finding the Treasure: Locating Catholic Religious Life in a New Ecclesial and Cultural Context*, vol. 1 of *Religious Life in a New Millennium* (Mahwah, N.J.: Paulist, 2000).

6. It is important to note that this public responsibility is for what pertains to Religious Life. The "creeping clericalization" of Religious by the Vatican, which imposes on Religious the obligations of the ordained and blunts their prophetic witness in the Church, is an aberration that will be discussed in volume 3.

7. Robert Hale, O.S.B. Cam., former prior of the Camaldolese monastery in Big Sur, California, gives a beautiful brief account of his own decision to enter the order in *Love on the Mountain: The Chronicle Journal of a Camaldolese Monk* (Trabuco Canyon, Calif.: Source Books and Hermitage Books, 1999), 109–13, which illustrates well the idealism that, even when immature, underlies a genuine vocation to Religious Life.

8. The prophetic role of Religious in the Church was dealt with at some length in chapters 4 and 10 of *Finding the Treasure*.

9. See, e.g., Canons 573, 587, 597–98, 602, *CCL*, 1983.

10. This raises many questions around membership that were discussed at length in chapter 2 of *Finding the Treasure*.

11. The distinction between these lifeforms was dealt with in some detail in chapter 9 of *Finding the Treasure*.

12. Although there are a few points with which I might disagree, the article on vocation promotion by Seán D. Sammon, "Last Call for Religious Life," *Human Development* 20 (Spring 1999): 12–27, is well worth consideration.

13. I will take up this issue in much greater depth in chapters 6 and 7 below.

14. Cf. *P.C.* 15; *L.G.* 6, 44; *E.T.* 3, 39–41 and 5, 52, in Flannery, vol. 1.

CHAPTER TWO

1. For purposes of simplicity, in what follows I will use the terms *candidate* and *candidacy* not only for the prenovitiate stage (which traditionally was called the postulate) but for the entire process of initial formation up to profession. Initial formation includes both candidacy in this sense (postulancy and novitiate) and the period of temporary profession, i.e., the entire process culminating in perpetual profession.

2. In 1982 CARA published a study by a religious sociologist, Kristen Wenzel, O.S.U., entitled *Turnover and Burnout Among Vocation and Formation Directors: An Exploratory Survey* (Washington, D.C.:

Center for Applied Research in the Apostolate, 1982), in which she analyzed the problem and suggested strategies for confronting it.

3. See note 10 below for details of this movement.

4. A major contribution is the book by prison chaplain, Helen Prejean, C.S.J., *Dead Man Walking: An Eyewitness Account of the Death Penalty in the United States* (New York: Vintage Books, 1994). The book was made into an award-winning film and is now available as *Dead Man Walking*, videorecording (New York: PolyGram Video, 1996). An opera based on the book opened in San Francisco in the fall of 2000.

5. See volume 1, chapter 6, note 18 on the theory that today's birds are descendants of the aviary dinosaurs. Ritamary Bradley suggested that this evolutionary fact is a good metaphor for the evolution of Religious Life from its preconciliar form, marked by size, power, and resources, to its current form, which is much less overwhelming but perhaps no less significant.

6. R. Scott Appleby, in "Surviving the Shaking of the Foundations: United States Catholicism in the Twenty-First Century" in Katarina Schuth, *Seminaries, Theologates, and the Future of Church Ministry: An Analysis of Trends and Transitions* (Collegeville, Minn.: Liturgical Press, 1999): 1–23, especially 1–2, refers to the postconciliar youth as the least catechized generation in U.S. Catholic history.

7. I dealt extensively with the identity crisis and confusion in Religious Life following the Council and in the context of emerging postmodernism in *Religious Life in a New Millennium*, vol. 1, *Finding the Treasure: Locating Catholic Religious Life in a New Ecclesial and Cultural Context* (New York/Mahwah, N.J.: Paulist, 2000), especially in chapters 3, 5, and 6.

8. See *L.G.* 5, 39 (Flannery, vol. 1) on the universal call to holiness and 4, 33 on the baptismal call to mission and ministry.

9. A subject that requires serious sociological analysis is the "cohort confusion" among Religious who are in their twenties, thirties, forties, and even fifties at the present time.

10. In May of 1997, "Fertile Fields" became the first national, intercongregational gathering organized by women Religious under fifty for women Religious under fifty. Shaped by the vision of Dedra Serafin, S.C., Kristin Matthes, S.N.D., and Judy Eby, R.S.M., "Fertile Fields" later gave birth to a variety of efforts by women Religious under fifty to cooperate in shaping the future of Religious Life. Later that same year, an internet discussion list—FERTILEFIELDS—was initiated by Dedra Serafin, S.C., and Fran Fasolka, I.H.M.

Many "Fertile Fields" participants started congregational-specific gatherings, while others initiated intercongregational connections. Although activities began after "Fertile Fields," the ongoing "Younger Sisters' Intercommunity Alliance," which encompasses social justice, recreational, prayer, and spiritual experiences, was established officially in March 1999 in St. Louis, Missouri, by Jan Hayes, R.S.M., and Toni Temporiti, C.PP.S., and other younger sisters in that locale. In March of 1999, *Giving Voice,* the first intercongregational newsletter that targets the audience of women Religious under fifty and fosters intergenerational dialogue, was initiated by Judy Eby, R.S.M., Jan Hayes, R.S.M., Kristin Matthes, S.N.D., and Toni Temporiti, C.PP.S. In June of 2000, "Fertile Fields 2000" took place under the leadership of Carolyn Giroux, O.S.U., Jean M. Moore, F.S.P.A., and Dedra Serafin, S.C.

11. Victor W. Turner, *The Ritual Process: Structure and Anti-Structure* (Chicago: Aldine, 1969).

12. Walter J. Ong, *Fighting for Life: Contest, Sexuality, and Consciousness* (Ithaca, N.Y.: Cornell University Press, 1981).

13. Several years ago I suggested the analogy between Religious and artists and I continue to think it is a useful one. See *New Wineskins: Re-imagining Religious Life Today* (New York/Mahwah, N.J.: Paulist, 1986), 34–38.

14. Considerable discussion and writing have been done on the role of the spiritual director in the formation program, especially the pros and cons of the spiritual director playing some role in the evaluation process and/or discussing the directee's process with the formator. This is not the place to discuss the issue, but I am of the opinion that the director should play no role. I have two reasons for this position. First, spiritual direction is aimed at the spiritual development of the candidate as a person, regardless of whether she decides to continue in Religious Life. It should, therefore, not involve any kind of prejudice toward or against the choice of Religious Life. Second, spiritual direction will only be really effective if the directee can be completely open with the director without fearing that anything she confides could be "used against her" in the evaluation process. Even if the candidate gives permission to the director to communicate with the formator or vice versa, she may come to resent the use of that permission or to feel violated if it is used. My own opinion is that unless some issue of consummate importance involving the possibility of grave harm to the candidate or someone else such as suicidal inclinations, financial fraud that involves the congregation, alcoholism or

drug abuse, or sexual abuse of another person is at stake the spiritual director and the formator are best advised not to cross the communication wires.

15. John of the Cross specifies as the primary practice and purpose of the first stage of a serious Christian spiritual life (by which he means not the very beginning of turning from sin to God but the setting out on the path of holiness) the loving imitation of Christ. "First, have an habitual desire to imitate Christ in all your deeds by bringing your life into conformity with his. You must then study his life in order to know how to imitate him and behave in all events as he would" (*The Ascent of Mount Carmel* I, 13, 3–4). The text is available in English in *The Collected Works of Saint John of the Cross,* rev. ed., translated by Kieran Kavanaugh and Otilio Rodriguez, revisions by Kieran Kavanaugh (Washington, D.C.: Institute of Carmelite Studies, 1991): 101–349.

Ignatius Loyola says essentially the same thing in his *Spiritual Exercises,* which, in the "second week," intend to bring the exercitant to an "election" or definitive choice of and for Jesus Christ as the center of his or her life (Exercises 169–89). The Exercises are available in English translation in George E. Ganss, *The Spiritual Exercises of Saint Ignatius: A Translation and Commentary* (St. Louis: Institute of Jesuit Sources, 1992).

16. See Philip Sheldrake, *Spirituality and Theology: Christian Living and the Doctrine of God* (Maryknoll, N.Y.: Orbis, 1998), for an extensive explanation of this interrelationship.

17. The fascinating story of the Sister Formation Movement and the founding of the first graduate program in theology for laity in general and women Religious in particular (the Graduate School of Sacred Theology at Saint Mary's College, South Bend, Ind., 1944–70) is told in Gail Porter Mandell, *Madeleva: A Biography* (Albany, N.Y.: State University of New York Press, 1997), chap. 13.

18. Women need only look at Paula, Hilda, the two Gertrudes, the two Mechtildes, Catherine of Siena, Teresa of Avila, the leaders of the Sister Formation Movement and the Leadership Conference of Women Religious of the twentieth century to understand the central importance of theological formation for the work of holiness and leadership.

19. It is interesting that in very recent years candidates, especially younger ones, have shown a serious interest in learning about and experimenting with some of the devotional practices that older Catholics sidelined in the postconciliar period, such as the rosary,

stations of the cross, prayer before the Blessed Sacrament, and so on. This has caused some concern among formators who fear the backlash conservatism evident in many seminarians. Actually, this seems to be a misunderstanding of the phenomenon. Often these younger candidates are quite open-minded in regard to Church and dogma but are seeking an experience they never had of a "way," a spiritual discipline in which tested methods support the spiritual quest. Everything depends on how such practices and methods are taught and fostered, and where better to do this than in a formation setting, where experience can be monitored, discussed, and appropriated in a sound theological context?

20. I will discuss this thesis in chapter 9.

21. *U.S. Census Bureau Statistical Abstract of the United States: 1999*, 119th ed. (Washington, D.C.: U.S. Department of Commerce, 1999), 231.

22. In what follows I am inspired primarily by Margaret Wheatley's provocative study, *Leadership and the New Science: Learning about Organization from an Orderly Universe* (San Francisco: Berrett-Koehler, 1992), supplemented by Danah Zohar in collaboration with I. N. Marshall, *The Quantum Self: Human Nature and Consciousness Defined by the New Physics* (New York: Quill/William Morrow, 1990) and John Polkinghorne, *Quarks, Chaos, and Christianity, Questions to Science and Religion* (New York: Crossroad, 1997). I strongly recommend these three very readable volumes as resources for rethinking a number of issues in Religious Life today.

23. Wheatley, *Leadership and the New Science*, 48.

24. Ibid., 52–54.

25. See chapter 9 of *Finding the Treasure*.

26. This theory of charism is suggested by Margaret Susan Thompson in "'Charism' or 'Deep Story'? Toward a Clearer Understanding of the Growth of Women's Religious Life in Nineteenth-Century America," in *Religious Life and Contemporary Culture*, Theological Education Process, cycle 2 (Monroe, Mich.: Sisters, Servants of the Immaculate Heart of Mary, 1998).

27. A prospective novice once told me that she was entering her community in order to change it, specifically from an exclusively Roman Catholic one to one open to Protestants and especially non-Christians as well. She asked me if I did not think that a valid project. I told her that it made about as much sense as marrying a person to convert him. If one does not basically accept the other as he or she is there is no sound basis for the union. It is seriously questionable if

anyone should consider herself called to radically change someone else (or an organization or community) unless the latter requests such help. Practical experience suggests that such a conversion agenda is not likely to succeed. A necessary fundamental disposition in the person entering formation is the desire to become a member of the congregation as it now exists. Undoubtedly, in the future, she will participate in changing the congregation. But to enter with an agenda of remaking the congregation is a recipe for disaster.

CHAPTER THREE

1. In all that follows on commitment I will be using and/or referring to Margaret A. Farley's excellent work, *Personal Commitments: Beginning, Keeping, Changing* (San Francisco: Harper & Row, 1990). She defines and describes commitment on pp. 14–19.

See also the treatment, from the standpoints of theology and spirituality, of John C. Haughey, *Should Anyone Say Forever?: On Making, Keeping and Breaking Commitments* (Garden City, N.Y.: Doubleday, 1975).

2. A report of the Rutgers University National Marriage Project, released on July 1, 1999, reported that the marriage rate in the United States had dropped by 43 percent since 1950. According to the report Americans apparently still cherish the ideal of a happy and permanent marriage, but an increasing number do not expect to experience the reality and are opting for alternatives to traditional marriage rather than face the expected collapse of commitments.

3. Farley, *Personal Commitments*, 30.

4. The vastly increased life expectancy of first-world people exacerbates this concern because commitment is no longer a matter of twenty or thirty years but often of fifty, sixty, or even seventy. And the increased rate and magnitude of change in Church and society mean that any attempt to guess what lies ahead is completely futile.

5. Farley, in *Personal Commitments*, 40–45, offers a lengthy reflection on this subject, incorporating some of the most important historical contributions.

6. This is the title of one of May Sarton's journals (New York: Norton, 1968), in which she explores the mystery of self-integration through choice and commitment.

7. Cf. Jn 19:30 and Lk 23:46.

8. I strongly recommend Farley's fourth chapter in *Personal Commitments* in which she discusses the issue of keeping commitments.

9. A letter by Griffiths to Martyn Skinner in 1937, quoted by Shirley du Boulay, *Beyond the Darkness: A Biography of Bede Griffiths* (New York: Doubleday, 1998), 74.

10. Ibid., 97.

11. As Francis Moloney pointed out in *A Life of Promise: Poverty, Chastity, Obedience* (New South Wales: St. Paul Publications, 1984), especially in the preface, p. 15, and the chapter "Evangelical Imperatives," all Christians are called to follow Jesus, poor, chaste (chastity is a virtue to be practiced in all states of life, not just celibacy), and obedient. And this call is not merely a suggestion but an imperative. Consequently, calling the object of the vows of Religious "evangelical counsels" suggests that not all Christians are called to what the Gospel demands (thus making Religious Life not a specific form of baptismal life but a better form). In other words, the notion of "evangelical counsels" is theologically and biblically questionable.

12. Canonically all Religious are obliged to consecrated celibacy, poverty, and obedience no matter what vows they make. Canon 654 says that "By religious profession members assume by public vow the observance of the three evangelical counsels...." But Benedictines, for example, vow obedience, stability, and conversion of manners rather than consecrated celibacy, poverty, and obedience. (See note 14 below on Benedictine profession.) Male Dominicans make a single vow of obedience to the master general and his successors, with poverty and celibacy understood as integral to the apostolic spirituality of the Order. The Dominican vow formula can be found in nos. 199 and 211 of the Constitutions but in ch. I, art. I, 3, ii, it is specified that chastity and poverty are included in the commitment to Dominican life. An English translation is available as *Book of Constitutions and Ordinations of the Friars of the Order of Preachers* at www.op.org/curia/ConstOP/.

13. E.g., Jesuits make a fourth vow of "special obedience to the sovereign pontiff in regard to the missions" (see "The Constitutions of the Society of Jesus, with Their Declarations," no. 527, in *The Constitutions of the Society of Jesus and Their Complementary Norms: A Complete English Translation of the Official Latin Texts* [St. Louis: Institute of Jesuit Sources, 1996], 202, 204) as well as five additional "simple vows" enumerated in the Norms, pt. V, no. 134. The Sisters of Mercy make a fourth vow of "service of the poor, sick and ignorant" (see

Constitutions of the Sisters of Mercy of the Americas, para. 20 [Silver Spring, Md.: Sisters of Mercy of the Americas, 1992]).

14. This is perhaps clearest in the Benedictine profession, which probably was originally cast in the form of questions and answers and later embodied in a rite in which the novice placed on the altar (symbol of Christ) a written formulation of his total and free gift of himself to the service of God. It seems clear that even after the formula came to include stability, conversion of manners, and obedience, these could not be understood as undertaking three distinct legal obligations but as an undertaking of monastic life in its fullness and integrity.

For an excellent history of the development of profession from the earliest form of monasticism to the present time, which makes very clear the distinction between profession as total self-gift and particular vows that were later conceived of as specific legal obligations, see *RB 1980: The Rule of St. Benedict in Latin and English with Notes*, edited by Timothy Fry (Collegeville, Minn.: Liturgical Press, 1981), appendix 5 by Claude Peifer, "Monastic Formation and Profession," especially 449–66.

15. Canon Law actually captures well this nuance. The first canon (607) on the life says, "Religious life, as a consecration of the whole person, manifests in the Church a wonderful marriage brought about by God, a sign of the future age. Thus religious bring to perfection their full gift as a sacrifice offered to God by which their whole existence becomes a continuous worship of God in love."

16. For example, the vow of poverty in the United States exempts individual Religious ministering in Catholic agencies from income taxation.

17. I am grateful to Mary Katherine Hamilton, I.H.M., who pointed out to me the way in which what I have written about profession implies this feature, which I had never quite made explicit.

18. *Merism* is a literary device that consists in the use of extremes to encompass symbolically a larger sphere of reality. For example, in Psalm 139 the psalmist says to God, "O Lord, you have probed me and you know me; you know when I sit and when I stand....behind me and before, you hem me in....If I go up to the heavens...if I sink to the nether world, you are present," and so on. The extremes of sit...stand, behind...before, up...down are meant to signify everything in between, thus all action, all space.

On the hyperbolic character of biblical language see Amos N. Wilder, *Early Christian Rhetoric: The Language of the Gospel* (New York: Harper & Row, 1964).

19. Robert Ellsberg in *All Saints: Daily Reflections on Saints, Prophets, and Witnesses for Our Time* (New York: Crossroad, 1998), 298, speaks of the prophetic influence of Benedictine monasticism in medieval society: "Apart from its effect on the history of monasticism, Benedictine spirituality had an even wider influence on medieval society. For centuries the Benedictine monasteries presented the challenge of an alternative world, governed by the spirit of Christ. At a time of extreme social hierarchy, they presented an ideal of equality. At a time when manual labor was derided, they affirmed the spiritual value of work. During a time of cultural disintegration, they maintained islands of learning and civilization. In a time when violence was commonplace, they lived by the motto of Peace. The Benedictine monasteries represented a vision of health, wholeness, and ecology in a world badly out of kilter."

20. There is considerable debate about whether chastity or consecrated celibacy is a better formulation. I will discuss this issue in chapter 4.

21. Paul in 1 Cor 7:32–35 suggested that marriage constituted an impediment to total devotion to the "things of the Lord" and combined with the "eunuch text" in Mt 19:12 it supplied this now questionable interpretation of the ministerial function of celibacy.

CHAPTER FOUR

1. See, for example, Diarmuid Ó Murchú, *Reframing Religious Life: An Expanded Vision for the Future* (Middlegreen Slough, U.K.: St. Paul's, 1995), 102–10.

2. Francis J. Moloney, *A Life of Promise: Poverty, Chastity, Obedience* (New South Wales: St. Paul Publications, 1984), 74–78. Originally published as *Free to Love* by Dartman, Longman and Todd, 1980.

3. M. Esther Harding, *Woman's Mysteries Ancient and Modern: A Psychological Interpretation of the Feminine Principle as Portrayed in Myth, Story, and Dreams*, new and revised ed. (New York: Pantheon, 1955), 125.

4. For an excellent treatment of this aspect of virginity see Peter Brown, *The Body and Society: Men, Women and Sexual Renunciation in*

Early Christianity, Lectures on the History of Religious, vol. 13, (New York: Columbia University Press, 1988), 5–32. The whole volume makes fascinating reading, but a sense of the intersection between sexuality and society can be gotten from chapter 1.

5. Robert Ellsberg, in *All Saints: Daily Reflections on Saints, Prophets, and Witnesses for Our Time* (New York: Crossroad, 1998), supplies the stories of several men who renounced military service as incompatible with their Christian faith, e.g., Martin of Tours (288–89), some of whom suffered martyrdom for their stand as did many women virgins who refused to marry.

6. See Canon 604, *CCL,* 1983.

7. Canon 1191, 1 (*CCL,* 1983) defines a vow as follows: "A vow is a deliberate and free promise made to God concerning a possible and better good which must be fulfilled by reason of the virtue of religion." Chastity is not the free choice of a possible or better good but the obligatory practice of a required virtue. It is fulfilled by the practice of the moral virtue of chastity, not as an exercise of the virtue of religion.

8. Sandra M. Schneiders, *New Wineskins: Re-imagining Religious Life Today* (New York/Mahwah, N.J.: Paulist, 1986), 114–36, especially 119–26.

9. In *Religious Life in a New Millennium,* vol. 1, *Finding the Treasure: Locating Catholic Religious Life in a New Ecclesial and Cultural Context* (New York/Mahwah, N.J.: Paulist, 2000), chapter 1, I devoted an extensive discussion to the invalidity of this position.

10. A recent important book on this subject is Walter E. Conn, *The Desiring Self: Rooting Pastoral Counseling and Spiritual Direction in Self-Transcendence* (New York/Mahwah, N.J.: Paulist, 1998).

11. Bede Griffiths, when asked by a member of a film crew, "What is the meaning of life?" replied, "The meaning of life is love and there are two ways to love. One is through a dedication of the whole of your life to the spirit and the working out of that dedication. The other is to love another human being so profoundly that that initiates you into the divine love" (cited in Shirley du Boulay, *Beyond the Darkness: A Biography of Bede Griffiths* [New York: Doubleday, 1998], 224).

12. *The Comedy of Dante Alighieri, The Florentine,* Cantica III, "Il Paradiso," trans. by Dorothy L. Sayers and Barbara Reynolds (Baltimore: Penguin, 1962), canto xxxiii, 145.

13. I discussed this issue in greater detail in "Celibacy as Charism," *The Way Supplement* 77 (Summer 1993): 13–25.

14. It should be noted that the general inadequacy of sex education that militated against formation in chastity was not peculiar to Religious Life. Most young people who married were probably as poorly prepared for the sexual aspects of marriage as young Religious were for the sexual aspects of celibacy.

15. See Nygren and Ukeritis, *FORUS*, 183.

16. See Margaret A. Farley, *Personal Commitments: Beginning, Keeping, Changing* (San Francisco: Harper & Row, 1986), especially 74–75.

17. For different approaches to this analysis see Jo Ann Kay McNamara, *Sisters in Arms: Catholic Nuns through Two Millennia* (Cambridge: Harvard University Press, 1996), who sees the history of women Religious as a two-thousand-year battle against male oppression, and Patricia Ranft, *Women and the Religious Life in Premodern Europe* (New York: St. Martin's, 1996), who sees that history as a testimony not only to male oppression but to the Church's promotion of women and women's promotion of themselves through an alternative lifeform in the Christian community.

18. See *Finding the Treasure*, chapter 9, for an overview of the development of congregations of simple vows.

19. A very interesting witness to the role of nuptial spirituality in Religious Life and to virginity as the focus and primary symbol of that spirituality is seen in Carol Lee Flinders, *Enduring Grace: Living Portraits of Seven Women Mystics* (San Francisco: Harper, 1993). This volume is an historically informed, consciously feminist treatment of seven women mystics who were all deeply imbued with the unitive mysticism that found its natural and most intense expression in the nuptial metaphor which they developed very explicitly and richly.

20. See Robert J. Schreiter, *Challenges and Directions of Religious Life at the Turn of the Millennium* (June 21, 1998), a privately printed transcript available from Catholic Theological Union in Chicago.

21. I have reflected at greater length on this issue in *Religion and Spirituality: Strangers, Rivals, or Partners*, The Santa Clara University Lecture Series (Santa Clara, Calif.: Santa Clara University, 2000).

CHAPTER FIVE

1. I put "closed" in quotation marks because the official position of the Catholic magisterium is that these issues were and are definitively settled and the official positions nonnegotiable, but that teaching

is not received by many Catholics who continue to discuss and debate these issues.

2. The furor occasioned by the appearance of Donald Cozzens' fine book, *The Changing Face of the Priesthood: A Reflection on the Priest's Crisis of Soul* (Collegeville, Minn.: Liturgical Press, 2000), in which he deals frankly with the sexual problems of the clergy surfaced the denial and avoidance of the issues by Church authorities and the common knowledge of the problems among clergy and laity.

3. Some estimate that as many as one in three girls have been sexually abused by adult males in their family context. The same studies say one in seven boys is a victim of incest. See Ellen Bass and Laura Davis, *The Courage to Heal: A Guide for Women Survivors of Child Sexual Abuse* (New York: Harper & Row, 1988), 20.

4. See Sandra M. Schneiders, *Beyond Patching: Faith and Feminism in the Catholic Church*, The Anthony Jordan Lectures (1990) at Newman Theological College, Edmonton (New York/Mahwah, N.J.: Paulist, 1991), 15. On pp. 15–31 I explain in some detail each member of the definition, and for those unfamiliar with the theory in this area I strongly suggest reading this section or something comparable.

5. See Douglas Burton-Christie, *The Word in the Desert: Scripture and the Quest for Holiness in Early Christian Monasticism* (New York/Oxford: Oxford University Press, 1993), especially 44–62.

6. See, e.g., Eugene Monick, *Phallos: Sacred Image of the Masculine*, Studies in Jungian Psychology by Jungian Analysts 27 (Toronto: Inner City Books, 1987); John A. Sanford and George Lough, *What Men Are Like* (New York/Mahwah, N.J.: Paulist, 1988).

7. Margaret R. Miles, *Desire and Delight: A New Reading of Augustine's Confessions* (New York: Crossroad, 1992), especially chapter 3.

8. See the excellent Catholic Theological Society of America presidential address by Margaret Farley, "The Church in the Public Forum: Scandal or Prophetic Witness?" in *Proceedings of the Fifty-fourth Annual Convention*, San Jose, June 8–11, 2000, vol. 55, edited by Michael Downey (Los Angeles: Saint John's Seminary, 2000): 87–101, in which she shows the negative effect of this fixation on the Church's role in public discourse.

9. Beginning with the work of Bernard Häring in the 1950s, Catholic moral theology has been undergoing a gradual revision. The work of Richard McCormick, Charles Curran, Margaret Farley, and Lisa Sowle Cahill among others has been courageous and groundbreaking. But the area of sexual morality has been perhaps the most institutionally dangerous field for any theologian. The controversy

surrounding the study commissioned by the Catholic Theological Society of America in 1977 and done by Anthony Kosnick and his associates, *Human Sexuality: New Directions in American Catholic Thought* (New York: Paulist, 1977), the removal of Charles Curran's mandate as a Catholic theologian because of his very moderate and widely shared position on contraception, and the punitive investigation of André Guindon, the author of the insightful volume, *The Sexual Language: An Essay in Moral Theology* (Ottawa: University of Ottawa Press, 1977) all testified to the official resistance to any development in the area of sexual morality. The effect of traditional moral theology on women is well presented by Lisa Sowle Cahill in *Women and Sexuality*, 1992 Madeleva Lecture in Spirituality (New York/Mahwah, N.J.: Paulist, 1992).

Two useful overviews of the development from physicalist toward personalist thought in moral theology are the following: Louis Janssens, "Personalism in Moral Theology," *Moral Theology: Challenges for the Future, Essays in Honor of Richard A. McCormick*, edited by Charles E. Curran (New York/Mahwah, N.J.: Paulist, 1990), 94–107, and Brian V. Johnstone, "From Physicalism to Personalism," *Studia Moralia* 30 (1992): 71–96.

10. See the illuminating study by Walter J. Ong, *Fighting for Life: Context, Sexuality, and Consciousness* (Ithaca, N.Y.: Cornell University Press, 1981), on this subject.

11. A good place to begin an introduction to women's mystical literature is the book by Carol Lee Flinders, *Enduring Grace: Living Portraits of Seven Women Mystics* (San Francisco: HarperSanFrancisco, 1993). The women mystics she treats are Clare of Assisi, Mechtilde of Magdeburg, Julian of Norwich, Catherine of Siena, Catherine of Genoa, Teresa of Avila, and Thérèse of Lisieux.

12. Ethel Spector Person, *The Sexual Century* (New Haven, Conn.: Yale University Press, 1999), 171.

13. There is not a great deal of statistical data to be found about the percentage of the general population that is homosexually oriented, and there is debate about the accuracy of the numbers reported by different surveys. However, an extensive Internet search located a summary of the research literature on the prevalence of homosexuality from 1948 through 1998 at the Kinsey Institute's web page at: http://www.indiana.edu/~kinsey/bib-homoprev.html. Though they differed in actual percentages, all of the studies mentioned reported higher percentages of males than females who had had some same-gender sexual involvement. The general range

tended to be 6 to 9 percent of males and 2 to 5 percent of females surveyed.

14. The best source of information on numbers, motivations, behaviors, etc. of lesbian women in Religious Life that I have found is the article by Jeannine Gramick, "Lesbian Nuns: Identity, Affirmation, and Gender Differences," in *Homosexuality in the Priesthood and the Religious Life*, edited by Jeannine Gramick (New York: Crossroad, 1989), 219–36, whose work and research suggest that gay men significantly outnumber lesbian women in Religious Life. And, while the proportion of gay men to heterosexual men is far higher among male priests and Religious, this does not seem to be true of the proportion of lesbians to heterosexual women among religious. Donald Cozzens in *The Changing Face of the Priesthood* gives the best available statistics on homosexuality among priests and male Religious. In chapter 7, "Considering Orientation," pp. 97–110, Cozzens, using the admittedly less than adequate available data, estimates that in comparison with the 5 to 10 percent of gay men in the general population, 50 percent or more of priests are gay. In note 7, p. 99, he indicates that the percentage might be considerably higher among men in Religious orders.

15. A fascinating study of this subject in one congregation is the two complementary studies of friendship in the Immaculate Heart of Mary Congregation of Monroe, Michigan: "The Official I.H.M. Stance on Friendship, 1845–1960" by Mary Ann Hinsdale and "P.F.s [particular friendships]: Persistent Friendships" by Nancy Sylvester in *Building Sisterhood: A Feminist History of the Sisters, Servants of the Immaculate Heart of Mary* (Syracuse, N.Y.: Syracuse University Press, 1997), 153–71 and 173–90 respectively.

16. Canon Law, 573, §2 (*CCL*, 1983) refers to the "evangelical counsels of chastity, poverty and obedience" as intrinsic to Religious Life.

17. A number of articles dealing with the issues and reports from the 1994 International Conference on Population and Development in Cairo and its follow-up meeting five years later in 1999 can be found on the web site at: http://communication.measureprogram.org/factsheets/cairo5.htm.

18. "LCWR Recommendations: Schema of Canons on Religious Life," 1977, *Records of the Leadership Conference of Women Religious*, CLCW 75/11, University of Notre Dame Archives. The LCWR criticized the "sexism in language" and "a disregard for the equality of women and men." My thanks to Sister Suzanne Delaney, I.H.M., of

LCWR and Kevin Cawley, archivist and curator of manuscripts at the University of Notre Dame, for their help in locating this reference.

19. *CCL* (1983), 606.

20. The much cited passage from *G.S.* I, 29, "...forms of social or cultural discrimination in basic personal rights on the grounds of sex, race, color, social conditions, language or religion, must be curbed and eradicated as incompatible with God's design..." is applied in the following sentence particularly to women even though the implications of this statement for Church order are often not acknowledged in theory or honored in practice. See Flannery, vol. 1.

21. The vituperation in a treatise like Tertullian's "Veiling of Virgins" is a classic case raising such a suspicion. The Latin text, *De virginibus velandis*, is available in *P.L.* II: 887–914. An English translation is available in *The Ante-Nicene Fathers: Translations of the Writings of the Fathers Down to A.D. 325*, vol. 4, edited by Alexander Roberts and James Donaldson (Grand Rapids, Mich.: Eerdmans, 1985–1987), 27–37.

22. Of particular note is the development of increasingly oppressive legislation on the subject of cloister. The (in)famous bull of Boniface VIII in 1298, *Periculoso*, imposed in perpetuity papal enclosure on all women Religious. Surprisingly, in the wake of Vatican II, whose documents tended to encourage experimentation and development in all segments of the Church's life including Religious Life, a particularly oppressive document, *Venite Seorsum*, on contemplative orders, was published, attempting to reverse the very moderate progress they had made in the areas of self-development, inculturation in the modern world, and mutual interchange and support (in Flannery, vol. 1, 656–75). As recently as May 13, 1999, the Congregation for Institutes of Consecrated Life and for Societies of Apostolic Life issued an "Instruction on Contemplative Life and the Enclosure of Nuns," which is as repressive as *Venite Seorsum* and which makes liberal use of the nuptial metaphor to justify not only restrictive legislation applying only to women contemplatives but extraordinarily regressive strictures. The document is available in *Origins* 29 (Aug. 12, 1999): 155–64.

23. Legal provision for the consecration of virgins is made in *CCL* (1983), 604 and the liturgical rite for the consecration of virgins, *Mos virgines consecrandi*, which was promulgated by the Sacred Congregation for Divine Worship on May 31, 1970. The pertinent parts can be found in English in Flannery, vol. 2, 193–94.

24. A beautiful passage in the mystical writings of Gertrude of Helfta captures this reserve. Christ speaks to her about her life with him: "I [Jesus] have collected as in a treasure the riches of my grace, so that everyone may find in you [Gertrude] what he [*sic*] wants. You will be like a bride who knows all the secrets of her spouse, and who, after having lived a long time with him, knows how to interpret his wishes. All the same, it would not do to reveal to others the secrets of the spouse, as this grace of mutual intimacy belongs to her alone." Gertrude of Helfta, *The Herald of Divine Love*, translated and edited by Margaret Winkworth, CWS (New York/Mahwah, N.J.: Paulist, 1993), 87.

25. A helpful treatment of spiritual direction with people whose experience is deeply affected by this unitive dimension of the relationship with God can be found in Janet K. Ruffing, *Spiritual Direction: Beyond the Beginnings* (New York/Mahwah, N.J.: Paulist, 2000), especially chapters 4 and 5.

26. A very accessible treatment of metaphor as resource for theological discourse is Sallie McFague, *Metaphorical Theology: Models of God in Religious Language* (Philadelphia: Fortress, 1982), 32–42.

27. I discussed this topic in greater detail in *Women and the Word: The Gender of God in the New Testament and the Spirituality of Women*, 1986 Madeleva Lecture in Spirituality (New York/Mahwah, N.J.: Paulist, 1986), 20–37.

28. See Paul Ricoeur, *Interpretation Theology: Discourse and the Surplus of Meaning* (Fort Worth, Tex.: Texas Christian University Press, 1976), especially 45–69.

29. Although some women were chosen to remain virginal for the service of the gods as temple vestals and others may have found themselves single for all kinds of personal and social reasons that made them unmarriageable, virginity beyond the age of marriage was considered a tragedy. This is poetically reflected in the biblical "tale of terror" of Jephthah's daughter in Jgs 11:29–40, especially vv. 37–38. When she learns that her father has made a vow to offer her in sacrifice in return for his military victory she asks for a two-month reprieve, not to mourn her imminent death, but to grieve her virginity, i.e., that she will die without having fulfilled her destiny as a woman.

30. For an in-depth treatment of this issue, see Peter Brown, *The Body and Society: Men, Women and Sexual Renunciation in Early Christianity* (New York: Columbia University Press, 1988), especially chapter 1.

31. See the perceptive contemporary reflection on this topic in Kathleen Norris, "Maria Goretti: Cipher or Saint?" in *The Cloister Walk* (New York: Riverhead, 1996): 223–36.

32. The story of Perpetua, the young married woman of Carthage martyred in 203, recounted in "Martyrdom of Saints Perpetua and Felicitas," *Acts of the Christian Martyrs*, edited and translated by H. Musurillo (Oxford: Clarendon, 1972), is a striking example of a wife and mother who was a heroine among the early Christians.

33. It is important to note that young men who embraced perpetual continence were also defying social expectations. A young man, until he married, was also subject to the patriarchal power of his father's household and he was obliged both to carry on the family name and to serve the emperor by military service. Young men choosing virginity refused their social roles in patriarchal society but it might be argued that no initiative of men in respect to their own destiny was as radical as the corresponding assumption of initiative by women.

34. There is a long history of sexual rigorism, strongly influenced by misogynism, that dates from the first centuries of the Christian Church. For an enlightening analysis of this strain in the early Church see Brown, *Body and Society*, chapter 4, "'To undo the Works of Women': Marcion, Tatian, and the Encratites."

35. The earliest textual evidence of the practice of consecrated celibacy among Christians comes from Justin Martyr writing in the early second century in his *Apology* 15:1–5: "Many, both men and women of the age of sixty or seventy years, who have been disciples of Christ from their youth continue in immaculate purity....It is our boast to be able to display such persons before the human race." Given that Justin was writing in the early second century of people who had chosen virginity at least forty years before, the phenomenon of Christian virginity must be dated from a few decades after the death of Christ. See Justin Martyr, *Apologies*, translated with introduction and notes edited by Leslie William Barnard (New York: Paulist, 1966).

36. The struggle over the veiling of virgins in the Carthaginian Church to which Tertullian's treatise (see note 21 above) bears witness was wholly concerned with the behavior of women virgins in the liturgical assembly. If there was similar concern about analogous behavior among male celibates, it does not appear in the text.

37. Men who have chosen virginity have, in fact, used the marital metaphor to speak of their experience. It is common and frequent in the writings of such mystics as Bernard of Clairvaux and John of the

Cross. But the use of the metaphor, and the experience in which it is rooted, seems to require considerably more "spiritualization" in the case of men. Whereas women mystics seem to experience symbolic marriage to Christ with their whole body-persons, male mystics speak much more carefully of the "soul" as the bride. This is understandable given the homosexual overtones of the metaphor of male marriage to a male Savior. This is a very delicate issue and I do not think it has been adequately analyzed. However, there may be some resources in the work on Wisdom christology emerging in both theology and spirituality. See the very perceptive article by Constance FitzGerald, "Transformation in Wisdom: The Subversive Character and Educative Power of Sophia in Contemplation," in *Carmel and Contemplation: Transforming Human Consciousness*, Carmelite Studies VII, edited by Kevin Culligan and Regis Jordan (Washington, D.C.: Institute of Carmelite Studies, 2000), 281–358.

38. On the content, date of composition, acceptance into the canon, and history of interpretation, see Roland E. Murphy, *The Song of Songs: A Commentary on the Book of Canticles or The Song of Songs*, edited by S. Dean McBride, Jr., Hermeneia (Minneapolis: Augsburg Fortress, 1990), 3–105.

39. Phyllis Trible, *God and the Rhetoric of Sexuality* (Philadelphia: Fortress, 1978).

40. Although the allusions to the Song of Songs pervade the Fourth Gospel, they are especially clear in the Easter christophany to Mary Magdalene. See Sandra M. Schneiders, *Written That You May Believe: Encountering Jesus in the Fourth Gospel* (New York: Crossroad/Herder, 1999), 189–201.

41. Trible, *God and the Rhetoric of Sexuality*, 145.

42. Like many other translations, the New American Bible marks each passage to distinguish the speakers. So it makes a decision for the reader that here the "Bride" (B) is speaking (although the woman is not said to be a bride), here the "Lover" (G—for God!), and here the chorus. But the need to do so makes it clear that the text itself is sometimes ambiguous.

43. Trible, *God and the Rhetoric of Sexuality*, 145.

44. Ibid., 162: "Never is this woman called a wife, nor is she required to bear children. In fact, to the issues of marriage and procreation the Song does not speak. Love for the sake of love is its message."

45. Interestingly, the NAB assigns this passage to the Bride, who is then presented as speaking of herself in the masculine!

46. Some of the more important are the following: Ambrose, *De Virginitatis*, *P.L.* 16.386–545, available in English as *The Nun's Ideals*, translated by James Shiel (Chicago/London/Dublin: Scepter, 1963); Augustine, *De sancta Virginitatis*, *P.L.* 40.395–428, available in English as *Holy Virginity*, part I, vol. 9, in *The Works of Saint Augustine: A Translation for the 21st Century*, translated by Ray Kearney, edited with introduction and notes by David G. Hunter (Hyde Park, N.Y.: New City Press, 1999), 65–107; Gregory of Nyssa, περί παρθενίας, *P.G.* 46:317–416, available in English as *On Virginity*, in *Gregory of Nyssa: Ascetical Works*, translated by V. W. Callahan, Fathers of the Church 58 (New York: Fathers of the Church, 1967); John Chrysostom, *De Virginitate*, *P.L.* 48.533–96, available in English in *John Chrysostom: On Virginity, Against Remarriage* translated by Sally R. Shore (New York: Edwin Mellen Press, 1983); Methodius, Συμποσίον των δέκα παρθενων ἤ περί ἀγνείας, *P.G.* 18:27–240, available in English as *The Symposium*, translated and annotated by H. Musurillo, Ancient Christian Writers 27 (Westminster: Newman Press, 1958); Origen, *In Canticum Canticorum*, *P.L.* 13.57–198, available in English as *The Song of Songs: Commentary and Homilies*, translated and annotated by R. P. Lawson (Westminster, Md.: Newman, 1957).

47. The latest document from the Vatican insisting on the total physical separation of women Religious in contemplative orders from the rest of the Church as well as from society and even from other contemplatives (see note 21 above) makes massive appeal to the nuptial theme as legitimation for this restorationist and even repressive legislation. It is striking that the document addresses only women contemplatives, not men, marking its use of the nuptial theme as deeply patriarchal.

48. Cf. Carol Lee Flinders, *Enduring Grace: Living Portraits of Seven Women Mystics* (San Francisco: HarperSanFrancisco, 1993), 126.

49. For a good synthesis of the tradition and of the feminist critique and reconstruction, see Rosemary R. Ruether, *Sexism and God-Talk: Toward a Feminist Theology* (Boston: Beacon, 1983), 93–115.

50. For a brief summary introduction of the classical pagan tradition on friendship, see Sharon H. Ringe, *Wisdom's Friends: Community and Christology in the Fourth Gospel* (Louisville, Ky.: Westminster John Knox, 1999), 69–71.

51. See Mark F. Williams, *Aelred of Rievaulx's Spiritual Friendship: A New Translation* (Scranton, Pa: University of Scranton Press, 1994), 31.

52. Aristotle, *Nicomachean Ethics*, translated by Terence Irwin (Indianapolis: Hackett, 1985). See IX, 1155a–72a for Aristotle's treatment of friendship. See especially 1157a–b on equality and 1158b on friendship between unequals.

53. Gertrude of Helfta, in *The Herald of Divine Love*, book III, chapter 50, hears Christ say to her: "My divine eyes rejoice ineffably in looking at you, for by bestowing upon you so many and so varied gifts of my grace, I made you beautiful in my sight." Jesus gives to Gertrude, who is deeply sensitive to her own unworthiness, all that she needs to enjoy a genuine equality with him. Constance FitzGerald has explored the theme of equality and mutuality between the mystic and Christ in "A Discipleship of Equals: Voices from Tradition—Teresa of Avila and John of the Cross," in *A Discipleship of Equals: Toward a Christian Feminist Spirituality*, edited by Francis A. Eigo (Villanova, Pa.: Villanova University Press, 1988), 63–97.

54. For a fuller explanation of this Johannine theme, see Schneiders, "A Community of Friends (Jn 13:1–20)," in *Written That You May Believe: Encountering Jesus in the Fourth Gospel*, 162–79.

55. John of the Cross, *The Collected Works of Saint John of the Cross*, rev. ed., translated by Kieran Kavanaugh and Otilio Rodriguez, with revisions and introduction by Kieran Kavanaugh (Washington, D.C.: Institute of Carmelite Studies, 1991), 676.

56. This oft-repeated anecdote is not found in Teresa's writings but has been passed down in the tradition of Carmel.

57. This exchange is cited by Carol Lee Flinders in *Enduring Grace*, 190, without reference.

58. Gertrude of Helfta, *The Herald of Divine Love*, book III, ch. 51.

59. Ibid., book III, ch. 50.

60. A. Néher, "Le symbolisme conjugal: Expression de l'histoire dans l'Ancien Testament," *Revue d'Histoire et de Philosophie Religieuses* 34 (1954): 30–49.

61. See, for example, T. Drorah Setel, "Prophets and Pornography: Female Sexual Imagery in Hosea," in *Feminist Interpretation of the Bible*, edited by Letty M. Russell (Philadelphia: Westminster, 1985), 86–95.

62. It is the consensus of most Johannine scholars that this pericope is non-Johannine, but it was obviously precious enough to the early Church that it was interpolated into the Fourth Gospel to maintain its canonicity and prevent its loss.

63. Gertrude of Helfta, *The Herald of Divine Love*, book III, ch. 16.

64. Catherine of Genoa, *Purgation and Purgatory* and *The Spiritual Dialogue*, translation and notes by Serge Hughes, introduction by Benedict J. Groeschel, preface by Catherine de Hueck Doherty, CWS (New York/Ramsey/Toronto: Paulist, 1979).

Chapter Six

1. See Erik Erikson, *The Life Cycle Completed* (New York: Norton, 1982), 67.

2. *Perfectae Caritatis*, the conciliar decree on the renewal of Religious Life, actually presents a very mature understanding of the authority of the leaders in a Religious congregation as an exercise of responsibility among one's brothers or sisters (cf. *P.C.* 2, 25, in Flannery, vol. 1), and this approach is reflected in the section on obedience in *Vita Consecrata*, the Apostolic Exhortation of John Paul II issued after the 1994 Synod of Bishops on consecrated life, which speaks of the unifying and communitarian role of obedience as practiced among sisters and brothers in the community.

3. Ronald Rolheiser in his book on Catholic spirituality, *The Holy Longing: The Search for a Christian Spirituality* (New York: Doubleday, 1999), 114–22, discusses the unrealistic expectations many have of the Church, among them the hope that the Church will be a kind of family. His observations are applicable to a similar misconception about Religious Life on the part of some people seeking entrance at the present time but also among some who lament the demise of the kind of family-style community life they experienced in preconciliar times.

4. A very poignant description of the effect in one Religious community of this intrinsically conflictual structure is the chapter "Procrustes' Bed" in the biography of Sister Mary Madeleva Wolff, the poet and visionary founder of Saint Mary's-of-the-Wasatch College in Utah and later president of Saint Mary's College, Notre Dame. See Gail Porter Mandell, *Madeleva: A Biography* (Albany, N.Y.: State University of New York Press, 1997), 103–15.

5. The U.S. Census Bureau, in its March, 1998 "Current Population Report" noted that the fastest growing marital category was the currently divorced category, which more than quadrupled, from 4.3 million in 1970 to 18.3 million in 1996 (3 percent vs. 10 percent of the population over age eighteen). A December, 1999 survey of 4,000 adults by the Barna Research Group (available at: www.barna.org) showed that 25 percent of all adults have been

divorced at least once, and, surprisingly, that the percentage of divorces among religious adherents is as a whole larger than the nationwide average. Only Catholics and Lutherans, at 21 percent, are below the norm, as are atheists and agnostics (also 21 percent). Mormons (24 percent), mainline Protestants (25 percent), Jews (30 percent), Baptists (29 percent), and nondenominational Protestants (34 percent) all surpassed the average.

6. According to the U.S. Census Bureau, 19.2 percent of all children live below the poverty level. Of these, 36.8 percent were African American, 36.4 percent were Hispanic, and 15.4 percent were white (*U.S. Census Bureau Statistical Abstract of the United States: 1999*, 119th ed. [Washington, D.C.: U.S. Department of Commerce, 1999], 483).

7. *The State of America's Children: A Report from the Children's Defense Fund* (Boston: Beacon, 2000) reports that there are currently about 850,000 homeless children and youth nationally, over 200,000 of these preschool age (p. 88). Also, foster care placement is one of the two main risk factors in family homelessness; 44 percent of homeless mothers lived outside their homes at some point during childhood (p. 90).

8. As of 1997, the jail population in the United States included 306,500 whites and 349,500 nonwhites, and inmates under sentence of death included 1,876 whites and 1,406 nonwhites (*U.S. Census Bureau Abstract: 1999*, 231). Considering that currently 83.5 percent of the U.S. population is white, these figures are astounding.

9. According to the Children's Defense Fund, an estimated 13 million children under age six, and millions more school-age, are cared for at least part-time by someone other than their parents. Also of note are the facts that (1) only one in ten children eligible for assistance with child care is getting any help; (2) the average yearly salary of a child care worker is $14,820, less than that of parking lot attendants; and (3) juveniles are more likely to be the victims of crime in the hour after the end of the school day than at any other time (*The State of America's Children*, 46).

10. A very detailed presentation of the large-scale 1986 study on incest that first reported such widespread incidence of sexual abuse is Diana E. H. Russell, *The Secret Trauma: Incest in the Lives of Girls and Women*, rev. ed. (New York: Basic Books, 1999); see especially 59–74.

11. In a chapter entitled "The Gender of Violence," author Michael S. Kimmel reports that men are overwhelmingly more violent than women, citing U.S. Department of Justice figures that, of those arrested for rape, men constitute 99 percent, for murder 88 percent, for aggravated assault 87 percent, and for family violence 83

percent. He also reports that domestic violence is the leading cause of injury to women in this country, and that between one-third and one-half of all women are assaulted by a partner or spouse at some time during their lives (*The Gendered Society* [New York: Oxford University Press, 2000], 242–63).

12. The U.S. Bishops became so aware of this problem that they published a statement, "Always Our Children," in October, 1997. The original statement is available in *Origins* 27 (1997): 285–90. The statement was then revised and reissued in July, 1998, and this version is available in *Origins* 28 (1998): 97–102.

13. For an excellent overview of how the practice of Jesus, as presented in the Gospels, challenges the conventional wisdom about family values, to say nothing of the right-wing version of this agenda, see Carolyn Osiek, "Jesus and cultural values: Family life as an example" *Hervormde Teologiese Studies* 53 (September, 1997): 800–814.

14. One of the most striking recent examples of this is the Southern Baptist Convention's resolution at their national meeting in June, 1998 that amended their essential statement of beliefs, "The Baptist Faith and Message," to include the declaration that a woman should "submit herself graciously" to her husband's leadership just as the church "willingly submits itself to the headship of Christ" (*New York Times*, 10 June 1998). This amendment marked the first change in thirty-five years to "The Baptist Faith and Message." In a surprising show of independence, the Baptist General Convention of Texas, the largest state organization (2.7 million members) in the 15.7-million-member denomination, repudiated the directive on wives' submission. The executive director of the Texas convention, Reverend Charles Wade, stated, "There's a partnership in Christian marriage....any attempt to put women 'in their place' or somehow limit the contribution that women might have in church goes against the whole spirit of Christ" (*Dallas Morning News*, 9 November 1999).

15. The conciliar document, Decree on the Apostolate of Lay People, *A.A.* (available in Flannery, vol. 1.), presents a developed theology of lay participation in the mission of the Church and places special emphasis on the fact that laity, by virtue of their roles in family, professions, and the realities of the secular order, have a particular vocation to the evangelization of these areas of human experience.

16. John W. Pryor in "Jesus and Family—A Test Case," *Australian Biblical Review* 45 (1997): 56–69, argues that Jesus did not intend to "shatter the patriarchal family." However, the burden of his article is that Jesus so relativized the claims of biological family in favor of

discipleship and its demands that he essentially agrees with authors who draw the conclusion that the patriarchal family is radically subverted by Jesus' teaching and practice.

17. Carolyn Osiek and David L. Balch, *Families in the New Testament World*, The Family, Religion, and Culture Series (Louisville, Ky.: Westminster John Knox, 1997), 132–33, interpret this text as Jesus' legitimation of nonmarriage by a divorced male, contrary to Roman legislation. This is certainly the most plausible interpretation in light of the text's context in the divorce passage. I think there is something to be said, however, for the suggestion by Francis J. Moloney, *Disciples and Prophets: A Biblical Model for Religious Life* (New York: Crossroad, 1981), 112 and notes 19–20, that the saying may have been provoked by attitudes toward Jesus' own celibacy that was imitated by divorced (and other) Christians in Matthew's community.

18. As Osiek and Balch, *Families*, 124–25, explain and illustrate from stories contemporaneous with the Gospels, the ancient world, Roman, Greek, and Jewish, in which Christianity was born, also regarded family as a penultimate rather than an ultimate value. In Roman society, for example, the state had a higher claim on the citizen than the family. However, producing and raising a family was itself a duty to the state. The Christian choice of celibacy was not only a relativization of family but a repudiation of the state's claim on the reproductive capacity of the person. See Peter Brown, *The Body and Society: Men, Women and Sexual Renunciation in Early Christianity* (New York: Columbia University Press, 1988), especially chapter 1, "Body and City," on this point.

19. The sociological term *fictive family* does not imply that the family in question is unreal but that it is not based on biological relationship but on some other kind of agreement.

20. Elisabeth Schüssler Fiorenza, *In Memory of Her: A Feminist Theological Reconstruction of Christian Origins* (New York: Crossroad, 1985), 147.

21. In Jn 4:22, in the context of the controversy between Jews and Samaritans about the proper place for true worship, Jesus tells the Samaritan woman that "salvation is from the Jews."

22. Obviously, this is the perspective of an early Christian community. Its supersessionist implications are today recognized as potentially anti-Semitic and theologically dangerous. On this topic see Mary Boys, *Has God Only One Blessing? Judaism as a Source of Christian Self-Understanding* (New York/Mahwah, N.J.: Paulist, 2000), especially

chapter 5, 75–89, for an argument against and alternative to supersessionist interpretation of the New Testament.

23. Although the passage is patriarchally constructed as if addressed only to men, it is clearly intended for all and so the term "wife" would be better rendered "spouse."

24. The differences among the lists of what the disciple must renounce (e.g., Luke includes "wife" which Mark does not) are significant for interpretation of the individual Gospels. My purpose here, however, is to sketch the overall pattern of Jesus' teaching on the subject of family and discipleship.

25. The formulation of this saying in Mt 10:37, "Whoever loves father or mother more than me is not worthy of me, and whoever loves son or daughter more than me is not worthy of me" clarifies the meaning. Jesus is not recommending hatred of relatives in the modern sense of emotional revulsion and desire to harm but using a Semitic construction of preference in which the two possibilities are "love" and "hate" with love marking preference for the loved.

26. For good commentary on the family-relativizing texts, see Joel B. Green, *The Gospel of Luke*, The New International Commentary on the New Testament, edited by Ned B. Stonehouse, F. F. Bruce, and Gordon D. Fee (Grand Rapids: William B. Eerdmans, 1997) in the sections on the individual texts.

27. As Joseph A. Fitzmyer acknowledges in his commentary, *The Gospel According to Luke (X–XXIV)*, Anchor Bible, vol. 28A (Garden City, N.Y.: Doubleday, 1985), 995–96, it is clear that although sayings such as that of Lk 12:49–53 bear the marks of community influence on the Jesus tradition, it is not valid to ascribe all such texts and/or their content exclusively to ecclesial formulation.

28. It is important to emphasize that Jesus was not talking about dishonoring parents (cf. Lk 18:20) or using religion as a pretext for denying support to aging parents (cf. Mk 7:10–13; Mt 15:5–6). Jesus is clear that the fourth commandment of the Decalogue is binding. But preferring Christ, even to parents, might be required in the case of conflict.

29. The exegesis and interpretation of the scene at the foot of the cross is notoriously difficult. I propose an interpretation which raises some questions about the identity of the disciple and the significance of this identity for the interpretation of the passage in "'Because of the Woman's Testimony...,'" in *Written That You May Believe: Encountering Jesus in the Fourth Gospel* (New York: Crossroad, 1999), 211–32.

30. Most translations render the Greek ἀδελφούς "to my brethren" or "brothers." The masculine plural in Greek as in older

English is inclusive when the group referred to or addressed includes both males and females, which is virtually certainly the case of the community of Jesus in John. A better contemporary translation therefore would be "brothers and sisters" rather than the archaic "brethren." "Brothers" is not really correct.

31. For a discussion of the progressive shift in moral theology on this point, see Brian V. Johnstone, "From Physicalism to Personalism," *Studia Moralia* 30 (1992): 71–96.

For a thorough development of the theory of sexuality as language see André Guindon, *The Sexual Language: An Essay in Moral Theology* (Toronto: University of Ottawa Press, 1976). See also Lisa Sowle Cahill, *Women and Sexuality*, 1992 Madeleva Lecture in Spirituality (New York/Mahwah, N.J.: Paulist, 1992) and Margaret A. Farley, *Just Love: Sexual Ethics and Social Change* (New York: Continuum, 1997) for presentations more sensitive to feminist concerns.

32. For a very good analysis of the effect of Jesus' message on the relationships of his discipleship group see Adriana Destro and Mauro Pesce, "Kinship, Discipleship, and Movement: An Anthropological Study of John's Gospel," *Biblical Interpretation* 3 (1995): 267–84.

33. I will discuss friendship as the fundamental relationship of celibate community in chapter 8.

34. Probably most small communities of two people are perfectly healthy, nonexclusive, nondependent relationships. Nothing in this section is intended to call all two-person local communities into question.

35. See Jeannine Gramick, "Lesbian Nuns: Identity, Affirmation, and Gender Differences," *Homosexuality in the Priesthood and the Religious Life*, edited by Jeannine Gramick (New York: Crossroad, 1989): 219–36, especially 231.

36. *U.S. Census Bureau Abstract: 1999*, 62.

CHAPTER SEVEN

1. From the Synoptic Gospels one would gather that Jesus' ministry lasted a year or slightly more. John mentions Jesus' activity at three successive Passover seasons, which suggests a slightly longer ministry, between two and three years.

2. John Dominic Crossan, "Jesus and the Kingdom: Itinerants and Householders in Earliest Christianity," in *Jesus at 2000*, edited by Marcus J. Borg (Boulder, Colo.: Westview, 1998), 21–53, proposes the interesting and rather convincing hypothesis that at least some

of the "pairs" were composed of a man and a woman, married or not. See especially 39–40.

3. *Didache*, commonly known as *The Teaching of the Twelve Apostles*, was probably written sometime between 50–100 C.E. and gives us a glimpse into an early Christian community, including its tensions between householders and itinerant charismatic preachers. See *Early Christian Fathers*, newly translated and edited by Cyril C. Richardson, et al. (New York: Macmillan, 1970), 161–79.

4. Cf. *Didache* 10:7.

5. Cf. *Didache* 11:3–6.

6. Cf. *Didache* 11:7–12.

7. For a good explanation of the meaning of stability, which is not merely physical presence in the monastery but an interior disposition of heart toward perseverance in the monastic life and its daily practice of community life, work, prayer, and the practice of virtue, see *RB 1980: The Rule of St. Benedict in Latin and English with Notes*, edited by Timothy Fry (Collegeville, Minn.: Liturgical Press, 1981), appendix 5 on "Monastic Formation and Profession" by Claude Peifer, 463–65.

8. Bernard McGinn notes, "What [Clare] refused to compromise on was her commitment to a life of total poverty....she induced Francis to give the 'poor ladies' of San Damiano a 'form of life' expressing this central spiritual value." *The Flowering of Mysticism: Men and Women in the New Mysticism: 1200–1350,* vol. 3 of *The Presence of God: A History of Western Christian Mysticism* (New York: Crossroad, 1998), 47–48.

9. A fascinating account of the extremely mobile congregations of women in the United States, told particularly through the lens of the history of the Sisters of St. Joseph of Carondolet, is Carol K. Coburn and Martha Smith, *Spirited Lives: How Nuns Shaped Catholic Culture and American Life, 1836–1920* (Chapel Hill, N.C./London: University of North Carolina Press, 1999). They highlight how the double marginality of gender and religion was overcome by the zeal, inventiveness, and tenacity of the early leaders.

10. Crossan, "Jesus and the Kingdom," 42.

11. Ibid.

12. Ibid., 38–39.

13. There are other dimensions to obedience, namely, unitive and communitarian ones, as there are to the other vows, but the focus here is on ministry.

14. A few Religious Orders, e.g., some Franciscans, have attempted to live an absolute poverty in which even the congregation owns nothing. While this disposition gives a powerful witness to gospel poverty, it usually has to be mitigated in some way since no one, individually or corporately, can actually live without any resources. The balance achieved in most ministerial congregations between corporate ownership and individual nonownership, which we will discuss in detail in treating poverty in volume 3, has its dangers but is probably better suited both for successful ministry and for corporate witness.

15. For a summary of the problem and of emerging responses in the religion/ecology discussion, see Mary Evelyn Tucker, "The Emerging Alliance of Religion and Ecology," in *Doors of Understanding: Conversations in Global Spirituality in Honor of Ewert Cousins*, edited by Steven Chase (Quincy, Ill.: Franciscan Press, 1997), 97–124.

16. Benedict, for example, commanded the cellarer (the monk in charge of material goods) to "regard all utensils and goods of the monastery as sacred vessels of the altar....He should not be prone to greed, nor be wasteful and extravagant with the goods of the monastery, but should do everything with moderation and according to the abbot's orders" (ch. 31, 10–12). See *Rule of St. Benedict*, 229.

17. This challenge has been raised especially by the geologian Thomas Berry, a Passionist priest who has led the movement for recognizing the "universe story" as the primary master narrative of the human race enjoying a certain normative priority over particular sacred stories. For a brief introduction to his thought, see Thomas Berry, "The Universe, the University and the Ecozoic Era," in *Doors of Understanding*, 79–95.

18. Crossan makes the point that in the context Paul is asking whether he does not have the same right as other apostles to be accompanied by a "sister wife," but since he, by his own claim, was willingly celibate he could hardly have had in mind an actual spouse.

19. Crossan, "Jesus and the Kingdom," 39.

20. Unfortunately, when the men in question are clerics, the hierarchical principle, sometimes exacerbated by male insecurity, inferior ministerial preparation in comparison with their women colleagues, lack of experience, and semiconscious "turf instincts," often leads to an exercise of unjust and oppressive power by men. For this reason, women Religious often find it much easier to work with Brothers or laymen than with clerics.

21. Crossan, "Jesus and the Kingdom," 42.

22. For an excellent treatment of this topic see the short monograph by Sharon H. Ringe, *Wisdom's Friends: Community and Christology in the Fourth Gospel* (Louisville, Ky.: Westminster John Knox, 1999).

23. Patricia Wittberg, in *Creating a Future for Religious Life: A Sociological Perspective* (New York/Mahwah, N.J.: Paulist, 1991), 11–81, devotes three very insightful and illuminating chapters to a discussion of these three sociological models of community. I will be referring to her work in the section on community.

CHAPTER EIGHT

1. This term was coined, apparently, by the sociologist Wade Clark Roof, as a designation for postdenominational Baby Boomers. See his *A Generation of Seekers: The Spiritual Journeys of the Baby Boom Generation*, with the assistance of Bruce Greer et al. (San Francisco: HarperSanFrancisco, 1993).

2. Sociologists of American religion point out that the so-called Baby Boom generation and Generation X are the most religiously illiterate generations in American history. This is a situation that has to be recognized and addressed in formation programs.

3. For a theologically and sociologically realistic and challenging presentation of what participation in the Church community means and does not mean, see Ronald Rolheiser, *The Holy Longing: The Search for a Christian Spirituality* (New York: Doubleday, 1999), especially chapter 6, "A Spirituality of Ecclesiology," 111–40.

4. There are a number of older orders, such as Benedictines, Franciscans, and Carmelites, that have both male and female branches, and in recent years some of these "spiritual families" have made serious efforts to increase collaboration between the branches. Among the groups that CARA classifies as "emerging religious communities" 27 percent admit both men and women. (See Bryan T. Froehle and Mary L. Gautier, and CARA Staff, *Catholicism USA: A Portrait of the Catholic Church in the United States*, vol. 1 of Catholicism 2000 series [Maryknoll, N.Y.: Orbis, 2000], 136–39, on new communities.) In established canonical congregations and orders, even those with male and female branches, actual living together of men and women in the same house is rare.

5. The best treatment of homosexuality in the priesthood that I have found is Donald B. Cozzens, *The Changing Face of the Priesthood: A*

Reflection on the Priest's Crisis of Soul (Collegeville, Minn.: Liturgical Press, 2000). In chapter 7, "Considering Orientation," (97–110), Cozzens estimates that 50 percent or more of priests are gay. In note 7, p. 99, he indicates that the percentage might be considerably higher among men in Religious orders.

6. The best source of information on lesbian women in Religious Life that I have found is Jeannine Gramick's article, "Lesbian Nuns: Identity, Affirmation, and Gender Differences," in *Homosexuality in the Priesthood and the Religious Life* (New York: Crossroad, 1989), 219–36, whose work and research suggest that gay men significantly outnumber lesbian women in Religious Life. And, while the proportion of gay men to heterosexual men is far higher among male priests and Religious than between gay and straight men in the general population, this does not seem to be true of lesbians in relation to heterosexual women in Religious Life.

Robert Nugent, in "Addressing Celibacy Issues with Gay and Lesbian Candidates," *Horizon* 24 (Fall 1998): 15–25, suggests that there is also a significant difference between the experience of lesbianism and that of male homosexuality. They are not parallel experiences, and women and men candidates of homosexual orientation cannot be dealt with in similar fashion.

A recent study presented by Cynthia Nordone, "New Perspectives on Religious Life: Gifts and Insights of Lesbian and Gay Religious," *Proceedings of the Eleventh National Congress of the Religious Formation Conference, October 7–10, 1999* (Silver Spring, Md.: Religious Formation Conference, 2000): 95–102, makes some important observations about the role of homosexual Religious in community life.

7. Cf. A. W. Richard Sipe, *A Secret World: Sexuality and the Search for Celibacy* (New York: Brunner/Mazel, 1990). Sipe, on the basis of his extensive clinical work with priests, estimates that about 2 percent of the clergy "can be said to have achieved celibacy" (p. 67) and another 8 percent to "enjoy a present condition so refined and in which the practice of celibacy is so firmly established that the group can be said to have consolidated the practice of celibacy to such a degree that it approaches the ideal" (p. 68).

8. For a good treatment of the nature of intentional community and an extensive bibliography on the subject, see Patricia Wittberg, *Creating a Future for Religious Life* (New York/Mahwah, N.J.: Paulist, 1991), 11–35, 160–64.

9. Some recent works on cults and their victims are Marc Galanter, *Cults: Faith, Healing, and Coercion* (New York: Oxford University Press,

1999); Margaret Thaler Singer, *Cults in Our Midst: The Hidden Menace in Our Everyday Lives,* with Janja Lalich (San Francisco: Jossey-Bass, 1995); and Michael D. Langone, ed., *Recovery from Cults: Help for Victims of Psychological and Spiritual Abuse* (New York: Norton, 1994).

10. Religious communities appear to go through cycles of foundation, consolidation, flourishing, and diminishment, which either call forth a rebirth or end in dissolution. The two basic studies of this pattern, both chiefly concerned with male communities, are Raymond Hostie, *Vie et mort des ordres religieux: approches psycho-sociologiques* (Paris: Desclée de Brouwer, 1972) and Lawrence Cada, et al., *Shaping the Coming Age of Religious Life* (New York: Seabury, 1979).

The most important recent studies of life expectancy of women's Religious congregations are Helen Rose Fuchs Ebaugh, *Women in the Vanishing Cloister: Organizational Decline in Catholic Religious Orders in the United States* (New Brunswick, N.J.: Rutgers University Press, 1993) and Patricia Wittberg, *The Rise and Fall of Catholic Religious Orders,* SUNY Series in Religion, Culture, and Society, edited by Wade Clark Roof (Albany, N.Y.: State University of New York Press, 1994).

11. See RB1980: *The Rule of St. Benedict in Latin and English with Notes,* edited by Timothy Fry et al. (Collegeville, Minn.: Liturgical Press, 1981), 267. In chapter 58, 7–8: "The concern [in receiving new members] must be whether the novice truly seeks God and whether he shows eagerness for the Work of God [i.e., the Divine Office], for obedience and for trials. The novice should be clearly told all the hardships and difficulties that will lead him to God."

12. See Sandra M. Schneiders, *New Wineskins: Re-imagining Religious Life Today* (New York: Paulist, 1986), especially 246–52, and "Formation for New Forms of Religious Community Life," *The Way Supplement* 62 (Summer 1988): 63–76.

13. See statistics in notes 5 and 9, chapter 6, above.

14. See Josephine Massyngberde Ford, *Redeemer, Friend, and Mother: Salvation in Antiquity and in the Gospel of John* (Minneapolis: Fortress, 1997); Eldo Puthenkandathil, *Philos: A Designation for the Jesus-Disciple Relationship: An Exegetico-Theological Investigation of the Term in the Fourth Gospel* (Frankfurt: Peter Lang, 1993); and Sharon H. Ringe, *Wisdom's Friends: Community and Christology in the Fourth Gospel* (Louisville, Ky.: Westminster John Knox, 1999).

15. For a concise treatment of this material, see Ringe, *Wisdom's Friends,* chapter 3, 29–45. The classic assumption of the ancient tradition on friendship into the literature of Religious Life is the treatise *De Spirituali Amicitia* by the twelfth-century monk Aelred of

Rievaulx. It is available in a good modern translation as *Aelred of Rievaulx's Spiritual Friendship: A New Translation* by Mark F. Williams (Scranton, Pa.: University of Scranton Press, 1994).

16. For an excellent treatment of the issue of the masculinization of Wisdom in the Logos terminology of John's Prologue, see Elizabeth A. Johnson, "Jesus, the Wisdom of God: A Biblical Basis for Non-Androcentric Christology," *Ephemerides Theologicae Lovanienses* 61 (1985): 261–94, especially 284–89.

17. A very accessible and reliable treatment of Wisdom in the Old Testament is Roland E. Murphy, *The Tree of Life: An Exploration of Biblical Wisdom Literature*, The Anchor Bible Reference Library (New York: Doubleday, 1990), especially chapter 9, "Lady Wisdom," 133–49.

18. The major Old Testament texts on Lady Wisdom are Job 28, Proverbs 8, Sirach 24, Baruch 3:9–4:4, and Wisdom 7–9.

19. See especially the Prologue, Jn 1:1–18, and Jn 15:11–17 on the friendship of Jesus with his own.

20. A good place to start one's study of this theme is with the New Testament data on Jesus' closest biological relative, Mary. The ecumenical study, *Mary in the New Testament: A Collaborative Assessment by Protestant and Roman Catholic Scholars*, edited by Raymond E. Brown, Karl P. Donfried, Joseph A. Fitzmyer, and John Reumann (Philadelphia: Fortress/New York: Paulist, 1978), gives a very balanced presentation of all the data.

21. *Inclusio* is a literary device in which persons, words, refrains, structures, themes, actions, or some other formal or material elements in a text are used both to begin and to end a section, thus marking it off as a unity.

22. Although the masculine metaphor for the divine parent is used here it is not exclusive in John's Gospel. In Jn 3, in the conversation with Nicodemus, divine filiation is described as birth from above, i.e., through a feminine God-image.

23. For a brief summary, see Ringe, *Wisdom's Friends*, 69–71.

24. A collection of studies documenting and analyzing the various dimensions of the problem caused by the inequality among members of clerical institutes that have nonordained members is *A Concert of Charisms: Ordained Ministry in Religious Life* edited by Paul K. Hennessy (New York/Mahwah, N.J.: Paulist, 1997).

25. For an historical study of the evolution of originally lay monastic life into a two-tiered social system in which brothers became, in effect, a servant class in relation to the ordained monks, see Bruce

Lescher, "Laybrothers: Questions Then, Questions Now," *Cistercian Studies* 23 (1988): 63–85.

26. As noted in chapter 7, note 17, Thomas Berry has been especially influential in calling for a resituation of the human story, including biblical revelation, within what he calls the "universe story." Berry's thought is readily accessible in the book of his essays, *The Dream of the Earth* (San Francisco: Sierra Club Books, 1988), especially chapter 10, "The New Story," 123–37. A seemingly whimsical but actually very serious presentation of this universe story is Brian Swimme's *The Universe Is a Green Dragon: A Cosmic Creation Story* (Santa Fe, N.M.: Bear & Company, 1984).

27. E.g., the 1997 National Assembly of the Leadership Conference of Women Religious passed a resolution calling on all members (leaders of Religious congregations in the U.S.) to promote and celebrate within their communities Earth Day, April 22. The official publication of the Global Concerns Committee of the LCWR, *Resolutions to Action* 8 (March 1999) contains brief reports from many congregations about specific actions taken to promote ecological awareness and practice. The LCWR has committed itself to ecologically sound practices in its own national office, has had leaders in the ecological movement as main speakers at National Assemblies, and promotes the ecological commitment and projects of individual congregations.

28. An excellent presentation of the challenges and possibilities for a theology of religions is Jacques Dupuis, *Toward a Christian Theology of Religious Pluralism* (Maryknoll, N.Y.: Orbis, 1997).

29. The second member of verse 23 in the text is my translation of ἄν τινων κρατῆτε, κεκράτηνται, which makes no mention of "sins" and in which the verb "to hold" does not mean "to retain" but to "hold fast."

30. An article by Retta Blaney, "Survey Reveals Growth in Orders' Associates," *National Catholic Reporter* (May 26, 2000):7, supplies statistics on the remarkable increase in numbers of people associated formally but not as members with Religious congregations. They total more than 25,400, an increase of 19,000 in the five years from 1995–2000.

31. This entire mystery is set forth in John 14, on the Spirit life of the community after the departure of Jesus.

CHAPTER NINE

1. One of the better expositions I have encountered of the struggle over community today is Judith A. Merkle, *Committed By Choice: Religious Life Today* (Collegeville, Minn.: Liturgical Press, 1992), especially 117–24.

2. See, for example, Nancy Schreck, "The Forces That Push Us Toward and Pull Us Away from Community," *Horizon* 25 (Spring 2000): 7–15.

3. There have always been women Religious living the hermit or anchorite forms of the life, but they have been few in number after the desert period and not normative.

4. An engaging example of these dynamics is available in Carol K. Coburn and Martha Smith, *Spirited Lives: How Nuns Shaped Catholic Culture and American Life 1836–1920* (Chapel Hill, N.C./ London: University of North Carolina Press, 1999).

5. This, however, has to be questioned in light of the eremitical tradition that still has adherents today.

6. Thomas Merton struggled throughout a good part of his mature life with the extreme uniformity of Trappist life and eventually obtained permission for a modified hermit life within the context of the monastery.

7. I proposed the terms "group living" and "living singly" as alternatives to "living in community" and "living alone" respectively in an article, "Formation for New Forms of Religious Community Life," *The Way Supplement* 62 (Summer 1988): 63–76. In *New Wineskins: Re-imagining Religious Life Today* (New York/Mahwah, N.J.: Paulist, 1986), published two years earlier, I was still using "living alone" as a neutral term covering all forms, positive and negative, of living community life outside a group setting (see 252–55). But it became clear to me that this was not only confusing because it equated community exclusively with group living but also that it promoted a presumption of the normativity of group lifestyles. By 1988 I was trying to distinguish community as theological reality from lifestyles by suggesting different vocabulary.

8. For a good description and interpretation of Merton's two periods of modified solitude, see William H. Shannon, *Silent Lamp: The Thomas Merton Story* (New York: Crossroad, 1992), 152–62 and 248–62. During the latter period, which began in 1965 and involved a more complete solitude (but still not absolute since he continued

to teach the novices and to join the community for some meals and liturgies), Merton wrote his best work on monastic life in which he both criticized the current state of monasticism and proposed reforms. In other words, he was not alienated from monastic life or from his community but deeply involved in their development.

9. This separate space might be a small apartment, a separate area of a large community dwelling, a cottage or hermitage on the grounds of a Religious congregation, or some other type of individual quarters. What the dwelling provides is freedom from the relatively continuous presence of other people during the time the Religious is at home.

10. I have some problem with the implied accusation that the intensified need for solitude of some Religious whose ministries are particularly public and high-profile is a kind of selfish refusal to make the effort to build community during their "time off." It is quite possible that maintaining a high level of interpersonal interaction both in ministry and in their living situation constitutes a real psychological imbalance, especially for more introverted personalities. Being actually present to and active in community for such people might be much better achieved in some other manner, and according to some other rhythm, than by actual continual physical presence in a group-living situation.

11. See Thomas Merton, *Day of a Stranger*, introduction by Robert E. Daggy (Salt Lake City: Gibbs M. Smith, 1981) for his own description of his hermitage life, and *The Hidden Ground of Love: The Letters of Thomas Merton on Religious Experience and Social Concerns*, selected and edited by William H. Shannon (New York: Farrar, Straus, Giroux, 1985), especially his correspondence with the Sufi Abdul Aziz, 43–67, for his reflections on the importance of solitude. Merton also wrote an important essay on the meaning of solitude in the spiritual life, "Notes for a Philosophy of Solitude," in *Disputed Questions* (New York: New American Library of World Literature, 1965), 139–60, and a book, *Thoughts in Solitude* (New York: Farrar, Straus, Giroux, 1958).

12. Actually, most of what has been said could, with some modifications, be applied in stabile monastic orders as well.

13. As noted in chapter 6, in the United States only about one-fourth of households is a traditional nuclear family of husband and wife and their biological children (*U.S. Census Bureau Abstract: 1999*, 62).

CHAPTER TEN

1. I treated the issue of affiliation of laypeople in terms of the "membership issue" in volume 1, chapter 2.

2. Raymond Hostie, *Vie et mort des ordres religieux: approches psychosociologiques* (Paris: Desclée De Brouwer, 1972).

3. Lawrence Cada, et al., *Shaping the Coming Age of Religious Life* (New York: Seabury, 1979).

4. Erving Goffman, "The Characteristics of Total Institutions," in *A Sociological Reader on Complex Organizations*, edited by Amitai Etzioni and Edward Lehman (New York: Holt, Rinehart and Winston, 1980), 319–39.

5. See Patricia Wittberg, *Creating a Future for Religious Life: A Sociological Perspective* (New York/Mahwah, N.J.: Paulist, 1991), "Outward Orientation in Declining Organizations: Reflections on the LCWR Documents," in *Claiming Our Truth: Reflections on Identity by United States Women Religious*, edited by Nadine Foley (Washington, D.C.: LCWR, 1988), 89–115, *Pathways to Re-Creating Religious Communities* (New York/Mahwah, N.J.: Paulist, 1996), *The Rise and Fall of Catholic Religious Orders: A Social Movement Perspective*, SUNY Series in Religion, Culture, and Society, edited by Wade Clark Roof (Albany: State University of New York, 1994), and "Ties That No Longer Bind," *America* 179 (September 26, 1998): 10–14.

6. Wittberg, *Creating a Future*, 11.

7. Ibid., 11–22.

8. I will say more below about the desire for community among newer members, a desire that can be either neurotic or quite valid and healthy, depending on its meaning in a given context.

9. Wittberg, *Creating a Future*, 36–37.

10. Ibid., 37–44. A fascinating artistic depiction of the subversion of bureaucracy is the recent film, *The Cider House Rules*, based on the novel of the same name by John Irving (New York: Ballantine, 1994). It raises deep questions about both the necessity for and the limits of intentional community and the ultimate incapacity of bureaucracy to handle the *humanum* as social.

11. Wittberg, *Creating a Future*, 61–62.

12. A beautifully written and very appreciative account of Amish life is offered by a non-Amish artist, Sue Bender, who spent a period of time among the Amish to learn about their quilt-making. In her book, *Plain and Simple: A Woman's Journey to the Amish* (San Francisco: HarperSanFrancisco, 1991), Bender shows both how satisfying life in a

healthy intentional community can be, especially because of the strong primary ties among members, but also the severe limitations it places on members and the restriction of outside resources that it involves.

13. See Wittberg, *Creating a Future*, 71.

14. Ibid., 74–75.

15. Margaret Wheatley in *Leadership and the New Science: Learning about Organization from an Orderly Universe* (San Francisco: Berrett-Koehler, 1992), says on p. 135: "A self-organizing system has the freedom to grow and evolve, guided only by one rule: It must remain consistent with itself and its past. The presence of this guiding rule allows for both creativity and boundaries, for evolution and coherence, for determinism and free will."

16. *Giving Voice* 1 (December 1999), a newsletter for Women Religious under 50, which grew out of the Fertile Fields conference for this cohort of women, was devoted to the issue of communal living. The articles give strong testimony to the desire of these younger Religious for real community living, which most seem to understand as some form of group living.

From another perspective and in another publication, a young woman who entered Religious Life only a few years ago wrote a very nuanced article on how a variety of lifestyles could be integrated into a true community of hearts and minds. See Julie Vieira, "The Changing Models of Religious Life," *IHM Journal* (Spring 1999): 20–23.

17. Two sequential chapters in *Building Sisterhood: A Feminist History of the Sisters, Servants of the Immaculate Heart of Mary* (Syracuse, N.Y.: Syracuse University Press, 1997), "The Official IHM Stance on Friendship, 1845–1960" by Joan Glisky and "PFs: Persistent Friendships" by Nancy Sylvester, describe the dynamics by which real friendship was born and survived in a climate which officially proscribed it.

18. Good examples are Carol K. Coburn and Martha Smith, *Spirited Lives: How Nuns Shaped Catholic Culture and American Life, 1836–1920* (Chapel Hill, N.C./London: University of North Carolina Press, 1999), on the Sisters of St. Joseph of Carondelet and *Building Sisterhood*.

WORKS CITED

Acts of the Christian Martyrs. Edited and translated by H. Musurillo. Oxford: Clarendon, 1972.

Aelred of Rievaulx. *Aelred of Rievaulx's Spiritual Friendship: A New Translation* by Mark F. Williams. Scranton, Pa.: University of Scranton Press, 1994.

Ambrose. *De Virginitatis. P.L.* 16:386–545. Available in English as *The Nun's Ideals*. Translated by James Shiel. Chicago/London/Dublin: Scepter, 1963.

Appleby, R. Scott. "Surviving the Shaking of the Foundations: United States Catholicism in the Twenty-First Century." Introduction to *Seminaries, Theologates, and the Future of Church Ministry: An Analysis of Trends and Transitions*, 1–23, by Katarina Schuth. Collegeville, Minn.: Liturgical Press, 1999.

Aristotle. *Nicomachean Ethics*. Translated by Terence Irwin. Indianapolis: Hackett, 1985.

Augustine of Hippo. *De sancta Virginitatis. P.L.* 40:395–428. Available in English as *Holy Virginity*, part I, vol. 9. In *The Works of Saint Augustine: A Translation for the 21st Century*, 65–107. Translated by Ray Kearney. Edited with introduction and notes by David G. Hunter. Hyde Park, N.Y.: New City Press, 1999.

Bass, Ellen and Laura Davis. *The Courage to Heal: A Guide for Women Survivors of Child Sexual Abuse*. New York: Harper and Row, 1988.

Bender, Sue. *Plain and Simple: A Woman's Journey to the Amish*. San Francisco: HarperSanFrancisco, 1991.

447

Berry, Thomas. *The Dream of the Earth*. San Francisco: Sierra Club Books, 1988.

———. "The Universe, the University and the Ecozoic Era." In *Doors of Understanding: Conversations in Global Spirituality in Honor of Ewert Cousins*, 79–95. Edited by Steven Chase. Quincy, Ill.: Franciscan Press, 1997.

Blaney, Retta. "Survey Reveals Growth in Orders' Associates." *National Catholic Reporter* (May 26, 2000): 7.

Book of Constitutions and Ordinations of the Friars of the Order of Preachers. Available at www.op.org/curia/ConstOP/.

Boys, Mary. *Has God Only One Blessing? Judaism as a Source of Christian Self-Understanding*. New York/Mahwah, N.J.: Paulist, 2000.

Brown, Peter. *The Body and Society: Men, Women and Sexual Renunciation in Early Christianity*. Lectures on the History of Religions, vol. 13. New York: Columbia University Press, 1988.

Brown, Raymond E., Karl P. Donfried, Joseph A. Fitzmyer, and John Reumann, eds. *Mary in the New Testament: A Collaborative Assessment by Protestant and Roman Catholic Scholars*. Philadelphia: Fortress/New York: Paulist, 1978.

Burton-Christie, Douglas. *The Word in the Desert: Scripture and the Quest for Holiness in Early Christian Monasticism*. New York/Oxford: Oxford University Press, 1993.

Cada, Lawrence, et al. *Shaping the Coming Age of Religious Life*. New York: Seabury, 1979.

Cahill, Lisa Sowle. *Women and Sexuality*. 1992 Madeleva Lecture in Spirituality. New York/Mahwah, N.J.: Paulist, 1992.

Catherine of Genoa. *Purgation and Purgatory* and *The Spiritual Dialogue*. Translation and notes by Serge Hughes. Introduction by Benedict J. Groeschel. Preface by Catherine de Hueck Doherty. Classics of Western Spirituality. New York/Ramsey/Toronto: Paulist, 1979.

Coburn, Carol K., and Martha Smith. *Spirited Lives: How Nuns Shaped Catholic Culture and American Life, 1836–1920*. Chapel Hill, N.C./London: University of North Carolina Press, 1999.

Code of Canon Law: Latin-English Edition. Translated by Canon Law Society of America. Washington, D.C.: Canon Law Society of America, 1983.

The Comedy of Dante Alighieri: The Florentine. Cantica III, "Il Paradiso." Translated by Dorothy L. Sayers and Barbara Reynolds. Baltimore: Penguin, 1962.

Conn, Walter E. *The Desiring Self: Rooting Pastoral Counseling and Spiritual Direction in Self-Transcendence*. New York/Mahwah, N.J.: Paulist, 1998.

Constitutions of the Sisters of Mercy of the Americas. Silver Spring, Md.: Sisters of Mercy of the Americas, 1992.

The Constitutions of the Society of Jesus and Their Complementary Norms: A Complete English Translation of the Official Latin Texts. Saint Louis: Institute of Jesuit Sources, 1996.

Cozzens, Donald. *The Changing Face of the Priesthood: A Reflection on the Priest's Crisis of Soul*. Collegeville, Minn.: Liturgical Press, 2000.

Crossan, John Dominic. "Jesus and the Kingdom: Itinerants and Householders in Earliest Christianity." In *Jesus at 2000*, 21–53. Edited by Marcus J. Borg. Boulder, Colo.: Westview, 1998.

Destro, Adriana, and Mauro Pesce. "Kinship, Discipleship, and Movement: An Anthropological Study of John's Gospel." *Biblical Interpretation* 3 (1995): 267–84.

Didache. In *Early Christian Fathers*, 161–79. Translated and edited by Cyril C. Richardson, et al. New York: Macmillan, 1970.

Du Boulay, Shirley. *Beyond the Darkness: A Biography of Bede Griffiths.* New York: Doubleday, 1998.

Ebaugh, Helen Rose Fuchs. *Women in the Vanishing Cloister: Organizational Decline in Catholic Religious Orders in the United States.* New Brunswick, N.J.: Rutgers University Press, 1993.

Ellsberg, Robert. *All Saints: Daily Reflections on Saints, Prophets, and Witnesses for Our Time.* New York: Crossroad, 1998.

Erikson, Erik. *The Life Cycle Completed.* New York: Norton, 1982.

Farley, Margaret A. "The Church in the Public Forum: Scandal or Prophetic Witness?" In *Proceedings of the Fifty-fourth Annual Convention, San Jose, June 8–11, 2000.* Vol. 55, 87–101. Edited by Michael Downey. Los Angeles: Saint John's Seminary, 2000.

———. *Just Love: Sexual Ethics and Social Change.* New York: Continuum, 1997.

———. *Personal Commitments: Beginning, Keeping, Changing.* San Francisco: Harper and Row, 1990.

Fiorenza, Elisabeth Schüssler. *In Memory of Her: A Feminist Theological Reconstruction of Christian Origins.* New York: Crossroad, 1985.

FitzGerald, Constance. "A Discipleship of Equals: Voices from Tradition—Teresa of Avila and John of the Cross." In *A*

Discipleship of Equals: Towards a Christian Feminist Spirituality, 63–97. Edited by Francis A. Eigo. Villanova, Pa.: Villanova University Press, 1988.

————. "Transformation in Wisdom: The Subversive Character and Educative Power of Sophia in Contemplation." In *Carmel and Contemplation: Transforming Human Consciousness*, 281–358. Carmelite Studies VII. Edited by Kevin Culligan and Regis Jordan. Washington, D.C.: Institute of Carmelite Studies, 2000.

Fitzmyer, Joseph A. *The Gospel According to Luke X–XXIV*. Anchor Bible, vol. 28A. Garden City, N.Y.: Doubleday, 1985.

Flannery, Austin P., ed. *Vatican Council II: The Conciliar and Postconciliar Documents*. 2 vols. Grand Rapids: Eerdmans, 1975 and 1984.

————. *Vatican Council II: More Postconciliar Documents*. 2 vols. Northport, N.Y.: Costello, 1982.

Flannery, Austin P., and Laurence Collins, eds. *Light for My Path: The New Code of Canon Law for Religious–Digest, Source Material, Commentary*. Wilmington, Del.: Michael Glazier, 1983.

Flinders, Carol Lee. *Enduring Grace: Living Portraits of Seven Women Mystics*. San Francisco: Harper, 1993.

Ford, Josephine Massyngberde. *Redeemer, Friend, and Mother: Salvation in Antiquity and in the Gospel of John*. Minneapolis: Fortress, 1997.

Froehle, Bryan, and Mary L. Gautier, and CARA Staff. *Catholicism USA: A Portrait of the Catholic Church in the United States*. Vol. 1 of Catholicism 2000 series. Maryknoll, N.Y.: Orbis Books, 2000.

Galanter, Marc. *Cults: Faith, Healing, and Coercion*. New York: Oxford University Press, 1999.

Ganss, George E. *The Spiritual Exercises of Saint Ignatius: A Translation and Commentary*. St. Louis: Institute of Jesuit Sources, 1992.

Gertrude of Helfta. *The Herald of Divine Love*. Translated and edited by Margaret Winkworth. Classics of Western Spirituality. New York/Mahwah, N.J.: Paulist, 1993.

Glisky, Joan. "The Official IHM Stance on Friendship, 1845–1960." In *Building Sisterhood: A Feminist History of the Sisters, Servants of the Immaculate Heart of Mary*, 153–7. Syracuse, N.Y.: Syracuse University Press, 1997.

Goffman, Erving. "The Characteristics of Total Institutions." In *A Sociological Reader on Complex Organizations*, 319–39. Edited by Amitai Etzioni and Edward Lehman. New York: Holt, Rinehart and Winston, 1980.

Gramick, Jeannine. "Lesbian Nuns: Identity, Affirmation, and Gender Differences." In *Homosexuality in the Priesthood and the Religious Life*. Edited by Jeannine Gramick. New York: Crossroad, 1989, 219–36.

Green, Joel B. *The Gospel of Luke*. The New International Commentary on the New Testament. Edited by Ned B. Stonehouse, F. F. Bruce, and Gordon D. Fee. Grand Rapids: William B. Eerdmans, 1997.

Gregory of Nyssa. περί παρθενίας. *P.G.* 46:317–416. Available in English as *On Virginity*. In *Gregory of Nyssa: Ascetical Works*. Translated by V. W. Callahan. Fathers of the Church 58. New York: Fathers of the Church, 1967.

Guindon, André. *The Sexual Language: An Essay in Moral Theology*. Ottawa: University of Ottawa Press, 1977.

Hale, Robert, O.S.B. Cam. *Love on the Mountain: The Chronicle Journal of a Camaldolese Monk*. Trabuco Canyon, Calif.: Source Books and Hermitage Books, 1999.

Harding, M. Esther. *Woman's Mysteries Ancient and Modern: A Psychological Interpretation of the Feminine Principle as Portrayed in Myth, Story, and Dreams*. New and revised ed. New York: Pantheon, 1955.

Haughey, John C. *Should Anyone Say Forever?: On Making, Keeping and Breaking Commitments*. Garden City, N.Y.: Doubleday, 1975.

Hennessy, Paul K., ed. *A Concert of Charisms: Ordained Ministry in Religious Life*. New York/Mahwah, N.J.: Paulist, 1997.

Hinsdale, Mary Ann. "The Official IHM Stance on Friendship, 1845–1960." In *Building Sisterhood: A Feminist History of the Sisters, Servants of the Immaculate Heart of Mary*, 119–50. Syracuse, N.Y.: Syracuse University Press, 1997.

Hostie, Raymond. *Vie et mort des ordres religieux: approches psycho-sociologiques*. Paris: Desclée De Brouwer, 1972.

Irving, John. *The Cider House Rules*. New York: Ballantine, 1994.

Janssens, Louis. "Personalism in Moral Theology." In *Moral Theology: Challenges for the Future. Essays in Honor of Richard A. McCormick*, 94–107. Edited by Charles E. Curran. New York/Mahwah, N.J.: Paulist, 1990.

John Chrysostom. *De Virginitate. P.L.* 48:533–96. Available in English in *John Chrysostom: On Virginity, Against Remarriage*. Translated by Sally R. Shore. New York: Edwin Mellen Press, 1983.

John of the Cross. *The Collected Works of Saint John of the Cross*. Rev. ed. Translated by Kieran Kavanaugh and Otilio Rodriguez, with revisions and introduction by Kieran Kavanaugh. Washington. D.C.: Institute of Carmelite Studies, 1991.

Johnson, Elizabeth. "Jesus, the Wisdom of God: A Biblical Basis for Non-Androcentric Christology." *Ephemerides Theologicae Lovanienses* 61 (1985): 261–94.

Johnstone, Brian V. "From Physicalism to Personalism." *Studia Moralia* 30 (1992): 71–96.

Justin Martyr. *Apologies*. Translated with introduction and notes edited by Leslie William Barnard. New York: Paulist, 1966.

Kimmel, Michael S. "The Gender of Violence." In *The Gendered Society*, 242–63. New York: Oxford University Press, 2000.

Kosnick, Anthony. *Human Sexuality: New Directions in American Catholic Thought*. New York: Paulist, 1977.

Langone, Michael D., ed. *Recovery from Cults: Help for Victims of Psychological and Spiritual Abuse*. New York: Norton, 1994.

"LCWR Recommendations: Schema of Canons on Religious Life." In *Records of the Leadership Conference of Women Religous*. CLCW 75/11. University of Notre Dame Archives, 1977.

Lescher, Bruce. "Laybrothers: Questions Then, Questions Now." *Cistercian Studies* 23 (1988): 63–85.

Mandell, Gail Porter. *Madeleva: A Biography*. Albany, N.Y.: State University of New York Press, 1997.

McFague, Sallie. *Metaphorical Theology: Models of God in Religious Language*. Philadelphia: Fortress, 1982, 32–42.

McGinn, Bernard. *The Flowering of Mysticism: Men and Women in the New Mysticism 1200–1350*. Vol. 3 of *The Presence of God: A History of Western Christian Mysticism*, 3 vols. New York: Crossroad, 1998.

McNamara, Jo Ann Kay. *Sisters in Arms: Catholic Nuns through Two Millennia*. Cambridge: Harvard University Press, 1996.

Merkle, Judith A. *Committed by Choice: Religious Life Today*. Collegeville, Minn.: Liturgical Press, 1992.

Merton, Thomas. *Day of a Stranger*. Introduction by Robert E. Daggy. Salt Lake City: Gibbs M. Smith, 1981.

—. *The Hidden Ground of Love: The Letters of Thomas Merton on Religious Experience and Social Concerns*. Selected and edited by William H. Shannon. New York: Farrar, Straus, Giroux, 1985.

—. "Notes for a Philosophy of Solitude." In *Disputed Questions*, 139–60. New York: New American Library of World Literature, 1965.

—. *Thoughts in Solitude*. New York: Farrar, Straus, Giroux, 1958.

Methodius. Συμποσίον των δέκα παρθενων ἤ περί ἀγνείας. *P.G.* 18:27–240. Available in English as *The Symposium*. Translated and annotated by H. Musurillo. Ancient Christian Writers 27. Westminster: Newman Press, 1958.

Miles, Margaret R. *Desire and Delight: A New Reading of Augustine's Confessions*. New York: Crossroad, 1992.

Moloney, Francis J. *Disciples and Prophets: A Biblical Model for Religious Life*. New York: Crossroad, 1981.

—. *A Life of Promise: Poverty, Chastity, Obedience*. New South Wales: St. Paul Publications, 1984.

Monick, Eugene. *Phallos: Sacred Image of the Masculine*. Studies in Jungian Psychology by Jungian Analysts 27. Toronto: Inner City Books, 1987.

Murphy, Roland E. *The Song of Songs: A Commentary on the Book of Canticles or The Song of Songs*. Edited by S. Dean McBride, Jr. Hermeneia. Minneapolis: Augsburg Fortress, 1990.

————. *The Tree of Life: An Exploration of Biblical Wisdom Literature*. Anchor Bible Reference Library. New York: Doubleday, 1990.

Néher, A. "Le symbolisme conjugal: Expression de l'histoire dans l'Ancien Testament." *Revue d'Histoire et de Philosophie Religieuses* 34 (1954): 30–49.

Nordone, Cynthia. "New Perspectives on Religious Life: Gifts and Insights of Lesbian and Gay Religious." *Proceedings of the Eleventh National Congress of the Religious Formation Conference, October 7–10, 1999*, 95–102. Silver Spring, Md.: Religious Formation Conference, 2000.

Norris, Kathleen. "Maria Goretti: Cipher or Saint?" In *The Cloister Walk*, 223–36. New York: Riverhead, 1996.

Nugent, Robert. "Addressing Celibacy Issues with Gay and Lesbian Candidates." *Horizon* 24 (Fall 1998): 15–25.

Nygren, David J., and Miriam D. Ukeritis. *The Future of Religious Orders in the United States: Transformation and Commitment*. Foreword by David C. McClelland. Westport, Conn.: Praeger, 1993.

Ó Murchú, Diarmuid. *Reframing Religious Life: An Expanded Vision for the Future*. Middlegreen Slough, U.K.: St. Paul's Publications, 1995.

Ong, Walter J. *Fighting for Life: Contest, Sexuality, and Consciousness*. Ithaca, N.Y.: Cornell University Press, 1981.

Origen. *In Canticum Canticorum*. *P.L.* 13:57–198. Available in English as *The Song of Songs: Commentary and Homilies*. Translated and annotated by R. P. Lawson. Westminster, Md.: Newman, 1957.

Osiek, Carolyn. "Jesus and cultural values: Family life as an example." *Hervormde Teologiese Studies* 53 (September, 1997): 800–814.

Osiek Carolyn, and David L. Balch. *Families in the New Testament World.* Family, Religion, and Culture Series. Louisville, Ky.: Westminster John Knox, 1997.

Patrologia cursus completus: Series Graeca. Paris: J. P. Migne, 1857–1866.

Patrologia cursus completus: Series Latina. Paris: J. P. Migne, 1844–1855.

Person, Ethel Spector. *The Sexual Century.* New Haven, Conn.: Yale University Press, 1999.

Polkinghorne, John. *Quarks, Chaos, and Christianity: Questions to Science and Religion.* New York: Crossroad, 1997, orig. 1994.

Prejean, Helen. *Dead Man Walking: An Eyewitness Account of the Death Penalty in the United States.* New York: Vintage, 1994.

Pryor, John W. "Jesus and Family—A Test Case." *Australian Biblical Review* 45 (1997): 56–69.

Puthenkandathil, Eldo. *Philos: A Designation for the Jesus-Disciple Relationship: An Exegetico-Theological Investigation of the Term in the Fourth Gospel.* Frankfurt: Peter Lang, 1993.

Ranft, Patricia. *Women and the Religious Life in Premodern Europe.* New York: St. Martin's, 1996.

Ricoeur, Paul. *Interpretation Theory: Discourse and the Surplus of Meaning.* Fort Worth, Tex.: Texas Christian University, 1976.

Ringe, Sharon H. *Wisdom's Friends: Community and Christology in the Fourth Gospel.* Louisville, Ky.: Westminster John Knox, 1999.

Rolheiser, Ronald. *The Holy Longing: The Search for a Christian Spirituality*. New York: Doubleday, 1999.

Roof, Wade Clark. *Generation of Seekers: The Spiritual Journeys of the Baby Boom Generation*. With the assistance of Bruce Greer et al. San Francisco: HarperSanFrancisco, 1993.

Ruether, Rosemary R. *Sexism and God-Talk: Toward a Feminist Theology*. Boston: Beacon, 1983.

Ruffing, Janet K. *Spiritual Direction: Beyond the Beginnings*. New York/Mahwah, N.J.: Paulist, 2000.

The Rule of St. Benedict in Latin and English with Notes, RB 1980. Edited by Timothy Fry. Collegeville, Minn.: Liturgical Press, 1981.

Russell, Diana E. H. *The Secret Trauma: Incest in the Lives of Girls and Women*. Rev. ed. New York: Basic Books, 1999.

Sammon, Seán D. "Last Call for Religious Life." *Human Development* 20 (Spring 1999): 12–27.

Sanford, John A., and George Lough. *What Men Are Like*. New York/Mahwah, N.J.: Paulist, 1988.

Sarton, May. *Plant Dreaming Deep*. New York: Norton, 1968.

Schneiders, Sandra M. *Beyond Patching: Faith and Feminism in the Catholic Church*. The Anthony Jordan Lectures, Newman Theological College, Edmonton, 1990. New York/Mahwah, N.J.: Paulist, 1991.

———. "Celibacy as Charism." *The Way Supplement* 77 (Summer 1993): 13–25.

———. *Finding the Treasure: Locating Catholic Religious Life in a New Ecclesial and Cultural Context*. Vol. 1 of *Religious Life in a New Millennium*. New York/Mahwah, N.J.: Paulist, 2000.

———. "Formation for New Forms of Religious Community Life." *The Way Supplement* 62 (Summer 1988): 63–76.

———. *New Wineskins: Re-imagining Religious Life Today*. New York/Mahwah, N.J.: Paulist, 1986.

———. *Religion and Spirituality: Strangers, Rivals, or Partners?* The Santa Clara University Lecture Series. Santa Clara, Calif.: Santa Clara University, 2000.

———. *Women and the Word: The Gender of God in the New Testament and the Spirituality of Women*. 1986 Madeleva Lecture in Spirituality. New York/Mahwah, N.J.: Paulist, 1986.

———. *Written That You May Believe: Encountering Jesus in the Fourth Gospel*. New York: Crossroad/Herder, 1999.

Schreck, Nancy. "The Forces That Push Us Toward and Pull Us Away from Community." *Horizon* 25 (Spring 2000): 7–15.

Schreiter, Robert J. "Challenges and Directions of Religious Life at the Turn of the Millennium," June 21, 1998. A privately printed transcript available from Catholic Theological Union in Chicago.

Setel, T. Drorah. "Prophets and Pornography: Female Sexual Imagery in Hosea." In *Feminist Interpretation of the Bible*, 86–95. Edited by Letty M. Russell. Philadelphia: Westminster, 1985.

Shannon, William H. *Silent Lamp: The Thomas Merton Story*. New York: Crossroad, 1992.

Sheldrake, Philip. *Spirituality and Theology: Christian Living and the Doctrine of God*. Maryknoll, N.Y.: Orbis, 1998.

Singer, Margaret Thaler. *Cults in Our Midst: The Hidden Menace in Our Everyday Lives*. With Janja Lalich. San Francisco: Jossey-Bass, 1995.

Sipe, A. W. Richard. *A Secret World: Sexuality and the Search for Celibacy*. New York: Brunner/Mazel, 1990.

The State of America's Children: A Report from the Children's Defense Fund. Boston: Beacon, 2000.

Swimme, Brian. *The Universe Is a Green Dragon: A Cosmic Creation Story*. Santa Fe, N.M.: Bear & Company, 1984.

Sylvester, Nancy. "P.F.s [particular friendships]: Persistent Friendships." In *Building Sisterhood: A Feminist History of the Sisters, Servants of the Immaculate Heart of Mary*, 173–90. Syracuse, N.Y.: Syracuse University Press, 1997.

Tertullian. *De virginibus velandis*. *P.L.* II:887–914. An English translation is available as "Veiling of Virgins" in *The Ante-Nicene Fathers: Translations of the Writings of the Fathers Down to A.D. 325*, 27–37, vol. 4. Edited by Alexander Roberts and James Donaldson. Grand Rapids, Mich.: Eerdmans, 1985–87.

Thompson, Margaret Susan. "'Charism' Or 'Deep Story'? Toward a Clearer Understanding of the Growth of Women's Religious Life in Nineteenth-Century America." In *Religious Life and Contemporary Culture*. Theological Education Process, Cycle 2. Monroe, Mich.: Sisters, Servants of the Immaculate Heart of Mary, 1998.

Trible, Phyllis. *God and the Rhetoric of Sexuality*. Philadelphia: Fortress, 1978.

Tucker, Mary Evelyn. "The Emerging Alliance of Religion and Ecology." In *Doors of Understanding: Conversations in Global Spirituality in Honor of Ewert Cousins*, 97–124. Edited by Steven Chase. Quincey, Ill.: Franciscan Press, 1997.

Turner, Victor W. *The Ritual Process: Structure and Anti-Structure*. Chicago: Aldine, 1969.

U.S. Census Bureau Statistical Abstract of the United States: 1999. 119th ed. Washington, D.C.: U.S. Department of Commerce, 1999.

U.S. Conference of Catholic Bishops. "Always Our Children," revised and reissued. *Origins* 28 (1998), 97–102.

Vieira, Julie. "The Changing Models of Religious Life." *IHM Journal* (Spring 1999): 20–23.

Wenzel, Kristen. *Turnover and Burnout among Vocation and Formation Directors: An Exploratory Survey.* Washington, D.C.: Center for Applied Research in the Apostolate, 1982.

Wheatley, Margaret. *Leadership and the New Science: Learning about Organization from an Orderly Universe.* San Francisco: Berrett-Koehler, 1992.

Wilder, Amos N. *Early Christian Rhetoric: The Language of the Gospel.* Cambridge, Mass.: Harvard University Press, 1964.

Wittberg, Patricia. *Creating a Future for Religious Life: A Sociological Perspective.* New York/Mahwah, N.J.: Paulist, 1991.

———. "Outward Orientation in Declining Organizations: Reflections on the LCWR Documents." In *Claiming Our Truth: Reflections on Identity by United States Women Religious*, 89–115. Edited by Nadine Foley. Washington, D.C.: LCWR, 1988.

———. *Pathways to Re-Creating Religious Communities.* New York/Mahwah, N.J.: Paulist, 1996.

———. *The Rise and Fall of Catholic Religious Orders: A Social Movement Perspective.* SUNY Series in Religion, Culture, and Society. Edited by Wade Clark Roof. Albany, N.Y.: State University of New York, 1994.

————. "Ties That No Longer Bind." *America* 179 (September 26, 1998): 10–14.

Zohar, Danah, in collaboration with I. N. Marshall. *The Quantum Self: Human Nature and Consciousness Defined by the New Physics.* New York: Quill/William Morrow, 1990.

INDEX

Acedia, 348
Adultery, 194
Aelred of Rievaulx, 191
Aquiba, Rabbi, 184
Aristotle, 191
Associations, 365–70
Augustine, 120, 168, 274
Authority, 63–64

Benedict, 111, 254, 274, 288
Benedictines, 138, 313
Boniface VIII, Pope, 143
Bureaucratic organizations,
    359–65

Cada, Lawrence, 356
"Calvin and Hobbes"
    (Watterson), 93–94
Camaldolese monks, 313
Carmelites, 138, 313
Catherine of Genoa, 199
Catherine of Siena, 189, 254
Celibacy, 10–11, 29–31,
    62–63, 112, 160–200,
    406–7; as charism,
    117–59; communitarian
    motive, 112, 144–51,
    154, 156–57, 159;
    definition, 117–19;
    distinctiveness of vow,
    125–32; family and,
    201–47; feminism and,
    173–200; fidelity and,

98; free choice and, 30,
135–37; homelessness
and, 253, 257–58,
271–73; invalid
motivations, 140–41; as
legal obligation, 106–7;
ministerial motive, 113,
144–51, 154, 156–57,
159; motivations for,
118, 132–34, 137–51;
nonnatural character of,
129–31; patriarchy and,
109; perpetuity of
commitment, 154,
155–56; prayer and,
172–73; sexual
revolution and, 160–64;
terminology of vow,
119–24; theological
aspects, 126–27;
unitive/mystical motive,
111, 141–44, 153–54,
158, 178; valid
motivations, 141–51;
witness value of, 131; *see
also* Chastity; Nuptial
metaphor; Virginity
Charism: consecrated
celibacy as, 30; spirit of
the congregation, 23,
74–75, 76
Chastity, 120, 122–23,
168–69, 171, 172; as

463